# AT 40:

## ASIAN AMERICAN STUDIES
## @ SAN FRANCISCO STATE

*Self-Determination*

*Community*

*Student Service*

Asian American Studies Department
College of Ethnic Studies
San Francisco State University
2009

**Editorial Committee**
Jeffery Paul Chan
Malcolm Collier
Lorraine Dong, Coordinator
Daniel Phil Gonzales
Marlon K. Hom
Russell Jeung
Allyson Tintiangco-Cubales
Wesley Ueunten

Copy Editors
Lorraine Dong
Brian Folk
Steve Wake

Design Subcommittee
Steve Wake, Designer
Mai-Nhung Le
Valerie Soe

Design and Layout: Steve Wake, Wake Media Productions
Printed in USA by Thomson-Shore, Inc.

© 2009 by Asian American Studies Department,
    San Francisco State University

Asian American Studies Department
College of Ethnic Studies
San Francisco State University
1600 Holloway Avenue
San Francisco, CA 94132
www.sfsu.edu/~aas

# Contents

## COMMUNITY

## CONTRIBUTIONS

## APPENDICES

## AUTHORS

# AT 40:
# ASIAN AMERICAN STUDIES
# @ SAN FRANCISCO STATE

## INTRODUCTION

子曰
吾十有五而志於學
三十而立
四十而不惑
五十而知天命
六十而耳順
七十而從心所欲 不踰矩

The Teacher said:
At fifteen my ambition is to learn;
At thirty I am established;
At forty I am not confused;
At fifty I know my destiny;
At sixty my ears go with the flow;
At seventy I follow my heart without transgression.

> – Chapter 2, "On Governance" 為政, in *Lunyu* 論語 (often known in English as "The Analects of Confucius") – ca. 5th century BC

On March 20, 1969, Asian American Studies at San Francisco State University was born and became the first AAS program in the United States when a settlement was signed at San Francisco State College to establish the country's first and still only School (now College) of Ethnic Studies. This was one substantial result of the Third World Liberation Front (TWLF) Strike that began on November 6, 1968.

Amidst the militant activism, reactionary administrative and government politics, police suppression, and violence that mainstream media effectively sensationalized as anarchical clamor and influential negative imagery for mass consumption, serious work toward democratization of post-secondary education was ongoing at "State." The TWLF was a coalition of six student organizations (in alphabetical order): the Asian American Political Alliance (AAPA), the Black Student Union (BSU), the Intercollegiate Chinese for Social Action (ICSA), the Latin American Student Organization (LASO), the Mexican American Student Confederation (MASC), and the Philippine (now Pilipino) American Collegiate Endeavor (PACE). The TWLF led the movement and – with the support of the Students for a Democratic Society (SDS), other radically politicized, predominantly white student groups, progressive faculty and administrators, particularly members of the American Federation of Teachers (AFT), and a broadly representative group of progressive leaders from our local communities – won their demand for a School of Ethnic Studies. The School was comprised of four distinct ethnic components: American Indian Studies, Asian American Studies, Black (now Africana) Studies, and La Raza (now Raza) Studies.

United under the rubric "Asian American Studies," and functioning under the basic principle of self-determination and related values, the three Asian American student organizations, together with supportive faculty and ethnic community members, immediately began to build a curriculum. In early September 1969, Asian American Studies offered its first courses. The original curriculum consisted of a combination of pan-ethnic and ethnic-specific Chinese, Japanese, and Pilipino American courses.

"AT FIFTEEN OUR AMBITION IS TO LEARN" 吾十有五而志於學: During the first fifteen years of existence, a young, idealistic, and street-smart AAS at SF State learned what it meant to operate as a field of academic study, not only in terms of knowledge and presentation of subject matter and research methods but also in terms of the practice of realpolitiks necessary to survive and thrive in the unique environment of higher education.

Life for those who continued to work in the School of Ethnic Studies after the Strike was not easy, but sacrifice and very hard work enabled the Asian American program to survive and grow through the 1970s and 1980s.

"AT THIRTY WE ARE ESTABLISHED" 三十而立: At thirty, Asian American Studies was no longer seen just as a passing phase, or an illegitimate unscholarly "bastard." On October 22-24, 1998, a student-led conference, entitled "Dreams, Realities, and Challenges in Asian American Studies: Asian Pacific Islander Americans Commemorating the 30th Anniversary of the SF State Third World Student Strike," was held to evaluate the growth and development of AAS. A new generation of faculty, not present at the 1968 Strike and all holding doctoral degrees, was hired over time and became the majority of the faculty. The number of Asian ethnic-specific courses doubled to include the specific study of Korean Americans, Vietnamese Americans, and Asian Americans of Mixed Heritage. New, pioneering areas of specialized focus in AAS were also established by then, including Asian American creative writing, photographic exploration, Asian Americans of Mixed Heritage studies, Asian American community health, and Asian American children's literature. An AAS major was established in 1997 and an AAS master's program was approved in 1999, amidst growing concerns about institutionalization, corporatization, domestication, and internationalization, and how these factors might cause AAS to deviate from the original ideals and founding principles rooted in and emanating from the Strike.

"AT FORTY WE ARE NOT CONFUSED" 四十而不惑: For forty years, the initiators of AAS struggled to develop an academic discipline out of nothing. More importantly, they fought to uphold the revolutionary values of the Strike to make academe accountable to the people and the community. For this, at various times and in different circumstances, they have been honored, misunderstood, or criticized by both the academy and the community.

This collection presents for the first time the direct, unfiltered description of the journey of the founding members of Asian American Studies – joined by those who followed – in their own words. The former is our first generation of Asian American faculty, followed by the latter 1.5 generation faculty who were present at the Strike, left for their advanced degrees, but returned to SF State, and the second generation of Asian American faculty who were just young children during the 1960s.

The seven essays in "Hopes" relate the aspirations of the 1968 student strikers and the later generation of students who mobilized in 1997 to work with faculty and administration to establish the AAS major (see also Appendices 1-2). "Invention" is a restatement and explanation of the values and principles that served as the bases for the construction of Asian American Studies, from 1969 to 2008 (see also Appendices 3-5). This section describes the department's incredibly robust growth from six FTEF (full-time equivalent faculty) to 15.6 FTEF, and the expansion of the program from seventeen courses in 1969 to forty-one undergraduate and eleven graduate courses in 2008 (see also Appendices 6-13). To date, the department remains the largest AAS department in the nation with specific individual ethnic units, faculty, and courses dedicated to the study of Chinese Americans, Filipino Americans, Japanese Americans, Korean Americans, South Asian Americans, Vietnamese Americans, and Asian Americans of Mixed Heritage.

In "Teaching," five faculty share teaching pedagogies that make their courses unique even within the discipline of Asian American Studies. In "Community," the trials and tribulations of incorporating and merging academe and community reveal a challenge that has yet to be totally overcome, especially with the emerging institutionalization of "Community Service Learning." In the final section entitled "Contributions," seven AAS faculty share their writings and research. Representing the perspectives of the first, 1.5, and second generations of AAS faculty at SF State, they exemplify new ways to confront and effectively address some of the important Asian American Studies issues facing us today.

All articles are the opinions and perspectives of the writers and do not necessarily reflect that of the entire department. Those that are more historical in nature have gone through verification and multiple reviews, corrections, and additions by many individuals involved with the initiation and continuation of AAS at SF State. Every attempt has also been made to be as accurate as possible with the listings and spelling of names in the appendices. Unfortunately, due to the passage of time and the loss of contact with some individuals, it is difficult to achieve one hundred percent accuracy. With this in mind, the editorial committee apologizes in advance for any unintentional omission or misspelling of names.

### UNPREDICTABLE POSSIBILITIES

At forty, Asian American Studies at San Francisco State is not confused. We remember our origins and remain dedicated to our founding principles. On the eve of the fortieth anniversary of the 1968 Strike, Asian American Studies had lost a substantial portion of our self-determination when the decision-making process over budget, curricular offerings, and replacement faculty was subjected to administrative fiat. But a united front of AAS faculty and students led to a powerful reaffirmation of our origins and rights. This collaboration has sparked another era for AAS, where students are again engaged as welcome voices and minds with real presence and participation in the department, and with the potential to influence AAS in a new direction and to the development of a new structure.

We will continue to evolve and in another ten years of struggle, we hope that "at fifty we know something of our destiny." Meanwhile, welcome to our journey: from our beginning to the present, and the unpredictable possibilities for the future of Asian American Studies.

*Editorial Committee*

Jeffery Paul Chan
Malcolm Collier
Lorraine Dong
Daniel Phil Gonzales
Marlon K. Hom
Russell Jeung
Allyson Tintiangco-Cubales
Wesley Ueunten

December 31, 2008

# HOPES

ON STRIKE! Origins

1968 Aspirations

Self-Determination BA

# ORIGINS: PEOPLE, TIME, PLACE, DREAMS

*Malcolm Collier and Daniel Phil Gonzales*

Asian American Studies at San Francisco State was the product of efforts by Asian American students, faculty, and community members to effectively address pressing academic and community issues. Although our backgrounds and motivations were varied, we had shared concerns and goals. As participants in the initiation and development of this first curricular program of its kind, it is our purpose here to present a brief retrospective on the origins of Asian American Studies.[1]

Beyond the influences of the Civil Rights and Black Power movements of the 1960s and a broad range of concurrent domestic and international movements, the founders of Asian American Studies had personal experiences with particular forms of racial and ethnic exclusion and restriction suffered by Asian American communities, and held in common, perceptions of racial, cultural, political, and socioeconomic inequities in American society. Because our ethnic and class origins were diverse, our motivations were also varied. Consequently, adherence to a single, sanctioned political paradigm was not a requirement for participation in our activities, but a critical awareness of social and political contradictions of America and a deep concern for the practical needs of Asian American communities were expected from all involved.

## A SEARCH FOR EQUITY

The development of a "Third World" perspective that recognized common issues of race, class, and access to political power led Asian American student organizations, with the assistance of some faculty and community leaders, to form alliances with each other and with other Third World groups. These alliances were intended to address pressing community issues, provide mutual aid, and increase community-centered political power. The most immediate motivating factor was a broad frustration

with academe because of its traditional racial and class inequities and its gross irrelevance to the needs of Third World students and their communities. Such frustrations were not exclusive to San Francisco State College, but a particular confluence of factors contributed to the unique direction taken by Asian American student, faculty, and community activists at San Francisco State.

Most of us – then students – involved in the creation of Asian American Studies at San Francisco State began our formal education in US schools in the late 1940s and early 1950s, a time of ultra-conservative sociopolitical conformity associated with the Cold War and the McCarthy era. For Asian Americans and all "non-whites" there were extreme pressures to assimilate toward an idealized White Anglo Saxon Protestant (WASP) cultural model. As the United States moved into the 1960s, the influence of the Civil Rights Movement and the growth of the so-called "counter-culture" began to weaken the social rigidity that marked the 1950s. When we arrived at San Francisco State in the mid- to late 1960s, we found a campus awash in a ferment of experimentation and new ideas. However, like most of our earlier formal schooling, the existing college curriculum was largely disconnected from the lives and worlds of our families and communities.

At San Francisco State, we met others from our communities and engaged in discussions about our social, economic, and cultural circumstances with a frequency, scope, and depth that we had never done before, exploring and modifying the few methods taken from the classroom and related texts that best fit the task. At the core of these discussions was a developing articulation of the needs and desires of our communities that we were both witnesses to and participants in.

We were becoming aware that existing institutions did not effectively meet these needs and desires. We shared a hope – soon frustrated – that "higher education" would provide us with increased knowledge and skills to address issues important to our communities. As we learned to describe and define our circumstances, issues, hopes, and expectations, we searched the college for language courses, history classes, literature classes, and courses in different branches of the social sciences, looking for content and meaning relevant to our experience.

We found little.

We found no Pilipino language course, Mandarin classes but no Cantonese classes, and literature courses that did not include readings from Asia, let alone anything written by or about Chinese, Japanese, or Filipinos in America. Asian Studies provided little that informed Asian American students about our places of ancestral origin.

Whatever our varied backgrounds, even our limited knowledge of our own family stories made us aware that THERE MUST BE HISTORIES of Chinese, Japanese, and Filipino Americans in the United States, though we usually lacked detailed knowledge of these histories. We found that courses in the History Department contained little regarding Asians in America. A number of Chinese Americans signed up for a history class on immigrant and racial minorities in America, taught by Moses Rischin, a nationally recognized scholar, and found scant content on Asian immigration or the history of Asians in America. One student asked why there was nothing of substance about the Chinese in America. She was told that "This course deals only with significant minority groups" (Irene Dea Collier and Gale Ow, personal communication, 24 July 2008).

A few progressive instructors in various disciplines assigned the *Autobiography of Malcolm X* as required reading. It provided profound insight into the dynamics of Black society and American racism, and was a basis of comparison for other Third World American experiences but it did not directly touch on Asian Americans.

Those of us with interests in social work and teaching knew from our own observations that there were few Asian Americans in those fields. We envisioned using our college education to become trained professionals, equipped with the skills and knowledge necessary to address the issues and needs of our communities. The hard reality was that even these programs – ostensibly intended and designed to prepare students for "real world" circumstances – had virtually no awareness of or evident concern for our communities, nor did they provide the skills and knowledge that we so much desired. There was an absence of the most fundamental reference to the existence of Asian Americans from the general curriculum, just as it had been missing in our earlier schooling.[2]

In blunt contradiction to the daily recited pledge that described the United States as "one nation, under god, with liberty and justice for all," formal education at all levels presented students from cultural minority groups with extremely limited access to information about either their historical or their contemporary cultural and social circumstances. Apparently, our histories, cultures, and communities were not part of the American "all"?

White students were provided multiple opportunities to obtain knowledge about their place in American history, culture, and society but we were not. As our understanding of the extent of these omissions grew, so did our feelings of exclusion. This was an obvious violation of the principles of democracy that we were taught as children and adolescents and that we wanted to believe.

Beyond the equity issue there was also the pragmatic question – how can a society that claims to be democratic and pluralistic operate as such if the full range of its socio-cultural character is not recognized and addressed? The evidence presented in our academic setting pointed away from "liberty and justice for all" and toward cultural dismissal and racialized restriction instead.

We felt the College should do better.

## COMMUNITIES

Our desire for change was, ultimately, shaped by our community circumstances. A variety of historical realities and new trends were shaping those communities in the late 1960s.

Starting in the late 1950s and accelerating through the 1960s, Chinese American families were moving out of San Francisco Chinatown into other neighborhoods at a steadily increasing rate. Many of these families were comprised of second generation parents with third generation children, but some were also families formed by the arrival of wives and children after the war. These migrations were also related to the gradual opening up of public sector employment to Asian Americans and other "non-whites" in the same time period, as well as the decline in legalized housing discrimination.

Even as some long-term residents moved out, new immigrants moved into Chinatown in ever larger numbers. There was a rapid increase in the numbers of new immigrant children in local schools and on the streets. They were the newest neighbors.

The pressures brought by the growing population began to expand Chinatown to the west and the north. New immigrants were joining some students' mothers in the sewing factories – unseen and unknown to Chinatown outsiders – and new immigrant-owned businesses were opening up on Stockton Street. Immigrant youth were joining existing street organizations or forming their own peer groups that were often identified as "gangs" whether they were engaged in anti-social activity or not. By 1968, immigration had major impacts on San Francisco Chinatown: housing shortages, more traffic congestion, new businesses, crowded schools, the need for more jobs, youth and family problems, and health concerns to name just a few. The old, familiar Chinatown struggle for survival took on new dimensions, with new issues that were expanding geometrically, in part because they were going unaddressed by both traditional Chinatown organizations and the government agencies that served the wider society.

Concurrently, historical and political tensions and hardships festered below the surface of the community. Chinese American students were very much aware of familial fears of the immigration authorities. They knew that their family names were often changed and "false." They knew that there was tremendous danger to being labeled "communist" and that silence, not protest, was seen as a virtue.

What history lay behind these fears?

The social and political structure of the Chinese American community had been long dominated by conservative elements that suppressed progressive movements but their often crude tactics were losing their effectiveness by the mid-60s. These conservative elements had declining influence with both the families that were moving out and the new immigrants. Their inability to address the changing needs and tensions of the community was undermining their power. The federal War on Poverty was starting to bring money into the community that could provide needed services as well as new bases of social and political power. These resources from outside further weakened the old power structure that was politically disinclined, as well as poorly prepared, to make use of these new opportunities. Actually, the stereotypic view that "Chinatown takes care of its own" – a view abetted by the conservative organizations – initially resulted in Chinatown being left out of the federal War on Poverty plans in San Francisco. It took action by younger, college-educated Chinese Americans activists to get the federal government to include Chinatown in War on Poverty programs (Alan S. Wong, interview, 18 May 2008). This new generation of college-educated Chinese Americans, both American-born and immigrant, was beginning to show up in social service related roles in Chinatown. By 1968, they were agitating for wider recognition of and response to the pressing needs of Chinatown. They would later provide some of the community support for the student Strike at San Francisco State.

Some issues affected all three of the larger local Asian American communities. In the mid- and late 1950s, the San Francisco business and political elite spawned a major redevelopment plan that targeted the Fillmore District, a heavily Black populated area between Market Street and Geary Boulevard, and a Japanese American populated area above Geary between Octavia and Divisadero, and the Central City (now called the South of Market or SOMA) with a large and growing Filipino American population.

While the core area of Chinatown successfully resisted redevelopment, there was a strong threat of encroachment by powerful corporate interests from the business district to the south and from the east where Chinatown/Manilatown merged with the old produce market (where the Golden Gate Plaza Towers now stand). The expanding financial district was threatening low-income housing and small businesses essential to the local community at the very moment that the need for more housing and community-based businesses was growing. Single-room occupancy (SRO) housing on Kearny Street, including the International Hotel (I-Hotel), which housed both Filipino and Chinese American residents, was inadequate for the large families arriving from the Philippines as a result of the Immigration Reform Act of 1965.

While Chinatown expanded north and west to accommodate new arrivals, new immigrants from the Philippines concentrated heavily in the Central City/South of Market and the Inner Mission District. By the late 1960s, the area had become a very visible and dynamic Filipino community with issues that paralleled those of Chinatown. The City's redevelopment project very quickly razed buildings that included SRO hotels and four- and six-unit "flats" in an area ranging from Third to Fifth Streets and from Mission Street down to Harrison Street. By the late 1960s, redevelopment was facilitating the similar destruction of low-cost housing, mostly "residential hotels" or SROs, from Market Street all the way north to Washington Street, along Kearny and Montgomery Streets, soon to be replaced by corporate skyscrapers such as Bank of America, Standard Oil, Wells Fargo, the Transamerica tower, and Holiday Inn.

This sweeping demolition affected the Kearny Street population most directly, decimating the Filipino manong/bachelor community within a few years. The symbolic center of this change was the I-Hotel, located on Kearney between Jackson and Washington Streets on the eastern border of Chinatown.

Filipino American students, whose political consciousness had been wakened by the Civil Rights and anti-war movements, and the struggles of farm, hotel, and restaurant workers, turned their attention and energy to the plight of the manongs of Kearny Street and the needs of the recent immigrants residing in Central City. These activities further encouraged student interest in Filipino American history. This history was immediately evident in the "manong and manang" generation of fathers, uncles, a smaller number of aunts and other women, and all those many fictive "uncles" not by sanguineal relationship but by title of address. They told stories from the 1920s and 1930s about work in the fields of Hawai'i, California, and Washington, and the canneries of Alaska, as well as those about their service in the US military in

World War II. Filipino American students heard accounts of their elders' experiences and how they responded to actions that they called "prejudice." They were told about union organizing, successes and losses, and about making good times from bad.

The same forces that threatened Chinese American and Filipino American communities were at work in the Fillmore District as well, where Japantown was still recovering from the damages of wartime "relocation" to American concentration camps. Redevelopment demolition in the Fillmore was in full swing in 1968. Its destructive impact affected the Japantown residents along with the Black community. The resulting displacement of people and most of the older businesses was as permanent as it was obvious. Taken together with the concurrent, sometimes resulting, movement of many Japanese American families into the Richmond District, other parts of the city, and outlying suburbia in the 1950s and 1960s, the redevelopment process raised major questions about the future of the Japanese American community in San Francisco. Would it survive at all?

These circumstances also raised questions among younger Japanese Americans about the history of their communities in America. In particular, they were beginning to seek explicit and complete discussion of the World War II internment that most of their families had endured. In the context of more open discussion of racism and civil rights issues during the late 1960s, the importance of the Japanese American experience was obvious. Questions about the camps were often treated with silence or terse dismissals by the older generations that experienced them. Why? Many sansei (third generation) Japanese Americans were frustrated by the lack of meaningful responses. They were looking for additional sources of information about Japanese American history.

On a certain level, the Asian American students of the time were following in the footsteps of their own parents and communities. When Chinese and Filipino American men worked hard and long enough to raise the funds to bring wives and family from Asia after World War II, they were laying a very emphatic claim to a permanent place in America. However conservative some of their political views may have been (some were quite extreme in their conservatism!), they knew about the struggles of their predecessors as well as their own. They were asserting their rights and challenging the old order by establishing families, seeking new avenues of employment, and moving into neighborhoods where the land was still covered by racial covenants meant to exclude them. They too were concerned with equity and inclusion. Some went further, by forming and joining labor unions, and taking public stances on community issues. Seen in the context of this dynamic, it is not at all surprising that many of their children were concerned and active as well.

## STUDENT ORGANIZATIONS

In conversation among ourselves, between classes, or in the very crowded and noisy Commons or on Muni going from and to our own neighborhoods throughout the city, we discovered that our questions, our concerns, our frustrations, and our growing anger were collective matters, not simply individual issues. This realization led to a desire for action and the formation of new activist student groups rooted in but extending beyond ethnic community experiences. Ethnic-specific Asian American student organizations officially recognized by San Francisco State were already in place. These were usually the traditional type, with emphases on socializing, fellowship, and a modicum of cultural reflection, and little interest in social or political activism. Our growing desire for collective action required the creation of new organizations that supported ethnic identity, enabled community advocacy, and promoted public activism.

Three Asian American student organizations formed in 1967 and 1968: the Intercollegiate Chinese for Social Action (ICSA, 1967), the Philippine (later Pilipino) American Collegiate Endeavor (PACE, 1967), and the Asian American Political Alliance (AAPA, 1968), the latter of which had a largely, but not exclusively, Japanese American membership at San Francisco State. Unlike preexisting student groups, these were politically-charged organizations.

The class and cultural backgrounds of the students who populated these three organizations were quite varied. The effects of ethnic and racial prejudice on the sociocultural realities of Asian American circumstances in the 1950s and 1960s make use of such terms as "working class" or "middle class" imprecise and misleading, so it is with caution that we offer broad descriptions of the membership background for these activist student groups.[3]

Most of the Chinese American students in ICSA were nominally "second generation": they were born in the United States, the children of families formed by the arrival of wives from China, who were sometimes accompanied by older children. These wives joined husbands who had come earlier, often twenty years or more, usually as "paper sons." Some ICSA members, however, were third, fourth, and even fifth or more generation Chinese Americans. Some were born in China, having come to San Francisco in the 1950s.

Despite these "generational" differences, almost all ICSA members had longtime family connections to America, either directly or through a history of "split families." This variation of the extended family structure occurred where two or more generations of fathers, grandfathers, and great grandfathers had lived much of their lives in the United States while their wives and children were forced to remain in China due to restrictive US immigration laws. Through these multigenerational connections, ICSA members had a basic awareness of a longer Chinese American history in America, although they usually had limited specific knowledge of it.

Most ICSA members were local, and many lived in San Francisco Chinatown for all or most of their lives. Some had moved out, many remained. Several came from small towns in northern California with very old Chinese American histories like Isleton, Weaverville, and Marysville. Most had parents who worked in sewing factories, restaurants, and small stores, or ran small businesses. Only a few had parents with better paying jobs in mainstream employment. All were the first generation in their families to attend college, most were working their way through school, and many still lived with their families in their local community.

PACE members had somewhat similar backgrounds: most were children of men with earlier histories in the United States who, because of changes in immigration laws in 1946 and their US military veterans' status, were able to bring wives from the Philippines and start families after World War II. In 1968, there was a near even distribution in PACE between members born in the Philippines and those who were second generation. Because of the truncated history of Filipinos in America, very few were third or fourth generation and those were usually of mixed heritage. Many had fathers or other relatives who belonged to the "manong generation" – men who arrived between 1899 and 1935. Like their Chinese American counterparts, they too had an awareness of the earlier "bachelor society" Filipino American experience. Most were also working their way through college and were from well-established Filipino American communities throughout Northern California, ranging from Salinas Valley in the south to Stockton and Central Valley in the east. Their activism was informed by the farm labor movement which was, as is now often forgotten, started by groups with Filipino leaders and majority members (the Agricultural Workers Organizing Committee) that were later joined by the better-known Mexican American union (the National Farm Workers Association) to form the United Farm Workers. They were also intensely curious about the colonial history of the Philippines and the impact of America's relatively recent colonial control on Philippine and Filipino American culture and society.

Both ICSA and PACE had some members who joined the work force right out of high school or served in the US military before going to college. There was nothing unusual about this. In fact, it was very typical of the general population at San Francisco State College at the time.[4]

AAPA was mainly, though not totally, a Japanese American organization. Unlike PACE and ICSA, most AAPA members were sansei and their family backgrounds were more varied in economic status, occupations, and schooling, although almost all their families had the World War II "camp experience" in common. They did not have as many older members but like the other groups, they were largely from Northern California with community concerns that reflected their varied rural and urban origins. Their somewhat more "Americanized" backgrounds and more differentiated social origins may partially explain why the Japanese American students – sometimes individually, sometimes collectively – took slightly different positions from each other and from the other Asian ethnic organizations. AAPA members seemed often more ideologically grounded and were more likely to espouse a pan-ethnic "Asian American" perspective (as reflected in the name of the organization) than the other two groups.

The three organizations saw themselves as community-focused, not simply traditional campus student groups. Prior to the Strike for example, ICSA was primarily concerned with community activities and engaged in a variety of social service endeavors. These included academic tutoring programs, social and recreational work with youth groups, and issue-based community advocacy intended to draw public and governmental attention to needs for improvements in public housing and the development of more social services in Chinatown. Consequently many ICSA members were more involved with the community service element of the organization than with on-campus activities.

AAPA members were developing community-based concerns and activities related to redevelopment and issues associated with wartime internment. They were also involved in the then very new concept, "Asian American," and the related developments of cultural and political consciousness and the growing movement stemming from them.

PACE actively supported the I-Hotel resistance to eviction that began in 1968 and advocated for community opposition to the destructive effects of business-oriented development both north and south of Market Street. They encouraged intergenerational political activism and organized youth groups in SOMA, the Mission, and Bernal Heights. Some PACE members developed a critical perspective of the Philippine government, particularly the Marcos administration – well before the 1972 declaration of martial law – while the Marcos family enjoyed tremendous popularity in the Philippines and among Filipino communities the world over. When anti-Marcos critics, including some members of PACE, began to voice their criticisms publicly, they were soon labeled "communist-inspired" radicals by the conservative leadership elite of their own ethnic community.

Community activism and service had substantial formative influence on all three organizations, which, despite the overlay of ideological rhetoric, were shaped by the pragmatic needs and immediate issues of their respective communities. ICSA, PACE, and AAPA members tended to identify as community people who were going to college, and not as college students who were going back to the community. Given their backgrounds and living circumstances this was an accurate and understandable self-perception. This shared self-concept would continue to affect attitudes, beliefs, operating values, principles, and the direction of their activism long after the Strike and after leaving San Francisco State.

## IDEOLOGY

The public language of those involved in the Strike, including many from the Asian American student groups, was often phrased in the ideological style of the time, with references to Mao Zedong (spelled Mao Tse-tung at the time), Frantz Fanon, and Malcolm X. This language, together with the radical nature of some of their demands, disguised the actual diversity of political perspectives within the three Asian American student groups. There was something of a shared "Third World" perspective, an identification of racism as a major problem in American society, and a strong emphasis on development of a "social consciousness," but the ideological forms expressed and applied by the student organizations and their members differed among and between them.

The demand for and eventual creation of an Asian American Studies program with Chinese, Filipino, and Japanese American components reflected an element of cultural nationalism that was largely driven by the desire for more knowledge about their own communities and cultures that had been previously denied them. This produced a clear "anti-assimilation" perspective, which conflicted not only with the very real pressures to assimilate and acculturate in the United States but also with universalistic tendencies within Marxism that promise superficial recognition of cultural minorities while limiting their access to power. Our ideological perspectives were correspondingly complex.

Some members of the three groups saw themselves as revolutionaries, influenced by international Marxism or domestic militant socialist groups. Others were inspired by the Civil Rights Movement and related traditions, by political movements in Asia, by local activism around issues affecting their own communities and families, or by familial environment.[5]

None of the three groups forced a strict orthodoxy on their members, instead tolerating a range of eclectic personal political perspectives and beliefs. The core standard was a commitment to community and to the particular goals of the organizations.[6] At San Francisco State, whatever the rhetoric, the reality was that the dominant ideological perspective was idealistic, democratic pragmatism.[7]

## THE CAMPUS

San Francisco State College of the mid- and late 1960s was a place where traditional, academic practice was constantly questioned. In addition to the Civil Rights Movement, the "counterculture," with its origins in the white middle class, challenged both conventional standards of behavior and concepts of knowledge. By 1968, the anti-war movement was gaining strong momentum. The world-renowned "Experimental College" has been oft-cited as the most evident expression of this ferment. Its proponents saw the Experimental College as an officially sanctioned venue for trials of innovative teaching methods and techniques, and for the presentation of alternative content that was not in the standard curriculum. Critics saw it as a vacuous waste of resources. While the Experimental College was primarily concerned with the alternative educational interests of the white cultural majority, it was also the setting where a few courses that clearly served as precursors of Ethnic Studies were first offered. Equally important, the Experimental College established precedents for university recognition of new and different areas of study, and the legitimacy of providing funding and credit for such offerings.

Most San Francisco State students lived and worked off campus. As with the Asian American student population, the majority of the students at San Francisco State came from families with "working class" backgrounds and jobs to match, although that did not preclude their families from achieving middle-class, home-owning status. Many faculty came from similar origins and were the first in their families to go to college, often with the benefit of the GI Bill following World War II. Classes were relatively small, compared to today, and the faculty were very accessible to students.

The campus was primarily a "teaching institution" and faculty tended to see teaching as their primary activity. There was also a small progressive and active faculty union. Asian American and Third World activists saw some major deficiencies among these positives: despite a few classes on aspects of Black or other ethnic experience in the Experimental College, the openness of the campus to experimentation on subjects of interest to white students and faculty contrasted with the general lack of attention to the absence of programs or course content related to American Indian, Asian American, Black, Latino, or Mexican American experience. Additionally, the Black student population, which approached 12% in the late 1950s and early 1960s, had declined to under 4% by 1965, the number of US-born or schooled Latino students was very small, and there was growing evidence that suggested certain groups of Asian American students were also underrepresented. The Third World student groups began to examine course titles and content and the admissions process, interests that led to the first major confrontation with the administration.

## EOP and the Prelude to the Strike

Higher education in California was governed by a state-wide "Master Plan for Higher Education." This template for the entire state education system defined a three-part structure for higher education: the University of California (UC) system, the California State College (CSU) system, and the Community College system (then commonly referred to as junior colleges). There were some very positive aspects to the plan, not the least of which was a substantial philosophical and financial commitment to the idea that higher education should be available to anyone who wanted it. On the negative side, it provided a hierarchal structure, with the UC system on top and the junior colleges at the bottom. Analyses of admissions data caused our attention to be drawn to mandates in the master plan about the functions and interrelations among the different areas in the system. We were led to the conclusion that the plan fostered maintenance of a social class system in which many Black and other minority students were being shunted into junior colleges and often dead-ending there. We concluded that the admissions process was exclusionary by design and in effect.

We discovered a category called "Special Admissions." Special admits were students who did not meet standard GPA (grade point average) and SAT (Scholastic Aptitude Test) score requirements but who were admitted on the basis of "special qualifications" – most frequently athletic abilities proven in high school sports. It occurred to us that, if there can be special admissions for good athletes, why can't there be special admissions for students who come from underrepresented communities, especially when their lack of full academic qualifications was often the result of their schools being poorly funded and operated?

The Asian American student groups joined other Third World student organizations to form the "Third World Liberation Front" (TWLF).[8] The TWLF pushed for expanded special admissions for minority students and the provision of associated support programs for such students to succeed academically. Buoyed by federal funding via the Economic and Educational Opportunity Acts, similar programs were being proposed nationwide as "Educational Opportunity Programs" (EOP).

The San Francisco State College administration dragged its feet on these requests and the student groups organized a major sit-in of the campus president's office in the late spring of 1968. This was the first coordinated effort by the TWLF and provided a training ground for the later Strike. The end result, after some confrontations with police, was the establishment of a campus EOP, including some expansion in special admissions and a variety of special classes, tutoring, and support services for the new EOP admits in the fall of 1968.[9]

## The Strike

From our perspective, the Strike was an important element, but only one part of the origins of Asian American Studies. The "glamour" and excitement of periods of open conflict like the Strike often serve to obscure the reality that any new vision becomes successful only with subsequent implementation, involving long and arduous effort, which is often anything but glamorous. The last forty years have seen many important innovations that had potential for positive social change fail due to poor implementation and lack of follow-through. To dwell too long on the Strike might tend to obscure the importance of what followed. It is not the purpose of this essay to recapitulate the history of the Strike but rather to clarify its character and describe its impact on the subsequent development of Asian American Studies at San Francisco State. To that end, we will address selected aspects of that crucial moment in the origin of AAS and the other units in Ethnic Studies on the campus. It should be understood that the Strike was a chaotic affair, and the logic and order of its history is most often a much later reconstruction.[10]

As the fall term opened in 1968, the skeleton of an agenda shared among the student organizations in the TWLF directly addressed the deficiencies of SF State. The immediate triggers of the Strike were disputes over treatment of Black lecturers working in support programs for EOP students. The Black Student Union (BSU) and TWLF quickly articulated a wider range of issues that reflected collective anger and frustration caused by the inability or unwillingness of the institution to deal with the needs of minority students and communities. These concerns were presented as a series of demands, ten from the Black Student Union and five from the TWLF (see Appendix 2 for the list of demands).

The most important demand was the first TWLF demand that "a School of Ethnic Studies for all of the ethnic groups involved in the Third World Liberation Front be set up with the students in each particular ethnic organization having the authority and control of the hiring and retention of any faculty member, director, or administrator, as well as the curriculum in a specific area of study."[11] At that time, a "school" was a separate academic administrative unit within the larger San Francisco State College. What the demand sought was the establishment and enabling of an academic unit with a substantial degree of control and autonomy over its internal processes. This demand for a "school" flowed from the TWLF's core principle of self-determination. More importantly, the demand demonstrates that the TWLF member groups understood the need for as much autonomy and independence as they could acquire within the larger college structure. It is this demand and its ultimate partial acceptance by the administration that made the development of Ethnic Studies programs, especially Asian American Studies, unique in comparison to related efforts at other colleges and universities.

The Strike was not simply a confrontation between students and authority, whether the authority was in the form of the campus administration or the police. On one hand the college administration repeatedly called in large numbers of police to "maintain order," but on the other hand, prior to the imposition of S.I. Hayakawa as President, they also bowed to faculty pressures from the diminutive but potent American Federation of Teachers (AFT) and its allies, and allowed campus-wide debate on the issues. The latter included several massive colloquiums where the TWLF and other groups and individuals were able to explain and justify their demands to overflowing audiences at the largest venues on SF State. These colloquiums were cablecast throughout the campus. There were follow-up meetings with and presentations to individual schools and departments. Students in the TWLF learned to detail, explain, and discuss their demands to a wide range of different groups and coordinated those presentations with each other. The larger student body and faculty were able, if they wished, to gain a better understanding of the issues and the players. These opportunities for extended and repeated explanation and communication drew many previously uncommitted students as well as a number of progressive faculty, into active participation in the Strike. Some faculty participants, like Jim Hirabayashi, believe that the participation of the union had significant impact on the behavior of the administration, both during and after the Strike, with positive results for the development of Ethnic Studies (Hirabayashi, personal communication, 18 July 2008). However, many of the striking faculty were terminated in a vicious post-Strike purge that the Hayakawa administration denied ever occurred.

Although alternately and appropriately called the "Third World Student Strike," not all third world students supported or participated in it. For a variety of reasons, many continued to go to class and, conversely, the greater number of students who did strike and walk the picket lines were white, as were the great majority of faculty who supported the strike demands. It was a complex affair in complex times.

The many communities of the Bay Area were also very much involved in the Strike, though most treatments of Strike history focus disproportionately on campus activity. At the start of the Strike, the TWLF immediately moved to seek outside support. ISCA, PACE, and AAPA engaged in meetings and held forums intended to cull support from individuals and organizations in their respective ethnic communities. Some of these forums, especially those held in Chinatown, drew large crowds and significant press coverage. Community leaders supporting the Strike, and student strikers themselves, presented the Strike to the public as being far more than a student-versus-college administration affair. Growing numbers of leading community figures began to show up on the campus picket lines. Several unions also publicly supported the Strike and sent members to join the picket lines. The intent, which was successful, was to define the issues to the public in larger political terms and to prevent the students from being isolated and vulnerable to police attacks.[12]

The college administration and the TWLF both experienced many internal disagreements. Neither had full control of their supporters' actions. As the Strike continued, it attracted people with agendas ranging from political to personal who wanted to be seen and heard. Some were confrontation "groupies" with little real interest in the goals of the TWLF. The resulting chaos was further aggravated by an intense and often aggressive, militaristic police presence, given purpose and encouragement by highly publicized political figures like San Francisco Mayor Joseph Alioto and California Governor Ronald Reagan.

For students and faculty, the tactical reality of the Strike required the presentation of a unified front. The TWLF's internal unity and cooperation with elements of the Student for a Democratic Society (SDS) were, however, actually real and not merely for appearance value. The TWLF experience was positive in many respects, providing important practical learning and an exciting sense of collective effort and success that many participants remember with considerable fondness and which have continued to shape their political perspectives to the present. The camaraderie and productive interactions with people from different student groups enriched inter-group understanding and provided very valuable lessons in the building of a political movement. Collaboration among the students and community activist groups, however conflicted and imperfect, demonstrated a potential for future collective actions.

Conversely, it sometimes seemed that the operative word in "Third World Liberation Front" was "front" – behind which discord, mutual misperceptions, and other problems festered. As one participant put it shortly after the Strike, "underlying all this effort was a faith that by 'acting as if it were so' the myth (of unity) would at some imperceptible point cease to exist and merge into the realm of reality. Underlying this facade...was a pattern of recurring contradictions and disunity" among the groups which this participant attributed to incomplete political consciousness and an overemphasis on "self determination."[13] Each group had its own agenda and frequently had only limited understanding of the needs and positions of the other groups. For example, the BSU tended to see themselves as the "vanguard," believing that what was best for the Black experience, Black students, and Black community was best for everyone else and that their views and goals were the truly progressive and correct ones. Consequently, they did not always coordinate their activities with the rest of the TWLF and even negotiated separately for Black Studies resources during the settlement of the Strike.

There were also obvious and serious gender issues. The leadership of TWLF and the public leadership of the various student organizations were overwhelmingly male and some of the men did not treat the women with respect. This led to conflict and frustrations for the women activists during the Strike. There was a general failure to address their concerns and to recognize the full extent, substance, and value of their contributions. Strikers with strong intellectual and philosophical commitments to gender equality sometimes found themselves in confrontations within the TWLF and the member student organizations.[14]

The gains of the Strike came with substantial cost. Many strikers and some community supporters were arrested, spending varying amounts of time in jail and in court. Others were beaten by the police. One unfortunate member of ICSA was overlooked in the chaos following a day of mass arrests and languished in jail for weeks as his relatives refused to bail him out and the student organizations assumed he had been bailed out by relatives. This is just one example of tensions with family that some members of ICSA, PACE, and AAPA experienced as they were castigated and ostracized by family members for their activism. While the student organizations received some community support, they were also subject to extreme criticism from many other segments of their communities who encouraged the authorities in their attempts to suppress the Strike by whatever means. Many students, both strikers and non-strikers, lost academic progress, delaying their graduation. This was the period of intense military activity in Vietnam, so male strikers ran significant risk of losing their student deferments and being drafted; some were able to regain their deferments but others had more difficulties.[15]

The larger campus also paid a price. The Experimental College did not survive – some striking faculty suspected that it was a specific target for defunding by the Hayakawa administration. A procedure for offering experimental courses was institutionalized, but the spirit of freewheeling experimentation and alternative approaches to learning was stifled. Many strikers and observers of the Strike have commented that much of the larger dynamic and positive energy on campus faded after the Strike. The reasons were varied but an important factor was that the Strike created schisms in many of the traditional departments between those faculty who supported the Strike and those who opposed it. Bitterness over these divisions remained for many years.

While the period following the Strike was one of positive, creative opportunity for programs like Asian American Studies, the climate campus-wide was not so happy. Additionally, the Trustees and the San Francisco State administration promptly put in place a host of new regulations that were intended to end forever the climate of unfettered debate that they believed helped to spawn the Strike. Consequently, students today are faced with many restrictions on their activities, and the opportunity and space for real public debate on campus are far more constrained than before 1969. Administrators at San Francisco State, especially the campus president, now operate with a degree of arbitrary and unchecked authority that would have been shocking to many in 1968.

## THE RELEVANCE AND LEGACY OF THE STRIKE TODAY

Our goals during the Strike were both simple and ambitious. On a broad scale we wanted the college to become a place in which Asian American history, culture, and communities – which is to say the realities of the Asian American experience – would be accepted as legitimate areas of study at the university level. This was a dream, a push for inclusion and redefining what is American. We wanted Asian Americans to be seen as Americans, not at the price of assimilation and "acceptance" but through a change in the conception of America to one that was broader and more varied in its character. We saw this as an issue of equity; if college is intended to provide students with knowledge and understanding of their society and culture, then it should include ours. But there was a pragmatic aspect to this dream too. We believed that if Asian American students could be provided with a solid understanding of Asian American realities, past and present, that they/we emerge both better individuals and better prepared to help provide for the needs of our communities. We also had hopes for specific learning and skills to assist that end.

We were seeking a change in the character and focus of the college, of academia in general. We wanted a connection between college and communities, believing, hoping, that such connections would be to the long-term benefit of the communities and, secondarily, the college. We wanted the college to serve the communities, not to remove or "rescue" students from their communities.

How relevant are these concerns today? In some

arenas, little has changed in the intervening forty years. The overall content of American schooling remains as resolutely ignorant as ever. It has regressed and is tragically continuing in that direction. In California, for example, the state framework for social studies instruction in the public schools developed in the 1980s did a reasonably good job of including Asian Americans and other ethnic groups in the curriculum, with short-term improvements in the content of textbooks, but this effort has not succeeded over time. Few schools actually implemented any portion of the state framework as it related to Asian Americans and more recent textbook adoptions are scarcely better in their coverage of Asian Americans than those used in 1968. Recent pressures from the "Leave No Child Behind" presidential/congressional project have made the situation in elementary and secondary schools even worse. Such national standards routinely ignore the existence of Asian Americans, much less their local needs, while leaving little incentive or time for teachers and schools to include them on their own initiative.[16]

Nor is improvement on a college level necessarily to be assumed beyond the confines of Asian American Studies programs. While Asian American populations have exploded and spread across the country, the pressures for assimilation are as high as ever and the notion of who and what is genuinely "American" has only slightly expanded. An appropriate understanding and inclusion of Asian American issues and experience within the curriculum of many traditional departments has remained fragmentary or shallow since 1968.[17] Given this reality and the fact that most students still arrive at college with little or no knowledge of the Asian American experience, the importance of strong, community conscious Asian American Studies programs at the college level is even more important than it was forty years ago.

While the growth of Asian American populations in California and in the San Francisco Bay Area ensures a strong Asian American student presence at San Francisco State, system-wide changes in admissions requirements as well local priorities in student recruitment since 1990 are resulting in the exclusion, once again, of whole groups of potential students, including some Asian American populations. This growing problem is much more difficult to address today because the consensus for inclusion and broad financial support for higher education is now historical rather than contemporary. It has been replaced by stricter standards for admission, matriculation, and graduation, elitist attitudes among legislators and administrators, and much higher tuition, fees, and student cost of living.

On a larger stage, the goal of a more inclusive concept of "American" is as important today as it was then. The hostility and exclusion experienced by Chinese, Filipino, and Japanese Americans in the past is now, in a period of increased "security concerns," visited on all new immigrants and many ethnic groups, including some Asian American groups with a history of many generations in the United States. While the residential, employment, social opportunities, and acceptance of many Asian Americans are substantially improved since the establishment of Asian American Studies in 1969, the price of acceptance continues to be a significant degree of assimilation and a casting away of important aspects of ethnic, familial, community, and individual culture and identity.

The Strike was settled on March 20, 1969, with many but not all of the TWLF demands met, the most important success being the creation of an independent School of Ethnic Studies that housed four separate programs: American Indian Studies, Asian American Studies, Black Studies, and La Raza Studies.[18] As a consequence of this victory, AAS (and the other programs) was able to establish itself with more autonomy concerning curriculum development, instruction, and faculty hiring than most other Asian American Studies programs with less institutional independence.

Another legacy of the Strike stems from the fact that THREE separate student groups, each primarily associated with a particular Asian American ethnic community, represented Asian American interests during the Strike. The AAS curriculum at San Francisco State developed strong ethnic-specific content and perspective. The internal governance structure for AAS that evolved after the Strike reflected these distinct, ethnic-specific interests. These topics are discussed in greater detail and length in essays that follow.

Beyond the immediate creation of the Asian American Studies Program, the most important product of the Strike for Asian American communities was a generation of students who participated in the Strike and in the subsequent creation of the AAS Department. Their experience provided them with organizing skills, a shared commitment to community, political sophistication, and considerable self-confidence. They had learned that sustained, organized action could produce results, that coalition efforts – while difficult to build and maintain – can be effective, and that it is important to establish a coherent intellectual foundation for action. Many went on to become important leaders and political players in their own communities, in large part because they were willing to challenge authority and had the discipline to move new ideas from concept to reality.

## NOTES

1. In addition to direct personal knowledge, this essay draws on minutes of the General Planning Group, minutes from individual planning groups, position papers, and a variety

of other departmental documents and notes from the time period. Due to the large number of these documents and the complexity of the subject, we have chosen to provide specific references selectively, as seems useful. We are also indebted to lengthy conversations and communications with Jim Hirabayashi, George K. Woo, Irene Dea Collier, and Juanita Tamayo Lott, as well as more limited comments by Penny Nakatsu, Jeffery Chan, Bette (Inouye) Matsuoka, Laureen Chew, and Richard Wada. The views presented here, however, are those of the authors and we are solely responsible for any errors and oversights. Because the early operation of AAS was generally collective in character, we have generally not named individuals except when deemed essential. A fairly complete listing of those involved in the program during the first two years is provided in Appendix 1.

2. There are exceptions: During her years in parochial schools, Juanita Tamayo Lott reports attention was given to some aspects of the Asian American experience, including Japanese American "internment" in World War II and farm labor movements (personal communication).

3. We argue that defining class status for the families of Asian American students at San Francisco State is both difficult and potentially misleading, except to note that none could be said to belong to the upper class! The distinction between working class and middle class could be very problematic in the 1968 social realities of Chinese and Filipino American families, although perhaps a little easier to define for Japanese Americans. For example, what is the class background of a Chinese American student whose parents are partners in a Chinatown hardware store but whose mother also works in a sewing factory and whose father works as a waiter? What defines class status?

4. Almost all the Asian American student activists were US citizens, although at least one ICSA member was holding a green card during the Strike as a result of being stripped of citizenship for illegal entry. Some of the students in the Latin American Student Organization (LASO), a Third World Liberation Front (TWLF) organization, were also non-citizens. Legal risks made involvement in Strike activities more risky for such students. Some were actually deported or chose the alternative of voluntary departure as a result of their involvement in the Strike.

5. Lott, for example, credits much of her political activism to the influence of labor organizers among her relatives, as well as to the influence of the nuns at the parochial schools she attended. Irene Dea Collier cites the influence of family emphasis on helping other people and concern for being a good person.

6. This did change somewhat in the 1970s, as is discussed in a separate essay.

7. On a non-pragmatic level, some of the more self-described "militant" members of the Asian American student groups, both during and subsequent to the Strike, believed in the principle of armed resistance and acted accordingly, practicing martial arts, obtaining small arms, and engaging in weapons practice. These actions were considered ridiculous by some of the other members of the student organizations, either on moral grounds or because their own experience and knowledge convinced them the idea was absurd or, in some cases, because they noted that some of the most enthusiastic "militants" had a dangerous lack of knowledge of the mechanical function of the weapons, much less their proper care and maintenance.

8. The TWLF was comprised of the Black Student Union (BSU), the Latin American Students Organizations (LASO), the Mexican American Student Confederation (MASC), and three Asian American student organizations, AAPA, ICSA, and PACE. There was no formal American Indian representation in the TWLF but Richard Oakes and a number of others spoke for their interest during this period, although their energies were already given to planning the occupation of Alcatraz Island.

9. EOP students who arrived in the fall of 1968 included a number of people who were to play an important role in the Strike and the subsequent development of AAS, including one of the authors of this essay, Dan Gonzales.

10. The 1998 commemorative conference program book for the 30th anniversary of the San Francisco State Third World Student Strike entitled, *Dreams, Realities, and Challenges in Asian American Studies*, provides a decent summary of the Strike. The essay, "Strike! Asian Americans in the Third World Student Strike," was written collectively by AAS students Jerry Dear, Katherine General, Susan Jeong, Lynne Wong, and Nancy Yin.

11. The original version of the demand was for a school of "Third World" Studies. The change to "Ethnic Studies" was a political compromise, made with serious reservations.

12. See Appendix 1 for the names of some of the community supporters.

13. Dittoed position paper by Penny Nakatsu, 1970.

14. Lott recalls a scene in which Nakatsu confronted Jerry Varnado on these issues, calling him a "male chauvinist pig." Lott notes that it was a memorable scene because Nakatsu was so small and Varnado so large. While Lott claims to have shrugged off the treatment, Irene Dea Collier notes that the situation became even worse after the Strike when she, Lott, Bette (Inouye) Matsuoka, and others were hired into staff positions and became subject to both gender prejudice and associated perceptions by some in the School of Ethnic Studies to whom secretaries exist only to be bossed around by people in higher status positions. These and related issues carried over, unresolved, for many years after the Strike.

15. Pat Salaver, the principal founder of PACE, was sentenced to federal prison after the Strike for refusing to serve in the US military, and suffered many of the adverse circumstances resulting from having a federal felony on his record.

16. This last comment on the situation in California draws from information provided by Irene Dea Collier, a former ICSA member and later a community educator and public school teacher who has worked on State standards and textbook adoptions issues.

17. An example is an argument the authors had in the 1980s with a leading Black political science scholar at San

Francisco State, who asserted that the history of racial politics in California could be addressed with only cursory attention to Asian Americans because all racial political matters are "derivative of Black politics" – a truly mind-boggling example of ignorance, arrogance, or denial.

18. The School was not officially a "school" for several years and the four separate units were called "programs" initially, becoming "departments" only after going through a specific series of administrative procedures. Black Studies is now called Africana Studies, La Raza Studies has become Raza Studies, and American Indian Studies subsequently known as Native American Studies, has later changed back to American Indian Studies.

# A Journey to 20 Days in the "Hole"

*Laureen Chew*

*LOCATION: THE WOMEN'S FACILITY (JAIL) INSIDE THE HALL OF "INJUSTICE" ON BRYANT STREET, SAN FRANCISCO: 1968*

Women are screaming:

"ON STRIKE, SHUT IT DOWN!
ON STRIKE, SHUT IT DOWN!"

THE BUILDING IS SHAKING...(the men are also shouting; they're a floor below/or above us)

"ON STRIKE SHUT IT DOWN!
ON STRIKE SHUT IT DOWN!"

THE BUILDING IS SWAYING....

"ON STRIKE SHUT IT DOWN!
ON STRIKE SHUT IT DOWN!
ON STRIKE SHUT IT DOWN!"

JESUS.... I CAN'T SEE WHAT'S HAPPENING UP FRONT!

HEY, WHAT'S GOING ON?

(I HEAR) A LOUD WHOOSH...BANG.... UGG!

THE ENTIRE ROW OF WOMEN SITTING ON THE BENCHES ATTACHED TO CAFETERIA TABLES ARE MERCILESSLY...VIOLENTLY... SWEPT AGAINST THE WALL...BY HIGH-PRESSURE FIREHOSES.

I'M ONE OF THEM....

ALL IS QUIET.

"PIGS" ARE COMING IN SWINGING... WOMEN SCREAM...WOMEN FALL...PIGS CONTINUE TO SWING THEIR BATONS AND BEAT WHOEVER IS IN FRONT OF THEM.

A GUNSHOT GOES OFF!!!!

NOW IT'S DEAD SILENCE!

I'm drenching WET...scared...pissed...fed up with being stuck here in the Hall of Injustice, arrested, charged with crimes that I thought were my constitutional rights... wishing the PLers (Progressive Labor folks) would just shut the fuck up with repeating "ON STRIKE SHUT IT DOWN!" shit....
I can't wait to get out of this hell-hole.
What am I doing here?????

## Beginning Years

I am a daughter of a Chinese immigrant mom, an American-born Chinese dad. I did not speak much English prior to entering kindergarten at Washington Irving Elementary School, a public school in San Francisco's Chinatown North Beach area. The school was ninety-nine percent Chinese, and my classmates came from similar language and immigrant backgrounds. I am a baby boomer, born in 1948, not too long after the repeal of the Chinese Exclusion laws. I was born into a family that experienced both pre- and post-Chinese Exclusion-era America, where American disdain for anything Chinese was the rule rather than an exception.
My dad was a bartender at the Chinese Sky Room (a nightclub at the end of Chinatown). Mom worked in the sewing factory part-time until I went to high school. I have a brother 18 months younger than I.

School was pretty "cool" in Chinatown. I don't think I loved learning; "learning" consisted of memorizing and pleasing the teacher by doing well in tests. I do not remember school teaching "critical thinking skills." I remember "conforming" as the key to being a good student, to never rock the boat. Of course that was also reinforced at home....

SOCIALIZING is what I loved about school.

My daily routine from the age of six was: go to "American" school, do homework, then go to Chinese school from 4:00 to 6:00 p.m. Come home, do more homework, eat dinner. We had television from about age seven. I remember the Donna Reed Show, Ozzie and Harriet, and the Three Stooges.

While television fed my knowledge of how white people lived and acted at "home," my contact with white folks was minimal.

My daily observances of what white folks were like had much to do with the images I saw when I walked to "Chinese" school from Vallejo and Montgomery to Stockton and Clay Streets. Walking on Broadway Street everyday provided me with images of what white folks were like.

Broadway Street during the 1950s was the height of the nightclub era. I was not oblivious to the fancy restaurants, and glamorously dressed white folks patronizing the clubs. I remembered Vanessi's Restaurant, Joe's Restaurant and Enrico's. There were also nightclubs like Finnochio's with the transvestite "floor shows." People would line up in front of the club dressed in their long beautiful gowns, gloves, and minks. This was a mere block away from my home. It felt like a different, enticing, and definitely more desirable world. I never saw a Chinese among them; no folks of color, period.

It was pretty "heady" stuff for a kid like me to observe on a regular basis. It encouraged my fantasy of a life outside of my own. That, along with my periodic purchases of Photoplay and Modern Screen magazines, enlightened me on how Hollywood and white folks lived.

My own world was busy, if mundane. Any free time on the weekends included playing with the kids who lived in the six-unit building where we lived, or those around the block on Vallejo and Montgomery Streets. My brother and I would, with the kids in the neighborhood, walk to the school playground that was a block and a half away. However, that rarely happened. My mom was a safety freak. Crossing the street on Broadway and Vallejo often proved too much for her to handle. After all, we might be hit by a car, so staying inside the small apartment we lived in was "life" for me.

Mom did not have any family here but we were part of a large extended family on my father's side. He had seven brothers and sisters; one sister had thirteen kids, one had five, and another sister had four kids.

Much of my early years were filled with birthday parties and visits with aunts and cousins. The closest aunt was my father's second-oldest sister, my yee goo ma. She was the one who lived on Kearney Street, behind a clothing storefront.

She was only four blocks from our place and my fondest memories were those of playing with her grandkids on Kearney, between Jackson and Columbus Streets. Roller-skating, playing tag, hide and seek, jacks, marbles, and hopscotch kept my life interesting. Playing in the streets was popular since both playground and indoor space was sparse.

No doubt life was simple...and, at times, downright boring and repetitive. It was a SF Chinatown Chinese American world. Anyone who was not Chinese was an outsider, "gwei lows." "Those" people were a mystery, a curiosity to me.

My American/Chinese school routine lasted from the age of six to about fourteen. Loved "American" school, hated Chinese school.

American school signaled to me several things. Speaking Chinese was not allowed. Teachers used to ring this huge bell into kids' ears during recess and yell "Speak English" if they spoke Chinese. We were "allowed" to be Chinese once a year...on Chinese New Year. On that holiday, many of the girls would dress up in sequined Chinese costumes for school. I sure felt special for being validated as "Chinese for a day."

American school was more "fun" than Chinese school. The teachers were more approachable, there were field trips, we had art projects, and the stories we read were definitely more interesting than what I read in Chinese school.

I attempted to be as American as I can at home. I began with speaking English to my brother, then to my dad, and lastly to my mom. Whoa! I stopped with my mom. She would yell at me if I responded to her in English. "You know I don't speak THAT language, so use CHINESE when I speak to you."

I despised my mother for making me speak Chinese. She didn't know that in American school, we were not allowed to speak it. Only the FOBs spoke Chinese, and they were treated as if they were "retarded."

I learned early to be ashamed of my mom. I did not dare to show her that. She was a tough lady who demanded respect. I had no choice but to obey her in every respect, e.g., speak Chinese, as well as go to Chinese school.

There is something to be said about growing up in Chinatown. Despite the fact that American school demanded total assimilation as the path to "glory in America," my day-to-day reality was that I had to use Chinese. I could not shop or negotiate relationships with folks in Chinatown if I did not speak the language. I did not want to be a total "jook-sing," one who had no

Chinese-ness, and was a "scum" in the eyes "real" Chinese folks.

## Catholic School and a Brave New World

My mom was a bit weird in terms of her religious bent. Growing up on Montgomery and Vallejo Streets, none of my friends who also had immigrant parents went to "church." My mom attended St. Mary's Church on Stockton and Clay every Sunday, and, my brother and I were required to go with her.

I believe I was eight and my brother six when she decided to be baptized. We were baptized soon after and St. Mary's Chinese Mission became a huge part of "my life."

I attended "American" school there in seventh and eighth grades as well as went to Chinese school there in the evenings. My mom was asked to put me in the girls' drum and bugle corps, so my Saturdays were occupied. Sunday was reserved for Mass and more Catechism.

The corps monopolized my life from ages ten until eighteen. It was a brilliant way to keep me out of "teenage" mischief, as well as exposing me to a world outside of Chinatown. I no longer am able to recall the long list of state and county fairs, or suburban parades and competitions I participated in. The most memorable for me were John F. Kennedy's inauguration in Washington DC, and Chiang Kai Shek's last presidential election celebration in Taiwan.

St. Mary's in the late fifties and sixties had a decidedly Chinese American "flavor." Folks who ran the activities in the church were American-born, spoke predominantly English, but also had strong Cantonese-speaking skills. Their aspiration was to be "assimilated," to be accepted/respected/loved by "white folks."

Most members of the church worked government jobs. I learned, either consciously or unconsciously, to be impressed with Chinese Americans who had jobs outside of Chinatown. Having a job outside the "community" was making it; that was being "upwardly mobile."

By the time I was fourteen, Chinatown life began to feel...stagnant. The routine, while comforting, was feeling a bit confining. The gossiping, whether it was heard when food shopping with my mom, at family functions, or hanging out in her sewing factories, was repetitive. We did not have a car, and therefore, rarely left the area. I constantly thought to myself: there must be a more exciting life outside of Chinatown.

When I heard that I was accepted to Notre Dame de Victories High School in 1962, I was I was ecstatic. I would be meeting new people. I would be visiting their homes and participating in activities outside of Chinatown. It was so exciting just thinking about it.

Thank you God!!!

It is an understatement to say I had high expectations for Notre Dame des Victoires (NDV). I did not know what EXACTLY to expect. But, there is something delusional about going to a "prized" school. I had to believe that it would be a great experience. Why would it be a "prized" school if it was anything short of FABULOUS?

Well, it was not fabulous. To this day, more than forty years later, my memories of NDV remain painful ones. I suppose it is similar to Chinese Americans who lived their lives outside the protective confines of Chinatown during that era. By 1962, the Chinese Exclusion law had been repealed twenty years earlier. Yes, the Civil Rights movement was well on its way, with ground-breaking decisions like Brown vs. the Topeka Board of Education.

Unfortunately, changing laws and having a Civil Rights movement that was disconnected from those who were not black or white, did not insure appropriate behavioral changes for those of us who were attending predominantly white schools. NDV represented the "status quo" of the time. The five girls of color in my freshman class (four Chinese, one African American) were on the bottom of the social/cultural "food chain" of the school.

My high school years was the first time I experienced "innocence" being taken from me, where the world as I knew it, where my sense of self, which had been previously supported, nurtured, and secure, totally fell apart, disintegrated. I did not understand any of it.

Coincidentally, it was also the first time my parents had a business outside of Chinatown.

We owned a laundry on Polk Street between California and Pine Streets. People who patronized us were white, predominantly white men, and gay (this was before the Castro was popular).

It was the first time I saw my parents interact with white folks.

I did not understand why my dad was called a "stupid Chinaman" at our laundry when we misplaced a white man's sock.

I did not understand why dad never yelled back when he was racially insulted. He masked his humiliation by nodding his head laughing as he was insulted.

My mom, on the other hand, did not laugh. She would deny losing anything and say something like: "you left at home, not here." She "didn't take no shit."

I did not understand why I hated being Chinese in high school. I blamed my parents for being Chinese. I blamed the both of them for not having friends at NDV. I did everything I could to make their lives miserable. Yelling at them was my normal response to anything they requested of me.

Why did I despise being Chinese?...because I never measured up to the white girls at NDV. My clothes were homemade, they looked "dorky," often made from reject fabric my mom received free from her sewing factory. My hair was a disaster. We had no money for the hairdresser. My mom gave me home perms. But she never timed the perm correctly. My hair was this unsightly mess. I hated her for making me even uglier than I felt.

Truth be told, I acted like an orphan in high school. Never went to mother-daughter fashion shows, mother-daughter breakfasts, mother-daughter teas, etc. My mom never stepped foot in NDV for the entire four years. I was elated she sat in the back of the church when I graduated.

I ended my high school experience not understanding my anger, and self hate. I hated, just hated the fact that I was born Chinese. Hated the language, hated the values put on being a Chinese girl (no dating, no dances, no leaving the house, etc.), hated NDV. Hated that we could not afford anything the other girls had: a car, store-bought clothes and shoes, vacations (what's that?), owning a home.... RACE and CLASS, RACE and CLASS. They were not separate issues.

My mom's retort to me was: "what do those white folks know? They have no culture. We, on the other hand have more than 5000 years of Chinese culture." Five thousand years of Chinese culture? So what? We're in America. They don't care about Chinese culture.

It was confusing to me, the mixed messages I received from the Chinese American adults. I knew they did not think much of "white folks." That they feared them, didn't trust them, etc....Then at the same time they wanted to emulate them, be accepted by them.

## SAN FRANCISCO STATE AND BEYOND

I wanted to "go away" for college. Unfortunately my parents spent their money on NDV. I had to pay for college myself. In addition, I was a girl, and "good" girls did not move away from home at the age of seventeen or eighteen. San Francisco State College was my only choice.

I loved SFSU. The teachers were inspiring; they were funny. Learning was fun, but not easy.

I reacquainted myself with classmates from Washington Irving, St. Mary's, and from Chinese school. Reconnecting with them was both comforting and reassuring. Having friends from the past made the adjustment of coming from a small to large school much easier.

However, after a year or two of hanging out with a particular group of Chinese Americans, I again felt like a misfit. The girls were devoting too much effort and time to snatching a boyfriend, hoping to be engaged before graduation, and married shortly after.

I tried to fit in by doing the same. But the Chinese guys just were not interested in me.

Maybe I was too loud? Not pretty enough? Too opinionated? Too caustic? Too direct? It did not help that I asked them out on dates, instead of vice versa. "Women's lib" was not a mindset for my male contemporaries of

Chinese descent.

I met Judy Gin while working at the library. She was godsend. We connected...in a manner that was similar to relationships I had in K-8 schooling. Judy grew up in South San Francisco when it was predominantly white. The racism she confronted in K-12 was achingly like mine, and she coped with it similarly...by wishing that she was not Chinese.

Judy was different than me because she had broader interests. She explored activities on campus. I, on the other hand, was still abiding by my mother's dictates... go to school, work at school, and then go to the family laundry to help. I had no idea what was happening on campus.

One day Judy came to the library during my work hours and was really excited about a meeting that was convening on campus. She urged me to go. She told me I would like it, as well as identify with the content. Her excitement was contagious.

I had a sneaky suspicion that going to this "meeting" might not be something my parents would approve of. Judy said something about Black people and how they were angry, like us. My folks did not have good things to say about Black people; they told us they were troublemakers. The riots on TV fueled that image.

I still had a lot of anger to work through because of my high school experiences. Anything that would help me work that through seemed reasonable to me.

I went to that packed meeting. For the first time in life, I heard life stories from Black, Chicano, and other Asian Americans that mirrored my own. The anger expressed was coupled with reasons why. Specific examples of racism were presented; it is because of racism that I have been made to feel inferior, and be inferior.

I was finally getting some answers....

The details of my day-to-day involvement with the Third World Liberation Front Strike are blurry now, forty years later. Many days were spent marching, meeting, and being involved in a host of community activities in Chinatown. More traumatic personal outcomes included a month-long jury trial, being found guilty of three misdemeanors, sentenced for twenty days, appealing, seeking probation, being denied,...and spending twenty days in jail during the summer of 1970. What has not diminished with time is recalling the tremendous sense of camaraderie, and, totally audacious attitude that we can change an unjust world.

The Strike gave me "permission" to explore and reacquaint myself with a Chinatown I did not know. Issues of poverty, language loss, and job discrimination all surfaced for me during that time. This fact was evident: that as students we understood and embraced working in, and for, the community – for Chinatown.

I worked as a "houseparent" at a home for runaway

girls. It was named: "Mok Lan" and was sponsored by the Salvation Army. I lived there part-time and worked with girls who had "drug problems." I could not believe the extent to which drugs were prevalent in Chinatown, and how the Chinese Playground was a popular place to get "high." Working with the girls and their mothers helped me understand my issues with my own mom.

During the week I also tutored, with other Strikers, at Commodore Stockton School (now called Gordon J. Lau). The kids were new immigrants, who, like myself, had few English skills entering school. They came from homes where parents were working in low-paying Chinatown jobs, again similar to myself. It was inspiring and rewarding working with them. My decision to become a teacher was largely due to what I learned of myself from working with them.

Then there was a Saturday Junior League afterschool program. It was funded by the SF Junior League and I was selected to coordinate the program with the Activities Coordinator at Cameron House. It was an interesting experience because Cameron House at that time was serving predominantly American-born Chinese kids...kids from the "Richmond" or "Sunset." I did not feel the immigrant kids were always welcomed at Cameron House, particularly by the ABCs. At times, I made my anger known that this would not do.

There was so much going on in Chinatown in the late 1960s and the 1970s. I cannot begin to list all that the Strikers and I were involved with. It was a time of transition in Chinatown politics. Chinatown was moving from a community that was forced to "take care of its own" to one that would be different, that would include voices and funding outside. College students were seen as a force from the "outside."

I was part of the first generation of Chinese Americans who "reaped" the benefits of the "Civil Rights" movement. Government programs, in response to "righting the wrongs" of the past, allowed many of us opportunities that previous generations did not have.

Federal funds supported such programs like "Teacher Corps," which was committed to funding "minority" students to receive their teaching credentials and return to teach in their communities. I was able to become an elementary teacher and teach during the 1970s due to that.

During the late sixties and seventies, federal funds, with language from the 1964 Civil Rights Act, supported nation-wide bilingual cross-cultural programs. I taught in a federally funded Chinese bilingual cross-cultural program in Chinatown in the 1970s. I remember I could not believe the first time I walked into a bilingual class at Commodore Stockton School. I heard the kids speaking Chinese and the teacher actually using the language for instruction.

I could not believe it! My entire education taught me to discard my Chinese language, culture, and values. I was ashamed of speaking it and was embarrassed by my mom who ONLY spoke Chinese. It was never acceptable for us to use it in American school. In fact, my mother was told not to speak to us in Chinese by my elder cousins because it would retard our English, and I would speak accented English.

Here I was, in a classroom of Chinese immigrant second graders, learning both English and Chinese in American school and doing well. They were not silent, they were not disengaged, they were thriving and excited by learning. It was liberating for me to see and experience. Teaching in the program had to be the highlight of my entire career. It was new, and therefore creative, politically engaging, and fulfilling.

By the time I arrived at SFSU in that late 1970s, I had quite a few experiences in being an "advocate" and community worker within the context of a "new" Chinatown. I continued to work with ethnic coalitions in the area of education, specifically bilingual cross-cultural education. New community agencies started, e.g., Chinese for Affirmative Action, Self-Help for the Elderly, EOC (Economic Opportunity Council), Youth Council, and Youth Service Center, to name a few.

They were exciting times. They were times in the community where the dreams and hopes of Civil Rights, and the TWLF Strike actually took form in real/tangible activism. For me, that period cannot be replicated; that mixture of "idealism" and "reality" being one and the same.

Coalitions with other ethnic groups to reach common goals continued here at SFSU. However, it has not been as easy as it was for me when I was teaching at SF Unified Schools. The politics here are different; the issues of protecting one's turf are more intense, and the stress of individual achievement versus the common good is blurred (to put it mildly). Yet the College of Ethnic Studies remains a reminder that it began as a "coalition" struggle, and its survival will depend on that.

It saddens me to see how younger people of color now believe it is solely because or their "merit" and "skill" that they are now able to enter fields traditionally excluding us generations before. These opportunities did not materialize with a white power structure suddenly having an "epiphany" and wanting to make it "right." They were "won" with the "blood, sweat, and tears" of those before them. Many Asian Americans now have no clue how the Civil Rights movement benefits them.

I credit the TWLF Strike for inspiring me to re-examine myself and my "place" in America. My Chinatown experiences, coupled with experiences of the TWLF Strike, developed a subsequent desire to make things "right" for the underserved, no matter what job I held or "visible" role I pursued.

Change, commitment, community....These words are forever etched in how I live my life due to my participation in the TWLF Student Strike. Simply put: if there is to be change, it is not only for the individual, but the "whole" or community, and, that change cannot occur without commitment and hard work in collaboration.

The months of striking, the month-long trial, the year of waiting for an appeal, and the subsequent twenty days I spent in jail (the "hole") as a Striker represented my commitment, optimism, and belief that "change" can and must occur. I suppose I can say that those twenty days in the "hole" carved a path for me to become "whole," both professionally and personally.

# A Short Piece on the San Francisco State Strike

*Bette (Inouye) Matsuoka*

I was asked to write a reflective piece about my involvement in the 1968 San Francisco State Strike and about other women I knew who were also involved.

Three friends whom I would like to particularly write about are Penny Nakatsu, Miyo Ota, and Jane Maki Tabata. They have been my friends for forty years.

What got us involved? I think I can collectively speak for the four of us and say that it was, quite simply, our desire for social change and social justice, and our commitment to activism. Our liberal and often radical and passionate ideals strengthened during that time of unrest in the late 1960s. We were all members of the Asian American Political Alliance (AAPA), "ah-pa," a fairly new student organization on campus.

I remember AAPA as a small group made up mostly of Japanese American and Chinese American students. With no disrespect to any of the other former female members, I also remember Penny and Miyo as probably the two most active women in the group. Shortly before the Strike, AAPA was a part of the Third World Liberation Front (TWLF) on campus. When momentum was building around the Strike, it was their persuasiveness and perseverance that got AAPA individuals to take a firm stand to fully support the Strike, not only by walking out of our classes, but to commit to its activities.

Penny's involvement was one of leadership. She was brilliant, articulate, and at the forefront as a major spokesperson for our organization. She was highly visible among the backdrop of male peers and male leaders because she was often the only woman spokesperson at the on-campus convocations and teach-ins. She also represented us at organizational and community meetings. She publicly spoke up against President S.I. Hayakawa and argued for the inclusion of a Japanese American Studies program at San Francisco State. Soon after the Strike ended, Penny developed and wrote much of the curriculum that is still being taught today.

Miyo also held her own among the leadership of strikers. She was a born organizer. Her accomplishment in assisting the Strike was seen in her efforts with grassroots organizing. Miyo was responsible for raising funds for legal defense and assigned us to go to public places such as the Fillmore or Avalon Ballrooms to collect donations. She asked us to make and sell food, attend teach-ins, pass out pamphlets in and around the campus, join the picket lines, and attend the rallies.

I recollect Maki had excellent oral and written communication skills, and handled information and community outreach. She was responsible for developing and securing liaisons between AAPA and Japanese American organizations in San Francisco and Berkeley. She worked with churches such as Pine Methodist and Glide Memorial. Her contacts were with community leaders such as Rev. Lloyd Wake and Janice Mirikitani. Both Lloyd and Janice became loyal supporters of the student strikers, due largely to the efforts of Maki and others, who educated them on the Strike's significance.

There were other women whom I also remember from this time. Donna Nomura and Masayo Suzuki were founding members of AAPA. During the Strike, Donna, I believe, was committed to legal defense work. Masayo, an Art major, designed, printed, and sold posters to raise funds. There were women in other groups who were working alongside of us as well; to name a few: Judy Seto, Laureen Chew, Irene Dea Collier, and Juanita Tamayo. Judy, Laureen, and Irene were members from the Intercollegiate Chinese for Social Action (ICSU). They were instrumental on campus and in the development of Chinese American Studies and the Asian American Studies Department. In the community they worked with social agencies and organizations in Chinatown. Juanita did the same for Filipino American Studies. She was a member of the Pilipino American Collegiate Endeavor (PACE) and also became the first secretary in Ethnic Studies.

As for my involvement, I can't think of any one major contribution that I made during this time. Nor was there any particular assignment that I became attached to, or involved with, that stands out in my mind. Reflecting on my role now, I was just one of hundreds of strikers. In order to keep the mechanics of our cause ongoing, I pretty much did ground-level tasks wherever needed. Since attending classes wasn't an option, I spent time away from the picket lines and rallies, going to meetings, collating flyers, collecting donations, making picket signs, and even speaking at a few teach-ins with Penny. This was nothing special, since all of us collectively shared in these responsibilities. Today, the women whom I knew from this time still joke around and agree that "it was the men who were out there being visible, and it was the women who did the work."

Although I only remember fragmented pieces of the events that took place during the Strike, the significance of this time for me was the building of relationships and friendships in the midst of building Ethnic Studies. What seems incredible to me now is that everyone mentioned here (with the possible exception of Masayo or Donna) was in their sophomore or junior year in college. And most likely, none of us was even twenty-one and old enough to vote. It is awesome to believe that students at such a young age could help create change in the dynamics of institutionalized education and public policy.

I can still see the faces of other women in the TWLF, and once in a while, a mentioned name would connect with a figure or an incident. The Strike connected women from all walks of life who joined together to fight for a cause. It was a time when we shared not only our commonalities and sensibilities, but also a respect and recognition of our diversities. Had it not been for the Strike and these circumstances, I don't think I would have had the opportunity to meet such a diverse group of women. Forty years later, the particular women in this essay still remain remarkable and formidable. I am fortunate to still know most of them today.

# Looking Back

## (May 18, 2008)

*Alan S. Wong*
*(as told to Irene Dea Collier)*

*The following are excerpts from an interview with Alan S. Wong, one of the first instructors in Chinese American Studies.*

I was asked to teach Chinese in America (a history class) in fall 1969. At the time, the only published books on Chinese were Rose Hum Lee's The *Chinese in the United States of America* and Gunther Barth's *Bitter Strength*. Neither one was quite what I needed, so I had to develop my own sources. I had a knack for spotting important articles on Chinese Americans and I used razor blades, cut newspaper articles, and put them in a scrapbook. When we had mimeograph machines, I had the articles retyped, filed, and categorized with the help of Irene Dea Collier. I also took many slides of current issues regarding youth, health, and seniors with the help of John Rink. These were the materials that I used for my classes. If we had the technology that we have now, the job would have been so much easier.

The juvenile delinquency issue was very visible and seniors were dying in single room hotels with no kitchens and one shared toilet per floor.

Despite these problems, President Lyndon Johnson's War on Poverty Program refused to give any money to Chinatown. The attitude was that "Chinatown takes care of its own." Rev. Larry Jack Wong, Rev. T.T. Tam, Diana Ming Chan, and I organized a tour of Senior Community Single Room Occupancy (SRO) Hotels with the National EOC (Economic Opportunity Council) members. During this tour, the EOC members witnessed firsthand the appalling living conditions of Chinatown's seniors. The EOC members were shocked into action and San Francisco Chinatown was included as a "target area" for funding through the War on Poverty Program.

It was a time of great upheaval and I jumped at the chance to take on many jobs that reflected the times. I started out at the Chinatown YMCA, then worked as a community organizer in the War on Poverty Program where I helped, with others, establish Self-Help for the Elderly, Planned Parenthood, and Tenant's Associations in Ping Yuen, Manilatown, and North Beach Housing Projects. I had also worked with Ron Dellums in the Concentrated Employment Program in the Mission District. When George Washington High School erupted, I was assigned as ombudsman from the Metropolitan YMCA to help students resolve their differences.

What brought me to San Francisco State was the Third World Liberation Front's desire to inhabit the full bungalow which was shared with the Black Student Union and the College Y. The College Y staff member was extremely uncomfortable, felt forced out, and left. I transfered into her job and shortly thereafter, the demand for Ethnic Studies touched off a student strike. A photograph showed Rev. Larry Jack Wong, Rev. Harry Chuck, Yori Wada, his son Richard, Edison Uno, and myself in the demonstration, supporting the student strike.

All this activism had some effect. When I taught the Sociological Profile course, I wanted to take the students to the Wong Family Association, but a Chinatown elder refused to let me enter because he said I was a "communist." Funny thing was, the FBI agent assigned to Chinatown knew me and was in my Community Bible Class! Still, I was "persona non grata" in many circles. Even my pastor accused me of being an "ultra-liberal gadfly." I said, "I didn't come to worship you; I came to worship God."

Despite the difficulties in that first semester of Ethnic Studies, the caliber of the students was good and some were very inquisitive. There was a great deal of dialogue between the students and the faculty members. Among the students, there were different reactions to my involvement. Some were receptive; some were not. Even for the students at the time, many said I was too radical.

In 1968 the juvenile delinquency issue kept escalating.

Judge Harry Low and George Woo tried to get the Chinatown establishment to understand the needs of the immigrants and young people in gangs. The Chinatown Youth Council was formed and held meetings. Even so, by 1971, the street gangs took over Chinatown, smashed windows, slashed theater seats, and ate at restaurants and refused to pay. An Espicopal priest asked to hold a Council of Churches meeting at my church and while in atttendance, I answered questions about gang activity taking place in Chinatown. The next morning, my photo was on the front page of the *San Francisco Examiner* and I received a warning that the gangs were about to target me for speaking to the media. Dianne Feinstein, now a US Senator, offered to put me up in her home.

For some reason, I never felt the intensity of the criticism; I just continued what I thought needed to be done. With other grassroots leaders, I helped establish more organizations to address youth and economic issues: the Summer Youth Program, Educational Opportunities Program, and Asian Incorporated. In the political arena, I was President of the Chinese American Democratic Club in 1969. I ran for public office in 1966 for the Democratic Central Committee and in 1982, 1986, and 1989 for the Community College Board. In most of them, I placed first.

At home, all the credit goes to my wife, Rachel. She did a wonderful job raising our two children, Kimberly and Kevin. I have beautiful grandchildren, ages 9, 7, 5, and 3. Rachel is from Greenville, Mississippi and attended a segregated school in a one-room schoolhouse. She graduated with a college degree in Texas and taught in San Francisco.

I withstood the criticism. My faith helped me. The issues don't die, even after all those years.

# ETHNIC EDUCATION:
# ITS PURPOSES AND PROSPECTS

*James A. Hirabayashi*

*NOTE: The following paper was presented at the Second Annual Conference on Emerging Programs at University of Washington, Seattle, 7-9 Nov. 1974, when James Hirabayashi was Director/Dean of Ethnic Studies at San Francisco State College.*

## INTRODUCTION

In this essay I will focus on some basic assumptions underlying the education of certain ethnic minorities in this country, the problems of articulation with traditional educational systems, and future prospects given this condition. When I say certain ethnic minorities, I make a distinction between all ethnic minorities which refer to: "any group which is defined or set off by race, religion, or national origin, or some combination of these categories"[1] and those ethnic groups who consistently experience forms of social and economic discrimination in our society. Specifically, I will relate to Black, Mexican, Latin, Asian, and Native Americans. I do not wish to imply that this definition only distinguishes these groups, but the primary push for the redefinition of education for the ethnic minorities has essentially come from members of these ethnic groups.

Before beginning with the theme of this essay I will make my biases explicit. I am an advocate of separate Ethnic Studies programs and am an active participant in one such program. My direct experience in program development has been primarily with the Asian American Studies program and as an administrator of the School of Ethnic Studies at San Francisco State University. As a result, the following analysis will rely heavily upon the events at San Francisco State, the site of one of the initial confrontations to start an independent Ethnic Studies program. Finally, I am formally trained in the field of anthropology.

## ETHNIC EXPERIENCE AND ETHNIC EDUCATION

Given the fundamental principles underlying our society, it seems inevitable that certain ethnic minorities in this country should ultimately rise in protest of the existing conditions. After years of adapting to a situation of inequity and noting the discrepancies between the society's ideal values and behavioral norms and attitudes in regard to many phases of their lives, it is surprising that they should have waited so long. Perhaps in terms of a long historical perspective it will not be assessed so, but the events of the tumultuous Sixties appear to be a culmination of pent-up emotions exploding into action. Undoubtedly one related factor was the push for gradual social change during the Fifties on the part of the liberals with the ultimate goal of integration of the ethnic minorities into the mainstream of American life. There was a certain style used, characterized by legal analyses, deliberate strategies, and the mobilization of people for non-violent confrontations. However, these events were quickly to be followed by spontaneous and more extreme forms of direct confrontation in the urban centers where there were concentrations of low income ethnic populations. For them, conditions had become too drastic; it became a matter of survival to act for the changes; economic and social conditions were too slow in evolving and emotions could no longer be contained.

The thrust on educational institutions came somewhat later but rests essentially on the same assessment of the conditions operating within the American society. However, inasmuch as the educational institutions are one of the major means of socializing future citizens, a re-examination of these institutions is particularly crucial in considering the process of social change. In the quest for social change, reform in education is a necessary part of the general process of change to better life conditions for these ethnic minorities.

Most of the early essays concerning the need for the development of Ethnic Studies based their rationale upon an emotional assessment of the life conditions of ethnic groups in our society. This was certainly legitimate in view of the situation as outlined above when the development of concerns about the plight of the ethnic minorities was intricately interwoven with concrete events such as discrimination in housing, employment, and other forms of inequity. These events relate essentially to a question of racism and therefore an emotional evaluation was a natural outcome of the situation. However, it is not the fact of racism *per se* that gives us the rationale for Ethnic Studies; it only gives us the reason for the development of the rationale. The correct way of developing a rationale for Ethnic Studies is to recognize its legitimacy and to create a positive base from which to construct a meaningful program for the people it is to serve. To build a rationale on the basis of racism results in negativism, and this is not a healthy base upon which to develop a creative program.

The recognition of the legitimacy of Ethnic Studies essentially rests upon an assessment of American society as a pluralistic society. Public and social science ideologies and theories concerning the relations of ethnic groups to American culture and society can be classified into three main types: (1) conformity to dominant society standards (assimilation); (2) biological, cultural and social blending into a new synthesis (acculturation); and (3) preservation of significant portions of the original culture and society within the context of the American society (pluralism). It would appear, from a cursory assessment of the literature, that the majority of the public and social science views are either explicitly or implicitly formulated in terms of the first type with an underlying assumption of an eventual assimilation to "middle class standards." It would seem that this goal motivated the actions of the liberals of the Forties bent upon easing the ethnic minorities into one mainstream of American life. This view and the second view, i.e., the "melting pot synthesis," both postulate a unitary model with the expectation that people conform to the model.[2] Of the two, the second type is much more palatable to the ethnic minorities, for at least there is some attention paid to the variety of unique cultural experiences which are a part of their lives. However, there is an assumption that cultural traits from a variety of sources are resynthesized into a new unitary model which would provide an *equally meaningful model* for all people.

When the conceptualization is made in terms of a unitary model, regardless of the sources of the model, ethnic groups are seen as assimilating from divergent cultural backgrounds to some single uniform American culture. Let us examine the case of the migrant ethnic groups for illustrative purposes. A large number of social scientists' assessments of the adjustment of the migrant ethnic groups in America have used a particular type of the acculturation-assimilation model. Briefly, an ideal type is postulated for the original culture and society and likewise an ideal type is conceptualized for the American culture and society. Ethnic groups are then studied in the new setting and their adjustments assessed in terms of "how far they have diverged from the original culture and society" and "how close they have come to the American culture and society." Some ethnic groups are then considered "more progressive" than others because they have assimilated more rapidly. Consider the assessments made of the Japanese Americans where they have often been labeled "model minorities."[3] They are assessed as having made good adjustments to the degree that they have conformed closely to the ideals of middle class society.

There are several underlying assumptions in this type of acculturation-assimilation model. There are assumptions that the idealized models on both ends of the continuum are correct assessments of the realities and there is a further assumption that the change moves along a continuum. However, there are, in fact, many differences in levels and orders of abstractions which are subsumed when a single model is generalized for the original culture which the migrant is purported to have brought with him to the new setting. Differences in the ideal-behavioral, regional, class, rural-urban and other norms have been subsumed to generate the single "idealized" model. That the migrant population is a self-selected sample which may deviate from the idealized norms, and that it usually comes from specific segments of the original society are facts that are ignored. In short, the conceptualization of the original culture and society of the migrants is usually an over-generalization which disregards the special situation and conditions of the migrants. The expectation that everyone moves along a continuum is based on the assumption that we have had in the past, do have in the present, and will have in the future a uniform culture and society.

Thus we have migrants bringing their "cultural baggage," whatever segments of the original society from whence they come, and whatever conceptualization of the ideal values of the original society, and adapting creatively to the new environment as they assess it. They do not recreate the original culture and society in totality for that is impossible. What they do is to develop new meanings and relationships adapting old forms where they can, but in novel ways. The important point here is that factors in the particular environment of the new setting will most certainly affect the kind of adaptation that takes place. The development of ethnic communities cannot be an exact recreation of the original cultural form in the new environment, nor is it a uniform adaptation to some generalized ideal which subsumes the particular settings of these ethnic communities. The distinctive resolution of any ethnic group should not be evaluated simply as a movement away from some "ideal" toward some other "ideal." Rather, it should be viewed as a creative development, an evolutionary development rather than a horizontal movement; and it is an ever continuing process.

I have used the example of recent migrant ethnic groups to illustrate the adaptive process to the general society. The migration of the Black people is quite distinct. They were torn from their social and cultural contexts in Africa and forcibly resettled, by and large and consciously, in a socially fragmentary fashion. The slave traders and plantation owners broke up social groups in order to maintain an oppressive social and economic control over them. In spite of this social and cultural oppression, traits and trait complexes survived and combined with new adaptations to develop into unique cultural forms in the new setting. If I do not elaborate further here it is because I am not as familiar with the details of this process (and these should initially be developed by Black people themselves), but we need not belabor the point that Black culture and society has many characteristic traits and a style which distinguish it from that of "middle class" America, and that it is a viable and evolutionary entity.

The Native Americans, of course, were not migrants but the original settlers of this continent. In spite of long-term governmental policies which were designed either to eliminate or to assimilate them (the ultimate goal of the Bureau of Indian Affairs was to work themselves out of a job after assimilation was complete), the Native Americans who were not completely decimated by social and cultural genocide through wars, disease, and social and economic oppression continued to evolve their own unique distinct lifestyles.

Thus the Black and Native American situations differ from that of recent ethnic migrants insofar as time of contact is concerned, but in each case the minorities continued to evolve a unique style of living. Therefore, regardless of the group in question, no one can seriously question the existence of ethnic communities with lifestyles which vary from that characterized as "middle class America." This fact, coupled with the existence of racism in its many forms,[4] gives rise to several specific educational needs among those who grow up, live in, and relate to these communities. These needs fall into two major categories: those which pertain to the understanding of the minorities themselves as members of ethnic communities; and those which pertain to the relationship between that ethnicity and the total society. As it has been one of the functions of educational institutions to facilitate the discovery and internalization of a "correct" model for individuals in our society, it becomes necessary to challenge traditional education which has generally been based on a normative philosophy with an assumption of assimilation to a single uniform society. To the extent that the traditional educational system assumes a unitary model for all members of the society and to the extent that it does not relate directly to the perceptions and conceptions of the ethnic minorities, the ethnic minorities cannot readily find meaning for themselves if a positive understanding of their primary experience is prevented. Moreover, racism compounds their problem for their primary experiences are judged negatively.

There are those who contend that the traditional educational system no longer holds assumptions which prevent the ethnic minorities from dealing with primary issues of their ethnicity because certain corrections have been made now, and ethnic content is being added to the traditional curricula; but I will argue that basic changes have not been made. Moreover, the traditional educational system is resisting changes which will allow Ethnic Studies to develop the postulates needed to serve the primary needs of ethnic education. The main thesis of this essay is that the basic assumptions underlying traditional education do not accommodate concepts and perceptions of the ethnic minorities without immediately distorting them. And without fundamental changes in traditional education, I remain an advocate of separate Ethnic Studies programs.

## THE UNIVERSITY SETTING

The university, in its broadest definition, is characterized as a place for learning where knowledge and new ideas are developed, where students are prepared for useful lives in our society, and a place where self-awareness and intellectual development are promoted. Although there are many sources we may use for an assessment of the university and its purposes, I shall take one by my colleagues at San Francisco State University, for not only do they review the meaning of the university experience for students, but they do so in the context of the events which led to the strike of 1968. Let us first begin by examining their views on how institutions fit into other aspects of the total culture and society in terms of their social ideologies:

A fully developed ideology provides individuals and groups with a frame of reference that includes assumptions, projected ideals, and expected patterns of behavior and processes...mature ideologies include assumptions about: (1) the nature of the universe and man's relation to it; (2) the nature of man and his relation to his fellows; (3) the purpose of institutions and their relationships to individuals and groups; (4) ideal goals and purposes of individuals to be nurtured by institutions and society; and (5) appropriate processes and acceptable behavior providing the means suggested by (1) through (4) above.[5]

They also describe the university as an institution which has at least nine different lives: life as an explorer, preserver and transmission belt, processor and quality controller, quasi-home, tribal rite, critic, change agent, place for self-discovery, and as a corporation.[6]

In a traditional educational institution, if we assume as an objective a uniform culture and society, a single uniform normative ideology would suffice as there would be compatible assumptions underlying the ideology. However, because of the diversity of the lifestyles of the people who make up this nation, the assumptions underlying the ideology of middle class society must be called into question. Let us isolate one of the assumptions contained in their definition of a mature ideology, the nature of man and his relation to his fellows, and view it in conjunction with one of the "lives" of the university experience, life as a place for self-discovery. If the life styles for the ethnic minorities are at variance with that of "middle class" America, as has been argued above, it follows that the ethnic minorities cannot achieve self-understanding if they approach self-discovery with assumptions and perceptions other than their own. Unless ethnic education sees the development of a rationale based on their own assumptions, all other goals become diverted. The "lives" of the University as an institution, if they rest on middle class assumptions, do not serve the basic needs of the students from ethnic communities.

Given these differences, the issue of control of Ethnic Studies programs becomes paramount. The irony of the strike at San Francisco State is that the very people who were forced to recognize Ethnic Studies are the self same people who now sit in judgment of everything that is done. All programmatic developments, all staff appointments require ultimate approval by those in charge of the institution. If we isolate the assumptions underlying the "ideal goals and purposes of individuals to be nurtured by institutions and society" (No. 4 above), and take that in conjunction with one of the lives of the institution as a corporation, we can readily determine what administrators are charged to do, and there is immediate and basic conflict. Specifically, the conflicts come out explicitly in almost all decision making procedures in the development of the program. Questions such as: Do all of the courses meet the academic standards? Are the teachers qualified to teach? Does the format in terms of which the course is conceptualized fit into the existing curriculum? All are judged in terms of standardized traditional criteria and ultimate fit into the general educational system. Here I am not necessarily charging administrators with conscious and malevolent intent, I am merely pointing out that the pervasive nature of the basic assumptions underlying the system are never made explicit, but they affect the nature and kind of adjustments forced upon Ethnic Studies at every turn. Thus, the issue of control is not simply a Machiavellian grab for power, as many have characterized those who press for Ethnic Studies, but it is an insistence upon the fundamental necessity of defining ethnic education on its own terms.

## EDUCATION, RESEARCH AND STUDIES[7]

The discussion thus far has remained rather abstract. To illustrate the pervasiveness of the assumptions underlying traditional education, it may be instructive for us to examine the relation between traditional education, conventional research, and ethnic education. Conventional education and research rest upon certain assumptions which have resulted in a total disregard of the particular needs of the ethnic minorities to understand themselves, and they have not contributed a body of data for the explicit purpose of the education of the ethnic minorities as either individuals or as members of their communities. Why is this so? The answer comes from the inquiry: What motivates a conventional researcher to do research?

One of the primary motives is the validation of his activities in the eyes of his peers. Consider those activities. The basic conceptual framework which he uses, the theories which are based on the framework, the hypothesis he derives from those theories, and the methodology which he uses to generate the data to test the hypotheses, all are based upon certain specialized assumptions underlying that particular discipline. The results of any research are then evaluated in terms of what contribution it makes to the further clarification and development of the conceptual framework and the associated body of data of that discipline. Central to the motivations of any given researcher is that he contributes to the goals of that discipline and the structure of the conventional research community demands this kind of accountability. If this is so, then those who are "researched" necessarily remain "objects" to be used as sources of "data," data based on their conceptualizations, for those academicians to further the development of their own disciplines.

It is true that some of these academicians may empathize with "the people" and in addition to his primary motivation discussed above, may be motivated to "help" the people as in the case of some applied behavioral scientists. However, it still remains that the conceptualization of the problem and the articulation of solution continue to be inextricably bound to the particular conceptual framework of the behavioral scientist and is not based on the conceptualization of the members of the community. Basically any definition of "help" rests on value judgments of what is ultimately good. Therefore, any value judgment of what is good for the community must arise from the people's own understanding of themselves and their lives.

The way in which the people of the community remain "objects" becomes clearer – when we examine how the "data" about the people are used. Since the results of the research are presented in terms of conventional social science disciplines, as browsing in any university library will readily show, these data are primarily available to the very academicians who give it validation, due to an elitist bias on the part of the same academicians. Further, when we examine the funding of applied social science research and any implementation of these in action programs, we must question the role of values and motivations of those supplying the funds. Those values, inasmuch as they are based on "outside" perspectives, cannot be the same as those of the community members. As stated above, even if the welfare of the community is claimed as a motive, the perception of this is in terms of persons other than the members of the community so that at best it becomes arbitrary, imposed, and paternalistic.

## RATIONALE FOR AN ETHNIC STUDIES

In the redefinition of Ethnic Studies and research we must look at the issues both in terms of the content and process. For not only do we challenge the relevancy of the basic conceptualizations made of us by traditional academia, but also the very processes of discovery and education which have become alienated from the people concerned. In traditional education, the academic elite are considered to be the repository of "information" and as Freire characterizes this "banking concept of education" the data become deposited in the students.[8] But in true education it is necessary for individuals to become actively involved in the process of their own education.

We learn and come to understand ourselves and our world views, i.e., the way we see ourselves in relation to all else, only when we undertake this process of understanding as active participants. To the extent that we relinquish being active participants in this task, we become alienated from ourselves; for what we are talking about is not the objective world as such but our perceptions of it. Our forms of thought, concepts, and complex of ideas are not isolated, static entities "out there" in the objective world. Our feelings, our aspirations, and motivations are the result of an ongoing process, historically derived to be sure, but uniquely combined at any given time. Any investigation of this process cannot contribute to the development of our self-awareness if it is based upon other than meaningful themes and concepts to us. To the extent that we accept definitions of ourselves based on the conceptions of others, to the extent that we try to find meanings from these definitions based on other than our own understanding of our primary experiences, do we become alienated. Moreover, if we accept norms imposed on us and if we use those norms to pattern our behavior regardless of our life experiences, we will estrange ourselves from those very experiences and this process leads ultimately to our dehumanization. Thus when our cultural context is penetrated by outsiders, and their descriptions are then imposed on us (as in negative stereotyping) in disrespect

of our own views, this imposition inhibits our self-awareness by curbing it. Therefore, it is absolutely essential that self-understanding be based on an active participation in the process itself. A closed cycle has existed in traditional education which did not include meaningful research and knowledge for the education of ethnic minorities and thus the university has been prevented from fulfilling its proper role for the ethnic minorities.

Ethnic education must be relevant for the ethnic minorities and their communities. The codification of reality must be made in terms of symbols derived from the people themselves which begins with the language and the universe of the participants. It follows that this process must be tied closely with actual events as they occur in the community setting. Thus, ethnic education must be tied closely to community involvement and research: community people involved in education and the educational community involved in the ethnic community.

Ethnic education must include the following foci in research and studies: a re-examination of the historical experiences of the people concerned, a thorough study of the community and its culture, and the articulations of the lives of those people with the total society of which they are a part. It is particularly crucial in its initial stages that we give free rein to the development of the humanities and creative arts, for free expression of the life experiences is the basis upon which ethnic education must build new knowledge and self-understanding.

Whatever the focus, it is essential to begin with the codifications of reality based on the people's conceptions, and abstractions from this must not violate the fundamental codifications. Any subsequent ideas and approaches, then, must constantly be evaluated in terms of the basic criteria set up to achieve ethnic education in terms of whether they accomplish these tasks.

## CONCLUSIONS: SUMMARY AND PROSPECTS

To summarize the basic necessities of ethnic education: it must deal directly with the life experiences of the ethnic minorities and deal with it by codifying that reality in terms of the conceptions and perceptions of those who are living that life. It must take care that in the process of abstraction, it does not destroy the linkage between the primary experience and the conceptualizations that follow from it. To ensure relevance for the ethnic minorities, and to ensure the proper linkage in this process, it is necessary for ethnic education and the community to engage in this process together. An ethnic community must be an integral part of the process of research and studies and the results must be directly relevant and applicable to that community.

As long as the university as an educational institution continues to operate in terms of its existing set of assumptions, the successful implementation of Ethnic Studies programs is seriously curtailed from the outset. The particular issue of fundamental assumptions underlying educational philosophy is seldom of concern to the traditional departments, as they accept the basic assumptions and practices of the traditional educational system: but we only need to point to cases such as the attempt to hire Angela Davis at UCLA to show that should any program challenge the system's definition of purpose and process, the issue is always settled in favor of the system.

Although I count among my non-ethnic colleagues many who have been sympathetic and have gained a measure of understanding of our position, I remain rather pessimistic of the prospects of ethnic education within the context of traditional educational systems. There are inevitable and overwhelming forces represented by consistent and persistent articulations with the operations of traditional education which militate against the implementation of the fundamental precepts of ethnic education, making the outlook for change discouraging. I do not say, thereby, that the effort has been for naught for there have been some changes, not only in the minds of the ethnic population, but in challenges which have forced adjustments on the part of traditional systems. Perhaps enough of these adjustments may call into question the basic assumptions underlying their operations, but that is yet to come. My perceptions of the situation as an administrator of an Ethnic Studies program is that the odds are overwhelming, and that gradually the total forces of the system will wear us down. In the words of Denis Goulet: "...this has been the way of all ideological flesh....our society secretes its own gastric juices to polish the rough stones of dissent into smooth pearls of conformity."[9]

Since this resistance to accommodate is implicit and disguised, the adjustments of traditional educational systems to ethnic education have been inadequate. Various responses to pressures brought by ethnic minorities include piecemeal and token accommodations, for example the requirement of primary and secondary teachers to take a few units in Ethnic Studies so that they can then "relate" to students coming from that cultural background. Were it so simple, we could have long since solved many of the educational issues for the ethnic minorities. To take another example, university administrators "solved the problem" by adding ethnic content into the traditional disciplines and have even created "paper degrees" by assembling enough of these courses for a major in Ethnic Studies. This is no solution at all, for the fundamental concepts and perceptions are still those of the traditional disciplines which I have argued do not address the basic issue of codification of reality into symbols based on the perceptions of the ethnic minorities. Often the failure of those programs is pointed to with delight on

the part of the detractors of Ethnic Studies as proof that they did not have substance, quality, or standards. To the extent that forces in the dominant society have been able to divert the purpose of ethnic education, such factors guarantee failure for the ethnic minorities are quick to recognize that it does not serve their needs at all.

It is not correct to merely lay all the blame on those outside of ethnic education. To the extent that we who are involved fail to recognize the fact that, after all, we are also creatures of the total society and that we have internalized those implicit assumptions in terms of which this society operates, we often neglect to question the assumptions underlying traditional education and thus, we do not need outside oppressors. We function very well in that respect ourselves.

So our task is difficult and will take time. Perhaps my pessimism concerning the educational system is justified, and ultimately it will grind us down to the point where Ethnic Studies will be indistinguishable from any traditional department or program. When that time comes, the battle will have been lost and we will only be able to gain solace in the fact that there may have been some overall effect upon the system and upon those ethnic minorities who have been involved in its development. But when that time comes, and if the situation for the ethnic minorities is not such that they are able to relate in a positive way to their own life experiences, it will be time to do something else.

## NOTES

1. Milton M. Gordon, *Assimilation in American Life* (New York: Oxford UP, 1964) 27.
2. For a recent view of the "melting pot theory" see S.I. Hayakawa, "The Meaning of the Melting Pot." *San Francisco Examiner* 9 Mar. 1974: 11.
3. Stanley Sue and Harry H.L. Kitano, eds. "The Model Minorities." *Asian Americans: A Success Story?* Spec. issue of *The Journal of Social Issues* 29.2 (1973): 1-9.
4. For a recent examination of the racism issue, see Harry Kitano, *Race Relations* (Englewood Cliffs, NJ: Prentice Hall, 1974).
5. Devere Pentony, Robert Smith, and Richard Axen, *Unfinished Rebellions* (San Francisco: Jossey Bass, Inc., 1971) 55-56.
6. Pentony, Smith, and Axen 1.
7. The following comments of this section have been excerpted from James Hirabayashi, "Research and Studies," *Proceedings of the National Asian American Studies Conference II*, July 1973 (Davis: U of California, 1973).
8. Paulo Freire, *Pedagogy of the Oppressed* (New York: The Seabury Press, 1973).
9. Denis Goulet, "Development or Liberation." *International Development Review* Sept. 1971.

## BIBLIOGRAPHY

Freire, Paulo. *Pedagogy of the Oppressed*. New York: The Seabury Press, 1973.

Gordon, Milton M. *Assimilation in American Life*. New York: Oxford University Press, 1964.

Goulet, Denis. "Development or Liberation." *International Development Review* Sept. 1971.

Hayakawa, Samuel I. "The Meaning of the Melting Pot." *San Francisco Examiner* 9 Mar, 1974.

Hirabayashi, James. "Research and Studies." *Proceedings of the National Asian American Studies Conference II*. Davis: University of California, 1973.

Kitano, Harry H. L. *Race Relations*. Englewood Cliffs, NJ: Prentice Hall, 1974.

Pentony, Devere, Robert Smith, and Richard Axen. *Unfinished Rebellions*. San Francisco: Jossey-Bass, Inc., 1971.

Sue, Stanley, and Kitano, Harry H.L., eds. *Asian Americans: A Success Story?* Spec. issue of *The Journal of Social Issues* 29.2 (1973).

# Dismantling a Monolithic History:
## Revisiting the Creation of the Baccalaureate in Asian American Studies at San Francisco State University

*Jeanne Batallones, Darren Lee Brown, and Jerry Dear*

### Preface

*Darren Lee Brown*

When drafting histories, there is a tendency to lump together experiences as a uniform voice of dissent, conflating differences between individuals in favor of a monolithic master narrative. Of the many writings concerning the creation of Ethnic Studies and Asian American Studies (AAS), one notices the general lack of voices in favor of academic jargon – an example of streamlining the past to fit a theoretical framework. In most cases, the role San Francisco State University (SFSU) played in creating Ethnic Studies and AAS is minimized, or at worst, totally disregarded in favor of top-tier institutions of higher learning like UC Berkeley. Given the number of historical revisions of the late 1960s, the need to draft a history from SFSU students' perspectives of the 1990s became paramount.

Pivotal activists integral to establishing the major – Jeanne Batallones, Darren Lee Brown and Jerry Dear – were contacted to draft recollections of the period regarding the tenth anniversary of the baccalaureate at SFSU. As soon as drafts were exchanged, it was apparent that our motivations, albeit similar, were in fact different. For some, AAS faculty, community activists, and the social-historical context of the 1990s influenced their passion and drive to establish the baccalaureate. For others, issues regarding social justice, identity politics, and pure jealousy came to the forefront. Despite these differing motives, all three leaders came from various disciplines (Accounting, Political Science, and Creative Writing) in addition to their diverse ethnicities (Filipino American, Mixed Heritage, and Chinese American), gender, and class backgrounds.

The following essays portray the heterogeneous composition of the Asian American student body, which played an integral part in establishing the major. Inspired by the Third World Liberation Front, these students took it upon themselves to disrupt the complacent air of AAS at SFSU in the late 1990s. For some, this meant working with the establishment, playing by the rules to get things done. For others, the petition to establish the major had distinct ties to the greater Asian American communities. Lastly, these essays invoke an unavoidable dilemma – how can Asian American Studies remain "radical" while becoming incorporated within academia? Hopefully, these varying recollections can shed light on this question for future generations of Asian Pacific Islander American activists, leaders, and students.

### Continuing the Legacy of Self-Determination and Community: A Personal Reflection

*Jeanne Batallones*

In the summer of 1996, I enrolled in a summer program offered at San Francisco State University (SFSU) called the Philippine Area Language Overseas Study (PALOS). It was a pilot program organized by a group of professors from the Asian American Studies (AAS) and International Relations departments at SFSU, in partnership with the University of the Philippines (UP). The program brought professors from UP to SFSU to teach Filipino American students about Philippine history, society, and culture.

During the program, community activists from Filipino Civil Rights Advocates (FilCRA) conducted a workshop using a timeline covering the history of organizing in the Filipino community. The timeline ended in the 1990s with one of the main issues being the fight to save affirmative action and defeat Proposition 209 – the California Civil Rights Initiative – which proposed to end affirmative action programs in California. One of the presenters was Bill Sorro, a veteran Filipino activist and leader in the fight for the International Hotel. I did not know it then, but this experience would have a lasting impact on me and my political development.

The following semester, I enrolled in Asian American Studies 680 – Asian American Community. The class was taught by labor organizer Vitus Leung, who invited a variety of community speakers who introduced current issues affecting Asian Americans in the Bay Area, including a speaker from Chinese for Affirmative Action (CAA). At the conclusion, the same message of "get involved" was reinforced and I could not ignore the sense of responsibility that I felt. At the end of class, I approached Leung and asked him if there was an organization similar to CAA, but for Filipinos. It was then that I was introduced to Filipinos for Affirmative Action (FAA) and their Executive Director Lillian Galedo, another veteran activist leader in the Filipino community.

A week later, I phoned Galedo and she scheduled a meeting with me. When I arrived, she had a whole stack of documents for me to review and told me about a campaign they were leading to defeat Proposition 209, the same initiative that Bill Sorro was organizing around. It turned out that Galedo was also the chair of FilCRA and FAA was its fiscal sponsor. Soon after my first meeting with Galedo, I was making weekly trips to Oakland to work on the Filipinos Against 209 campaign and I joined FilCRA's Bay Area Chapter.

Through FilCRA, I joined campaigns to stop other attacks on immigrant communities such as No on Proposition 227 to defend bilingual education, the fight to win Filipino veterans equity legislation, and the mass mobilization in Watsonville to support strawberry workers. The more involved I became in the community, the stronger my commitment grew to fighting for social justice, making everything that I was learning in the classroom concrete and real, giving me a sense of purpose and compelling me to change my academic direction.

Prior to PALOS, I had just returned to SFSU after nearly dropping out. When I first began my studies as an Accounting major at SFSU in 1992, I developed a track record of continuously enrolling in business courses and failing them. After I was academically dismissed from SFSU, I did not know what I would do with my life. I was stuck between working two meaningless jobs, contemplating if I was cut out for college and I hadn't even told my parents that I was kicked out of college. I also considered that maybe college was not for me.

Seeking guidance on what I should do, I met with an academic advisor. After reviewing my transcripts, she pointed out my interest in taking several AAS classes. However, we were surprised to learn that no such major existed. Upon her advice, I inquired about this with

faculty in the Asian American Studies Department.

That semester, I took Asian American Children/Teen Literature with Lorraine Dong and scheduled a meeting with her to talk about my interest in pursuing a degree in AAS. I expressed how upsetting it was to learn that students were not able to pursue an AAS undergraduate degree. This meeting catalyzed a yearlong campaign to fight for our right to major in a field that represented the experience of Asian Americans at SFSU.

During our meeting, Dong revealed that a proposal to obtain an AAS major had already been developed and submitted by AAS Department Chair, Marlon Hom. However, the proposal was stalemated and lacked the necessary political support to move the proposal forward. This revelation made it clear that this issue needed to be led by student organizing and advocacy. I put to use the organizing skills I had gained from the community and worked with Dong and Hom to organize a committee of students to campaign for the major. Through mass letter-writing, petitions, and media attention, we showed the administration that calls for the major could not be ignored and the major was approved in the fall of 1997.

Words cannot express my excitement and relief when after a six-year journey, I finally walked the stage to receive my diploma. In addition to my academic experience, I had also become immersed in Filipino community organizing and the fight for social justice. As soon as I graduated, I was offered a job as a Youth Employment Counselor at West Bay Pilipino Multi-Services, an organization founded by community members who were active in the Third World Student Strike at SFSU.

In 1998, the Asian American Studies Department at State held "Dreams, Realities, and Challenges in Asian American Studies," a conference commemorating the 30th Anniversary of the Third World Student Strike. During a Filipino American roundtable discussion, Theo Gonzalves argued that unlike thirty years ago, my generation – the "30 and under" generation – lacked a point of reference which to draw from. Unlike that of the sixties, who had the anti-war and Black liberation movements, our generation didn't have politically charged events to draw from. I thought about what he said and concluded that personally, I did have a point of reference, and it began with the PALOS program where I learned about my history and was encouraged to serve my community. Through classes like this, I realized that the Third World Strike was more than a moment in history; it symbolized an ongoing struggle for self-determination that continues today.

Everything that I have learned, both inside and outside SFSU, originated from a movement forty years ago, and my generation has a responsibility towards continuing this legacy and upholding its principles of being rooted in self-determination, community, and liberation.

While some may argue that this movement no longer exists, I would argue that it does. It has been carried out in the community, continues at SFSU, and exists in my generation of activists, community workers, writers, and scholars who understand that so long as the fundamental problems continue to exist in our community, there is a basis for us to continue this legacy and see ourselves as part of an ongoing movement for social justice and revolutionary change. Makibaka! Huwag Matakot!

## RECTIFYING AN ACADEMIC WRONG: SAN FRANCISCO STATE UNIVERSITY, UC BERKELEY, AND ASIAN AMERICAN STUDIES

### *Darren Lee Brown*

The 1990s were a turbulent period in California. During Pete Wilson's administration, a variety of anti-immigrant and anti-affirmative action legislative acts passed (Propositions 187, 209 and 227). Student-led movements against these proposals peppered college campuses; however, for some, these responses were bittersweet. Asian American student involvement at San Francisco State University (SFSU) was barely noticeable, and most student groups were generally apathetic, non-political, and preoccupied with throwing parties or going skiing. On the other hand, UC Berkeley (UCB) appeared more politically aware and organized as a result of having additional monetary resources. Yet, being knowledgeable about the legacy of the Third World Liberation Front and the founding of Ethnic Studies at SFSU made me question the erasure of SFSU's role by UCB students and scholars.

The fall of 1994 marked a dramatic change in my life. I transferred to SFSU from Laney College to pursue a degree in Political Science. The transition from a junior college to a four-year institution was the least of my worries. I had moved from the rather comfortable city of Alameda to the heart of San Francisco Chinatown to live with my grandmother. Previously, William Sato's Asian American Studies (AAS) courses at Laney College inspired me to lead the Asian Pacific Islander Student Association and my subsequent involvement with Ohana Cultural Center and Asian American Theater Company. Even though AAS was not offered as a major at SFSU, I knew that someday I would teach or work in a related field. Perhaps at the time, I felt living in Chinatown would give me an edge above my contemporaries, even if they held degrees from the "superior" college across the Bay.

Interactions between me and UCB students through Hapa Issues Forum and Cal Asian Lesbian, Bisexual & Gay Alliances Younited were interesting, to say the least. I was envious of such groups forming at UCB, but resented the general "book-bred" application of AAS devoid of anything remotely anti-establishment. Consequently, I was branded as an outdated relic of the 1960s from "State" or, rather bluntly, a student longing to attend UCB. This stigma combined with UCB's AAS major motivated me to establish the baccalaureate at SFSU.

One of the first courses I enrolled in at SFSU was "Chinese in America" taught by Vitus Leung. I approached him after lecture and asked, "Why isn't Asian American Studies a major?" He replied, "Good question. Why not?" Leung's response provided the seed for questioning why, despite high enrollment, AAS was not a major, thus furthering my interest. Shortly afterwards, I dropped Political Science as my major when the white instructor of "Contemporary China" claimed, "the Chinese consider me Chinese." I immediately dropped the course and went back to my temporary home, Chinatown, while he taught students Chinese table manners.

Pedagogically speaking, courses in AAS at SFSU used the word "community" quite freely. Looking back, I don't think most of us knew what community entailed; however, avoiding a definition allowed students to forge their own meanings. In a sense, the alliance forged with Jeanne Batallones and Jerry Dear, despite our differing backgrounds, epitomized "community," persistence and resiliency in the face of the establishment. We knew that talks between the faculty and the administration were at a stalemate. We took it upon ourselves to draft letters, distribute petitions, and in Jeanne's case, storm the State Chancellor's office, to create the major.

In retrospect, it happened rather quickly and perhaps too soon. The establishment seized the opportunity to satiate demand and stifle student upheaval. My envy of UCB resources may have clouded my desires to rectify an academic wrong, but nevertheless re-institutionalized AAS. However, the birth of the major represents maintaining the legacy of student-led movements alive at SFSU. With increasing tuition fees and an ever-changing student population, I wonder if such movements are a thing of the past.

## TRANSFORMING AND PRESERVING A THIRTY-YEAR LEGACY

### *Jerry Dear*

The spring semester of 1997 marked a year of unexpected endings and beginnings. Prepared to complete my creative writing degree that semester, I could have graduated as planned, but something compelled me to continue exploring the Asian American Studies (AAS) coursework at San Francisco State University (SFSU). Like interlocking pieces of a puzzle, each class filled a void in my life, beckoning towards my innermost being and connecting me to my cultural roots, my Chinese American heritage.

While pursuing a creative writing degree, I had segued into a minor that had emerged from the climactic strike of 1968 – The Third World Student Strike – a momentous event that erupted at the height of the Civil Rights Movement, spearheading and giving birth to the College of Ethnic Studies at SFSU. The progressive movements of the past paved the way for future generations, and I among others sought to preserve that legacy.

Academic research has always been a mainstay in my education, and Lorraine Dong, who taught the very first AAS proseminar class, launched this class with a mere four students, planting a seed in me that gradually germinated and led me into the library and information science field. Research comes in many shapes and sizes, but historical and cultural research – the kind that invigorates your curiosity and challenges you to come to grips with your heritage and identity – catalyzed a profound inspiration that fueled my interest in Asian American Studies, so I resolved to use my writing to help transform this minor into a major.

Along with Jeanne Batallones, Darren Lee Brown, and the support of many AAS students and faculty, we embarked on a quest to propel this minor to the next level – establishing a baccalaureate degree. The AAS minor had remained dormant for nearly thirty years. Where would we start? I figured that with respect to English grammar rules, we needed to master them before we could break them. This was, after all, the 90s, not the 60s. We couldn't exactly march to the administrative offices of the upper echelon and topple down the university's pillars. No – we needed a plan. Hence, what started as a small project that spring semester ignited into a semester-long campaign, one that pooled the collective efforts of our fellow classmates and AAS professors.

First, we needed to engineer a diplomatic means of resolving our dilemma. The fall semester had already started, and I had planned to graduate at the end of the year, so I banded with my fellow classmates to formulate a plan. In a cramped office which barely accommodated three people, we drafted a letter asserting our predicament, collected statistics to justify our cause for the Asian student population, and sought to impress upon the Administration the dire nature of our situation, understanding full well how bureaucratic mechanisms could hinder our academic goals. Next, we contacted the State Chancellor's Office in Sacramento periodically, attempting to ascertain the status of the Asian American Studies BA degree proposal. Thirty years had passed, and the program remained stagnant. Meanwhile, our letter underwent countless revisions, based on feedback contributed by our fellow classmates and AAS faculty.

After weeks of silence and uncertainty, the good news finally arrived – the AAS degree proposal passed quite easily at the state level, which signified a symbolic victory – but the real question still lingered in the balance: Could we graduate by the end of the year? Imagine my surprise when the Registrar's Office informed me that I could not earn a bachelor's degree in Asian American Studies because no code existed for such a major. This unforeseen technicality unleashed a storm of emails between the AAS Department (initiated by Department Chair Marlon Hom) and the administration. What ensued was this: To earn my degree, I would need to fill out the appropriate applications, obtain numerous signatures, and submit the paperwork to one of the administrative deans. In my case, I would have to fill out twice as much paperwork – one for a degree in Creative Writing, and the other, in Asian American Studies. Was it worth the trouble? You bet. I figured this: Play by their rules and see what happens. Navigating through the labyrinthine maze of paperwork required precise timing, but I persisted, and lo and behold, the AAS degree was conferred to me.

If there was any lesson to be gained from this experience, it was this: Take risks and persevere. As the saying goes, "Nothing ventured, nothing gained." This was one battle that was well worth the fight in what has escalated into an ongoing war in academia. Like the Asian American immigrant groups who fought to claim their citizenship in America, as an enduring bastion of a culturally relevant curriculum in higher education, the College of Ethnic Studies at SFSU continues to excel as a legitimate academic discipline in the California State University system. Embracing risks and perseverance in the face of failure and disappointment can only move us forward, for through our struggles we grow stronger and wiser. And through the power of education, we can continue to preserve this forty-year legacy. May the Asian American Studies Department at SFSU continue to nurture new leaders whose dreams and visions will only bring greater benefit to our communities and a stronger presence in our society. In the words of American activist Marian Wright Edelman, "Education is for improving the lives of others and for leaving your community and world better than you found it."

# TOWARD THE FIFTH DECADE
## OF ASIAN PACIFIC ISLANDER AMERICAN
## STUDIES AND SCHOLARSHIP:
## RECOLLECTIONS OF 1968-2007

*Juanita Tamayo Lott*

*This essay is dedicated to James Akira Hirabayashi and William Julius Wilson and has been edited from a presentation prepared for the US Library of Congress National Conference to Establish an Asian Pacific American Collection, October 4-5, 2007.*

In spring 1973, I was a young bride new to Washington, DC. I experienced cultural shock. For the first time, I saw a sleepy southern town with Blue Laws, women with pearls and white gloves, and men with Panama hats and white shoes. *The Washington Post* and *Washington Star* displayed daily headlines on ending the Vietnam War and on congressional hearings on Watergate. I was finishing my University of Chicago master's thesis, "An Explanation of Racial Prejudice and Discrimination in Terms of Group Antagonism: Mexican Americans and Japanese Americans in Twentieth Century California;" preparing for the federal employment exam; and searching for a job. I was a home-sick Asian Pacific American looking desperately for other folks who looked like me so we could commiserate over a home-cooked Asian meal. In my spare time, I would go to the Library of Congress, as libraries and books have always been a joy since childhood. It was a house filled with endless treasures. I found great comfort in the Library of Congress, specifically the Jefferson Building's rotunda reading room. In 1973, anyone could walk into that magnificent room; browse the card catalog; request specific books for reference; and sit at the wooden desks to read, reflect, and write pretty much until closing time. In those first few weeks as a Washingtonian, I borrowed 89 books on racial minorities and ethnic groups, including Asian and Pacific Americans. I skimmed through them, listing every single one.

Today, in the fall of 2007, I am a mother of grown men, no longer looking for a job, nor desperately seeking other Asian Pacific Americans with whom to share good Asian food. I am reconnecting with Asian and Pacific American Studies pioneers of the first decade and meeting young scholars and fresh leaders for the fifth decade and next century of Asian Pacific American Studies, such as those at the University of Maryland, College Park. I am very grateful that we are able to gather – pioneers, seasoned scholars, and young scholars – on this historic occasion to collectively establish an Asian Pacific American Collection at the Library of Congress. I wish to take this opportunity to discuss four Asian Pacific American initiatives with which I have been associated and that are important in understanding Asian Pacific American scholarship and research over the past forty years.

## ASIAN AMERICAN STUDIES AT
## SAN FRANCISCO STATE SINCE 1968

In the beginning of 1968, the student population at SF State was approximately seventy-five percent white, nine percent "Oriental/Filipino," five percent Black, two percent "Mexican American," and one-half percent American Indian. A coalition of minority student organizations merged and became known as the Third World Liberation Front (TWLF) to advocate for the educational needs of Third World students. The groups included the Asian American Political Alliance (AAPA), Black Student Union (BSU), the Intercollegiate Chinese for Social Action (ICSA), the Latin American Students Organizations (LASO), the Mexican American Student Confederation (MASC), and the Pilipino American Collegiate Endeavor (PACE). Although the Strike was minority-based in origin, many white students also participated. Among the most visible non-TWLF student organizations were the Students for a Democratic Society (SDS) and its Progressive Labor Party (PLP), both already active in the anti-war movement.[1]

Spawned by the 1960s Civil Rights Movement, the Asian American Studies Department at San Francisco

State is among the oldest Asian American Studies programs in the United States. The program was launched in fall semester 1969 with eighteen courses in four areas: Asian American Studies, Chinese American Studies, Filipino American Studies, and Japanese American Studies. James A. Hirabayashi served as the first coordinator/chair of Asian American Studies and was subsequently appointed to be the first director/dean of the School of Ethnic Studies, under which Asian American Studies resided. The other components of Ethnic Studies in 1969 were Black Studies, La Raza Studies, and Native American Studies. For historical and research purposes, it is useful to note what that first curriculum and faculty were:

| | |
|---|---|
| AA 20 | Conversational Cantonese – Mary Yang |
| AA 60 | Introductory Pilipino – Felicissimo Velasquez |
| AA 105 | Practical English Skills for Asian Americans – Jeffery Chan |
| AA 110 | Asian American Communities and the Urban Crisis – Kenji Murase |
| AA 115 | Asian Perspectives on Western Literary Traditions – Kai-yu Hsu |
| AA 116 | Asian Perspectives on Contemporary Literature and Ideas – Jeffery Chan |
| AA 117 | Asian American Workshop, Creative Writing – Jeffery Chan |
| AA 119 | Curriculum, Research, and Evaluation – James Hirabayashi |
| AA 120 | Chinese in America – Alan S. Wong |
| AA 130 | Chinese Art – William D.Y. Wu |
| AA 135 | Chinese American Community – Larry Jack Wong |
| AA 140 | Japanese American Social Psychological Profile – Dudley Yasuda and Karl Matsushita |
| AA 145 | Japanese Americans in the United States – Edison Uno |
| AA 155 | Selected Topics in Japanese American Studies – Joe Kamiya |
| AA 160 | Introduction to Ancient Pilipino History – Carolina Borromeo |
| AA 165 | Philippine Arts – Joaquin Legaspi |
| AA 179 | Pilipino Community Workshop – Jovina Navarro |

The AAS faculty included some tenured professors from traditional departments. Several held graduate degrees from the California State College system and doctoral degrees from the University of California, Berkeley, Stanford, Columbia, Princeton, and Harvard. Other faculty were community leaders or professionals in various institutions including the Chinese Culture Center, American Friends Service Committee, University of California Medical Center, Economic Opportunity Council, YMCA, and the Civil Rights Committee of the local Japanese American Citizens League. They joined other minority faculty, including the recently departed Black Studies pioneer and professor Asa Hilliard and the late Life Sciences professor George Araki, who effectively supported student demands for a School of Ethnic Studies in the historical San Francisco State Third World Student Strike of 1968.

The introductory narrative for the Asian American Studies course listing for fall 1969 stated:

> The Asian American Studies program will be offered under the auspices of the School of Ethnic Studies during the Fall Semester, 1969. The Asian American Studies program is open to both Asian American and other students interested in Asian American Studies. The curriculum is designed to meet the need of students (1) who wish to pursue a personal interest in Asian American Studies; (2) who will be teaching Ethnic Studies subjects in elementary, secondary and college level institutions; (3) who plan to work in ethnic communities in a professional capacity as lawyers, health socialists, psychologists, social workers, sociologists and counselors.
>
> The Asian American Studies curriculum is thus designed to serve people and to understand people who have unique experiences in the American society. The primary focus is to look at the "whole human being" within relevant context. It is an interdisciplinary approach; a humanistic historical and social science convergence for the understanding of the Asian Americans in our society. The individual and his community are viewed at the primary level and more importantly, from the Asian American perspective. It is necessary to examine the cultural heritage and the historical development of the Asian American communities in the American setting. Further, a re-examination of various past and prevailing views of Asian American minorities by others must be made and then a re-assessment of the Asian American community must be developed from the Asian American perspective. Finally, there must be a continual re-synthesis of meanings and experiences as Asian Americans in the total American society.
>
> Within this context, this perspective is different from both the traditional middle class view of the minorities and the view of the traditional peoples and cultures of origin offered by regular Asian departments. It is complementary with the latter for it is important to study the traditional cultures in their own setting but for us, the

focus becomes one of understanding whereby selected cultural forms are re-formulated in the new cultural setting here in the United States. The focus is on the relation between the traditional cultural forms and the migrants so as to lead to knowledge to the adaptive processes of the Asian Americans and for the thorough understanding and meaning of these processes, both for the Asian Americans and others from the perspective of the Asian Americans.[2]

On the 30th anniversary commemoration of the San Francisco State Student Strike in October 1998, its legacy was summed up as follows:

> In 1994, the School of Ethnic Studies was renamed the College of Ethnic Studies, which to date remains the only one of its kind in the nation. The term "Asian American" itself has grown to "Asian Pacific Islander American." At present the Asian American Studies Department has expanded to include Vietnamese Americans, Korean Americans, and Asian Americans of mixed heritage. Of the three original Asian American student organizations from the strike, PACE is the only surviving one that is working side by side with many other Asian Pacific Islander student groups that have sprouted since 1968. AAS faculty and students have not forgotten the original objective of community activism and have continued to work with various community organizations. SF State recently established a baccalaureate AAS major, with the first class graduating in May 1998. An AAS Master of Arts program is pending from the Chancellor's Office. Of SF State's total 26,982 student population in fall 1997, 35.1% are Asian Pacific Islander while only 13.4% of the total 1,572 tenured/tenure-track faculty are of Asian Pacific Islander descent. Such is the thirty-year legacy of the Third World Student Strike for Asian American Studies at San Francisco State University.[3]

For its first forty years, Asian American Studies at San Francisco State has effectively focused on teaching and service. Its unique position, as the first, most enduring, and most heterogeneous Asian American Studies Department in the United States, has produced faculty, graduate students, counselors, and staff who mentor and graduate hundreds of Asian Pacific Islander American students and other students who have gone on to be catalysts and leaders in many walks of life since 1968. Towards the fifth decade of Asian American Studies and scholarship, it is appropriate and strategic to compile, research, analyze, and synthesize the intellectual capital, contributions, and tradition of Asian American Studies, beginning with the seminal role of students, faculty, and graduates of San Francisco State.

## The Office for Asian American Affairs, DHEW, and other Asian Pacific Islander American Federal Initiatives, 1971-1980

Asian American Studies, and the more inclusive Asian Pacific Islander American Studies, began not in the ivory tower or think tanks but inherently from the ordinary lives and work of Asian Pacific Islander Americans who struggled with the American ideals of freedom and the rule of law, yet lived the paradox of separate but equal through the 1960s. It was primarily a local phenomenon, becoming alive in institutions of higher education where well-established Asian American populations lived and worked. Just as important, Asian American Studies also evolved within the larger historical forces of post-World War II active civic engagement of minority and immigrant Americans who were veterans, permanent residents, citizens, and US-born children. These 20th century Americans – people of color outside the mainstream, many of whom were military veterans and union members – raised their children and grandchildren to partake fully of American society and to demand that their history and contributions be recognized and documented. They entered college with the GI Bill; built suburbia with veterans housing benefits; established the American GI Forum; organized citizenship classes; undertook voter registration drives; petitioned for family members to immigrate to the United States; and built the dominant US industrial economy in the 20th century.

These local examples of civic engagement succeeded in part due to a federal environment that extended from the New Deal through the Great Society. President Kennedy called the best and brightest to public service, especially to Washington, DC. In the implementation of economic, employment, educational opportunity programs, and the enforcement of civil rights statutes, Asian Americans heeded the call to go east. Asian Pacific Islander American pioneers in the nation's capital in the 1970s included Gwen Wong, a Los Angeles social worker, who served as project officer for the first federal social services grants contracts for Asian Pacific Islander American nonprofit organizations and went on to become the first Asian American manager in the Women's Bureau of the Department of Labor; Pete Jamero of Seattle, who served as a branch chief in the Department of Health, Education, and Welfare; and Patrick Okura, a psychologist at Boys Town, who left Nebraska to become special assistant to the Director of the National Institute of Mental Health. Asian Americans who grew up in Chinatown and the DC suburbs also joined the federal government, such as Robert Jew at the Office of Education (precursor to the Education Department) and Alan Seto at the US Census Bureau, and actively promoted Asian Pacific Islander American representation at the national level by recruiting and mentoring young Asian Pacific Islander Americans. In preparation for the 1980 Census, Seto recruited young Asian Pacific Americans in the West Coast and Hawai'i; he picked them up at the airport and, with his family, hosted them in their home until these new federal employees could find places of their own.

In 1971, the Secretary of the US Department of Health, Education, and Welfare established four units to assess and better meet the health, education, and welfare needs of American minorities and women. Four units paralleled the San Francisco State Ethnic Studies programs – the Office for Asian American Affairs, Office for Black American Affairs, Office for Native American Programs, and Office for Spanish-Surnamed American Affairs.[4] Toyo Biddle was the first director of the Office for Asian American Affairs. Phil Chin from San Francisco State served as analyst. Chin also founded the Asian Pacific American Federal Employees' Caucus with Art Bigornia from Vallejo, California who became one of the first Asian Pacific Islander American managers of the Social Security Administration. I joined Biddle and Chin in 1973 and the Office for Asian American Affairs became a coordinating point for federal services and policy-relevant research on Asian Americans through 1980.

The office managed the seminal analysis of the 1970 Census data, *A Study of Selected Socio-Economic Characteristics of Ethnic Minorities Based on the 1970 Census: Volume 2, Asian Americans*. Authored by Canta Pian, it provided national and local-level analyses of Chinese, Filipinos, Japanese, Koreans, and Hawaiians by immigration, population, education, employment, poverty, and income, using the 1960 Census data as a baseline. The office developed, compiled, and disseminated the first comprehensive reference on Asian Pacific Islander Americans, the 1976 classic six-hundred page *Asian American Reference Data Directory*. It also conducted early needs assessments of various Asian American communities such as the May 1977 *Asian American Field Survey: Summary of the Data*, which focused on characteristics of selected Asian American communities in low-income areas and those populations' needs for and use of health, education, and welfare services. Five groups in three cities – the Chinese in New York City, the Filipinos in San Francisco, and the Japanese, Koreans, and Samoans in Los Angeles – were surveyed. In 1978, the office held the first Conference on Pacific and Asian American Families and HEW-Related Issues.

As a representative for the Office of the Secretary, I served on the interagency group, the Ad Hoc Committee on Racial and Ethnic Definitions of the Federal Interagency Committee on Education, and was appointed to chair the committee's 1974-1975 working group that developed the report that served as the basis for promulgation of the first federal standards for racial and ethnic data, the 1978 Office of Management and Budget-issues Statistical Directive 15, "Race and Ethnic Standards for Federal Statistics and Administrative Reporting."[5] This directive guided the race and Hispanic categories for the 1980 Census and subsequent federal censuses and surveys of the population and federal administrative records.

Based in part on the 1970 Census analysis and development of Statistical Directive 15, the US Census Bureau requested assistance from the Office for Asian American Affairs in establishing the first Asian Pacific American federal advisory committee – the Census Advisory Committee on Asian Pacific American Populations for the 1980 Census.[6] With the full implementation of the 1965 amendments to the McCarran-Walter Act and the post-1975 resettlement of Vietnamese, Cambodian, Hmong, and Lao refugees, including Amerasian children, the 1980 Census became a watershed for complete and accurate enumeration of the increasing numbers and more heterogeneous profile of Asian Pacific Islander American populations. Asian Pacific Islander Americans became very visible, increasing their numbers in the US population.

Psychologist Freda Cheung was detailed from NIMH and Jonathan Chang from the Office of Education to the Office for Asian American Affairs to advise the Office of Refugee Resettlement between 1975-1980. Cheung addressed the psychological and cultural needs of primarily Vietnamese and Lao refugees who had been sponsored primarily by mainstream religious denominations. Chang and the Asian Pacific American Federal Employees Council lobbied to deliver culturally relevant educational services for refugee children. Cheung and Chang provided input into the design and conduct of the first panel surveys of the Southeast Asian refugee populations. The Office for Asian American Affairs was also instrumental in the creation of the Federal Advisory Committee on Bilingual Education that included Dorothy Cordova and Bok Lim Kim. Office staff accompanied Ling-chi Wang of San Francisco in his congressional testimony on the landmark 1974 Supreme Court case, *Lau v. Nichols* on equal educational opportunities for language minority children. The office advocated for the establishment of the Office of Asian Pacific Concerns in the Office of Education headed by Stephen Thom and the conduct of a major study in 1979 by the US Commission on Civil Rights on Asian Pacific Americans, *Civil Rights Issues of Asian and Pacific Americans: Myths and Realities*, managed by Laura Chin.

The office worked with the National Institute of Mental Health, particularly Patrick Okura and Ford Kuramoto, in establishing and implementing two major initiatives for APIAs: (1) the Pacific Asian Coalition, a national umbrella organization directed to training service providers and educators to fund and deliver mental health services to Asian Pacific Islander American communities and first led by Hawaiian Paige Barber, and (2) under William Liu, the Asian American Mental Health Research Center to conduct needs assessment and utilization research as well as to develop culturally sensitive research designs, method, and analysis. These federally-funded initiatives with ten regional areas in great part facilitated the creation of institutions and organizations to examine, serve, research, and document Asian Pacific Islander American populations and communities. Finally, the Office of Asian American Affairs recruited, hired, and mentored Asian Pacific Islander American interns, including Dana Takagi, Walter Wong, and Joyce Matsumori, who went on to be leaders and scholars in Asian American Studies and other disciplines.

By the early 1980s, other initiatives were underway to address Asian Pacific Islander American issues at the national levels including the Asian Pacific Congressional Caucus, Asian Pacific American caucuses of the Republican and Democratic parties' national committees, and several caucuses of professional organizations such as the National Education Association and the American Library Association. Also, the Federal Asian and Pacific American Council was established to focus on training and careers in federal service. In the 1990s, the National Asian Pacific Legal Consortium (now the Asian American Justice Center), the Asian Pacific American Institute for Congressional Studies, the Asian Pacific Islander Health Forum, and Asian Pacific American Labor Alliance set up Washington, DC offices. In addition, the Smithsonian Institution launched the Wider Audiences Program, directed by Marshall Wong, which set the stage for the Smithsonian Asian Pacific Islander American Program with Franklin Odo as founding director by the end of the 1990s. The US Census Bureau established Census Information Centers to directly provide data to underserved communities and re-charted the census racial and ethnic advisory committee for subsequent censuses after 1980. For the 2000 Census, the US Census Bureau launched a major advertising and partnership program with various populations and language minority groups, including Asian Pacific Islander American ones. Planning for the 2010 Census includes not only a Census Advisory Committee on Asian American populations but a separate one on Pacific Islander populations, consistent with the 1997 revisions to the OMB Statistical Directive 15.

Despite these evolving federal initiatives over the decades, research, analysis, and synthesis are sorely absent on these historical federal and national initiatives and events shaping the growth and visibility of the Asian Pacific Islander American population, particularly in the watershed decades of 1970s and 1980s. This is a glaring gap given the criticality and impact of federal policies on the American population, including Asian and Pacific Islander Americans. In my view, such historical and policy-relevant research is a pre-requisite conceptual framework for the future of Asian Pacific Islander American Studies scholarship, particularly given changing demography and geographic distribution in various time periods and cohorts. A broader policy and historical framework provide the larger context for the roots and continuing evolution of Asian American Studies beyond academia. More poignantly, the Asian Pacific Islander American pioneers who came to Washington, DC in the 1960s and 1970s, as well the trailblazers of Asian American Studies including community organizers, notably Yuri Kochiyama, are quickly approaching or are already in their retirement years. Pioneers such as Patsy Mink, Patrick and Lilly Okura, Michio (Mike) Suzuki, Bill Kochiyama, Edison Uno, Harry Kitano, and Royal Morales have passed on.

## DEMOGRAPHIC, GEOGRAPHIC, AND SOCIOECONOMIC DATA ON ASIA PACIFIC ISLANDER AMERICAN POPULATIONS AND ESTABLISHMENTS, 1960-2010

With the above history, the establishment of an Asian Pacific American Collection at the Library of Congress is timely and vital as the institutional repository of the US population. Such establishment is also poignant and personal for current and future researchers of the Asian Pacific Islander American populations. For those of us who advocate systematic and strategic research and scholarship in Asian Pacific Islander American Studies in order to contribute to a shared knowledge base and intellectual history, the critical formative decades of Asian Pacific Islander American Studies and federal initiatives on behalf of these populations in the mid-20th century must be recognized, researched, and documented.

National data in terms of statistics, policies, programs, and historical events on Asian and Pacific Islander populations exist, but reside in disparate collections including the National Archives and Records Administration, the federal statistical system, notably the US Census Bureau, and federal agencies, both civilian and military, particularly their libraries. While various libraries and bibliographic centers on Asian Pacific Islander American Studies exist, there is no central institutional repository. The Library of Congress with its wide array of electronic and other media resources plus its vast networks of specialty and popular libraries domestically and internationally is poised to be such a repository. This may not necessarily mean housing copies of every document but at minimum providing a central a map of various documents.

My particular interest is the vast knowledge produced with federal funds since the 1960s, including research grants, contracts, and training materials that impact the Asian Pacific Islander American population. For example, it would be useful to create an indexed and annotated catalog of federally-produced documents such as panel studies funded by the Office of Refugee Resettlement, DHEW in the 1970s and 1980s, or maps of the Asian American population produced by the US Census Bureau since the 1960 Census. An example of 1970s federally-funded studies include *An Analysis of Problems of Asian Wives of U.S. Servicemen* by Sil Dong Kim for the Demonstration Project for Asian Americans funded by the Office of Research Demonstration, Social and Rehabilitation Services, DHEW in 1975. A classic study was *Discriminatory Employment of Asian Americans: Private Industry in the San Francisco-Oakland SMSA* by Amado Y. Cabezas and Harold T. Yee of ASIAN Inc., one of the first policy research Asian American-owned firms. This study was under contract from the Equal Employment Opportunity Commission. A 1980s example is *The Adaptation of Southeast Asian Refugee Youth: A Comparative Study* by Ruben Rumbaut and Kenji Ima for the Office of Refugee Settlement, DHEW in 1988.

Several states and municipalities have also produced historical documents for consideration in an Asian Pacific American Collection at the Library of Congress; these include *Asians in Washington: A Statistical Profile* by Paul Ong, Joanne T. Fujita, and Sam Chin for the Washington State Commission on Asian American Affairs in 1976. In terms of periodicals, the New York-based magazine, *Asian American Perspectives: Bridge*, was a principal vehicle for creative expression "which captured the rich spirit of the Asian American experience," while also offering insightful analysis and documentation of Asian Pacific Islander American political participation and civic engagement during the 1970s and 1980s. The historical materials of Asian Pacific Islander American civil rights organizations, such as the Japanese American Citizens League, Chinese for Affirmative Action, Filipinos for Affirmative Action, and the Asian American Legal Defense Fund, are germane for this collection. The materials developed by cultural organizations that create and display various art media or chronicle impact of Asian Pacific Islander American arts and culture provide a synthesizing complement to more analytical works. This would include the collections of the Asian Pacific American Program at the Smithsonian Institution, Asian American Arts and Media that began the Asian American Film Festival in the Washington, DC area with the Smithsonian, and local universities and art/media institutes, such as the pioneering Visual Communications in Los Angeles and the nationally-focused National Asian American Telecommunications Association (NAATA), now known as the Center for Asian American Media (CAAM). The cultural material and artifacts of Asian Pacific Islander American museums,

such as the Wing Luke Museum in Seattle and the Japanese American National Museum in Los Angeles, could also be considered.

A long-time passion of mine is statistical data and statistical literacy. Compared to my graduate school days in the early 1970s, today there is a plethora of demographic, socioeconomic, and geographic statistics ranging from microdata to macrodata for various Asian Pacific Islander American demographic groups and business establishments at various levels of geography for historical, real, and prospective time. An Asian Pacific American Collection at the Library of Congress could benefit from a user-friendly classification and presentation of this mother lode, particularly given the multiple modes of data presentation as pioneered by Edward Tufte and continuing with the younger cohorts of technology-literate scholars.[7] In addition to accessibility of statistics in both aggregated and disaggregated forms, of great use would be the compilation and analysis of the reasons for collecting data, the theories and hypotheses that underlie particular types of data, their policy-context, their methodology, technical notes, changes over time, strengths and limits of the data, and appropriate uses of them to (1) inform pubic policy or decision-making and (2) contribute to public knowledge and institutional memory.

Finally, it would be wonderful to have a "Wise Elders Collection" in the Asian Pacific American Collection of the Library of Congress of the biographies, writings, and talk-stories of those who have contributed to public policies and relevant policy research on behalf of Asian Pacific Islander Americans. I think, for example, of Representative Patsy Takemoto Mink and the development of Title IX of the Higher Education Act and the Women's Educational Equity Act. Others include Senator Daniel Akaka and his longtime leadership on the rights and responsibilities of the US workforce, especially federal civil servants and the federal government as the model employer. I would also include non-Asian Pacific Islander Americans such Nampeo McKenney of the Census Bureau and Maria Gonzales of the Office of Management and Budget whose foresighted diplomatic, mentoring, and negotiating skills ensured the institutionalization of racial and ethnic data at the federal level and, importantly, the inclusion and advancement in the federal sector of analysts, demographers, and statisticians who represent the many faces of the US population. I would also include the legacy of Edward Gramlich for his long career of public scholarship, leadership, and service beginning in the 1960s as Policy Director of the Office of Economic Opportunity.

This quick overview brings me to my final area to include in an Asian Pacific American Collection at the Library of Congress – Filipino American Studies at the University of Maryland, College Park.

## Filipino American Studies, University of Maryland since 2006

Less than a year ago, Larry Shinagawa, then the newly hired Director of Asian American Studies at College Park, invited me to present at the Asian American Studies Speaker Series. On November 13, 2006, I spoke on "Looking Forward by Looking Back: Founding Principles, Standards and Unique Contributions of Asian American Studies." It was such a pleasure to be on campus to meet and speak with the Asian Pacific Islander American Studies students who were of all backgrounds and majors. I was reminded of the energy, commitment, and great potential of the 1968 San Francisco State Asian American Studies students and faculty.

I was particularly touched by the leaders of the student organization, the Filipino Cultural Association (FCA) with its fifteen-member executive committee led by Jonathan Sterlin, Ryan Herrera, and Maricel Hernandez. FCA was the catalyst for starting a Filipino American Studies program. At that point, Asian American Studies at College Park offered courses related to knowledge and experience of Asian Pacific Islander Americans generally and of Chinese, Japanese, and Korean Americans specifically with one Tagalog class. Thanks to FCA's superb focus, organizing abilities, community orientation, discipline, demeanor, and fundraising skills, Filipino American Studies was established at the University of Maryland, College Park in spring 2007. The first course is currently being offered in fall 2007, "Introductory Filipino American History," taught by Gem Daus, policy analyst for the Asian Pacific Islander Health Forum.

The establishment of Filipino American Studies at UMCP is an important milestone in Asian American Studies. First, it joins Filipino American Studies at San Francisco State as one of the few Filipino American Studies programs in any Asian American Studies department in the United States. Second, it was organically developed from the grassroots up by students with a wide range of majors from pre-medicine to criminology to communications. Many of the students had grown up in the well-established Filipino American communities since World War II of Oxon Hill and Fort Washington, Prince Georges' County where UMCP resides. Third, the students had broad support from Filipino American, Asian American, and other campus administrators and the Washington, DC area Filipino American and larger communities, ranging from the group, Before the Beltway: Filipino Americans in the Nation's Capital, to the National Education Association and the Asian Pacific American Labor Alliance. They also had the support of UMCP alumni, including Filipina Americans Angela and Christina Lagdameo who had led the struggle for Asian American Studies at College Park in the 1990s as

undergraduates. Angela was student body president.

Fourth, the establishment of Filipino American Studies at UMCP points to the next major area of research in Asian Pacific Islander American Studies – Southeast Asian and Pacific Islander. Of particular interest are the role of the US military presence in Southeast Asia and the Pacific Islands throughout the 20th century; the multi-generational legacy of colonization of Southeast Asian and Pacific Islander populations; and the disproportionate representation of Filipino Americans and Pacific Islanders in US military service over generations. Of equal interest is the growing proportion of these populations within the Asian Pacific Islander American population with their rising numbers in leadership in Asian American Studies and beyond.

Fifth, the establishment of Filipino American Studies, coupled with the continuing healthy growth of Asian American Studies at College Park, is a measure of the strategic role of Asian Pacific Islander Americans in the nation's capitol. The fact that we are talking about an Asian Pacific American Collection at the Library of Congress is a testament to the national and global significance of Asian Pacific Islander Americans for the future of the United States in terms of intellectual capital, public scholarship, institutional memory, and active civic engagement.

## NOTES

1. Jerry Dear, Katherine General, Susan Jeong, Lynne Wong, and Nancy Yin, "Strike! Asian Americans in the Third World Student Strike," *Dreams, Realities and Challenges in Asian American Studies: Asian Pacific Islander Americans Commemorating the 30th Anniversary of the SF State Third World Student Strike*, conference program book, San Francisco State University, 22-24 Oct. 1998 (San Francisco: Asian American Studies, San Francisco State University, 1998) 11.

2. Cover page, San Francisco State University, Asian American Studies, Fall 1969 Course Listings.

3. Dear, General, Jeong, Wong, and Yin 15.

4. A fifth office was the Women's Action Program, a reflection of the expansion of civil rights statutes at that time to include sex as a protected category along with race, color, national origin, and creed. Later, disability and age were added as protected categories.

5. Office of Management and Budget, 1978 Statistical Directive No. 15: Race and Ethnic Standards for Federal Agencies and Administrative Reporting, *Federal Register* 42: 19629-19270.

6. The Black Advisory Committee was developed for the 1970 Census. The Hispanic and Asian Pacific American ones were established for the 1980 Census and the American Indian/Alaskan one for the 1990 Census.

7. Edward Tufte, *The Visual Display of Quantitative Information* (Cheshire, CT: Graphics Press, 1985).

## SELECTED LIST OF REFERENCES

Dear, Jerry, Katherine General, Susan Jeong, Lynne Wong, and Nancy Yin, "Strike! Asian Americans in the Third World Student Strike." *Dreams, Realities and Challenges in Asian American Studies: Asian Pacific Islander Americans Commemorating the 30th Anniversary of the SF State Third World Student Strike*. Conference program book. San Francisco State University, 22-24 Oct. 1998. San Francisco: Asian American Studies, San Francisco State University, 1998. 8-15.

JWK International Corporation. *Summary and Recommendations: Conference on Pacific/Asian American Families and HEW-Related Issues*. HEW 100-77-0102. Washington: US DHEW, 1978.

Lott, Juanita Tamayo. *Knowledge and Access: A Study of Asian and Pacific American Communities in the Washington, D.C. Metropolitan Area*. Commissioned by the Arthur M. Sackler Gallery, the Freer Gallery of Art, and the Smithsonian Institution, 1988.

—. *Asian Americans: From Racial Category to Multiple Identities*. Walnut Creek, CA: Alta Mira Press, 1998.

Pian, Canta. *A Study of Selected Socio-economic Characteristics of Ethnic Minorities Based on the 1970 Census: Vol. 2, Asian Americans*. Washington: US DHEW, 1974.

—. *Asian American Field Survey: Summary of the Data*. Washington: US DHEW, 1977.

R.J. Associates, Inc. *Asian American Reference Data Directory*. HEW-100-76-0011. Washington: US DHEW, 1976.

San Francisco State University, Asian American Studies. Fall 1969 Course Listings.

# INVENTION

Creation & Survival

Placemat Literary Map

The First...

Reflections

Reflections

Crisis/Opportunity

# GOVERNANCE IN AAS: PRINCIPLES, STRUCTURES, AND PRACTICE

*Malcolm Collier and Daniel Phil Gonzales*

With the settlement of the Strike in March of 1969, there was an immediate need to establish Asian American Studies as a practical reality. This essay explores structures, strategies, and practices developed in that early period and their subsequent history. Issues and information related to development of curriculum and other programs of the department are handled separately. Our focus is on the period from 1969 to 1986, with more abbreviated discussion of subsequent developments.[1]

### INITIAL STRUCTURE AND GOVERNANCE

The Asian American Studies Program created in 1969 had a unique structural relationship to the larger college. The strike settlement provided for creation of an independent School of Ethnic Studies with separate Asian American Studies, Black Studies, La Raza Studies, and American Indian Studies components. Consequently, we had a degree of independence on a day-to-day operating basis and did not have to work within the immediate confines of any existing traditional academic schools or departments. We were still subjected to general college structures, procedures, and guidelines but the relative freedom of action was, and to a large extent still is, unique. No other Asian American Studies programs had this degree of freedom and autonomy during their inception. This independence, together with our origins in the combined efforts of three distinct Asian American student organizations, produced a unique governance structure, whose principles and practice continue to shape the department to the present.[2]

During the Strike of 1968-69, each of the Asian American student organizations (AAPA, ICSA, and PACE) were independent members of the Third World Liberation Front (TWLF).[3] Each had one vote in the TWLF, within which voting was by consensus, meaning that every group was independent in its own affairs and

all groups had to agree to any decision of the TWLF before it could move forward.[4] This consensus requirement was based on concepts of self-determination and solidarity, meaning that each group had the right to determine its own positions without imposition of the will of the majority and that the positions of the whole could only be successful if all members supported the positions. TWLF principles explicitly rejected the concept of majority power over a minority position or group. Additionally, the requirement for consensus was seen by some, privately, as preventing any particular interest group from packing meetings to force decisions they preferred during the chaotic and charged context of the Strike period. The principle of self-determination shaped one of the goals of the Strike: that courses and programs be created that addressed the experience of the different groups in the TWLF "from the perspective of" each group, not from the perspective of the majority.

When AAPA, ICSA, and PACE joined together to build the AAS Program starting in the spring of 1969, the principles of self-determination and consensus were adapted to the operation of the new program. The governance structure was as follows: Control of the program as a whole was in the hands of a "General Planning Group" (sometimes called the "AAS Planning Group") comprised, initially, of representatives from each of the three founding organizations. Decisions affecting the program as a whole were made by the General Planning Group on the basis of consensus – with each group having one vote. Decisions affecting only one group were the exclusive domain of that group and the other two groups had no say. Conversely, each group had veto power on any decisions affecting the whole.

This structure was reflected in the content of curriculum initiated in the fall of 1969. There were pan-Asian American courses, like "Asian American Communities and the Urban Crisis" and there were courses specific to particular Asian American groups, like "Chinese in America." For ethnic-specific areas of courses and programs, each group made its own decisions regarding courses, content, scheduling of classes, and the hiring of faculty, passing these decisions up to the General Planning Group for implementation and coordination. Creation of courses and selection of faculty for classes that dealt with Asian Americans in general were the domain of the General Planning Group, as was allocation of resources across the department and setting policy for the program as a whole, with consensus required on all such matters. It should be made clear that this was a consensus of groups, not individuals.

The ethnic-specific decision-making units of the program, originally based in the student organizations, soon came to be called the "area Planning Groups" – the Chinese American Planning Group, the Japanese American Planning Group, and the Pilipino American Planning Group respectively. Within each Planning Group, the decision-making process was up to that group; in practice this usually involved majority voting, although in most cases an attempt toward general consensus was still considered desirable. During the spring of 1970 the area Planning Groups became independent of informal organizations (neither recognized by the college nor legally incorporated bodies) in their own right rather than being linked directly to the student organizations. This separation from the student organizations occurred for various reasons. Essentially, AAPA and ICSA were fading away as campus organizations and on-campus student activity was increasingly taking place under the auspices of the Chinese and Japanese American Planning Groups and focused on efforts associated with the AAS Program. Only PACE remained as a viable campus organization after 1971, but even in that case AAS-related activities came to be handled by a Pilipino American Planning Group, not directly by PACE.

We also believed that AAS faculty and community should be involved, so the individual Planning Groups came to include faculty and community members. Although the Planning Groups were no longer composed exclusively of students, students remained the dominant participants in the program for several years. The expanded membership of the Planning Groups also allowed students who graduated to remain active in the affairs of the AAS Program. These changes were in keeping with a broader principle shared by all the groups, that there should not be any distinction among students, faculty, and community.

The college initially attempted to require formation of "Community Advisory Committees" from the Chinese, Filipino, and Japanese American communities which were intended to serve as checks on the students. Both a Chinese American and Filipino American

Advisory Committee were named but not a Japanese American one. Because the administration had no contacts in the communities, the resulting committees were almost totally comprised of supporters of the students. Although the advisory committees did not function as intended by the college administration and did not have a long official life, they helped provide an initial legitimacy for Asian American Studies and individual committee members often helped the new program as sources of information and guidance. Some of the first faculty came from among these community supporters.

## EARLY ACTIVITY

The General Planning Group met as needed until the first semester began in fall 1969, at which time it met weekly as an official class (AAS 119, "Curriculum and Instruction in AAS") and other times as needed, which was quite often. Dr. James (Jim) A. Hirabayashi served as the instructor of record for AAS 119 and as coordinator of the weekly meetings.[5] The General Planning Group continued to meet as the AAS 119 class (it was repeatable for credit) for several semesters, then simply met periodically as a governing body separate from the class. The Chinese, Pilipino, and Japanese American Planning Groups met on their own, usually off campus.

The tasks facing us in 1969 were immense. As the first AAS programs anywhere, there were no prior curriculum models, no books, no existing faculty, and no money for support staff.[6] By default, the process was largely in our hands as students, especially those in the General Planning Group, but while we did most of the work in setting up the program, we did not operate in a vacuum. We received assistance from friendly individuals among the few existing Asian American faculty on campus as well as guidance and advice from supporters within our communities. All of us were trying to define what an Asian American Studies might be.[7]

Courses and an integrated curriculum had to be created, faculty had to be found and hired, a schedule of classes for the fall needed to be set up and forwarded to the administration in proper form, those classes had to be publicized to students, students needed to register for classes, and much more. As the academic year of 1969-70 progressed, we then evaluated all the courses and instructors. We rehired the instructors or did not rehire, as the case might be. We dumped courses that did not seem to work and wrote up new ones to replace them. The entire curriculum was evaluated and redone in 1971 and 1972, with many courses either deleted or totally revised and many new ones designed. This process of evaluation and revision continued for many years.

When we could not find faculty to teach key courses, we taught them ourselves. We designed community-based programs and got funding for some of them. We debated the creation of a degree program in AAS, even wrote up a proposal according to state guidelines. We decided not to have a degree program and concentrated on obtaining General Studies graduation credit status for all the courses – a whole new arena of advocacy and associated paperwork. We also handled much of the day-to-day administration of the program. All of this was intensely time consuming and almost totally unpaid labor. "We worked our butts off" recalls one participant in the process.[8] We worked full time on the AAS program, took our own classes, and worked at paying jobs on the side. We also managed to graduate, eventually, sometimes a bit late.

The General Planning Group ran the department for many years, as reflected in an early one-page summary of "Departmental Structure," describing the different components of the department, their powers, and procedures for decision-making (see Appendix 4). This summary details the roles of the area Planning Groups and the general Planning Group but makes absolutely no mention of faculty, except for the department chair! This wording did not reflect a denial of power to faculty but rather that faculty were members of the Planning Groups along with students and other community-based members. This structure was highly irregular and, to some degree, illegal. TWLF Strike demands had included a formal role for students in the operations of the new programs created by the Strike settlement. This demand was denied in the Strike settlement due to legal constraints as well as administration resistance. Title 5 of the State Education Code, then and now, explicitly prohibits involvement of students in hiring and retention decisions. College rules did not and do not provide for student roles in the other areas of our activities in the Planning Groups. This is one of the reasons the formal connection between the AAS program and the Asian American student organizations was cut and replaced by the ethnic area Planning Groups. None of the Planning Groups, including the General Planning Group, officially existed as far as the college administration was concerned, although, as will be described shortly, some members of the administration chose to work with us unofficially.

An official structure was created to satisfy college rules and legal requirements. The program had a faculty director/chairperson who signed all the paperwork – course proposals, hiring papers, etc. – that required a chair's signature and represented the program officially.[9] It should be made clear that the director/chairperson was not simply a rubber stamp for the Planning Group. The director/chairperson facilitated the General Planning Group meetings and checked on the work of all the Planning Groups, keeping us informed as to campus requirements and deadlines, and served as the primary public voice for the program to the administration and the academic committees of the campus. They were also members of particular area Planning Groups and played important roles in shaping the program.

When it became necessary to have a formal Hiring, Retention, and (later) Tenure and Promotion committee (HRTP) for AAS, the program drew on sympathetic faculty in other departments to serve on the committee. These faculty signed off on decisions forwarded to them by the General Planning Group and the Department Chair. This was usually automatic but they would send back decisions that they felt were problematic. As the program/department became more established, some funding for office staff became available, as did student assistant money – these support positions were filled by individuals from the Planning Groups. Additionally, some special projects obtained grant money with associated staff money, again filled by students associated with the Planning Groups.

## STRATEGY

The ability of the Planning Groups, especially the General Planning Group, to carry out the tasks described was facilitated by an early strategic decision regarding how we would relate to the larger college, especially the administration. We set out to become proficient in the processes and procedures of the college, intent on using that knowledge, those processes, and those procedures for our aims. We would avoid direct confrontations whenever possible and we would use the educational rationales of the college for our own ends. We tried to make all paperwork as airtight and by-the-book as possible to eliminate any possible opening for rejection. None of this was a pretense, we really did want to do a good job and, in any case, we were forced to work though the existing procedures and requirements. In fact, we discovered that we usually did a better job of following campus guidelines than most traditional departments, who were often very casual about these matters. This approach served the Planning Groups very well through the years that followed and has continued to serve the department well to the present, although the strategy has always required maintenance of a delicate balancing act between our true and agreed principles and goals on the one hand, and the goals, forms, and functions of larger campus policies and state laws on the other.

We had to obtain technical information regarding college operations, including staffing formulas, budgeting, procedures for creating new courses, new departments, new degree programs, details of hiring practices, administrative shortcuts, and other seemingly obscure aspects of administrative operations that most regular faculty and even many department chairs rarely had to deal with. Jim Hirabayashi's assistance was critical in obtaining this information, as was the quiet cooperation of a number of key players in the administration.[10] The foremost example was Dean Daniel Feder, who ran training workshops for us on administrative procedures, staffing formulas, the political aspects of the state legislative budgetary process, and important details of administrative practice at the highest levels of the college. These workshops took the form of seminars that he held outside of regular campus working hours. By late 1969, Jim Hirabayashi was telling his colleagues in the Anthropology Department that he was working with a team of students who knew more about how the college worked than most of the regular faculty, tenured or otherwise. The information received in these sessions was of such tactical and strategic value that some veterans of the period believe that we might not have survived as a program without it.[11]

We also learned about campus politics, including the fact that while S.I. Hayakawa might be college president, the actual operation of the campus was in the hands of a small group of administrators. These administrators were generally conservative managerial types whose main concern was that the college be run smoothly and that recovery from the adverse impacts of the Strike proceeds with no more public disruptions. Also, unlike many modern college administrators, they came from a tradition in which different units in a college were expected to have considerable autonomy in their affairs. Consequently, if we could provide them with a well-run program that met college requirements, and caused them no bad publicity, they would give us considerable freedom to operate.

## CONSENSUS IN PRACTICE

The Planning Group structure operated for many years, including the requirement for consensus approval on all matters involving the department as a whole. Given the unfamiliarity of most people with consensus decision-making, it may be appropriate to discuss its characteristics further.

An important characteristic of a consensus-based system is that, while reaching decisions can sometimes be slow, when decisions are reached they can be implemented with great speed and efficiency because everyone has agreed and understands what needs to be done and why. Additionally, once broad-based policy and direction have been set by consensus then most associated decisions are made rapidly because the broader context and rationales have been thoroughly established. Naturally, in a consensus system some issues may be left unresolved or lead to bitter argument because consensus is not reached. This can be a problem if the issues are crucial or reflect deeply held positions. We did have some issues like this that left hard feelings and frustration regarding the consensus process, as is discussed separately. Whether such impasses or resulting bitterness is more or less desirable than a majority forcing decisions on an unwilling, perhaps bitter, minority is a matter of perspective, not a matter of objective fact.

Another potential difficulty arises if there is need for rapid response but the consensus required is of constituent groups who meet separately, as with our area Planning Groups. This was not a problem for us because of another operating principle, inherited from the Strike period: in an emergency, individual members of a group could speak for that group on their own. Consequently, when time demanded, the representatives from the area Planning Groups would act for their respective Planning Groups and the General Planning Group would make the decision on the spot. This practice also applied to minor or routine matters considered of insufficient importance to send back to area Planning Groups.

The General Planning Group arrived at consensus on most issues quite rapidly, in part because of shared perspectives and principles among the three groups and also because many decisions involved matters already thoroughly discussed in the area Planning Groups. The process was assisted by an operating principle that if you wanted a group's approval, say for a new "top" course, you must involve them in the early stages of planning so that by the time the course is ready for consensus approval it has already had input from everyone involved. You do not put a whole course or a project together on your own and then go ask for approval when there is no room left for real input; that does not work in a consensus system. This principle was also seen as important in a community context, that you should not plan a project for a community without having community participation in the planning from the start.

When there were major differences among the three groups, consensus could take time as each group's position was explained, contested, and reexamined, and adjustments or compromises made until all agreed. A consensus system forces a majority to listen to the concerns of the minority. Most of us did not see this as a deficiency but rather as a means of making sure that everyone's views were considered and that no action in the name of Asian American Studies would occur unless all of the groups were comfortable with the decision. We saw this process as required by the principles of self-determination. We did, however, have many and sometimes VERY long meetings, usually simply because we had so many tasks to address but occasionally because of the time required to arrive at a consensus.

Looking back, an exceptional characteristic of the early years was the degree to which everyone worked together and that, although there were sometimes bitter and lengthy arguments on particular issues, there was also a shared sense of commitment. Members of the General

Planning Group would readily step in to help and do whatever was needed at the moment. Despite the presence of many strong personalities, the Planning Group operation during the first two years (there were changes later) really was a collective process, not dominated by a few strong players – if we were not intimidated by the powers that be, we certainly were not going to be intimidated by each other! We were absolutely unafraid, either of the college administration or of the task that confronted us. Some of this was innocence regarding what we attempted to do and an overly optimistic expectation that we could make changes, but it was exciting.

## Long-term Consequences

The overall character of Asian American Studies at SF State was and continues to be significantly shaped by these early governance practices. We started and continue to operate as an independent department in an independent School of Ethnic Studies. While a number of other Asian American Studies programs have been able to achieve increasing autonomy over the years, the situation at SF State remains unique. This autonomy made possible a level of student and community involvement in the program during the early years that could not have been sustained had the department been situated in one of the existing traditional departments and schools. An initial consequence of this relative autonomy was considerable, although not unlimited, freedom in creating courses and hiring of faculty. We had space and time to experiment without immediate, full conformity to traditional academic practices and culture. Over the long term this fostered a rather independent attitude relative to the larger campus and the scholarly world.

The origin of the department in three separate student groups and the maintenance of that origin in the governance structure, principles, and practices of the department had impact that is still visible today. The dominance of ethnic specific courses in Chinese, Japanese, and Pilipino American Studies in the early days of the department and the continued programmatic, although numerically reduced, role of such ethnic specific courses in the department today originates in that structure and in those principles.

This early period helped foster a subtly different attitude toward community involvement. While most Asian American Studies programs emphasize community involvement, the early operating structure and practices of AAS at SF State blurred the distinctions between campus and community. Students and faculty were seen as being "of and in" the community first and at the university second, not the other way around. This attitude has continued to color the department's perception of itself relative to the communities, although this has also served to complicate that relationship.

## Changes and Controversies over Governance

While there are continuities, major changes have also occurred, reflecting both difficulties with the initial structure and adjustments to changing circumstances. The initial Planning Group structure and practices served well and operated with little debate as long as most participants were veterans of the Strike period, who had internalized the core principles of self-determination, solidarity, and consensus. With time, a number of problems and conflicts arose. The first was: how to maintain hard-earned knowledge, skills, practices and, above all shared perspectives and principles as people graduated or left and new people, both students and faculty, became part of the scene.

Although such changes did not occur at the level of the General Planning Group for several years, the problem of continuity was identified by fall 1970, when steps were made to bring new people into each of the area Planning Groups. New students were recruited and a new course (AAS 90, "Introduction to Methodology in Asian American Studies") developed to provide them information and training.[12] While these efforts were helpful, the problem of differential knowledge and experience proved very difficult – you cannot just teach or tell people about core knowledge and perspectives, they need to be lived.

Knowledge is power. During the first two or three years everyone was roughly equal in their knowledge and experience, able to operate as equals in meetings and in day-to-day activities, but this equality eroded in subsequent years. Veteran members of the Planning Groups started to dominate meetings, even if not by intent, because their wider knowledge and longer experience made their positions more compelling. They would talk to each other in meetings, using references to people, events, and processes outside the experience of more recent participants, further marginalizing newer members. We knew this was happening and could not discover an effective way to address it. It was the classical revolutionary problem, how to maintain revolutionary values and skills when the revolution is over. It is also a basic problem of group dynamics in many small organizations, and indeed is still a problem for the department today.

There were consequences to our ability to form consensus. It is harder to establish consensus agreement when operating from different levels of information and experience, when participants feel less than equal, or do not understand or accept the process of consensus decision-making. Challenges to the consensus model began to surface in fall 1973. Superficially these were associated with changes in the Japanese American Planning Group, although a wider range of factors were at work.

Many of the early players in the Japanese American Planning Group had graduated and moved on; a significant number of their replacements were both less familiar with past practices and more "Leftist" in ideology, including a strong contingent from the J-Town Collective. Several of the Japanese American faculty also fit this description, as did one faculty member in Pilipino American Studies.

These individuals brought a more explicitly and openly Marxist perspective to the program and were ideologically opposed to, as well as frustrated by, the consensus practices of the department. Their preference was for a structural model that reflected values of "democratic centralism" consistent with their own ideologies. This perspective was strongest in the Japanese American Planning Group, but not unique to it. The tensions over governance surfaced around the development of new "top" courses, those that dealt with Asian Americans in general, and around the issue of tenure, as will be discussed shortly.

Tensions over curriculum resulted from attempts to establish three new top-level courses – a pan-Asian American history course and two Asian American women's courses – without the full involvement of all three area Planning Groups in the early planning stages. Those proposing these courses felt that the need for representation of Chinese and Filipino American perspectives was satisfied by involving individual Chinese and Filipino Americans who shared their ideological perspectives in course planning, and by bypassing the Planning Groups. Many in the Chinese and Pilipino American Planning Groups saw this as too reminiscent of the way outside agencies, both public and private, would foist a variety of programs on their communities without substantive involvement of the communities in deciding what needed to be done and how. It was also seen as a direct contradiction to the principle of self-determination and associated existing departmental practice. As the groups also felt there were problems with the content and perspectives of the course (discussed in a separate essay), there were extended debates about the courses, which those proposing the course saw as stalling. The courses were eventually approved, but only after going through a process of input and approval from the individual Planning Groups.

Conflict on governance was now in the open and extended into 1975. While the Japanese American Planning Group was the primary source of specific proposals for change, it would be a mistake to view the conflict as simply contention among different ethnic groupings in the department. The position of the Japanese American Planning Group was more nuanced than can be presented here and the debate over procedures and governance was also to be heard within the other groups. Some people were sympathetic to the concerns of the Japanese American Planning Group, both in a general political sense and

with regard to the specific proposals for new "top" course content. Consequently, discussions in all three Planning Groups were lengthy and often contentious.

Larger political issues also affected discussions. Off-campus political organizations had instigated destructive ideological battles in Asian American Studies at UC Berkeley and other campuses during this period. Both the Chinese and Pilipino American Planning Groups successfully blocked attempts to make them more doctrinaire leftist in their membership and perspectives, choosing to maintain what most members saw as more pragmatic and flexible perspectives. These pressures were ongoing during this time, so many Chinese and Pilipino American Planning Group members were suspicious of proposals for changes within the department which were perceived as reflecting similar political agendas. In retrospect, the ability of AAS at SF State to survive the 1970s without the destructive ideological battles experienced in some other programs was, in large part, a product of the governance structure based on three separate Planning Groups and the consensus principle. This structure made it difficult for particular ideological interests to take control of the program because to do so they would have to take control of all three Planning Groups.[13]

The governance debate passed repeatedly from the General Planning Group to the area Planning Groups and back again through 1974 and 1975. Some in the Japanese American Planning Group argued that the consensus model benefited obstructionists and that the sometimes protracted discussions necessary to arrive at consensus were contrary to an efficient and progressive operation of the department. They proposed modifying or abandoning the consensus model and replacing it with another voting structure, inherent in which was also a de-emphasizing of the ethnic-specific Planning Groups and development of a more centralized process. The question, of course, was what exact form would any new structure and process take? These proposals were discussed and various alternative models mapped out and examined within the three Planning Groups. The basic problem was that any such shift would mean a significant change from the early principles of self-determination and autonomy that had informed the formation of the program. Critically, many saw a majority voting structure as a replication of the very phenomena of majority tyranny over minorities that had originally triggered the fight for programs like AAS and Ethnic Studies, as well as the Third World Strike itself.

The question came to a decision stage in spring 1975. In response to protracted debates and to new Japanese American Planning Group proposals and positions, the Chinese American Planning Group came in with a strong, formal position statement in favor of the existing structure. Because consensus was still required for changes in governance, this position meant that all proposals for change were blocked and the formal debate dissipated. The end of formal debate did not alter the reality that the issue had come up, in part, because changes were occurring in the department and the Planning Groups that would ultimately lead to alterations in departmental structure, processes, and procedures.

## The Tenure Issue

The debate over governance was intensified by concurrent discussions regarding the advisability of placing some or all full-time faculty on tenure track, including questions about how such decisions should be made, how such faculty should be evaluated, and what the consequences for AAS might be. This discussion started in the fall of 1971 with debate over whether the duties of full-time lecturers should be different than those of part-timers. Most people felt they should have more responsibilities and act in various ways as representatives of the program. By 1973, this discussion had evolved to encompass the question of tenure-track appointments.

At this time, faculty for ethnic-specific courses were selected by each of the area Planning Groups, not by the General Planning Group. If such a person was full-time and were to be put on tenure track, did the decision to do so belong to the General Planning Group or to the specific area Planning Group? The general feeling was that it had to be a General Planning Group decision because placing someone on tenure track would affect the program as a whole. However, that would mean the General Planning Group would be making decisions affecting a particular ethnic area, contrary to existing principles and practice.

More basic was whether AAS should even have tenured faculty. The Chinese American and Pilipino American Planning Groups felt that AAS had to build a tenured faculty, both for stability and to help maintain the independence of the program. They noted that we benefited from having a strong campus advocate for us, indeed for the whole School of Ethnic Studies, in the person of Jim Hirabayashi as Dean, but that we could not depend on him forever. We also were depending on friendly faculty from other departments to serve on committees to assist us in hiring matters, as well as on the cooperation of some high-ranking administrators on a range of issues. How long could that be maintained? All of our faculty were temporary lecturers and, for the most part, could not represent the department in official forums on campus. Our budget situation was weak; tenure-track faculty would tie down at least minimal funding for the program. There was a deep concern that so long as AAS existed in a temporary mode it was at the mercy of administrative whims and hostility.

Further, a number of lecturers were reaching two years of service in full-time appointments. Campus policy

(then but not now) was that lecturers who had been hired full-time for two years be placed into permanent positions or they had to be reduced from full-time. If we were to start putting people into tenure-track positions the time was now. Additionally, some argued that placing at least a few people on tenure track would force the administration to commit to a long-term future for the program.

Consequently, the General Planning Group recommended that Dan Begonia and George Woo be placed on tenure track, with questions about procedures and criteria for evaluation still to be worked out. In the fall of 1973, this decision was forwarded to the Hiring, Retention, Tenure, and Promotion (HRTP) Committee, then composed of three tenured faculty from other departments.[14] Prior to this, early in 1973, Jim Hirabayashi, as Dean of Ethnic Studies (not yet officially recognized as a school by the administration), had approached the administration regarding criteria for appointment and tenure in Ethnic Studies. He made a strong case that Ethnic Studies departments should not use the traditional academic criteria, arguing that traditional requirements for a PhD or other terminal degree were both unreasonable and irrelevant to Ethnic Studies. He proposed, with several pages of explanations and justifications, six criteria of his own. In order of importance they were:

1  Professional commitment to Ethnic Studies as an academic discipline.
2  Knowledge of and involvement in the ethnic community.
3  Teaching experience in the content area of Ethnic Studies.
4  Contributions to the development of Ethnic Studies programs.
5  Research and publications in the area of Ethnic Studies.
6  Formal education in the traditional academic setting.[15]

When the HRTP committee received the request to place Begonia and Woo on tenure track, the committee became concerned regarding the need for formal criteria, as well as procedures for dealing with this process. In December of 1973, they proposed to AAS and the three Planning Groups that Hirabayashi's six criteria be used as a starting point for criteria in Asian American Studies. They requested the Planning Groups to study the criteria, revise them as desired, and provide the committee with an approved set of criteria by late January 1974. When a response was not forthcoming by the deadline, they used the six criteria as a basis for placing the two nominees on tenure track, so when issues regarding procedures and criteria related to the tenure process were finally discussed in the General Planning Group and among the three area

Planning Groups beginning in March 1974, Begonia and Woo already were in tenure-track positions.

The discussions focused on several crucial issues: the benefits or liabilities of having tenured faculty, the procedures for deciding tenure-related questions within the department, the relationship between the General Planning Group and the HRTP committee, and the criteria by which tenure-track faculty might be selected and evaluated. Additionally, because Begonia and Woo were now on tenure track, there was the question of whether or not they should be kept on tenure track. Much of the debate fell into a pattern of opposing positions between the Japanese American Planning Group on the one hand and the Chinese and Pilipino American Planning Groups on the other.

Early in the process, the Chinese American Planning Group requested a decision from the General Planning Group to place Jeff Chan and Mike Ikeda on tenure track and to adopt a policy that all full-time faculty be considered for tenure-track appointments. The Japanese American Planning Group took the ideological position that tenure was used by universities to maintain an "Ivory Tower" mentality and control over faculty, implying that having no tenured faculty was more consistent with an anti-elitist democratic process. While not absolutely opposing placing people on tenure, they said that they had supported the appointment of Begonia and Woo contingent on resolving questions of criteria and procedure and that their tenure-track status should be suspended at the end of the academic year unless these issues were resolved.

The Japanese American Planning Group also raised questions regarding the six criteria, saying that they were a good starting point but too vague, and might make it hard for AAS to defend tenure-track faculty in the face of opposition from the administration, who could interpret the criteria in ways contrary to those intended by AAS. They also expressed concerns about the ability of the Planning Groups to control the hiring and evaluation process, as well as the activities of faculty once they became permanent. In response to this position and related concerns from within the other Planning Groups, the General Planning Group proposed that all tenure-track appointees be required to place a signed but undated letter of resignation on file with the department, so that the General Planning Group could fire them any time they desired. This idea was soon recognized to be unworkable but reflected deep ambivalence over the concept of tenure.

We were all concerned about the possible consequences of having a tenured faculty group, both positive and negative, and deeply worried about what criteria would be used by the college to grant tenure. Everyone understood there were implications for future governance practice in AAS, although no one appreciated how quick the impact would be. Despite these concerns, the Chinese and Pilipino American Planning Groups supported continued tenure-track status for the two faculty, noting that if their status were changed back to part-time faculty, the ability of AAS to have tenured faculty in place might be delayed by up to five additional years. They supported the criteria drafted by Hirabayashi and the right of the HRTP committee to apply those criteria, arguing that they were necessarily vague and provided flexibility for AAS to apply them as appropriate in different situations. They pressed the Japanese American Planning Group for alternative proposals.

Finally, in late April and again in May 1973, the Japanese American Planning Group came with position statements. They explicitly supported having tenured faculty, restated concerns already mentioned, argued for more explicit criteria, and noted that because tenured faculty would be ultimately independent of the Planning Groups it was crucial to have precise, unified procedures and criteria for use in the selection and evaluation process. The statement clearly articulated the inherent dangers, in terms of the existing character of the program, of having tenured faculty. Except for the renewed request for more explicit criteria, their formal position on tenure was now relatively consistent with the positions of the other two Planning Groups.[16]

However, the Japanese American Planning Group's position statement also articulated a proposal that tenure-track appointments be by majority vote of the three Planning Groups and the HRTP committee, thereby explicitly linking the discussion of the tenure issue to larger issues of governance. In associated discussion, the existing structure was attacked by one of the Japanese American faculty as obstructionist and inconsistent with a unified program in which people worked together. It was and is unclear that her position was that of the larger Japanese American Planning Group and the argument was ended by the chair of the Japanese American Planning Group noting that the issues related to tenure simply highlighted larger issues of decision-making that should be left for future discussion.

At the next meeting on May 21, 1974, with two of the HRTP members present, the Chinese American Planning Group presented their own position paper. This summarized their already described position and added to it a statement emphasizing the importance of the consensus requirement for decisions related to tenure issues.[17] In response, the Japanese American Planning Group reported they now felt that the tenure-track process did not have to be held up by debate over questions of procedure and criteria, and that they would support the continuance of Begonia and Woo on tenure track while the discussion on these issues continued.

This ended the immediate crisis and was the end of any real argument in AAS regarding the desirability of tenured faculty. Those who had pushed hardest for change in the consensus model soon left the program for other endeavors. There was continued discussion on procedure and criteria in the context of larger governance issues but not on tenure itself. Jeff Chan, Dan Gonzales, and James Okutsu were subsequently put on tenure track, so that by 1980 the department had five faculty who were either tenured or on tenure track.

In retrospect, there are ironic aspects of these debates. The Chinese and Pilipino American Planning Groups, strong supporters of the Planning Group structure and the associated consensus principle, pushed the appointment of tenured faculty, whose presence would help hasten the demise of that structure and significantly change the consensus model, while the Japanese American Planning Group was seeking to delay a process that would, in the end, bring the more centralized structure some of them desired, although not in the form they envisaged.

## NEW STRUCTURES, OLD PRINCIPLES REDEFINED

The 1974-75 contention over governance and tenure ended in reaffirmation of existing Planning Group structures and associated procedures but could not change the forces that were making that structure harder to maintain. Indeed, the creation of permanent faculty served only to spur change. The basic problems of unequal knowledge and experience became even worse within the area Planning Groups, increasingly aggravated by unequal presences on campus. By 1977, the Planning Groups became increasingly composed of faculty and community members, with a shrinking participation of students. While it was true many of the community-based members had previously been students or faculty active in AAS, they now had little regular contact with the campus. Most information on departmental affairs came to the Planning Groups via current faculty and conversely, faculty served as the primary representatives from the area Planning Groups to the General Planning Group. As intended, the permanent faculty were also becoming more involved as representatives of the department on campus and the day-to-day operation of the department was largely by faculty and staff.

Consequently, the ability of many Planning Group members to operate effectively declined while the power of the regular faculty in the Planning Groups increased. This situation did not encourage continued non-faculty participation in what could be time-consuming meetings. Faculty also began to feel that the Planning Groups were a drain on their time and perhaps not necessary when the decisions made were usually the same as the faculty would have made anyway. Although the Planning Groups continued to operate, they were in decline. By 1980, the area Planning Groups ceased to operate and the department

became a faculty-driven structure in which General Planning Group meetings were now simply departmental meetings of faculty. No real discussion and formal decision led to this end, it simply happened.

Nevertheless, certain long-held practices and principles remained; their form altered to fit new circumstances. The Planning Groups were gone but the ethnic-specific program areas remained, together with the faculty who taught those courses. The program areas and associated faculty came to be called "units" – as in the "Japanese American Unit" or the "Chinese American Unit." All affairs were now handled within a single governing body, composed of all the faculty of the department, both permanent and temporary. Not all temporary faculty participated in meetings but their right to do so was no different than that of permanent faculty – a pattern that continues to the present. Faculty associated with courses in the ethnic-specific areas were seen as having primary say over those areas and the group consensus model continued to operate in the sense that the department as a whole would not set policy for a particular ethnic area of the program without the consent of the faculty in that unit. In addition, a custom of attempting to reach collective consensus on all major decisions at faculty meetings was maintained, if not always adhered to.

This structure was in place in the early 1980s, when the department was faced with a major fight for survival following a complete overhaul of college graduation requirements, especially in the area of what had been called General Studies and would now be called General Education. The department's response to this challenge required a massive reconstruction of the AAS program, with many courses being deleted, many new ones created, and a whole new configuration of the curriculum necessary, as discussed separately. This effort, which entailed almost as much work as the early creation of the program itself, was handled by the faculty as a whole. Decision-making was done by the whole, but again, each unit was left to define its own area within the parameters of the larger plan, while everyone worked on the pan-Asian American courses.

As the situation entailed both the redesign of the AAS program and a wider political effort to get that program accepted by the college, this period also saw something of a re-creation of the larger Third World coalition of the Strike period. The four different departments in the School of Ethnic Studies worked collectively to strategize for and implement a united front to the larger college. Many of the same education and advocacy activities toward the wider campus of the Strike period were now recreated in a new form. The entire activity, which stretched over a period of five years, entailed one of AAS's most successful applications of the early strategic decision to bend the university's procedures and policies to our own needs. While the changes made meant the loss of important areas in the program, AAS emerged stronger than before, both internally and as a campus presence.

## CONCLUSION: BROAD PRINCIPLES OF OPERATION

The structure and practices that evolved by the early 1980s are essentially the same as those that the department operates under in 2008. The four-part structure of Asian American, Chinese America, Japanese American, and Pilipino American sections/units that originated from the Strike period continues to be reflected in the content of the programs today but has been expanded. Changes in Asian American populations and growth in the AAS program have led to the development of new "units" related to Vietnamese Americans, Korean Americans, and, to some degree, Asian Americans of Mixed Heritage. The consensus principle still operates in that the department as a whole will not make decisions for any one ethnic unit without the consent of the faculty in that unit and consensus is still the desired basis for all major departmental decisions. Decisions by majority vote are very rare and the only arena in which a formalized majority voting structure has been created is in selecting the department chair. This occurred in the early 1990s, partly to conform with campus-wide policies and also in response to internal conflicts over selection of the chair. With the gradual growth of a permanent, tenured faculty, the department soon had its own faculty-staffed HRTP committee, although under certain circumstances it was and is still necessary to pull in outside faculty.

The struggles and evolving character of the Asian American Studies Department from 1969 onward has produced a set of broad operating principles that are still in place today, if not always fully operative. Listed briefly they are:

1   Involvement of any particular community or group in a project, a course, or any other activity requires their involvement in the early planning stages, not simply their approval of an already completed plan.

2   The majority cannot speak for the minority; consequently any project, plan, or program that encompasses several groups requires the consent of all the groups affected.

3   Decide what we want first, and then decide how to fit or achieve that goal in the settings in which we operate. Do not make choices simply to meet the desires of the larger institution or other groups.

4   Survival within a larger institution requires making use of the processes and procedures of that institution, but for our own ends, not the ends of the institution.

5   The needs of students and community should be paramount in the decision-making and operation of the department. Scholarly research and faculty needs are only important insofar as they serve these primary needs, not by themselves.

Asian American Studies at San Francisco State was born and evolved in a particular set of circumstances, producing a unique direction relative to other Asian Americans Studies programs. An important aspect of this process was the development of the particular forms of governance and associated operating practices we have described. While the Department has become more conventional over time it still retains important aspects of its earlier origins and character.

## NOTES

1. In addition to direct personal knowledge, this essay draws on Planning Group minutes, position papers, and a variety of other departmental documents. Because of the large number of these documents and the complexity of the subject, we have chosen to provide specific references on a selective basis, as seems useful. We are also indebted to lengthy conversations with Jim Hirabayashi, George K. Woo, Irene Dea Collier, and Juanita Tamayo Lott, as well as comments by Penny Nakatsu, Jeff Chan, and Richard Wada. The views presented here are, however, ours and we are responsible for any errors and oversights. Because the early operation of AAS had a significantly collective character, we have generally not named individuals except when deemed essential. A fairly complete listing of those involved in the program during the first two years is provided in Appendix 1.

2. At this time and for many years after, the institution was known as "San Francisco State College." The College was organized into separate administrative units called schools, as in the School of Behavioral and Social Sciences, the School of Science, the School of Business, and so on, within which there were different departments. Asian American Studies was initially called a "Program" rather than a "Department," achieving recognition as a department only later. Likewise, the "School" of Ethnic Studies did not become officially a "School" for several years although the term was used from the beginning. Much later, with reorganization of the campus into a "University" the "School" became a "College" of Ethnic Studies. It should be noted that the original demand was for a "School of Third World Studies" not "Ethnic Studies."

3. The full names of the organizations were: Philippine (later Pilipino) American Collegiate Endeavor (PACE), the Intercollegiate Chinese for Social Action (ICSA), and the Asian American Political Alliance (AAPA). AAPA – at SF State – was a largely Japanese American student organization. The name reflected the more pan-Asian American outlook and philosophy of the organization.

4. The other members of the TWLF were the Black Student Union (BSU), the Latin American Students

Organizations (LASO), and the Mexican American Student Confederation (MASC). BSU also operated somewhat separately from the TWLF and had its own set of demands apart from those of the TWLF (see Appendix 2). There was no formal American Indian organization at the time, but Richard Oakes and a number of other American Indian students spoke for American Indian interests during the Strike. After the Strike, Bea Medicine and Luis Kemnitzer – faculty in Anthropology Department – played a major role in getting American Indian Studies courses and classes off the ground.

5. Jim (we rarely called him Dr. Hirabayashi!) was a tenured member of the Anthropology Department and had been an active faculty supporter during the Strike. He acted as a "Director/Chair" of AAS and was the official representative of the AAS program in settings where we – as students – were not supposed to exist. Above all, he was a superb team coordinator, adept at getting everyone's ideas heard and everyone working together, all without ever imposing his own views, although he would not hesitate to diplomatically tell us when he thought we were wrong. His importance in the early development of the AAS program cannot be overstated. He became Dean of the School of Ethnic Studies in the summer of 1970, but continued to take an active part in AAS affairs for many years, both in his role as Dean and as a member of the Japanese American Planning Group and associated community organizations.

6. In March 20, 1969, as part of the Strike settlement, the Asian American Studies Program at San Francisco State became the first AAS to be established in the nation, upon which time the work on courses commenced immediately. The first AAS classes were held at SF State in the fall semester of 1969. (UC Berkeley began its AAS classes slightly later in fall 1969 under the quarter system.)

7. The General Planning Group in fall of 1969 was composed of the following individuals: (a) from AAPA/ Japanese American Planning Group – Penny Nakatsu, Daro Inouye, Kay Nomura, Richard Wada, Masayo Suzuki, and Sharon Uratsu; (b) from ICSA/Chinese American Planning Group – Berwyn Lee, Mason Wong, Alfred Wong, George K. Woo, Eddie Chin, Ben Tong, and Malcolm Collier; (c) from PACE/Pilipino Planning Group – Ronald Quidachay, Edward de la Cruz, Juanita Tamayo, Ed Ilumin, Francisco Rosario, Daniel Phil Gonzales, and Arika Dacumas; and (d) AAS Director, Jim Hirabayashi. As with other essays in this set, in keeping with the collective nature of efforts in the early years of the program, we have generally not named people in the text, except with regard to faculty and some other individuals. Because so many people contributed to the efforts of the Planning Groups, singling out individuals by name would give a false impression of who contributed to the program.

8. Irene Dea Collier, personal communication, 1 Sept. 2008.

9. As long as AAS was a "program" rather than a department, the position was that of "director;" when AAS achieved department status, the position became that of department chairperson. Likewise, the "Dean" of Ethnic Studies was dean in name only until the university formally recognized Ethnic Studies as a "School." Jim Hirabayashi was followed, briefly, as Chair of AAS by Moon Eng. Jeff Chan became chair following Moon Eng.

10. Hirabayashi credits his ability to obtain cooperation from some of the administrators and other faculty to personal relationships from his successful career on the College of Behavioral and Social Science softball team! He also benefited from the fact that Donald Garrity had attended college with Jim's older brother, Gordon Hirabayashi. He was also an early member of the faculty union (American Federation of Teachers) and made use of that connection.

11. Students from other groups in the TWLF were also participants in these sessions but the other departments never developed the strong structural role of students in department operations that AAS did.

12. AAS 90 (later renumbered AAS 250) was used for this purpose for a number of semesters; later, other courses were used for a time to help train students for work in the program and to give them units for those efforts while AAS 250 became basically an introductory course in AAS. The current course ETHS 220 (Asians in America) is a direct evolution of AAS 90. The official instructor for the fall 1970 course was Neil Gotanda but the course was actually taught by Dan Gonzales, Penny Nakatsu, and Malcolm Collier.

13. The ideological conflicts that occurred in many other AAS programs at this time have sometimes been described as reflecting conflicts between "community radicals" and "academic reformers" – this dualism is irrelevant to the story of AAS at SF State. Everyone involved in the debates we are describing were clearly community-based and no one in the program at the time reflected the "academic reformer" perspective.

14. George Araki, Donald Lowe, and Kenji Murase.

15. Unpublished memo from Hirabayashi to Feder, 12 Mar. 1973.

16. Position papers, Japanese Planning Group, 23 Apr. and 13 May 1974.

17. Position paper, Chinese Planning Group, 21 May 1974.

# CREATION AND SURVIVAL:
# COURSES AND ACADEMIC PROGRAM,
# 1969-1986

*Malcolm Collier and Daniel Phil Gonzales*

When the Strike ended in March of 1969 there was no Asian American Studies program anywhere, no models, no existing courses, no real body of curriculum to draw on, almost no books in print for courses or reference, and no body of trained and experienced specialists who could teach the courses – nothing.[1] We had to invent Asian American Studies.[2]

## GETTING STARTED, 1969

Our major objective was to construct a curriculum to be offered in the fall semester of 1969. Courses had to be written and submitted for approval; faculty had to be hired; a schedule of classes needed to be set up, forwarded to the administration in proper form, and publicized to students; students had to be registered for classes; and much more. Who was to do this? In the absence of anyone else, the job fell to a cadre of students from the three Asian American student groups – AAPA, ICSA, and PACE.[3] There was assistance from sympathetic Asian American faculty on campus and from members of our communities, as well as a number of campus administrators, but most of the labor and organizational responsibilities were borne by the students. Work was coordinated and to a significant degree carried out by a collective body called the "General Planning Group."[4]

We set out to learn and to use the academic bureaucracy of the college. This activity was facilitated by the appointment of James (Jim) A. Hirabayashi as Asian American Studies program coordinator and the cooperation of Dean Daniel Feder.[5] After being approached by a representative of the Third World Liberation Front (TWLF), Feder agreed to conduct after hours seminars where he explained all of the academic and economic workings of the college, the relationships between the politics of the campus and the state college system, and the budgetary process of the state legislature. He assigned exercises to student representatives from the TWLF organizations that were designed to make them as facile as possible, given the pressure of time, with the assembly and presentation of course and curriculum proposals, required support materials, proper staffing classifications, syllabi, official forms, etc. Fewer than twenty students attended these workshops, but the products of their very disciplined labors became the basis for the first classes offered by the School of Ethnic Studies.

The first semester of Asian American Studies had eighteen classes, organized into four basic areas: six pan-Asian American offerings (or "top" courses as we called them), four Chinese American classes, four Japanese American classes, and four Pilipino American classes. As two of the Japanese American classes were separate sections of the same course, there were actually seventeen different course titles.[6]

Recruiting faculty was a particularly challenging task. Some of the choices of courses offered that first semester were decided on the basis of who was available with appropriate expertise to teach on short notice. The first AAS faculty included some who were working educators, either at SF State or elsewhere. Others were social service professionals working in community-based agencies, or individuals who had well established reputations as local ethnic historians and community-based scholars. As part of the course approval and scheduling process, the student-led Planning Groups provided course descriptions, goals, justifications, syllabi, and bibliographies but the class instructors bore the responsibility of developing lesson plans, exercises, tests, essay examinations, and other devices with which to measure student achievement of learning objectives. Consequently, the early development of the courses was a collaborative effort between the students participating in the AAS Planning Groups and the faculty hired to teach the courses.

## INSTITUTIONAL BARRIERS

The difficulties of getting our program curriculum accepted by the broader institution as a whole, both then and later, should not be underestimated. The negotiated Strike settlement provided for the nominal establishment of Asian American Studies and the other programs in Ethnic Studies, but each individual course proposed by any of our programs was required to be approved through the "regular" channels via a chain of committees – each with its particular membership combination of faculty and administrators – then by the higher campus administration and, in the instance of degree-granting programs, the system Chancellor's Office. The entire Ethnic Studies curriculum conflicted with the content and perspectives of many different disciplines on campus, all of whom had representatives on the committees through which our proposals had to pass. Virtually every course we proposed could be argued against on the basis of our alleged encroachment on the territory – "turf," as we said back then – of existing departments. Jim Hirabayashi, both as Coordinator/Chair of Asian American Studies and later as Dean of Ethnic Studies, spent much of his time in the first several years of Ethnic Studies fending off such challenges.

This circumstance presented us with a glaring and constant contradiction: we were attempting to change the pre-existing institution, and to present facts and perspectives that challenged the traditional order of established departments, yet our course submissions were assessed under procedures and guidelines set and applied by those very entities. In addition to the philosophical and factual combat likely to result in the course sanctioning process, several traditional departments stood to lose student enrollment to our newly established School – a very practical reason to oppose and suppress our advances.

Our desire to at least initiate the operation of the School of Ethnic Studies sometimes moved us to discomforting compromises following along the narrow path at the border of our "radical" intentions and the territorial resistance of the old order. The academic community was and is quite conservative, with many structural and institutional barriers to educational innovation and genuine institutional change.

## COURSE DEVELOPMENT AND REVISIONS, 1969-1970

The Planning Groups viewed the AAS curriculum of the fall of 1969 as preliminary, as a period of germination. Throughout our first year of instruction, the Planning Groups revisited, modified, and enlarged the entire curriculum. The eighteen classes offered in the fall of 1969 grew to twenty-three classes in the spring of 1970, involving twenty-two individual courses. By the fall of 1970 the program had developed a total of forty-four course titles, each with distinct content and perspectives reflected in their formal descriptions, justifications, goals, and syllabi. Of these, twenty-three were actually scheduled, with several courses being rotated in and out of the schedule, typically on a once-every-two-semester cycle.[7]

This job was immense, with all the planning work voluntary and unpaid, from meetings with community supporters to the development of curricular concepts, submission of proposals, and advocacy for their approval. Course proposals included a cover sheet with course title, brief description, the conceptual basis of the course, a course justification, and staffing formulas. Attached to this was a detailed course syllabus with course outline, teaching methods, and bibliography. The cover sheet was then on pale green paper, so they were called "green sheets" even when in later years they became pink and, now, white. The paperwork alone was voluminous but there was much, much more to be done.

Most typical academic departments generate new courses once every few years and always in the context of a well-established body of knowledge consistent with their extant curriculum. We were creating an entirely new field, which required substantial, often novel research and had many difficult decisions to make regarding content and perspectives appropriate to our goals. Course proposals, in the circumstances that we faced, required far more than filling out forms and supplying a possible outline. When materials were few – which was quite often – we had no choice but to do the best we could with what was available. We took the process seriously and wrote terse, but strong course descriptions, course justifications, and syllabi. We wanted to shape a comprehensive, well-integrated curricular program.[8] Valued and often crucial advice and assistance were given to student proponents by supportive Asian American and Third World faculty on campus and there was an ongoing dialogue with individuals in our respective ethnic communities who provided information, critiques, and suggestions.

The extreme rarity of readily available published materials that fit our curriculum development needs made the construction and offering of courses difficult. Following on our initial work, some instructors built resource development into the curriculum of their course. Phil Choy, for example, enlisted his students, as well as members of the Chinese American Planning Group, in painstaking searches for existing materials about Chinese American history. This included tasks like dividing up the whole card index of the college library and identifying every item in the library that had any reference to Chinese Americans. This information was painstakingly cumulated and printed as a "Chinese American Bibliography." He also had students go through all the microfilm newspaper records from local papers dating into the nineteenth century, listing every news article with references to Chinese Americans onto index cards. Some resource development required irregular activities. For example, the only comprehensive book on Chinese Americans was Rose Hum Lee's *The Chinese in the United States of America*, published in Hong Kong in 1960 and no longer available. When efforts to get it republished failed, some people in the Asian American Studies program made duplicate copies so that it could be used for instructional purposes.

Most instructors had to produce their own reading materials for classes, either compiling articles and/or original writings of their own. Phil Choy and Him Mark Lai, who taught the first classes in Chinese American history, authored their well-known *Outlines: History of the Chinese in America* directly from their teaching efforts at SF State, publishing it themselves in 1972, with a reprint by the Chinese American Studies Planning Group in 1973. Jeff Chan and others concerned with Asian American literature started identifying publications by writers like Louis Chu, Toshio Mori, and John Okada, which they then tried, with some success, to convince publishers to reissue. Eventually, Jeff Chan would join Frank Chin (who taught in the program in the spring of 1970), Lawson Inada, and Shawn Wong to produce *Aiiieeeee!* in 1974. Alan S. Wong, the director of the College YMCA and an early instructor in the program was, like Choy and Lai, a collector of anything and everything he could find on Chinese Americans and other Asian Americans. He made his files available to the program, as well as the mimeograph machines in the College Y, and used his student assistant money to hire students to work on the materials. Similar assistance came from individuals in the Japanese American community, some of whom, like Edison Uno, also taught courses for the program. Eventually, an informal group known as the "Japanese American Curriculum Project" came together, not only assisting the development of courses at SF State but also helping to define what should be presented regarding Japanese Americans in schools generally. In this manner, the program provided an outlet for people to bring forth their own skills, knowledge, and productions regarding their communities, their histories, and the larger arena of Asian American experience.[9]

## CURRICULUM STRUCTURE AND CONTENT

The early Asian American Studies curriculum had four major content areas: (a) social, cultural, and psychological topics courses, (b) historical courses, (c) literature, arts, and expression courses, and (d) community topics courses. This mix of course content flowed from what we wanted to know regarding our own communities, cultures, and origins. With time came a realization that there was a programmatic function to such a mix and it has been maintained in modified form to the present.

The curriculum also reflected a belief that different Asian American groups had developed new and legitimate cultural forms, societies, and identities as Chinese Americans, Filipino Americans, and Japanese Americans, distinct from being simply Chinese/Filipino/Japanese or American. We wanted our courses to explore the origins, content, and the dynamic character of these new cultural and social realities. We also believed that, because of shared experiences with American racism, culture, and society, there were commonalities as well as differences, within the experience of Asian Americans that needed to be addressed in the program.

Consequently, the courses were a combination of ethnic-specific offerings and pan-Asian American or "top" courses. The fall 1970 course listing included eleven Chinese American courses, seven Japanese American courses, eleven Pilipino American courses, and fifteen "top" courses. The presence of a strong list of ethnic-specific courses was a distinguishing characteristic of the program through the 1970s and, although later modified substantially, continues to be a feature of the program to the present. Ideologically, this mix flowed from the Strike-based principle of "self-determination" and resistance to the concept of majority rule over minorities. The development of many group specific courses also reflected our hunger for an opportunity, previously denied, to explore our particular communities, cultures, and origins.

The concept, gradually articulated, was that ethnic-specific courses would provide detail and depth regarding each group's experience in America "from the perspective" of each group, while the "top" or pan-Asian American coursework would be the venue for comparative examinations and collective efforts. Exactly how this was to be operationalized as a balance set between the ethnic specific and the top courses remained a subject of considerable discussion. On one hand the area Planning Groups generated many ideas and demands for courses specific to their communities but at the same time there was also explicit desire for more collective content and analysis.

The need for balance and the potential dangers of excessive emphasis on ethnic-specific content was best expressed by one of the General Planning Group members, who felt that the principle of self-determination could go too far: that we might end up with a set of disjointed ethnic pockets, each operating alone and without reference to each other and concentrating on cultural trivialities. She was concerned that the program not lose a political awareness, which she saw as necessary to enact real change and which she felt had to be based in "Asian American" and "Third World" perspectives. While no one disagreed with her identification of the importance of political awareness or even the possible dangers of too much emphasis on ethnic-specific coursework, many others did not see any contradiction between developing a larger political awareness and also having strong ethnic-specific components and course offerings. Conversely, she did not oppose the presence of ethnic-specific coursework but remained concerned that we create and maintain holistic, politically informed perspectives that unified the different groups.[10]

The challenge of maintaining such a balance continued through the 1970s. Various circumstances created a situation in which it was easier to develop group-specific courses but harder to develop solid cross-group courses and programs, particularly when there might be disagreements over content and ideological perspectives. In some sense this was good; courses that claim to address the realities of all Asian American groups should be well thought out and satisfactory to the perspectives of all the different groups. However, the common human tendency to follow the easiest road resulted in a period during which the curriculum was dominated by group-specific course work, with only limited pan-Asian American course offerings.[11]

This evolution can be seen with the courses in place in 1980. There was a total of fifty-seven courses: eighteen Chinese American area courses, ten Japanese American area courses, seventeen Pilipino American courses, and twelve pan-Asian American courses. Superficially, this appears well balanced, but the content of the "top" courses was in fact rather limited, with no general courses on Asian American literature, history, or social structure, and only limited coverage of arts and community.[12] In fact, the pan-Asian American curriculum was weaker in 1980 than it was in 1970, in part due to internal tensions related to this portion of the program during the 1970s, as has already been discussed in a separate essay. On the other hand, the course listings did reflect a significant interest in linkages between Asia and Asian America; every unit had courses that looked at such transnational relationships.

Through the 1970s we encountered a number of problems in presenting our program. We were never able to offer every course listed. Ideally, certain core courses would be offered regularly while others would rotate in and out, but this did not happen consistently. We discovered that a course had to be offered consistently and with the same instructor so that materials, content, and teaching methods could be developed into a solid package. A full rotation of all our courses would have required having a faculty who could also rotate in and out of employment, which was not practical, and courses that were not offered regularly did not build student history, so enrollment would suffer. Consequently, courses that were offered sporadically (or not at all) did not develop fully and their enrollment remained low. Throughout the 1970s we often found ourselves having to recruit and advertise to get adequate enrollment for many classes.

## TENSIONS OVER CONTENT AND IDEOLOGY

The mix of top courses in 1969 and 1970 was the product of cooperative efforts among the three Planning Groups, whose members had a history of working together during the Strike period. There were tensions and even bitter disagreements, but also significantly shared perspectives and commitments to solidarity that allowed for compromises and collaboration. While this collaboration did not disappear as membership in the Planning Groups evolved, the mid 1970s brought increased tensions over how to handle the pan-Asian American curriculum. Issues of political consciousness and course content became more contentious during a period in which some Leftist groups in the communities made efforts to take political control of some Asian American Studies programs. The program at San Francisco State was significantly insulated from such takeovers because of a governance structure that would have required gaining control of all three area Planning Groups, so we had fewer problems in this respect than other programs. However, the Japanese American Planning Group and faculty did come to include a significant number of members of the J-Town Collective. The Chinese and Pilipino American Planning Groups remained more varied in their membership but included members who shared important ideological perspectives with those in the J-Town Collective. Consequently, tensions developed which were manifested in conflicts over governance (discussed elsewhere) and course content in the pan-Asian American or "top" courses area of the curriculum.

At this time, two obvious gaps in the curriculum were the absence of a pan-Asian American history course and courses specifically dealing with Asian American women's issues. A member of the Japanese American faculty proposed two Asian American women's courses and a Filipino American faculty member with similar political perspectives put forward a proposal for an Asian American history course. There was little contention regarding the need for the courses but considerable debate on the process of planning the courses and on their content, which were intertwined. The established procedure for developing new "top" courses was that each of the Planning Groups had to be involved at all stages. Because those proposing the new courses wanted to control the political perspectives of the courses, they bypassed this process and recruited individual Chinese, Filipino, and Japanese Americans who shared their political perspectives to work on the courses, claiming that by so doing they were satisfying the need to gain the perspectives of each group in developing the courses. This approach, part of a larger conflict on governance, was rejected by the Chinese and Pilipino American Planning Groups, delaying approval of the courses.[13]

The debate over procedure was an important concern in its own right but was also a convenient proxy for conflict over ideological content in the proposed courses, which reflected significant Marxist content. Both the Chinese and Pilipino American Planning Groups were suspicious of course content that was seen as too explicitly ideological in character. Their memberships had considerable ideological diversity with a preference for keeping course content from being overtly tied to particular leftist perspectives. They were also concerned that hard line ideological content would appeal to only a narrow range of students, rather than the broad body of Asian American students whom the program hoped to attract and influence. Both groups also hoped to avoid the ideological battles that were engulfing other Asian American Studies programs at the time.

The loosely leftist perspectives of all parties discouraged open rejection of the courses on ideological grounds but the details of content festered. A specific concern was the inclusion of Engels' theories of history in the courses, especially in the women's courses. Even a casual reading of Engels' theories shows them to be extremely Eurocentric, even racist, in their explication of the evolution of societies and civilizations. Ironically, given their inclusion into the women's courses, they can also be read as sexist! Such perspectives were clearly contradictory to the critical attack on Eurocentric and racist perspectives which formed a core rationale for the Asian American Studies program. These concerns were not openly debated but circulated privately while open conflict focused on procedure.

In the end, both women's courses were approved following formal involvement of the Planning Groups in course planning. Because the issues of content had not been openly acknowledged, these remained unresolved and when the courses were first taught they included much of the original ideological content, leading to lack of unified support for the courses. Development of an Asian American history course was also required to involve the Planning Groups, although it remained dominated by the particular ideological perspective. It was offered on a trial basis but not made a permanent part of the curriculum until much later and in a completely different form.

The conflict left unresolved two programmatic problems: an unclear role for pan-Asian American coursework and a failure to deal positively with gender issues. While those pushing for the women's courses had recognized these as a major programmatic weakness, their particular approach failed to produce a productive solution, although the women's courses remained in the curriculum. Whether a different, less ideologically directed approach might have been more productive is open to question but the whole affair left unpleasant memories and clouded the larger gender problems in the program which would remained unaddressed, even undiscussed, for many years.

While these conflicts were difficult, they were mild compared to ideological battles at other Asian American Studies programs during the 1970s. Our disputes did not involve a conflict between campus-based "scholars" and community-based "activists" but rather contrasting approaches taken by different community-based activists. Campus-based scholars did not then exist in the Asian American Studies program at San Francisco State. The Strike at SF State had been much more intense and disruptive than similar events at other campuses and the administration was therefore often more cautious in dealing with the different programs in Ethnic Studies. This, together with the development of cooperative relationships between Asian American Studies and some members of the administration and the insulation of the program in a separate School of Ethnic Studies, produced a degree of autonomy for the program during these years. These circumstances reduced pressures to immediately hire academic-oriented faculty with PhDs. The faculty hired from 1969 to 1985 (including all the early tenure-track hires) were largely non-PhDs, most with roots in the student groups of the Strike period and with their feet firmly placed in their communities. They were much better placed to both resist and work with off-campus pressures, and the stability of the program was further enhanced by the decentralized, consensus-based governance structure under which AAS then operated. This structure made it very difficult for any one organized group to "take over." Consequently, the program at San Francisco State has had a higher degree of continuity of people and perspectives from its founding period than most other Asian American Studies programs.[14]

## GENERAL STUDIES

The courses offered in fall 1969 counted only as electives and could not be used to meet any college requirement beyond units. We quickly realized, as students ourselves, that this was a problem. If students were to explore Asian American subjects in any depth, the classes would have to be more than electives. The easiest and most effective way to achieve that goal was to have courses meet "General Studies" requirements, San Francisco State's term at the time for the broad range of "Liberal Arts" course requirements common in American higher education. Fortunately for us, the campus climate of experimentation in the late 1960s had resulted in a flexible structure for General Studies requirements. Rather than limiting choices to a small number of courses, the college set broad criteria for acceptable courses in basic subjects, science, social science, humanities, and arts, plus a senior seminar, with the result that students had many options. We had only to show that our courses met criteria for the areas of General Studies in which we wished to place them.

If challenged, we would then look to the larger list and point to approved courses in traditional departments that were similar in scope and ask "why not an Asian American Studies course?" Our argument then, as well later, was that Asian Americans are and have been part of America, so if Euro American students can get General Studies credit for courses that explore aspects of Euro American culture, history, and society (gaining more self knowledge of their own culture, history and society) it was only equitable that Asian American students could do the same and that, indeed, all students might benefit from such courses. We argued that in educating people for a plural, democratic society, everyone would benefit from our courses. This was carrying the struggle for legitimatization of Asian Americans as Americans forward.[15]

Consequently, we submitted the necessary proposals and justifications for our courses, with the result that by the fall of 1970, all but one course in the program could be used someplace in General Studies.[16] Students could now take a considerable number of our courses to meet specific requirements within General Studies. Initially, this was mainly an exercise in pragmatism but over the next year we began to think about this process more programmatically, especially in conjunction with discussions over the pros and cons of developing a BA major.

## THE DEBATE ABOUT A MAJOR IN ASIAN AMERICAN STUDIES

One of our major early decisions was to skip developing a BA major program in Asian American Studies. This action, which was thoroughly debated and examined, in many ways defines the department's perspectives at the time and illustrates the process by which major curriculum issues were addressed. This decision has been consistently misunderstood by outsiders and even by subsequent generations of Asian American Studies students and faculty at San Francisco State, so a detailed discussion is appropriate.[17]

Both the Black Studies and La Raza programs had developed BA major programs. Should we in Asian American Studies do the same? The question was first raised in March 1970 while seeking department status for the program, which was necessary for a more secure budgetary and structural relationship with the college. We initially thought that the departmental status and a BA major degree program were linked, but a meeting with Feder established that Asian American Studies could become a department without having a major, allowing us to move rapidly for departmental status while discussing the idea of a major as a separate issue. This extended discussion examined the pros and cons, the procedures necessary to establish major programs, and the requirements for maintaining such programs. There was a considerable range of viewpoints within and among the Planning Groups regarding a possible BA degree. Most people felt we needed more information, so we treated the issue just like a course proposal; that is, we decided to design a major and write up a formal proposal in the form required by the California State College system. This task was assigned to a committee with members from each of the area Planning Groups.[18]

The committee developed a proposal with several variations but all included a core of required pan-Asian American courses (fifteen units), an area of concentration (twelve to fifteen units minimum), and electives from outside Asian American Studies (nine to twelve units). The initial proposal had four possible areas of concentrations – community, humanities/creative arts, social science, and interdisciplinary – and explicitly defined the necessity that students have a firm comparative understanding of Asian American experience across the various groups. This plan was presented to the Planning Groups in February of 1971. The committee did not take a stand pro or con on the desirability of a having a BA but still said "this is what a BA program might look like." Further discussions in the area Planning Groups produced a revised structure with a core of pan-Asian American courses (nine units), an upper division concentration on advisement that formed a "unified" program (nineteen to twenty units), related units on advisement from outside Asian American Studies (twelve units) – for a total of forty to forty-one units. A senior project was also required, as was language competency in Cantonese, Japanese, or Tagalog, either via additional coursework or through equivalent proficiency. This was the proposal on which the final decision was made.

It was clear that this decision was too serious to be simply handled by the General Planning Group, so a joint meeting of all the Planning Groups was called for a Saturday, which lasted from early morning past nightfall. The committee's proposal and variations on it were examined and the larger question of the desirability of a BA then debated – hotly and for a long time. Those supporting a BA degree program stressed that a BA major provided an opportunity for really developing Asian American Studies as a discipline, that it would give credibility and standing in the college, be an opportunity for students to truly explore who they were, and gain a sound social and political consciousness under the direct supervision of the department. Some felt a BA would be affirmation of the legitimacy of Asian American Studies, providing more bases for support of the department within the college. A BA would give students a way to have their coursework in Asian American Studies formally recognized and validated. Not so explicitly stated was the idea that real departments had majors and that without one Asian American Studies would not be a real program.

Those arguing against creating a BA degree program did so on pragmatic and philosophical grounds. They questioned whether it was realistic to have a BA program. How many students would want to have a major with no clear application after graduation? Could the department even afford to support a major, they wondered – pointing out that a number of traditional departments were struggling to survive because a major required regular offering of a broad range of courses that enrolled only majors, often with low enrollments that caused problems with the administration. They questioned whether we were ready or capable of offering a BA major program. More important, they questioned how the BA would benefit students and community. What would a student gain from having a BA in Asian American Studies? Are we certifying them as "genuine Asian Americans" – stamped double A like the Texas AA brand rice sack? Can it get them a job? What does it lead to? Are they better able to serve the community? How? The community needed teachers; it needed social workers. Would the community gain more from having Asian American Studies majors or from some other approach? They pointed out that there were alternatives – having concentrations within other majors, having a minor, or building institutes and training programs – as the department was already doing with the "Nine Unit Block" program in conjunction with departments in Behavioral and Social Sciences. They argued that the communities would benefit more by having people return with degrees in social work, teaching credentials, planning, even business, and other traditional degree areas – but who also had strong coursework and consciousness-raising in Asian American Studies. Priority should go to establishing ways of serving many students rather than the few students who might want a BA in Asian American Studies. They pointed to the placement of Asian American Studies courses in General Studies as part of that process, saying that the more students we can get to take our courses and the more AAS courses they take, the more students we will reach and potentially influence.

This account does not do justice to the complexity of the positions on either side, nor to the ambivalence that many felt. But as the discussion continued there was a broadly shared and explicit priority expressed toward serving community and students, and relatively little concern with academic respectability, except as how that impacted the ability of the department to serve community and student needs and goals. Although the formal proposal from the committee had included discussion of the importance of providing a venue for scholarly research in Asian American Studies, this subject was not a major topic during the meeting. By evening it was clear that, while the Japanese American Planning Group generally supported having a BA program, the Chinese and Pilipino American Planning Groups were not convinced.

Lacking consensus, the matter was therefore put aside. Subsequently, the creation of an Asian American Studies minor was approved and put in place.

The intense debate left hurt feelings but also had been a venue for sustained discussion of our goals and possible alternative approaches to achieving them. One result was a reexamination of General Studies as an area of Asian American Studies activity. We came to see our activity in General Studies, and the General Education requirements that replaced it in the 1980s, as a core part of our program although it was and is not seen that way by the larger institution. Stated simply, the idea was that both students and communities would benefit most from having students attain traditional degrees but also take a comprehensive set of courses in GS (later GE) in Asian American Studies that would serve to make them socially conscious and better informed about their communities. Whether they were bus drivers, teachers, social workers, small business owners, city employees, or whatever, they would also be primed to be active members of their communities. A secondary product of the BA decision was more focused efforts on projects and activities that served communities and students.

In retrospect, the decision was a sound one at that time. The absence of a BA program allowed the department to be more experimental and flexible for many years, creating and dropping courses readily without having to commit to a set body of curriculum and, as will be detailed, able to respond creatively to serious threats to the program in the early 1980s. Equally important, the department's ability to establish a core of tenure-track and other faculty who did not have doctoral degrees was facilitated by the absence of a degree program. Had there been a BA degree the college administration would probably have been more aggressive in demanding more traditional degree qualifications in hiring. These elements in turn helped maintain a community-based focus on the program and a markedly independent attitude toward the larger academic world.

However, the decision should have been revisited in the 1980s, by which time the department could have offered a degree program without many of the negative consequences feared in 1971. By 1986 the department had developed a cohesive, stable curriculum, fully integrated into General Education requirements, that was producing a large enrollment capable of supporting a BA program. Starting a BA at that later time would not only have provided a degree for which student interest was building but would also have encouraged Asian American Studies at SF State to take a more aggressive role in defining what the larger field of Asian American Studies might be. As it was, the goal of having a BA major in Asian American Studies was not finalized until 1998.

## SURVIVAL IN THE 1980s

In the early 1980s we were faced with the greatest challenge since the Strike itself. San Francisco State became engaged in one of those periodic upheavals that afflicted universities as they respond to changing academic trends and real or imagined flaws in their own operations; in this case the attention was on graduation requirements. The 1960s had produced a very open and flexible range of choices by which students could address the traditional liberal arts breadth requirements common to American colleges and universities. In the late 1970s various parties on campus attacked this General Studies structure and argued that a more "rigorous" and "coherent" set of requirements be established in which students would no longer have the ability to choose from a large and varied "Chinese menu" of courses but instead would select from more limited clusters and groupings of options. (The term "Chinese Menu" was actually used by some of the proponents for changes!) Committees were formed, resolutions and guidelines passed, and a new "General Education Program" was created to replace General Studies.

Central to this new plan were "core" areas of knowledge that students should be exposed to and that were to be the purview of particular "lead" schools within the larger college, specifically the School of Science, the School of Behavioral and Social Science, and the School of Humanities and Creative Arts. Even within these schools, only certain courses would be eligible for General Education credit, and departments and schools outside of the lead schools would have only restricted ability to place courses into General Education. The threat to Asian American Studies and the School of Ethnic Studies was obvious and, we believed, not accidental! It was a rollback to pre-Strike days.

In response to this threat, a School of Ethnic Studies Council was created as a venue for sharing information across all the departments and for developing effective collective actions. This was somewhat a replay of the Third World Liberation Front from the Strike. Through this Council and associated activities, there was significant coordination of actions by the different departments and a generally shared set of strategies for responding to the challenges we faced. We agreed to seek the maximum possible inclusion of courses from the School of Ethnic Studies into the GE program based on demands for cultural equity and inclusion. We would demand that American Indian, Asian American, Black, and Raza students be given the same opportunity granted white students, as Americans, to use GE to explore their cultures, communities, and societies. We argued that as part of American society we must be included as a matter of equity. Essentially, we needed to educate the larger campus about Ethnic Studies so that they would respond more favorably to our interests when setting campus policies.

We also sought representation on campus committees with purview over the General Education structure and its components. This approach was handicapped by the low number of permanent faculty in the School of Ethnic Studies who were eligible for committees, and also by the governance structure of General Education, in which most of the seats on the committees went to people from the "lead" schools. Despite these difficulties, we were able to place people into key committees where they could protect our interests, keep us informed as to the actions and plans of the committees, and also serve to educate the larger campus regarding our concerns. Because of this activity, we were able to obtain some changes in the General Education structure and its implementation.

Significantly, we collectively took a different approach to "Ethnic Studies" requirements than other colleges and universities. Our approach was to get as many courses from the School of Ethnic Studies to count for as many different areas of General Education as possible, not to simply demand that all students take one or two Ethnic Studies courses. We took this approach so that we could maximize the opportunity for Third World students to take courses in Ethnic Studies for General Education credit. We felt this would benefit our students and also help us continue to offer a wide and diverse curriculum, rather than having mass enrollment in a handful of classes. At the same time we were able to push changes in the General Education requirements that effectively required all students to take two courses related to cultural diversity, and racial and ethnic minorities in America, although their choices were not limited to courses from the College of Ethnic Studies. By allowing other departments on the campus to offer courses that met these requirements we could more effectively argue for inclusion of our courses in other areas of General Education and by so doing so help neutralize the "lead" school concept.

The goal was to establish courses in Ethnic Studies departments as being equal to courses across the whole campus with regard to "Liberal Arts" experience rather than being concerned only with one small part of such requirements. Our position in Asian American Studies was that Asian Americans are part of America, that the social/historical experience and creative expressions of Asian Americans are as legitimate a part of the story of American society as those connected to the Euro American experience. We also argued that just as the literary and historical aspects of the Euro American experience are connected to larger global influences and traditions, so too are the experiences of Asian Americans. Consequently, if courses in the traditional departments can be used to meet requirements for the understanding of society, of human behavior, and of literary and artistic expression, so too should courses of a similar character in

Asian American Studies. We went further and proposed that limiting the ability of students to use Asian American Studies courses for such purposes would be a form of institutional racism, inasmuch as Asian American students would be denied the right to see and understand themselves as a part of national and international society and culture. We also argued that all students could potentially benefit from our courses by obtaining a more complete understanding of the whole scope of American society and culture.

We had to examine and change our curriculum to fit the new guidelines. The core problem was the severe limit placed on how many courses we could offer in the key "Segment II" area of General Education, which encompasses breadth requirements in Science, Social Science, and Humanities/Creative Arts. These limits were much lower than the number of courses we then offered in those areas for General Studies and the criteria for acceptance of courses into General Education were much tighter and more specific than under General Studies. The whole curriculum had to be reinvented, every course evaluated and either deleted or redesigned, and a whole body of new courses created. The paperwork required for new courses was far more extensive than previously, and we had far fewer people available to work on the job, as by 1980 the ethnic-specific Planning Groups were gone and with them all the students and community members who used to help with the operation of the department. Almost all the work was done by six permanent faculty (two of whom had to work in other departments) and four lecturers. This group met weekly and more often as needed.[19]

The result was a transformation of the curriculum. In 1980, before the changes, the department had fifty-seven courses, all but twelve of which were specific to particular Asian American groups. Of these courses, forty-nine were available for students to use in their GS programs.[20] In 1983, midway through the changeover into the new GE structure, the list was reduced to fifty courses, with eleven fewer ethnic-specific courses and six more pan-Asian American courses. Only twenty-two of these courses were in the new General Education program. Between 1983 and 1986 the General Education structure was revised further, at the cost of more courses, and then became locked into a stable form that has persisted, with amendments, to the present (fall 2008). Once the transition to the new GE structure was complete in the late 1980s, the character of the Asian American Studies curriculum was quite different; we had only twenty-six courses, over half of which were pan-Asian American courses, and there were only three to four courses specific to each Asian American group. All but three of our courses could be used in General Education. Retrospectively, what is remarkable is the new structure actually looked a lot like the structure put together for the first

year classes in 1969-70!

The elimination of many ethnic-specific courses while expanding the number of pan-Asian American courses was a direct result of ceilings placed on Asian American Studies offerings by the General Education structure. We had to collapse multiple ethnic-specific courses into single pan-Asian courses to stay within the limits. In the process we suffered losses to our programs but also made some gains. These gains included a complete reappraisal of the program and a consequently more coherent body of courses organized into clearly defined relationships and sequences. The relationship of pan-Asian American Studies courses to ethnic-specific courses had now been systematically addressed, and the parallel division of offerings related to creative expression, social and cultural experience, history, and community seen in the early days of the department now operated at both an ethnic-specific and pan-Asian American level. While the variety of opportunities for exploration in details of particular ethnic experience was gone, the curriculum had a structure and purpose that was readily visible and attractive to students. One consequence was a rapid increase in enrollment, which in turn allowed us to obtain new faculty positions during the 1980s.[21]

Because the program was more carefully planned and the courses sequenced and coordinated, a thoughtful student could take up to thirty-three units of GE coursework in Asian American Studies, and by doing so practically have a major in terms of units and coherent range of subject matter. Our GE structure really was a program now, whereas before it had been an assemblage of courses. We revised our minor program to fit the new curriculums and the impact was immediate; students discovered they could apply courses to both an AAS minor and GE, and the size of our minor program soared.

What we lost was equally significant. We lost the ability to support a wide range of specific, in-depth examinations of different Asian American communities, their character, and cultural expressions. We lost all our ethnic-specific community courses and almost all of our community-specific arts and performance courses. All courses that examined the relationship between Asian societies and Asian Americans were gone. We went from offering a more varied program with many different courses to offering multiple sections of high demand courses. We had more lecture classes and fewer activity and seminar courses. We gained structure and coherence at the expense of depth and variety. Not so immediately obvious, we lost our ability to easily innovate and to experiment with new subject matter and different approaches to instruction. Under the old GS program it had been easy to offer experimental and special topics courses and students could still use the course to meet GS requirements – if we liked the experiments we could turn them into new permanent courses that could be applied to GS requirements. All of that was now difficult, even impossible. As the student body became more diversified with Southeast Asian and Korean students it was harder for us to respond to those changes. Even if we did try new classes and they succeeded, our ability to place them into the General Education structure was much more circumscribed. The enrollment successes of the new structure were gratifying but they also greatly increased faculty workloads and encouraged complacency about our program. The new structure encouraged stasis, not innovation.

## LANGUAGE COURSES

One change in the 1980s that was not driven directly by General Education was the eventual dropping of our Cantonese and Pilipino language offerings. These had been much desired by early Planning Groups but over time we found them to be problematic. The most immediate difficulties were staffing and content. We found it difficult to find people qualified to teach the courses who also understood what we wished to accomplish. We wanted courses that upgraded the practical language skills of students who already had some exposure to the languages, with the aim of making them more effective in community settings. The instructors tended to approach the courses as standard foreign language courses and never developed solid curriculum that had the applied focus we desired. To be fair to the instructors, they were handicapped by a lack of instructional materials as the existing curriculum materials assumed students for whom both the languages and the culture were alien. These difficulties were compounded by enrollment issues; we found it hard to maintain enrollment beyond the first semester level courses. After many years of frustration, we negotiated arrangements with the Foreign Languages Department for continued partial offering of the courses. They have since continued to offer Pilipino language courses but have dropped the Cantonese courses. In the 1990s we instituted a one-year Vietnamese language course sequence and have continued to offer it until the 2008-09 budget crisis necessitated its cancellation. The whole arena of language instruction remains a subject to be revisited.

During the late 1970s and early 1980s we also offered courses directed toward preparing Cantonese and Pilipino bilingual teachers; these were tied to collaborative programs with the School of Education and were somewhat more successful. These courses were dropped from our program when the collaborative programs that they were part of ended.

## THE PAST AS FUTURE

This account of the Asian American Studies Department's response to major changes in campus graduation requirements in the 1980s is immediately relevant in 2008 as the campus is again in turmoil regarding graduation requirements. All signs point to major changes to liberal arts and other graduation requirements, with every reason to believe that the changes will not be favorable to Asian American Studies or to Asian American students. Unfortunately, many faculty from across the larger campus, whom we were able to educate regarding our programs in the 1980s, have now been significantly replaced with new faculty unfamiliar with past issues on the campus and often ill-informed regarding Asian American Studies and Ethnics Studies issues. So the campus-wide education we carried out in the 1980s will have to be done again. Some newer faculty in the College of Ethnic Studies are now more attuned to traditional academic values and have little interest in serving students through programs like General Education. Finally, while the administration of the campus in the past was more willing to give faculty and departments control over their own affairs, the new generation of administrators who started arriving in the late 1980s and early 1990s are practitioners of much more centralized and arbitrary control from on top and their power over the campus much greater than in the past. All this points to immense challenges facing Asian American Studies if the founding principles of the program are to be maintained into the future.

In the late 1990s, as described separately, the Department added a BA major in Asian American Studies as well as an MA program. While these developments have led to the creation of new courses, the undergraduate curriculum of the department has substantially the same character as that developed in the 1980s, and the structure and content of the BA program itself is based on the curriculum program developed at that time. That program in turn, while involving abandonment of many courses created in the exuberant experimentation of the 1970s, is remarkably consistent with the program hastily invented by the first Planning Group for the first year of classes in 1969-70.

## NOTES

1. There were courses at the University of Hawai'i with ethnic specific Filipino content that Robert Ilumin, Manuel Difuntorum, and Alex Soria drew on when they developed a list of proposed courses as the basis of Filipino American Studies
2. This essay is based primarily on our own knowledge as participants and on primary documents, including Planning Group minutes, position papers, memos, course proposals/

outlines, and other documents. This information has been supplemented with the collective input during 2007 and 2008 from a number of other participants from the time period, including lengthy conversations with Jim Hirabayashi, George K. Woo, Irene Dea Collier, and Juanita Tamayo Lott, as well as comments by Penny Nakatsu, Jeff Chan, and Richard Wada.

3. The full names of the organizations were Asian American Political Alliance (AAPA), Intercollegiate Chinese for Social Action (ICSA), and Philippine (later Pilipino) American Collegiate Endeavor (PACE).

4. See Appendix 1 for a list of people active in the first two years of the program. The decision-making structure of the program is detailed in "Governance in AAS" – also in this volume.

5. See "Governance in AAS" for further discussion of Jim Hirabayashi's role in the development of the program.

6. See Appendix 6 for a full listing of the first offerings in 1969.

7. See Appendix 7 for a list of the courses in place by fall 1970. A "course" is a titled body of curriculum approved by the college as available to be offered as a scheduled class. The number of classes offered each term is the number of courses actually scheduled and enrolled, including multiple sections. Consequently it is possible to have more classes than courses in any given semester by offering multiple sections of a course. Because most departments do not offer every course every term, most departments have more courses in place than classes actually offered.

8. In time we found out that most traditional departments did not take course proposals seriously and usually produced very minimalist proposals. While this might be possible in an established field, we did not have that luxury; we had to be more complete.

9. See Appendix 1 for a partial list of faculty and community members active in the early years.

10. Dittoed position paper by Penny Nakatsu, 1970.

11. See Appendix 8.

12. See Appendix 9 for courses in 1980.

13. See "Governance in AAS" for more discussion of process issues.

14. Jim Hirabayashi notes that the existence of a faculty union at SF State also served to moderate some of the actions of the administration in the early years of Ethnic Studies. The faculty union, although small, had supported the Strike and provided some body of ongoing support from across the campus.

15. See "Ethnic Education: Its Purposes and Prospects" by James Hirabayashi, reproduced elsewhere in this volume, for further examples of the rationales we used.

16. See Appendix 7 for details.

17. Some people erroneously believe that the campus administration did not permit us to have a major. Quite the contrary, it was our decision alone. Others have attributed our choice to ideological stances that were, in fact, not part of the debate in 1971. For example, objections to a BA as being "elitist" were not a major part of the debate at the time.

18. The committee was comprised of Malcolm Collier, Ed De la Cruz, Dan Gonzales, Penny Nakatsu, and Juanita Tamayo. Faculty support was provided by Jeff Chan, Phil Choy, Jim Hirabayashi, and Jovina Navarro.

19. See Appendix 11 for the list of faculty in 1981.

20. See Appendix 9 for a full list of courses in 1980, before the changes were made.

21. See Appendix 10 for course listings for late 1980s, which fully reflect the changes brought on by the new GE structure.

# MAPPING OUT LITERARY ASIAN AMERICA ON PAPER PLACEMAT AT THE JACKSON CAFÉ

*Shawn Wong*

In a fairly short period during 1969 and early 1970, the future of what we know about Asian American literature was forged by a series of meetings between four young Asian American writers: Frank Chin, a twenty-nine-year-old writer, former railroad worker, journalist, and Berkeley resident; Jeffery Chan, a twenty-seven-year-old Asian American Studies professor at San Francisco State and fiction writer; Lawson Inada, a thirty-two-year-old English professor and poet from Southern Oregon University in Ashland, Oregon; and me, a nineteen-year-old University of California, Berkeley student and aspiring writer.

I had spent my first two years of college, from 1967 to 1969, at San Francisco State, studying poetry and fiction under the mentorship of Irish poet James Liddy and the renowned American writer Kay Boyle, before transferring to Berkeley. I was dismayed, as many were, by the leadership of SF State under President S.I. Hayakawa and left for Cal. Although I transferred, I continued to take classes from Kay Boyle, essentially enrolled at two universities at the same time.

In the summer of 1969 at Berkeley, I asked myself, "Why am I the only Asian American writer I know in the world?" Are there any other Asian American writers? Why has no teacher ever mentioned one in high school or college?" I was ashamed to admit that these questions came to me so late. In the middle of completing an English literature major that included mostly dead British male authors, I was hungry for contemporary literature written by authors who were alive, who wrote about issues I was interested in, and who pushed the boundaries in fiction and poetry. While I searched for the answer to my questions, I read my Chaucer, dodged tear gas canisters at Berkeley, and went looking for other writers whenever Berkeley was shut down by strikes and demonstrations.

I asked my Berkeley professors for the names of Asian American writers, but they couldn't name any. I went back to SF State to see Kay Boyle who mentioned that one of her graduate students in Creative Writing was Jeffery Chan and he was writing fiction. I called Jeff in Asian American Studies and met with him – my first encounter with an Asian American writer. He was working on a novel entitled *Auntie Tsia Lays Dying*. Jeff also referred me to his friend, Frank Chin, who had recently published a short story, "Food For All His Dead," and who lived in Berkeley just blocks from me. It turned out we were all writing about someone dying or dead – a true bond.

I called Frank that same evening and introduced myself as a student at Berkeley who was interested in writing and had never met a published Chinese American writer. Chin replied, "Meet me at the Med in ten minutes. We'll talk." The Med, or Mediterranean, was a popular coffeehouse on Telegraph Avenue, just south of the university. To make a long story short, I met my first published Chinese American writer and drank my first cappuccino in the same evening.

A few months later, Frank and I found a book in Cody's Bookstore titled *Down at the Santa Fe Depot: 20 Fresno Poets*, an anthology edited by David Kherdian and James Baloian (Gilgia Press, 1970). In the book was the poetry of Lawson Fusao Inada, a Fresno, California native writing about the multiracial west side of his hometown. Frank contacted Gilgia Press and was given Inada's phone number. We contacted him, identifying ourselves as "two Chinese American writers who have read your poetry and want to meet you." It turned out that Lawson had heard of Frank when they were both at the University of Iowa at the same time, but they had never met.

Lawson drove down from Ashland and met Frank and me at a publication party for Ishmael Reed's anthology *19 Necromancers From Now* (1970). Reed had included a chapter from Frank's unpublished novel, *A Chinese Lady Dies*, in the anthology. It was a significant meeting place because it forged an alliance not only between Lawson, Frank, Jeff, and me, but also between Ishmael Reed and other writers present at the gathering, including Al Young, Victor Hernandez Cruz, and Alex Haley. Two literary paths were constructed that evening in 1970 – one headed by Ishmael Reed, who was out to define something called American multicultural writing, long before "multicultural" became the iconic buzzword; and the other path headed by Frank, Jeff, Lawson, and me, who were out to search for what we thought might be a generation of Asian American writers who came before us, hoping that those names might form an Asian American literary canon.

In 1971 we started looking and found a lot of our people who told us that Asian Americans didn't write. We were told there were no Asian American books. None. No histories, no novels, no collections of poetry, no published plays, and certainly no anthologies of Asian American literature. They were wrong. We found that the novel *No-No Boy* by John Okada had been published in 1957 in an edition of 1,500 copies by Charles Tuttle Company and was *still* in print fourteen years later and still for sale for $3.00 in hardcover. We found Toshio Mori's 1949 collection of short stories, *Yokohama, California*, in a used bookstore for twenty-five cents. We found Monica Sone's memoir, *Nisei Daughter* (1953), still in print. We found that *Eat a Bowl of Tea* (1961) had been published by Louis Chu's friend, Lyle Stuart, a publisher known more for books on gambling and sex than great Asian American literature. And we found and interviewed writers such as Hisaye Yamamoto and Wakako Yamauchi.

At the same time, a Japanese American *sansei* poet, Janice Mirikitani, became influential in gathering all the young Asian American literary voices together to read at the famous Glide Memorial Methodist Church and elsewhere around San Francisco. When she called us to read our work, she was asking us to change the world. I met other young Bay Area writers at these reading, such as Jessica Hagedorn and Ntozake Shange. While in my senior year at Berkeley, I became the editor of the national newsletter for the Glide Urban Center. Young writers started to emerge out of Jeff Chan's classes at SF State like Russell Leong and Alan Lau.

At Berkeley I had studied with Jackson Burgess, who had taught both Jeff and Frank (as well as Maxine Hong Kingston) at different times. Lawson published his first collection of poetry, *Before the War: Poems as They Happened*, in 1971. UCLA published its first issue of *Amerasia Journal* in March 1971. In the issue was an essay about Jade Snow Wong's autobiography, *Fifth Chinese Daughter* (1950), by journal editor Lowell Chun-Hoon, and a poem by Ray Lou titled "A Poem for the People."

By 1971, I had graduated from Berkeley and started graduate school in Creative Writing back at SF State. I also moved into Kay Boyle's four-story Victorian mansion at 419 Frederick Street in the Haight-Ashbury. She taught me not only how to be a writer, but also how to live one's life as a writer. The house was filled with artifacts and memorabilia from her days living in Paris and elsewhere in Europe in the 1920s. One day I came home with a copy of the *Dubliners* tucked under my arm and she said to me, while we were both checking the mail, "I see you're reading Jim's book." A constant stream of writers, singers, artists, journalists, teachers, community activists, and even letters from Samuel Beckett entered through the front door of her house. She taught me that writing "was about belief" and that everything I write needed to be relevant to our lives. In graduate school, Kay converted me from a somewhat abstract language poet to a novelist and, in the process, I discovered my narrative voice. The first version of my novel, *Homebase*, began as a twenty-page poem. Several passages from the novel, prior to its publication in 1979 (published by Ishmael Reed's press, I. Reed Books), appeared in several of her poems, non-fiction essays, and even in a novel, *The Underground Woman* (1975). *Homebase*, of course, has Kay's influence and mentorship on every page. An earlier version of the novel was my creative writing master's thesis.

That same year I started graduate school, Frank, Jeff, Lawson, and I met at the Jackson Café in San Francisco Chinatown, and mapped out on a paper placemat the table of contents for an anthology of Asian American literature. For me, there were no college classes in Asian American literature, no professors, no credit, and no grades. I took various essays, book reviews, and interviews by the four of us and sat down to glue together these separate pieces and write a draft of the introduction for the anthology. The central piece to the introduction was an essay written by Frank and Jeff entitled "Racist Love." I remember Lawson writing in a letter the sentence, "We can pronounce Lillian Russell now, so we can speak for ourselves." After the four of us finished the introduction to *Aiiieeeee!*, we gave it to Kay Boyle, who read it and sent it back with pages and pages of handwritten notes. In spite of our combined youth and arrogance at believing we knew all about Asian American literature, we knew when to be students – we followed every one of Kay's suggestions for revision.

We didn't call ourselves literary scholars or historians – we were just looking for the writers and the literature we knew must have been there on the path before us. We called our research project the Combined Asian-American Resources Project, Inc. (CARP). By the end of 1972 we had completed a manuscript of *Aiiieeeee! An Anthology of Asian American Writers*, the first anthology of Asian American literature, and had started looking for a publisher, but the publishers we approached had never heard of Asian American literature and turned us down. While we were searching for a publisher, some of our CARP research for our anthology was published in *Asian American Authors* (Hougton Mifflin, 1972), a textbook edited by SF State professors Kai-yu Hsu and Helen Palubinskas.

In 1973, Roberta Palm, a young editor at Howard University Press, contacted me because she had read that I had won a literary contest sponsored by the Council on Interracial Books for Children and wanted to see my manuscript. Instead of sending her a children's book, I sent her the manuscript to our anthology. The following year, Howard University Press published *Aiiieeeee! An Anthology of Asian American Writers* in its inaugural year and the anthology quickly caught the attention of book reviewers everywhere from *Rolling Stone* to *The New York Times* to *The New Yorker* to Asian community newspapers. Now 34 years later the anthology continues to be lauded and reviled, often in the same essay or book by Asian American literary scholars. No matter who was praising it or who was taking exception to our definition of Asian American literature, everyone began their knowledge of Asian American literature with our anthology. It educated an audience to what Frank, Jeff, Lawson, and I were doing in our own creative work. "*Aiiieeeee!* named the canon," as UCSB Professor Shirley Geok-lin Lim once said at an Asian American literature conference.

The four of us, masquerading as a research project called CARP, also compiled interviews with Asian American actors, and collected oral histories of Asian communities and families. Much of our research is now housed at the Bancroft Library at UC Berkeley.

In 1976, when we couldn't get publishers to reprint Okada's novel, *No-No Boy*, we raised the money and republished the novel under the CARP imprint – our one and only venture into publishing. After we proved that the novel's time had finally arrived, we convinced the University of Washington Press to take over publication of the book. Recently *No-No Boy* sold its 100,000th copy. All this literary history got started forty years ago at SF State when an almost seventy-year-old Kay Boyle said she knew of an Asian American writer.

# UPON REFLECTION

*Philip P. Choy*
*June 28, 2008*

After 120 years, Chinatown, the oldest ethnic community in San Francisco remained a ghetto, its population of multi-generations regarded and treated as foreigners denied a place in America's history. The 1960s were tumultuous times for social change, triggered by the frustration of the Black community's long struggle for racial equality. America's celebration of race diversity was lip service. It took violent protests, campus strikes, and riots to shatter the complacency of America's maintenance of the status quo. History as written and taught was propaganda to promote white America's exploits to the disadvantage of minorities. In the case of the Chinese, we did not exist.

In the midst of the turmoil, teachers throughout the school districts of California requested information on the Chinese of America from the Chinese Historical Society of America (CHSA). To address the need, CHSA held a one-day seminar on April 17, 1969. Likewise seeking information, Alfred Wong from San Francisco State College (now San Francisco State University) called and asked if he and students could attend the seminar by volunteering. I replied that CHSA had enough volunteers among the membership and the event was already overbooked. Wong then threatened, "If you don't let us attend, we're going to bomb you!" Accepting the threat as revolutionary rhetoric, I replied, "Go ahead."

In attendance was Chester Cheng, a professor from San Francisco State who called the following day to ask me (as I was CHSA president at the time) whether anyone from CHSA would teach a course on Chinese American history in the History Department. I spoke with two CHSA founding members, Thomas W. Chinn, who was then regarded as the authority on Chinese American history and Chingwah Lee, but both expressed no interest. And, when there was no response from other board members, Him Mark Lai said he would do it if I taught the class with him. Together, we accepted the challenge.

When Him Mark Lai and I entered the classroom, students involved in the Strike sized us up. Confident that the material to be presented justified the cause for the Strike, I was not intimidated. Him Mark Lai, being the scholar that he is, insured that the course met, if not surpassed, academic standards. What the students' grades were I don't remember, but to this day, Gordon Chin swears I gave him a "D" and will never let me forget! Perhaps if I were to grade him today, he would receive an "A" for not forgetting the motto, "return to the community and serve the people." I do know we didn't flunk George Woo, because at the end of the class, George asked if we would consider teaching the class in the Asian American Studies Department. We agreed. Being self-employed, I had the flexibility to teach in the daytime while Him Mark Lai continued to teach in the evening.

Now, forty years after the Strike at San Francisco State, we have validated our presence in America without yielding to Anglo American dominance. We have reclaimed our history, defined our own identity, and shaped our own destiny. Now, forty years later, we have a piece of America's apple pie, baked by our own bakers. I never dreamed I would witness these changes in my lifetime. Participation in the Movement, and teaching at San Francisco State, are milestones in my life.

*Editor's Note: On October 9, 2005, Philip P. Choy and Him Mark Lai were awarded the San Francisco State University President's Medal in recognition of their contributions to the development and scholarship of Chinese American Studies. This is the highest honor that a California State University president can bestow upon an individual. Choy is currently Adjunct Professor of Asian American Studies at San Francisco State University.*

# Planning and Teaching the First Course in Chinese American History

*Him Mark Lai*
*July 1, 2008*

In late spring or early summer of 1968, some weeks after the April seminar on Chinese American history sponsored by the Chinese Historical Society of America (CHSA), I received a phone call from Chester Cheng, a professor in the History Department of San Francisco State College, inviting me to teach a pilot course on Chinese American history at the school. Since I still had to work at a full-time job as an engineer at Bechtel Corporation I felt that if I were to accept the offer I would have to have another colleague to share the load. After ascertaining that CHSA's Thomas Chinn was not interested in teaching such a course, I contacted Philip Choy and he agreed to team-teach with me.

At the time no university had ever offered or taught a full semester course on Chinese American history. Around 1960 I had taken a course on Asian American history from Stanford Lyman at the University of California Extension in San Francisco, which coincidentally also happened to be the former campus of San Francisco State College in downtown San Francisco. However, the course covered the histories of the Chinese, Filipino and Japanese communities, and, given the time constraint of a semester, was necessarily a broad-brush, mostly sociological, introduction to the subjects. Thus our pilot course was really the first college-level course in America concentrating solely on the history of the Chinese in America.

At the time, in spite of increased immigration after World War II, the Chinese population in America was less than 0.2% of the US population. Constantly faced with the effort to survive in a racist environment that had only begun to lighten in the post-World War II decades, there had been little effort by Chinese in America to systematically collect and preserve archival and historically significant documents, or to chronicle the community's history. On the other hand, due to cultural differences between Chinese and the non-Chinese, augmented by racism in the larger society, a large part of the voluminous writings on the Chinese lacked objectivity, and too often were deliberately sensational and prejudicial. This was the challenge that Phil and I faced in preparing for the course.

However, Phil and I did have some basis to be confident that we could handle such a course in Chinese American history since both he and I had been members of the CHSA since the mid-1960s and had participated in some of the spadework of the society on Chinese American historical research. Moreover, I had done research to write a series of articles on 19th century Chinese American history in the weekly *East/West* since the end of 1967, and then collaborated with Thomas Chinn and Phil Choy in compiling the syllabus *A History of the Chinese in California* that was published for the previously mentioned CHSA seminar in April 1969. Thus the essentials of historical experiences of the Chinese during the 19th century were already pretty well defined.

However, there was little written at the time on Chinese American history of the 20th century. I myself had only begun to examine that subject area. Fortunately, at that time I had the benefit of consultation and advice from Yuk Ow. Ow was a founder of the *Chinese Pacific Weekly* and at the time a research assistant at San Francisco State College. He had researched the history of the Chinese in California since the late 1940s, but he was too early in the field and hence was unrecognized. I personally benefited greatly from his expertise and suggestions.

During the summer of 1969 Phil and I had to embark on a crash program to prepare course outlines and lecture notes for the course. At the time the effects of the 1965 Immigration Act on the Chinese community was not yet evident, and the Chinese community was still overwhelmingly Cantonese. Thus the course began with a discussion on the history of Guangdong and its people. In my lectures in the course in subsequent years, I limited this part of the course to a discussion of the historical developments in China during and after the Opium War as being more relevant to 19th century Chinese emigration.

Two decades later I was to amplify and use some of the material on the history of Guangdong and its people as reading material for participants in the Chinese Culture Center's "In Search of Roots" Program. I had also included at the end of the course outline comparisons of the history of Chinese in continental United States with that of the communities in Canada and Hawai'i to explore how communities of people originating from similar social backgrounds developed under various different political and social environments.

During the course of teaching the pilot course, Phil and I found that there was too much material for a one-semester lecture course and we never had a chance to explore these sectors. Regrettably I was never able to schedule time to make these comparisons in offerings of the course during subsequent years. Although my interest in looking at Chinese American history from the perspective of the Chinese diaspora continued over the years, in Asian American Studies I taught Chinese American history as a part of American history.

The pilot course on Chinese American history was offered in the evening, and the students' average age was somewhat older than day students. A few had been active in the yearlong student strike that had resulted in the establishing of an Asian American Studies Program. The course was evidently substantial enough to satisfy the History Department's criteria, whatever they may have been. It was then transferred to the Asian American Studies Program the next time it was offered and it became a regular course in the program, superseding a course on Chinese in America that had been taught by Alan Wong during the same semester as our pilot course. Wong's course partially covered the same subject matter as our pilot course. To this day I do not know the details of the political maneuvering that may have occurred behind the scenes in the decisions to have two such similar course offerings.

I never did regard teaching as a career and taught only when responding to a request to fill a need. After the pilot course was successfully completed, Phil Choy took over for the next offering of the course. Subsequently, I taught at San Francisco State University from 1972 to 1975 and then at the University of California, Berkeley in 1978, 1979, and 1984. The challenge of teaching was of great help to me, in that I had to think through many Chinese American historical issues to reach rational and logical conclusions satisfactory to myself before I could present them to the students. At the beginning my perspectives on Chinese American history were not firmly formulated; as time went on I tended to concentrate on two aspects of Chinese American history: (1) as a part of the history of the American people, and (2) as a part of the Chinese diaspora. These perspectives reveal themselves more in my writings than in the classroom lectures.

Since I was already in my early forties, some fifteen to twenty years older than the core faculty in Asian American Studies, and also was only occasionally teaching a course, I never considered myself an integral part of the discipline, although I was supportive. This situation precluded my being in any position to exert any direct influence on the course of development of Asian American Studies. However, it also freed me from involvement in the internal politics, interactions, and power struggles that seem to arise inevitably in organizations where strong and ambitious personalities are involved. Not being in academia also meant that I am free to undertake research without having to worry about academic guidelines to justify funding, tenure, and promotions. As a member of the community, I am glad that I have had this opportunity to participate in helping to understand better the historical heritage of the Chinese American community.

*Editor's Note: On October 9, 2005, Him Mark Lai and Philip P. Choy were awarded the San Francisco State University President's Medal in recognition of their contributions to the development and scholarship of Chinese American Studies. This is the highest honor that a California State University president can bestow upon an individual. Lai is currently Adjunct Professor of Asian American Studies at San Francisco State University.*

# RAISING A RED BANNER...[*]

*Marlon K. Hom*

*Raising a red banner to resist the red banner 打著紅旗反紅旗！

*- Pro-Mao slogan on Liu Shaoqi - ca. 1966*

## PART ONE: GETTING FISCAL/PHYSICAL

### *Administrative Shift and Operational Shaft*

The year 1993 marked a turning point at San Francisco State University. Budgetary shortfalls led to a drastic increase in student fees, reduction of classes, and the termination of many lecturers, severely affecting student learning. The administration implemented a new "program priority" in resource allocation and a "dollar-based" budget. Departments that offered academic degrees (baccalaureate and master's degrees) were given prioritized support and each department would be responsible for its own operational expenses and lecturer salary compensation.

These new administrative measures were critical to the Asian American Studies Department at SF State (AAS) because AAS did not have a degree major, and hence had no program priority advantage. The departmental philosophy was to provide our students with knowledge learning rather than degree earning, because a few first-generation faculty considered the pursuit of an academic degree to be an elitist mentality from the "Ivory Tower." AAS focused on General Education (GE), a university-wide graduation requirement in the early 1980s, and made AAS classes accessible to as many students as possible. This safeguarded AAS from the "academic elitism" of focusing on degrees and majors versus a grassroots education that focused on outreaching widely to students. AAS was also committed to community service and many colleagues were part-time lecturers from community organizations. As temporary faculty, however, the employment of these lecturers was at the mercy of the budget. Hence, AAS was in a rather precarious and vulnerable situation under a "program priority" budget. AAS was large in size (enrollment) but zero in program (degree) outcome.

When the budget crisis hit in 1993-95, some senior colleagues who had seen similar crises during the infamous 1978 Proposition 13 period regarded the current crisis as exaggerated. This indifference revealed that those few AAS faculty missed a lesson in history: AAS survived and prospered during the post-Proposition 13 decade by finding and redefining the department's role in GE. Now, with the new administrative operational paradigm in the 1990s, AAS must determine:

- How to avoid being shortchanged by the new program priority budget allocation. It was suggested that GE *is* the department's program. But AAS is not the most popular (top) GE program. The top three departments at SF State used their GE enrollment count to support their BA and MA program/degree outcomes. AAS did not have a degree program.
- How to retain lecturers when the Collective Bargaining Agreement treated them as "temporary faculty." What can be done for lecturers in terms of programmatic needs and loyalty?
- How to ensure that student learning would not suffer. The university enrollment data in the late 1980s and 1990s showed that each semester over five hundred students could not enroll in AAS GE classes. The "waiting list" of students trying to get into AAS classes remained a "wailing list." No augmentation was given to AAS since 1993 to address excessive enrollment because AAS did not meet program priority support.

### *"Crisis Opportunity" Moment/Movement*

In 1993, AAS was still an amorphous program despite its GE success. Like Ethnic Studies elsewhere, most of its faculty still held on to traditional academic identities as anthropologists, historians, psychologists, sociologists, etc.; there was no disciplinary identity as an "Asian Americanist" despite the fact that AAS at SF State, officially established in March 1969, is the nation's founding AAS program. In curricular matters, AAS was wise to be involved in GE, but its survival in the 1990s became dependent solely on GE, a university-wide program beyond AAS control. GE could not be its academic identity. The claim of community involvement was mostly personal and individual, not institutional, participation. AAS program identity was not clearly articulated and its destiny at risk. AAS had to assess its survival and future: With degree programs, there would be institutional "program priority" support to mentor potential students to become future torchbearers of our paradigm. Without that, our AAS paradigm would not survive beyond one generation.

To remediate that, AAS must, in Maoist jargon, "raise a red banner to resist the red banner" – by using the institutional structure to define our own AAS institutional identity, to establish an independent and sustainable academic program identity and standard (red banner) based on our own paradigms of self-determination and community service, and to resist the institutionalized "red banners" of academic elitism prevalently seen elsewhere.

It was at this juncture in 1993 that I was elected the department chair. At that same time I was also recruited elsewhere. I used that as leverage to negotiate with Academic Affairs to make clear that AAS would have support to keep its GE role, and develop a new BA major and an MA degree; otherwise I would leave. I was assured that support for AAS's program development would come in the form of new tenure-track faculty recruitment.

### Hire Peter to Pay Paul

In fall 1993, AAS received approval for a new tenure-track recruitment for 1994-95, but the fiscal budget for 1994-95 only had funding for two classes available to lecturers. Tenure-track faculty's project- and grant-generated release time helped with lecturers' retention. It also helped that a tenured colleague who was on leave decided to resign. He agreed to remain "on leave" as long as university policy permitted, so that AAS could use his position for lecturer retention instead of losing it to the budget crisis. Still, several part-time lecturers could not be retained. The chair became the target of lecturer discontent and was accused of selling out lecturers while making new plans to hire tenure-track faculty.

Nobody seemed to know the budget difference between lecturer retention and new faculty recruitment, or how to manipulate the budget for both tenure-track faculty recruitment and lecturer retention. It was a situation where not everyone would be satisfied or happy when one could not separate the personal from the professional.

In order to address issues from all sides, it was best to put into practice tactical protraction, anticipation, and preemption in order to achieve the objectives of both new faculty recruitment and lecturer retention. Serving on and later chairing Academic Senate committees on academic and educational policies and faculty affairs allowed me to know the process. Being on the Senate Executive Committee and the Graduate Council also gave me insider's knowledge on the operational mechanics and protocols. The protracted move on faculty retention and recruitment was an upfront use of new faculty resources to retain lecturers on a year-to-year basis and at the same time recruit candidates for the new tenure-track position. If there were resources for lecturer retention, and if AAS conducted recruitment in good faith, there would be no accusation of mismanagement.

The job description for tenure-track faculty recruitment adhered strictly to the hiring policy provisions but with articulated specifics. The initial application pool was usually small, hence justifiable to request an extension to continue the search with minor revisions on the job description to encourage a larger pool. The administration agreed. Questions were raised when there was a request for a third-year extension. Citing both off-campus and on-campus examples that faculty recruitment often lasted for years without an ideal outcome, the administration knew and accepted that this was commonplace. As long as it was above board, tenure-track resources could be used for lecturer retention on a borrowed-time basis. Between 1993 and 2000, AAS searched for seven new positions as part of the promised program development support, and completed all seven appointments by 2000. Each position was parlayed into a multi-year search process. There would be at least two, sometimes three, new faculty positions concurrently under search annually. As a result AAS, had sufficient but "temporary" funds from the seven new tenure-track searches during the multi-year recruitment period to retain most of the senior lecturers and to hire some ABDs as lecturers for potential tenure-track positions. Since 1994, lecturers were also encouraged to earn a terminal degree with AAS sponsorship under the California State University (CSU) system's "Forgivable Loan" Program, so that they, too, could be considered for these tenure-track positions that require a terminal degree. This was to help lecturer retention and career mobility, not to promote academic elitism.

The entire faculty recruitment experience was a bittersweet one. There was the accusation of "selling out" to academic elitism, and buying into and promoting the PhD degree mentality, ignoring the fact that AAS had succeeded in defeating the management on the PhD-only criteria for hiring (see "Self-Determination" section below). The PhD degree meant nothing in AAS but it was a key to open the gatekeeping academic institution.

Some new PhD colleagues, regrettably, do have an elitist "3-self" mentality: self-absorbed, self-centered, and self-important. On a sweeter note, it was a faculty development success to witness three lecturers receiving terminal degrees and becoming tenure-track faculty with departmental support. The seven new tenure-tracks represented the attainment of ethnic and gender parity in AAS: one in Asian Americans of Mixed Heritage, one in Chinese American Studies, one in Chinese-Vietnamese American (tertiary migration) Studies, one in Korean American Studies, one in Pilipino American Studies, one in Vietnamese American Studies, and one for special faculty development. AAS grew from 8.75 faculty positions to 15.60, with a balanced gender ratio. In 2007-08, AAS still maintained 15.20 positions after the unexpected loss of .40 to the associate deanship appointment when the department was told there would be no reimbursement except on "good" budget years.

In playing this protracted maneuver, the department survived the lecturer crisis and more:

- The GE curriculum was intact.
- The department grew in both faculty ranks and new curricular offerings (Asian Americans of Mixed Heritage Studies, Vietnamese American Studies, Korean American Studies, children's literature, health studies, public policies, baccalaureate and MA degree courses, etc.).
- Some lecturers found upward mobility to tenure-track rank.

## Part Two: Being Historical/Hysterical

### Self-Determination and Self-Preservation

Self-determination and community activism were the paradigms of the Ethnic Studies movement in the late 1960s. Of all the AAS and Ethnic Studies programs, only the founding AAS program at SF State was able to safeguard this philosophy in faculty governance. AAS programs elsewhere submitted to the "publish or perish" and PhD-only requirements on tenure-track faculty hiring; non-doctoral-track activists in AAS were soon cast aside, at best staying as lecturers for a few years without security of employment. Beyond SF State, there was only one non-PhD faculty who was granted tenure and promotion to associate professor – a rare exception. PhD holders, hardly connected to the struggle in the late 1960s and early 1970s, were hired into AAS programs. With UC Berkeley and San Francisco State as exceptions, most faculty hiring were joint appointments with a traditional discipline controlling the promotion and tenure process, hence relegating AAS scholarship secondary to traditional scholarship. At research universities, community

involvement (unless to one's own professional community) would not be considered as part of the professional development criteria for tenure and promotion. This PhD-only "program cleansing" action in the early 1970s, known as "academic reform over community activism" in Ethnic Studies programs at most universities, forever shut out community activists from ladder-rank faculty appointment. From the early beginning, these AAS programs have betrayed the struggle for self-determination and community activism as an imperative of the AAS program paradigm.

At SF State, Jeffery Chan, a non-PhD lecturer, already had faculty status when AAS was established in March 1969. The Strike activists were mostly undergraduate students who later graduated in 1969-72. Sympathetic faculty leaders mentored some of them to attend graduate programs and professional schools. Those who remained active on campus became the core of the original AAS founding faculty. AAS was allocated six full-time-equivalent (FTE) faculty positions representing the Chinese, Japanese, and Pilipino American coalition. Five of them were filled by individuals who did not have a PhD; they gained tenure-track status by the mid 1970s, with an understanding that they would demonstrate a "doctoral equivalency" for tenure. Eventually all five received tenure and promotion through this understanding. Some activists who did not have the tenure-track opportunity felt bitter and betrayed. The SF State administration actually stopped non-PhD tenure-track hiring in AAS after the fifth appointment in 1976. The AAS faculty leadership knew, and began to hire doctoral-track faculty in 1980 and 1983, and again in 1986. On record, however, AAS rejected the "PhD-only" mandate while other units in the College of Ethnic Studies followed the PhD-only in their hiring.

In 1987, AAS openly disputed the PhD-only mandate from Academic Affairs and was denied two tenure-track appointments when the department was growing rapidly in student enrollment. During a meeting in 1988, when the new Academic Senate policy on tenure-track hiring was adopted to require a PhD or terminal degree, Associate Provost for Faculty Affairs, representing Academic Affairs, claimed that non-PhD hiring was no longer acceptable under the new policy, and insisted that AAS hire only PhDs and train the new hires to become AAS scholars. They reasoned that since none of the current AAS faculty were AAS specialists by academic training, then hiring a non-AAS doctorate would be no different. The AAS leadership maintained that since there was no AAS PhD program in any university, there should not be a PhD-only hiring mandate; it should be AAS's decision to define and determine its faculty's qualifications under the paradigm of self-determination on faculty governance.

The stalemate lasted for four years (1986-90). Academic Affairs was blatantly harassing the non-PhD AAS leadership who personalized the issue, engaging it as a personal affront and losing sight of a viable strategy for resistance and subversion. Elected as new Hiring Committee chair in 1990, I enlisted my former colleague, the late Yuji Ichioka, to apply for an open AAS position and help with this impasse we had with Academic Affairs. Ichioka was a perfect non-PhD scholar; his impeccable professional achievement showed that Academic Affairs was wrong and unprofessional because faculty hiring should be based on qualifications specific to the job description, and not solely on a PhD degree. In addition, the AAS Hiring Committee did not review Ichioka as a historian, which would have been the prerogative of the History Department. AAS evaluated him as an Asian Americanist, so it was within AAS's disciplinary integrity to judge Ichioka's qualifications. AAS argued that the definition of disciplinary expertise belongs to the department, as honored in any traditional discipline, and that AAS expects to be accorded with the same professional respect. This was not just a matter of AAS self-determination. Academic Affairs should not take this disciplinary integrity away from AAS unless the administration put it under receivership. If they did the latter, the Asian American communities would be mobilized to protest because AAS had done nothing wrong.

To end the argument, Academic Affairs did not dispute Ichioka as a *bona-fide* AAS specialist and offered him a tenured appointment, despite the fact that Ichioka did not have a terminal degree. Ichioka declined the offer. Academic Affairs also dropped the PhD-only mandate with an understanding that AAS, like all academic units on campus, would adhere to the same "PhD or equivalent terminal degree" criterion as articulated in the Academic Senate policy on tenure-track faculty recruitment. It was a fair settlement. If AAS expects the same respect accorded to any academic program, it should not seek special treatment.

AAS prevailed in this faculty governance fight. After a four-year delay, AAS concluded hiring three tenure-tracks in spring semester 1991: two associate professors and one assistant professor, all from the ranks of current lecturers. However, this victory also led to internal resentment because the solution basically eliminated an interest imbedded in this PhD fight: Some faculty believed in a *cause célèbre* for a Maoist-style "continuous struggle," instead of achieving parity and equity for AAS program and faculty development in the university community.

In fall 1993, AAS received the first new tenure-track position as promised. The plan was to apply the "equivalent terminal degree" provision of the university faculty hiring policy on a part-time lecturer who had a JD degree and was a well-respected community activist, a licensed attorney, and an expert in domestic violence. It would also have been an excellent move to advance gender and women studies in AAS. Ironically, some non-PhD senior colleagues did not support her candidacy because she did not have a PhD. The recruitment was extended and she left SF State for a federal government appointment. After several PhD hires, in 2005-07 AAS had another opportunity to exercise this "terminal degree" hiring provision with the consideration of an applicant with an MFA degree. This time, while the administration did not oppose it, AAS had to, again, overcome internal objection, this time, from a younger PhD faculty who accused the department leadership of "anti-intellectualism" in recruiting an MFA and not a PhD. Both scenarios reveal the disingenuous internal discord of the past twenty-five years over the PhD issue.

The internal tension over PhD was obsessive, irrational, and personalized. In the grassroots extreme, some colleagues generalized "research and publication" as an elitist PhD activity and incompatible with AAS, while in the ivory tower extreme, some considered the non-PhD colleagues professionally unproductive in research and publication. From the department chair's vantage, it was difficult trying to strike a balance between both extremes. At the university level, an institutional paradigm shift was happening when the administration began to prioritize its support for PhD faculty with research and not for teaching or service. The faculty community-at-large felt the administration intentionally valued research over first-rate teaching and service. Within AAS, this became a divisive issue due to the perceived inequity caused by such a shift in paradigm focus. In 1997, some younger PhD colleagues in AAS arrogantly stated that they were not hired for community service because they were "scholars" and not "social workers." In the department-sponsored 1998 conference on the 30th anniversary of the Third World Student Strike, a senior faculty publicly ridiculed PhD as irrelevant in AAS at SF State.

Neither the contempt for community service nor the simplistic anti-PhD posture should be considered professionally acceptable in AAS. This internal conflict only confirmed that AAS at SF State was having growth pains. Senior colleagues believed in their perpetual immortality – comfortable with tenure – and did not focus on mentoring anyone for succession into the next generation. For twenty-five years AAS did not sustain a discipline-based academic program to mentor students to carry on its own institutional torch in the academe. When AAS was promised with resources for expansion in the mid-1990s, new faculty were hired. Despite a careful search process, some, who were not our former lecturers, arrived already brainwashed by mainstream PhD arrogance. They found it difficult to embrace the community-based philosophy of our AAS program as their professional development priority. Eventually most left for research-based institutions.

In sum, AAS faculty development since 1993 has had its share of successes and failures in establishing a strategy for program development and succession. A pragmatic Chinese Marxist said it well in 1962: "A good cat is one that catches mice, be it white or black" – that is, outcome, not outward appearance, defines a good AAS faculty who, regardless of having or not having a PhD, contributes to our AAS program paradigm of self-determination and community service.

### Paradigm Realignment/Refinement

AAS degree program planning was a task that challenged the twenty-plus-year-old AAS program paradigm to educate students without offering an academic degree. The Asian Pacific Islander American (APIA) collegiate population, especially of Chinese, Filipino, and Vietnamese ancestry, grew rapidly in the 1980s and beyond the CSU Master Plan projection. CSU was behind on serving APIA students, leading to a system-wide commission review. In 1994, the CSU Chancellor's Commission reported that CSU needed to do more to address APIA students' educational needs. It identified AAS at SF State as "exemplary" in serving APIA students. It was a clear signal for AAS at SF State to move forward. Perhaps this commission review expedited our success to secure seven new faculty positions.

Armed with this document, AAS was able to plan for its academic program. In two years, it smoothly developed a Vietnamese American Studies Center, officially approved in fall 1996. The Center, dedicated to addressing the newest Asian American population in the post-Vietnam War era, was the first such program in US higher education institutions. AAS was able to add two faculty positions and develop three new courses in Vietnamese American Studies plus a Vietnamese language course.

Discussions on a baccalaureate major in the 1970s-80s ended with a decision to not offer a major. Since 1991, AAS began continuous but sporadic discussions on establishing baccalaureate and graduate degree programs. In the mid-1990s, some colleagues still felt that a degree program was inconsistent to the department philosophy, and that AAS majors would not find jobs after graduation. They maintained that GE should remain the focus at the undergraduate level to reach as many students as possible. There was also major reluctance for an MA program, despite the agreement that AAS needed to address the inequitable "quota admission" structure in the Ethnic Studies MA Program that rejected a lopsided number of APIA applicants, and more importantly, to mentor and prepare future specialists for either community service or

doctoral studies to carry on our AAS program paradigm. Despite calls for participation in the MA program planning, most non-PhD colleagues stayed away.

To find a common path, AAS conducted an extensive department survey of students. Its results showed an overwhelming student demand for an AAS BA major and MA as part of their educational experience at SF State. Still, faculty discussions progressed slowly. The main reason was that the planning group was not familiar with the new program proposal process. In spring 1996, re-elected as department chair, I took charge of the planning process and worked step-by-step with the faculty planning group. Within the same semester, two proposals, one for a baccalaureate major and one for a Master of Arts degree, were ready for administrative reviews after receiving consensus approval from the department faculty.

The move toward a degree program was not to challenge or undermine the success of AAS as a popular GE curriculum. The degree program was inclusive in group representation, and encumbered and protected our GE education philosophy while addressing the students' growing demand for an independent AAS major at SF State. To maintain a balance between the new program and departmental philosophy, the baccalaureate major proposal modeled its framework on the minor program established twenty years earlier by the senior colleagues as follows:

Module 1: Introduction to AAS (social sciences and humanities) (6 units)
Module 2: Asian American ethnic groups (18 units)
Module 3: Asian American community (3 units)
Module 4: Cross-group topics/electives (9 units)
Module 5: Senior proseminar (culminating experience) (3 units)

New courses were developed, not to replace any of the existing courses, but to make the major more comprehensive. To address the concern on career outcome, it was strategically designed as a thirty-nine unit major to encourage students to double major in another field without being burdened by heavy unit requirements from two majors that may delay their graduation. There would be balance and flexibility between ethnic-specific and cross-group (topical) courses, 45% and 55% respectively, so that students can develop a concentration (theme/genre specific or ethnic group specific) if they so choose through the multiple combination of taking group-specific and cross-group and elective courses in modules 2 and 4. The design also addresses post-graduation career concerns by limiting AAS majors to twenty-five students per semester, preparing them for both community service and graduate studies. This will also maintain GE education as a department program priority, and use GE as the support base for the major. The proposal met no opposition in the Academic Senate; it sailed through with flying colors.

The graduate program planning was originally designed as follows:

Module 1:  Theory    and    research    methodology
           (6 units)
Module 2:  Ethnic-specific    seminars    (Chinese
           American, Japanese American, Pilipino
           American, and Vietnamese American)
           (12 units)
Module 3:  Electives/concentration (9 units)
Module 4:  Project/thesis (3 units)

The objective in the ethnic-specific seminars was to ensure parity in learning about the four major groups in AAS as core values of self-determination. It was considered equitable in that all our MA graduates would be equally competent in the core groups. However, one ethnic group's seminar proposal was unavailable, thus holding up the entire planning process. Finally in 1996, the MA Planning Group gave up the core value ideals and replaced the ethnic-specific seminar design with topic/specialty seminars to resolve the impasse. The MA would be a flexible thirty-unit program in five modules of thematic learning, and consistent with our community service educational paradigm. It would prepare students for either community service or advanced graduate study or professional schools:

Module 1:  Research and methodology (3-6 units)
Module 2:  Topic seminars (immigration, literature,
           family-gender, etc.) (9-12 units)
Module 3:  Community seminars (health and public
           policy) (3-6 units)
Module 4:  Electives/concentration (3-9 units)
Module 5:  Project/thesis (3 units)

During its first step of review and approval at the Academic Senate, some representatives questioned the proposal as if this new AAS MA program would take resources from units they represented. There were also questions of disciplinary qualifications and curricular encroachment. It was obvious that some people felt an MA in AAS meant lending academic legitimacy to a department for which they did not have scholarly regard. These issues were their thinly disguised attempt to oppose AAS entry into graduate education. In response, they were reminded to read the materials in the AAS program proposal, that the reviews should be on its learning merit, and that AAS was an interdisciplinary academic unit. Suggestion of encroachment was without merit unless proven with evidence. AAS

graduate faculty's professional qualifications, all with PhDs from tier-one research universities, were beyond their challenge. It was at that moment during the Senate discussion that the university president unexpectedly spoke up, reminding the senators to judge the program's content, and that resources were his concern, not theirs. That said, the Senate ended the debate and passed the AAS MA proposal with overwhelming support.

However, Academic Affairs underwent new leadership and support for AAS vanished. From fall 1996 to fall 1997, there was no news to implement the degree programs. Repeated inquiries went unanswered. Finally, on the occasion for AAS to respond to an academic program review, I spoke up as department chair that I would not act on it, and that AAS faculty would not sign any university committee report, until the delay in implementing the two new AAS programs ended. When fall 1997 semester began, Jeanne Batallones met with fellow seniors Darren Lee Brown and Jerry Dear to organize other AAS students to spearhead a letter-writing campaign and a student petition with several hundred signatures to demand action. They also mobilized scores of students filing "Major Declaration" petitions to declare an AAS major despite the fact that such a major was not yet on record. (See articles written by Batallones, Brown, and Dear published elsewhere in this volume.) Suddenly everything came through. AAS graduated its first cohort of baccalaureate majors, including Batallones and her activist peers, in 1998. The students were able to graduate immediately with an AAS major in the same semester of program implementation because AAS was already offering all the required courses in fall 1997. The MA program began later in January 2000, after CSU headquarters conducted an external review of the proposal.

This again demonstrates that students continue to play a significant role in AAS. In fall 1968, student activism established AAS. In fall 1997, student activism helped to materialize the AAS baccalaureate and MA degrees.

On an interesting ending note regarding the degrees: When the first AAS major cohorts graduated, the department used the color red to represent AAS because red was seen as a positive color shared by the majority of Asian countries. When the Ethnic Studies MA students began to graduate, the color white was used to represent Ethnic Studies. AAS faculty initiated a proposal, with full support from Black Studies colleagues, to change the Ethnic Studies academic regalia color from white (representing Humanities and Arts in traditional academic regalia) to red which now symbolizes and acknowledges the revolutionary spirit of the 1968 Third World student struggle to establish Ethnic Studies. This also affirms Ethnic Studies as an independent college and not as a discipline under Humanities and Arts. This won Academic Senate and administrative approval.

## PART THREE: INCONCLUSIVE INCULCATION

### *Rises, Crises, and Prices*

The early 1980s, as a partial result of Proposition 13 (1978), ushered in a GE overhaul. In 1992-94, a fiscal crisis again brought about institutional (organizational and fiscal) changes. In both crises, AAS seized the opportunity to strategically move itself forward and, taking advantage of the momentum, to build up its program. In the 1980s, there were extensive GE involvement and enrollment expansion. In the late 1990s, there were tenure-track faculty development and degree program expansion. The result of this continuous motion maintained AAS as a major GE player and no longer an amorphous unit. With both degree programs firmly in place in 2000, and a strong presence in GE, AAS has distinguished itself besides being *the* founding AAS program. With a strong foundation built from the mid-1980s, it has defined and refined its own unique brand of community-based institutional paradigm in higher education: becoming a key player and an integral member on campus and in the community without being subservient to institutional culture and values. More important, while AAS programs elsewhere are trying to imitate traditional disciplines in faculty development and curricular matters, AAS at SF State continued to forge its own academic brand name with curricular innovation instead of imitation, and to be ahead of the game instead of following or playing catch-up. Despite receiving no additional institutional support other than faculty salary and basic office maintenance in the last fifteen years, AAS has transformed itself to become:

- The only AAS program with an extensive curriculum in General Education, and with the first AAS BA major and only AAS MA in the CSU system (see Appendix 12), institutionalizing red as the academic regalia color for Asian American Studies and Ethnic Studies by rejecting the color of white assigned for Ethnic Studies by the administration.
- The largest AAS department with 16 full-time tenure-track faculty positions, and in full and independent control of departmental hiring, retention, tenure, and promotion policies (see Appendix 13 for the 2008 roster of AAS faculty).
- The first AAS in the country to validate the studies of Asian Americans of Mixed Heritage with a dedicated faculty position.
- The first AAS to offer a variety of unique courses dedicated to topics such as Asian American children's literature, Asian American community health and wellness, and public policy.
- The first AAS to develop a cohesive Vietnamese American curriculum with courses in language, history, culture, and mental health.
- The only AAS program to institutionalize town-and-gown cooperation with community organizations in research and publication as well as community service.
- The first AAS to develop organized travel study programs to Asian American ancestral homelands (China, the Philippines, and Vietnam).
- The first AAS to develop a short-term inter-university program for student cohorts from another university to take AAS courses at SF State.

All these curricular development actions have their roots based on the program paradigm of student learning and service without betraying the founding principles of self-determination and community service. AAS success is based on proactive anticipation to realign and refine departmental interests without sacrificing its integrity.

Now, on its fortieth year, AAS appears to have everything in place – stability in enrollment and faculty development. What is the current state of AAS at SF State? There are more concerns and challenges on the horizon:

- The budget crisis of 2008 has reduced AAS faculty resources from 15.20 to 11.90. This appears similar to if not worse than the 1993 budget crisis. Most of the younger AAS faculty has no prior experience dealing with budget crises compared to the senior faculty who survived the crises of 1978 and 1993; and the former do not have experience confronting institutional oppression in the academe. With major reductions in classes (teaching) and continuous preference for professional development (research) that reduces classroom teaching, the 2008 crisis will be their initiation and baptism in the struggle for not just their professional survival but for safeguarding the AAS mission to serve our students.
- Institutionalization has led to a career paradigm shift among some faculty who prioritize non-teaching interest over classroom teaching. Some still avoid acknowledging themselves as Asian Americanists and value their traditional academic identity. Institutionalization has also led to an attitude of power worship among some faculty who cater to external management wishes over departmental interest and collegiality.
- Some AAS majors have considered a few AAS classes not challenging enough. Some also develop ambivalence towards faculty who are self-centered and

indifferent to student learning environment. Serious students are turned off by the "feel-good" and "groupie" pedagogy that alienate those who were not "in." AAS needs to create an environment to excite student excellence in learning, to stimulate a higher intellectual and social awareness, to better mentor and prepare students to serve the community or to go to graduate school, and not just to graduate to get out of school.

- Heritage language instruction was part of the core AAS curriculum in the 1970s. However, an ideal heritage language faculty – not just teaching the course as a foreign language – was difficult to find. Small in class size, language teaching is not resource-friendly. AAS in the past has given away small-class heritage language instruction on Cantonese and Pilipino (Tagalog) to maximize student enrollment. In 1997, AAS returned to heritage language instruction by offering Vietnamese but not Cantonese and Pilipino. AAS should re-assess its role on heritage language instruction in light of the university's internationalization agenda, which marginalizes heritage language learning. For example, Cantonese, the language of the Chinese American community, is not considered the official Chinese language and the Foreign Languages Department has ceased its instruction for years.

- Programmatic measures have been made to be inclusive beyond the original three Asian ethnic units (Chinese American, Japanese American, and Pilipino American) by adding courses on Korean Americans, Vietnamese Americans, Asian Americans of Mixed Heritage, and most recently South Asian Americans. Since the mid-1990s, several outreach attempts were made to include Pacific Islanders in AAS but without avail. AAS respects the self-determination of the Pacific Islander communities and their yet-to-be-determined decision to join AAS or not.

- While AAS has clearly articulated community service as an imperative in our paradigm for both faculty development (tenure and promotion) and student learning, AAS needs to re-articulate the spirit of service and volunteerism in our community service paradigm in response to (1) the university's institutionalized "community service learning" agenda that allows faculty to reduce class-teaching load and gives students additional academic credits to perform service activities in a class (i.e., earning five or six units for a normal three-unit class by piggybacking additional two to three units under "community-service learning"); and (2) career elitism that leads some faculty to prioritize their service to professional organizations and special interest groups over serving ethnic community service organizations.

Time brings changes and it is inevitable. Will the SF State AAS program paradigm – student learning and community service – survive future changes as faculty become more concerned with their careers than with the AAS program philosophy? Will the founding paradigm be sustainable after the program founders' retirement? Without mentoring and building a second generation to carry on the founding AAS philosophy in academe on the PhD level, will this philosophy be a one-generation only paradigm, as elitist careerism may eventually take over AAS at SF State, if not already in other academic institutions? Are the AAS program and faculty development strategies, implemented since the mid-1990s, too late to change this one-generation destiny? If yes, then without successors, the inevitable erosion and eventual demise of the founding program paradigm will be the ultimate price to pay for the hard-fought accomplishments of AAS's lonesome rise from institutional crises.

# The Vietnamese American Studies Center at San Francisco State University

*Mai-Nhung Le and Minh-Hoa Ta*
*in collaboration with Marlon K. Hom*

The history of Vietnamese Americans is a relatively recent one. The fall of Saigon on April 30, 1975 marked the end of the Vietnam War and US military involvement in Vietnam. This event led to the first large-scale migration from Vietnam to the United States. Prior to 1975, the majority of Vietnamese residing in the United States was scholars, students, and children and wives of American servicemen in Vietnam. Between 1951 and 1974, there were only 2,000 Vietnamese in the United States. It was an extremely small population. Spring 1975 witnessed the first wave of resettlement of Vietnamese who worked closely with Americans during the Vietnam War and Vietnamese who held high-ranking positions in the South Vietnamese government fearing persecution by the Vietnamese Communists. In spring of 1975, approximately 130,000 Vietnamese fled their homeland. The second wave of Vietnamese settlement in America began in 1977 and lasted until the mid-1980s. They consisted mostly of refugees of Chinese ethnicity who lived in Vietnam at the time and of Vietnamese who associated with the former South Vietnamese government. They escaped Vietnam by rickety wooden boats to neighboring countries and were known to the world as the "boat people." Thousands were temporarily quartered in refugee camps in Malaysia, Thailand, Hong Kong, and the Philippines, etc., and subsequently relocated under United Nations supervision. To discourage refugees from risking their lives crossing the perilous South China Sea where typhoons took high tolls in human lives on sea, the United States set up the Orderly Departure Program (ODP) in 1986. In 1987, the Amerasian Homecoming Act also brought over 30,000 children of American military and civilian personnel stationed in Vietnam during the war. And through the Humanitarian Operations (HO) program, the United States also admitted thousands of mostly former South Vietnamese soldiers who had suffered under the communist re-educational programs. The last group of Vietnamese refugees stranded in Hong Kong was repatriated back to Vietnam before July 1, 1997.

The majority of the relocated Vietnamese newcomers were placed in different regions of the United States to begin their new life. Many of them would later resettle to coastal regions which they consider more conducive to their lifestyle, namely California. There are nearly two million Vietnamese Americans today; the greater Los Angeles area and the San Francisco Bay Area are hubs for that population. In the City of San Francisco alone, there are 18,500 Vietnamese Americans, and about 92,000 live in Oakland and San Jose. Regions around Sacramento, Stockton, and Fresno also show a sizable Southeast Asian (Vietnamese, Cambodian, and Laotian) population.

By the mid-1980s, San Francisco State University (SFSU) witnessed a rapid growth in the Vietnamese American (VA) student population. There were over 400 students of Vietnamese ancestry. Besides the normal university-aged students, there were also many older, working-class Vietnamese students who returned to school because, in fleeing Vietnam, they lost their academic credentials from Vietnamese universities. Tuition at SFSU was still a bargain for them to claim a new four-year college degree. Today, there are 640 VA students, the third-largest group of Asian American student population behind Chinese and Filipinos. By the mid-1980s, the immigrant children had come of age, and by the mid-1990s, the American-born generation of immigrant parents was ready for higher education. Yet, despite the fact that so many Vietnamese Americans call the Bay Area their "home," there is a severe lack of educational programs linking the Vietnamese Americans to their resettlement community and their cultural heritage.

The Asian American Studies Department (AAS) recognized this historical development that has ushered in an underserved Asian American student population. Marlon Hom visited the "boat people" refugee camps in Hong Kong in summer 1987 and again, with Chuong Hoang Chung, in summer 1991. As part of the department's mission to maintain ethnic American cultural maintenance, AAS considered it a programmatic imperative to implement a new curriculum and provide academic mentorship for this emerging Asian American population. A full-time lecturer, Chuong Hoang Chung, was hired in 1987 and it became a tenure-track position in 1991. In preparation for a Vietnamese-specific unit in AAS, another tenure-track position was created in 1994 with Huong Hoai Tran, plus two part-time lecturers, Minh-Hoa Ta and Mai-Nhung Le. The latter two would later pursue doctoral studies under AAS sponsorship and become tenure-track faculty subsequently, Le in 1996 and Ta in 2000.

On October 11, 1995, with AAS support, Chung organized the first ever Be Dau Conference on Vietnam and the United States at SF State. The conference steering committee was made up of Vietnamese, Vietnamese American, and American war veteran communities whose hope was to move toward healing, convergence, and increased educational and cultural exchanges between Vietnam and the United States. The theme of the conference was in support of the establishment of US-Vietnam diplomatic relations. The conference drew strong reactions from both sides of the political spectrum in the VA community. There were vocal protesters who were anti-Hanoi government in the community as well as supporters who called for lifting of the US embargo against Vietnam. It was nonetheless an extremely successful academic event that called attention to and brought further interest in VA issues. After the conference, Hom, Chair of AAS, together with Chung, approached the university president to form an AAS academic program on Vietnamese America. With encouragement, Chung and Hom visited university campuses in Ha Noi and Ho Chi Minh City in January 1996 to assess the feasibility of including an international scholarly exchange in the new program proposal. Immediately after their return from Vietnam on February 5, 1996, AAS submitted a proposal, with support from the department faculty, for the formation of the Vietnamese American Studies Center (VASC) at SF State. The proposal focused on VA faculty development and the instructional curriculum to develop four specific venues consistent with AAS paradigms: (1) community outreach and service; (2) research and publication; (3) conferences and lectures; and (4) international scholarly exchanges.

SFSU President Robert A. Corrigan strongly endorsed the proposal and generously funded VASC a few months after the proposal was submitted. Chung was appointed the first center director and the Center became operational in fall 1996 as a part of the AAS Department.

VASC is the only academic center in the country dedicated to Vietnamese Americans. It aims to offer an academic program of study on the VA experiences, and to advance the knowledge and awareness of VA history, culture, and experiences through teaching, research, community service, and special events and activities. VASC fosters opportunities for students, faculty, and staff to become active and support social justice for the VA community. It also builds linkages between American academic institutions, local VA community-based organizations, and universities in Vietnam.

## FACULTY DEVELOPMENT

When VASC began operation in fall 1996, three faculty positions (FTEF) were affiliated to the Center, one of which is dedicated to a specialization in tertiary migration study, especially on Vietnamese Americans of ethnic Chinese ancestry. At that time AAS had four faculty of VA ancestry sharing these three FTEFs. They are the founding faculty members of VASC: Chuong Hoang Chung, Mai-Nhung Le, Minh-Hoa Ta, and Huong Hoai Tran, with Chung being the senior faculty of the group.

Chung was an experienced faculty before arriving at SF State in 1987. He had taught classes on Southeast Asian Americans and Vietnamese Americans, and especially on immigration and adaptation of Southeast Asian refugees in the United States. He was among the very few Vietnamese American professors teaching these courses at the time, and was very popular and well-received by Vietnamese American students as well as other Asian American students at SF State. Chung became a mentor to many VA students. Some of these students now hold prominent positions at universities across the United States.

AAS Department retained the VA faculty positions when Chung left SF State in 1998 for City College of San Francisco and when Tran left in 1999 to work for the private business sector. AAS also mentored new VA faculty by sponsoring VA lecturers to obtain their doctoral degrees and later to be considered for openings in the tenure-track (permanent) faculty rank. Both Mai-Nhung Le and Minh-Hoa Ta received their doctorates under this sponsorship program.

Of the three VASC tenure-track faculty positions established since 1996, Le, a specialist in community health, is currently the only active faculty member with tenure. In 2004, Ta, a multicultural education specialist in tertiary migration and cultural adaptation, became the full-time director of an Asian American Pacific Islander American student service unit at City College of San Francisco, but has remained active in VASC as a part-time lecturer with AAS. The tenure-track position on Chinese-Vietnamese American tertiary migration, vacated by

Ta, is currently under recruitment search. In 2008, Isabelle Pelaud, who was hired in 2001, decided to resign from VASC activities. Bac Hoai Tran who has taught Vietnamese language with the Center since 1997, was not scheduled to return to teach in 2009 due to severe cuts caused by the budget crisis.

## Curriculum Development

From 1989 to 1996, AAS offered only one course on Southeast Asian Americans (AAS 370, Southeast Asians in America). It was a highly popular course but responses from the students were mixed. Vietnamese American students, a majority in the class, considered the course not specific enough to their needs while other Southeast Asian students criticized the course for its imbalance for focusing too much on VA issues and neglecting other Southeast Asian American groups.

Responding to this curricular concern and in light of the formation of VASC, AAS 370 was redesigned in 1996 to focus entirely on Vietnamese Americans. Since there was no specialist on Southeast Asian Americans available at the time, the instructional curriculum on Southeast Asian Americans was postponed. AAS 370 was officially re-named as "Vietnamese in America" and anchors the VA curriculum.

Currently, the AAS curriculum covers a broad range of fields in VA Studies. It has reached curricular parity with other ethnic groups in AAS as each ethnic group offers three core courses in history, literature, and mental health. The VA unit comes out ahead by having a year-long language course not found in the other ethnic group curricula:

AAS 171-172 – Speak Vietnamese, I, II (Tran)
AAS 370 – Vietnamese in America (Le, Ta)
AAS 372 – Vietnamese American Literature (Pelaud, Tran)
AAS 375 – Vietnamese American Identity (Le, Ta)

These courses enroll about 250 students per academic year. Several thousand students have enrolled in these courses since 1996. As a result they have learned to bridge theory and "real" human experience. VA faculty have augmented their lectures with pertinent films and guest speakers who are prominent VA leaders, activists, politicians, writers, and poets.

When VASC became a part of AAS, it also impacted a curricular revision among the pan-ethnic (cross-group) courses in Asian American history, culture law, literature, arts, media, community, etc. All these courses revised their syllabi to integrate a VA component into their lesson plan. VA faculty would often be asked to be guest speakers in these cross-group courses.

By taking these classes in AAS, students gain an informed knowledge on Vietnamese in America, and VA students can discover and reclaim their ethnic heritage in America. For example, Mai Ly, a VA student wrote in 1999:

> I took AAS 370 to increase my understanding of the historical and emigration causation of the Vietnamese people to the United States. Throughout my higher education experience, there was not a course focused on Vietnamese population. I found the course to be relevant to my own personal and educational experience. It made me feel more connected to my cultural heritage and identification.

## Community Outreach and Services

VASC will always be a community-oriented Center with continuous efforts to consult with the community to chart out a course of action, and to define and broaden its future mission. On the home front, VASC appears in a guide of academic non-governmental and governmental agencies produced by the US Indochina Reconciliation Project (USIRP), a non-governmental organization (NGO) based in New York City.

In the last decade, the Center faculty and students have close working relationship with many community agencies such as the Vietnamese Youth Development Center, Southeast Asian Community Center, Ink and Blood, Huong Viet Community Center, East Meets West Foundation, Pacific Link, Vietnam Health, Education, Literacy and Promotion Project, etc.

In the community service area, Ta serves on numerous community agency boards, among which are VNHELP, Pacific Link, Northern California Transplant Donor Network, and the UCSF Vietnamese Health Promotion Project. As a partner in the AAS Access and Retention Project, Ta once directed an outreach program to encourage Southeast Asian (Vietnamese, Cambodian, and Laotian) high school students to attend college.

Le has been active in several San Francisco Bay Area health service organizations. She serves as board member of the API Wellness Center for their HIV/AIDS Anti-Stigma Campaign in the Chinese and Vietnamese communities, the UCSF/CAPS Health Project for Asian Women. Le is also active in the Global Education Opportunity program at the San Jose Evergreen Valley College District.

In June 2007, Le took seven SFSU students for seven days to New Orleans, Louisiana and East Biloxi, Mississippi, to study, document, and assess the needs of a rural Vietnamese American community that has received little attention from the media and governmental agencies after Hurricane Katrina. The goal of the project was to educate SFSU students about Vietnamese Americans in the US

South and promote civic engagement. Le partnered with the National Alliance for Vietnamese American Service Agencies (NAVASA) and Boat People SOS in New Orleans and Biloxi. SFSU Students conducted surveys on housing and business inventories and needs. They were involved in assisting with cleaning and remodeling a resident's home. They also recorded and conducted interviews with locals.

## CONFERENCES, RESEARCH & PROFESSIONAL WORKS

VASC organized a series of national and local conferences on social and political issues in the VA community as well as invited a gathering of VA artists from throughout the country. The Center tries to serve as a bridge between the academic world and the community. It is building a book collection and doing research pertaining to Vietnamese Americans. Ta was featured in the documentary entitled *Circle of Exchange* which won the Marin Film Festival award. Currently she directs an educational opportunity program for Asian Pacific Islander American students at City College, and is actively and professionally involved in the formation of a new Chinatown campus for City College of San Francisco, ensuring Asian immigrants the rights and access to pubic higher education.

Le has been extremely active in the arena of community and women's health issues. In 2001, she collaborated with AAS colleague Grace Yoo and secured funding for the first statewide conference on breast and cervical cancer among Asian American women. This brought about an awareness of preventive breast and cervical cancer screening among Asian American and Pacific Islander women. The conference was well received. Again in 2005, Yoo and Le organized another national conference on breast and cervical cancer survivors who are women of color. This conference made a strong impact on the attendees. Le was also Co-Principal Investigator for a study exploring risk factors of cervical cancer among young Asian American women through a Special Populations Initiative grant from the National Cancer Institute. Over 400 young Asian American women in Northern California were recruited and surveyed. A final report of this study was submitted to the *AANCART Special Populations Network* on March 31, 2005. For the "Asian American, Native Hawaiian & Pacific Islander Cancer Survivorship Conference" in July 2008, Le served on the planning committee, organized and hosted a panel discussion, and presented her own paper on "Developing Community-Academic Partnership Asian American Cancer Support Network and San Francisco State University."

Le also worked along with James Wu (a director and producer) to develop, create, and produce public service announcements – television, print, and media advertisements and transit billboards – urging Vietnamese American women to have Pap screening for cervical cancer. She worked as an associate producer/director, translating scripts and announcements into Vietnamese, and recruiting and directing the talent needed to produce six short television shows. Le served as a consultant for the Public Research Institute at SFSU on two research projects entitled "Reaching for Promoting Cervical Cancer Screening" and "Colorectal Screening in Vietnamese."

In 2002 VASC colleagues Pelaud, Le, Ta, and the Vietnamese American Student Association at SF State worked together and organized "East Coast/West Coast: Vietnamese American Writers, Poets and Performers" and in 2003, "East Coast/West Coast II: Vietnamese American Choreographers, Writers and Performers." These events featured the new generation of VA artists. About 400 people attended each event and the reception. These events received media coverage in local newspapers, bringing visibility to VA arts and culture.

In spring 2008, Pelaud, in partnership with colleague Grace Yoo, secured funding for VASC to cosponsor a conference entitled "Challenging the Myth: Uniting Community Summit Southeast Asian American Youth and the Judiciary System." The conference theme calls for community support for Southeast Asian American youth facing incarceration through methods of prevention, intervention, and re-integration. This conference brought together individuals and family members of the Southeast Asian community who must interface with the criminal justice and prison systems, social service providers, community organizers, and legal practitioners advocating for the rights of this underrepresented population to educate the public and share personal stories, best practices, and ideas for future movement-building collaborations.

## INTERNATIONAL SCHOLARLY EXCHANGES AND TRAVEL STUDY

The Center has hosted visiting scholars, rectors, directors, department chairs from Vietnam, faculty, and students. Visitors from Vietnam include those from Can Tho University, Thu Duc University, National University of Ho Chi Minh City, National Institute for Agricultural Projection and Planning in Ha Noi, the office of the National Assembly of Vietnam, Department for Home Affairs of Ha Noi City, and the Ministry of Foreign Affairs in Ho Chi Minh City.

The younger generation of Vietnamese Americans may be fluent in English, but have rather limited exposure to the history, culture, and language of their ancestors. VASC faculty believe a number of students with a Vietnamese cultural background would like to reconnect with their roots. In VA classes, many students including a number of non-Vietnamese students state that they are interested in learning the Vietnamese language and visiting Vietnam to understand the customs, history, and people. In the summers of 2005 and 2006, thirty-seven students joined the SF State and City College of San Francisco Vietnam Study Tour. The main aim of the Vietnam Study Tour is to expose students to the culture, language, and history of Vietnam as it relates to the courses taught by faculty in the AAS Department. Led by Ta, this two-week study tour provides students an opportunity to learn about Vietnam. Students took Vietnamese language course in the morning taught by Vietnamese faculty from Ha Noi National University. In the afternoon and on the weekend they visited old family homes, interacted with local people, visited historical landmarks, universities, and the ethnic minority community. The fifteen-day study tour included visits to local NGO orphanages and interaction with local university students. Since the Ministry of Foreign Affairs of Vietnam sponsored the program, participants received free tuition and lodging. The study tour impacted many students. Some students who participated in these two study tours described their experiences as "profound, life-changing, and incredible." Some also expressed an interest in returning to Vietnam in the near future to be involved in their social and educational programs.

In July 2008, Ta joined Marlon Hom to co-lead the "Chinese American Tertiary Migration History and Culture Study Tour" to Guangdong Province in China. This AAS travel study program provided a rare opportunity for American collegiate students of ethnic Chinese ancestry from Southeast Asian countries, especially Vietnam, Cambodia, and Laos, to gain onsite knowledge about their family's tertiary migration legacy. The July 2008 program was sponsored by the Chinese Cultural Education Foundation in Beijing and the Guangdong Overseas Exchange Association. They hosted this two-week, all expenses paid program. Twenty-six American participants (18 of them are of tertiary migration background from Vietnam and Cambodia), together with another 33 collegiate ethnic Chinese students from Indonesia, Malaysia, and the Philippines, visited the Han River Delta and the Pearl River Delta, from where many natives migrated to Southeast Asia for several hundred years, and then to North America since the late 1840s. Participants toured the regions from where their ancestors emigrated. They learned about the local culture, migration history, and family maintenance through lectures given by local scholars, and site visits to local emigration museums and various residential compounds built by emigrants in Southeast Asia and North America for their families who were left behind at "home" in China. They also learned about the decline of this homeland relationship since the 1950s.

This tertiary migration study tour again demon-

strated the coordinated professional relationship and cooperation between VASC faculty and other colleagues in AAS, with a shared interest to advance the issue of heritage maintenance among students of tertiary migration background. The study tour in July 2008 was extremely successful. The sponsor in China has expressed to Hom and Ta that they would sponsor another similar tertiary migration history and culture study tour program in 2009.

During the past twelve years, VASC has developed several projects with the Vietnam National University in Ho Chi Minh City and Ha Noi. Travel study tours for faculty and students at SF State and other interested institutions have been underway since the summer of 2000. Students have the opportunity to visit their ancestral land, learn the history, culture, and language of Vietnam, and get firsthand experience in understanding Vietnamese hospitality. VASC has continued to facilitate exchange programs with higher learning institutions in Vietnam for students and faculty. The Center continues to receive visitors from Vietnam and participate in joint projects between campuses.

## Future Direction

The VASC operational budget has diminished after ten years as the Center must now seek external support for its non-instructional activities. The year 2010 will mark thirty-five years of VA experience. VASC can engage in examining this legacy: What are the lessons learned? What are the new issues facing Vietnamese Americans in the new homeland, especially ethnic heritage maintenance? How should Vietnamese Americans deal with changes in the US-Vietnam relationship with regard to their homeland connection for the younger (i.e., American born) generation? How can we shape the new agenda for activism and community empowerment? How can the data of Census 2010 be used efficiently to inform organizations and agencies on the changes that took place? What are the race relation issues between Vietnamese Americans and other ethnic American groups?

These are important questions. VASC can address these issues by playing the lead role in facilitating dialogues among individuals, community organizations, and academic institutions to chart a plan of activities, combining both community efforts and academic endeavor to better serve the VA population.

# TEACHING

performance

pedagogy

Service

Internationalization

Pilgrimages

Activism

RESISTANCE

# Open the Light: Performing Filipina/o American Literature

*Allyson Tintiangco-Cubales*

## My First Day Teaching
### Asian American Studies 363 (AAS 363)

It was August 30, 2000, 4:10 in the afternoon. I pressed "play" on my rented CD player from San Francisco State's infamous Audio/Visual Department, "Sa buhay ko'y labis, ang hirap at pasakit. Ng pusong umiibig, mandi'y wala ng langit." The first few lines of Pinay's[1] rendition of *Dahil Sa 'Yo* struggled to emerge from the blown-out speakers of the ancient boom box, and echoed through the fog of thick silence in the classroom of more than fifty students sitting in rows and columns, about ninety percent of whom were Filipina/o American. It was standing-room only; some students were sitting on the floor not even a foot away from me and they could literally see the beads of sweat forming on my forehead. All their eyes were staring, wondering what the hell this rookie professor was trying to pull. A couple of students began to sing along as others started whispering to each other. I pressed stop. It was extremely quiet and so surreal that I almost thought I was dreaming my first day of teaching. Unfortunately as this first class unfolded, it could have easily been considered a classic teacher's nightmare.

I asked the students to take out a piece of paper and number lines 1 to 10. For number 1, I asked them to identify the title of the song and the artists or writers I had just played. For the remainder, I asked them to do the same for all the clips that I was about to play. I then proceeded to play a part of Bobby Banduria's *Brown Skin Lady*, then a clip from Julie Plug's premiere album, then a song from Kai, and a few other musical artists. I transitioned into playing a sample from Rex Navarrete's first CD and then I played a few cuts from *Infliptration*, the first Filipina/o American spoken word CD recorded in the San Francisco Bay Area by Aleks Figueroa. The last piece that I played was Kiwi's rare spoken word performance, *So You Call Yourself a Revolutionary?* At the end of the exercise (or "the diagnostic test") I asked the students to raise their hands if they knew all ten of the clips. All hands were down. Then I asked how many knew at least five. About three hands went up in the crowd of over fifty students. I was a little surprised at the lack of recognition of these artists because the majority of the artists I had played for them were local, and some of them were actually San Francisco State University graduates.

I asked the class, "Why do you think I had you listen to these tracks?" One bold Pinoy student in the front row cynically remarked, "To waste our time?!" First there was a big sigh in the air, and then a long "oooooooo," then the class started laughing hysterically. I could have just busted out in tears right then and there. I remember feeling like I was going to have a panic attack. I remember feeling like I was being attacked. Was it because I was new? Was it because I was young? Was it because I was Pinay? Why weren't the students feeling me? The room was spinning. I really just wanted to run out the door. Then it occurred to me that I still had about two hours more hours of the class to go. I took off my business suit jacket. The suit made me look like I was trying to look older and trying too hard to play a professor role in a badly written script. I tried to come back by saying in an annoying whiny voice, "Well, I played these Filipina/o American artists because I thought you would all know them and they could be our entry point into Filipina/o American literature. But I guess since none of you know them, you have a lot more to learn than I thought." The laughing died down. I thought I had won my first fight because I put my foot down as a "real" professor. Oblivious to my bad pedagogical move, I smiled and passed out the ten-page syllabus.

Ten was my favorite number that semester. I required the students to read ten books, complete ten writing assignments, write a ten-page paper for their midterm, and designated them only ten minutes for break during our three-hour class. As I read the ten-page syllabus aloud, nobody laughed when I made a joke about the ten-thing. While I was reading the syllabus, ten students had walked out and of those who stayed, ten were falling asleep and ten were rolling their eyes. After we read the tenth page of the syllabus, with only about ten minutes left before class was going to end, I asked the students to write a letter to themselves about the course and what they expected. One student sarcastically blurted out, "How many paragraphs should we write, ten?" Laughter filled the air. Ten began to look like my unlucky number.

Despite the dubious beginnings, after teaching AAS 363[2] for more than ten semesters, this course has transformed into its own legacy. In this essay, I describe the ways in which AAS 363, through the development of critical performance pedagogy, has become a space that transforms students into engaged learners, while it has transformed me into the kind of teacher my students deserve.

## My Second Day of Class: The Beginnings of a Critical Performance Pedagogy

It was not until the second day of class that I became a teacher. I traded in my business suit for a gold paisley jacket, skin-tight jeans, shades, black combat boots, and fuchsia streaks in my hair (the following semester this became a full florescent fuchsia wig). Before I entered, I asked one student to tell her classmates to put their chairs in a circle. Then I asked another student to be my dj and blast Jimi Hendrix's *Purple Haze*. After the first thirty seconds of Jimi's guitar intro, I strutted into class as my rendition of Rocky Rivera, the main character from their first reading assignment, Jessica Hagedorn's *The Gangster of Love*. I danced around for a bit, thoroughly rocking out air-band style. I took in the students' comments like, "Omigosh, what is she doing," and "She's crazy." I started shaking students' hands and began enjoying the laughter. I started asking students jokingly, "Do you like? Do you like?" After a lot of yes nods, I cued my dj to stop the music.

I began my lecture with flamboyant seventies vernacular mixed with a Tagalog accent, "Good afternoon, Class, your teacher has asked me to come into class to speak to you all. I heard you all read a book about me. Do you know who I am?" The class yelled out, "Rocky." I was shocked that so many had read the book assignment. I complimented them, "Yes, I'm Rocky, the rock star! Ah, you all are so good! You did your reading this week! Nice. OK, so today, I am going to reintroduce you to the real purpose of this class and I'm going to share with you the *Trajectory of Filipina/o American Literature*." So first, I asked the class what they thought the course was about. They yelled out things like, "hella reading," and "too

much work." Then I began to expressively re-describe what the course was about,

In this introductory course together we will take an exciting journey through P/Filipina/o/ American/Pinay/Pinoy literature. We will explore how this literature affects, documents, and creates Filipina/o American histories, identities, politics, and the epistemologies/subjectivities of Filipina/os in America. Through our journey we will use novels, short stories, poetry, performance, screenplays, comedy, spoken word, theatre, essays, music, and film to examine the diversity of themes, issues, and genres within the "Filipino American Community" and the legacy and development of a growing "Filipino American Cultural Renaissance." We will also use critical performance pedagogy to engage particular problems in the literature and in the community. Through group/team work, community service, and interactive lectures and discussions we will delve into the analysis, accessibility, and application of Filipina/o American literature. We will ask questions around the issues of – and intersections between – gender, race, ethnicity, sexuality, class, language, religion, tradition, colonization, access, citizenship, migration, culture, ideology, epistemology, politics, and love. The main questions that we try to tackle in this course are: **How does Filipina/o American literature represent, challenge, and/or change traditional notions of the Filipina/o American experience? How can literature be used to activate the possibilities of decolonization, activism, and social justice?**

Then I asked, "Do you know why it is important to learn about Filipina/o American literature?" And the same student who had the week before proclaimed that I was wasting his time, raised his hand and said, "Because our stories have never been told." He went on to talk about his K-12 experience as having ignored anything to do with Filipinos, especially books and history. Impressed with his ability to be critical, I pushed him further by asking him to list a bunch of Filipina/o American writers that he knew about. He got as far as Carlos Bulosan and Jessica Hagedorn. I asked the class to help him out and one student came up with Peter Bacho and another went out on a limb and yelled out Jose Rizal. This led right into my lecture. Borrowing heavily from Jean Vengua Gier's *Groundbreakers: The First Filipino Writers Published in the United States*, I created an interactive lecture: "Rocky Rivera's Rearticulated Trajectory of Filipina/o American Literature." As the students diligently took notes, it was evident that they were amazed at how many Filipina/o and Filipina/o American writers have published and performed in the United States.

As I lectured about this trajectory for the first time, I too was amazed at the how much the world of Filipina/o

American literature has grown. I was also angry that much of this has not been taught in their schools or in their other college courses. Along with their engagement in the content of the lecture, I was amazed at how engaged the students were in my performance of Rocky. There was clearly something magical about how performance could be used to engage the students. But it was beyond mere entertainment, the performance had a purpose, a purpose to expose a problem, a problem of Filipina/o American literary invisibility. This was the beginning of what I have named Critical Performance Pedagogy. Pedagogy is the art of teaching and learning. It is one's philosophy of education. Most deliberately, critical pedagogy aims to challenge oppression by developing a transformative education to pursue freedom. The purpose, content, and methods in the process of teaching and learning are carefully crafted to insure the goal of liberation. Critical Performance Pedagogy implements critical pedagogy in a humanizing manner that allows the purpose, content, and methods of performance to bring us closer to the goal of liberation. The trading in of my suit for my Rocky performance was about liberation because not only was I able to shed my physical expectations of what it meant to be teacher, I was also about tackling a problem with students. Critical Performance Pedagogy is in direct response or opposition to how we are forced and expected to "perform" on the stage, on TV, and in society and how these mainstream performances perpetuate stereotypes and lack critical representations of our identities. Particularly for Filipinas/os, our representations in the media and in society have been driven by the goals to make money versus community liberation or addressing particular problems facing Filipinas/os.

The nexus of Paulo Freire's *Pedagogy of the Oppressed* (1970) is the notion of critical pedagogy through the development of problem-posing education, which is directly opposed to the banking model of schooling based on teachers "depositing" information into the minds of students. To challenge the banking method, problem-posing education creates spaces for students and teachers to work together to develop a critical understanding of the problems in their world, including finding ways to pursue decolonization, freedom, and liberation. Ethnic Studies classrooms, including Asian American Studies, offer ideal settings for the practice of Freire's critical pedagogy. Particularly important to our work is Freire's development of the idea of praxis, which is the process that combines theory, practice, and reflection. Jeffery Duncan-Andrade and Ernest Morrell (2008) have developed Freire's process of praxis to "encourage students to become social agents, developing their capacity to confront real-world problems that face them and their community" (25). This cyclical process has five stages:

1  Identify a problem.
2  Analyze a problem.
3  Create a plan of action to address the problem.
4  Implement the plan of action.
5  Analyze and evaluate the action.

I build on this praxis and draw from Augusto Boal's (1971) development of the Freierian-based "Theatre of the Oppressed," which is interactive theatre that creates a dialogue between performers and audience members about problems in their communities. In Critical Performance Pedagogy, I aim to use performance in the classroom (both mine and my students') to pursue a critical dialogue on how the curriculum and literature presented in the course is directly connected to the cultures, histories, experiences, and problems faced in our communities with the aim of pursuing an education that is both humanizing and liberating. Critical Performance Pedagogy integrates Duncan-Andrade and Morrell's five stages of praxis through performative acts by both teacher and student.

In *Teaching to Transgress*, bell hooks argues:

Teaching is a performative act. And it is that aspect of our work that offers the space for change, invention, spontaneous shifts, that can serve as a catalysts drawing out the unique elements in each classroom. To embrace the performative aspect of teaching we are compelled to engage "audiences," to consider issues of reciprocity. (hooks 11)

To engage students to become "active participants in learning," I not only view teaching as performative act, I have also begun to see performance as a learning tool central to Critical Performance Pedagogy. Through critical performance, students can engage the process of praxis in a manner that allows for creativity and community building.

Josephine Lee, in her book, *Performing Asian America,* says "We must question the assumption that plays simply imitate a preexisting Asian American experience or identity and instead describe how race is constructed and contested by theatrical presentation" (6). Critical Performance Pedagogy allows for students to not only present the course content but it also allows them to challenge the literature and make direct connections between their lives and the problems that occur in the world in which they live. Through their performative acts they can challenge essentialized notions of their culture and identity, provide political commentary on social issues or history, and even use art as both therapy and activism. Through their performances students can also engage in critical cultural production that pushes us to look at particular issues in our families and community while also providing actions for healing and justice.

Embedded in critical performance pedagogy is a

critical discourse on culture. There are six major ways that culture is discussed through this pedagogy:

1   Cultural Past/Preservation: How we connect between culture and history. The effort of reclaiming and maintaining cultural heritage, but also being critical about how culture is defined and who has defined it for us.
2   Cultural Politics: How culture has been devalued, appropriated, commodified, and in some cases destroyed through colonialism and imperialism. How culture is related to ethnicity, race, and racism.
3   Cultural (re)Presentation: How culture is represented through literature, media, and popular culture. How media can be used to stereotype and essentialize cultural meanings. How media can be rearticulated to develop our own (re)presentations.
4   Cultural Practice/Praxis: How we theorize cultural practices and how culture is formed and transformed.
5   Cultural Production and Pedagogy: How we create and reproduce culture. How art and literature can produce new cultural meanings. How classrooms play a role in either oppressing cultures or becoming spaces for cultural liberation.
6   Cultural Power: How we use cultural work as a form of activism and service.

Through my example of Rocky, I began this cultural and critical performative dialogue with students.

As a teacher, I believe it is important to practice what we expect of students. At the end of my second day of class, I explained,

> Today I was a performer and next week you will perform. In this course, our classroom will become a stage, a stage where we can discuss and debate about how the literature challenges or affirms who we are and the world we live in. And our classroom will also transform into a community through our interactions. By the end of the semester we will use a community stage as our classroom and engage our larger communities outside of this class to share what we have learned from each other. Watcha you think?

As the students nodded, our purpose was set. Our stage was prepped and our community was being built. The students were ready to take on their first performance challenge. Although I have since re-structured the course to include Critical Performance Pedagogy in almost every element of the course, the remainder of this paper will focus on how Critical Performance Pedagogy is implemented in three of the course lesson plans/assignments: (1) Bulosanan, (2) Teaching Project, and (3) Final Show.

## BULOSANAN: REARTICULATING THE PHILIPPINE TRADITION OF BALAGTASAN[3]

"Bulosanan" is a critical pedagogy of performance. This lesson plan takes the form of the balagtasan, the traditional Philippine literary performance of poetical jousting, and rearticulates it for use in the classroom as a pedagogical tool to teach Carlos Bulosan's work, in this case his much debated semi-autobiography, *America Is in the Heart*.

Before describing the lesson plan to the students, I give a brief history of balagtasan. According to Philippine literary historians Jose Villa Panganiban and Consuelo Torres Panganiban, a balagtasan is a poetic debate that is unique to the Philippines. They write, "The holding of poetical jousts may be considered as peculiarly a Philippine literary tradition. We do not know of any other country that adapts the practice of poetical debates as a national literary activity" (197).

Some contend that the spoken word slam contests and Hip-Hop emcee battles – all forms of lyricism popular among youth, including many Filipinas/os – are in fact poetical jousts. In Los Angeles, the Festival of Philippine Arts and Culture (FPAC) has held an annual poetry slam contest that was inspired by the balagtasan. Unlike these more contemporary types of competitions, balagtasans in the Philippines were usually centered around a dual-faceted poetical theme that addressed political issues of the time. In balagtasans, two poets address the theme with opposing perspectives.

These poetical duologues were named in honor of Francisco Balagtas,[4] deemed the greatest Filipino poet of his time (he was born in 1788 and wrote until his death in 1862). Like Bulosan, Francisco Balagtas was born into poverty, and his words also made an impact on the political identity and ideological formation of Filipinos. Balagtas was a pioneer, writes E. San Juan:

> In the canon of Filipino literature, Balagtas' *awit*[5] is unquestionably the first anti-feudal poem of epic dimensions. It reflects in essence the struggle of different social classes at that crucial juncture in our history, the transition between two centuries spanned by Balagtas' lifetime. (2)

I briefly ask students to make connections between Bulosan and Balagtas, drawing out similarities between their socioeconomic class, political criticism, and their purposeful writing as a practice of freedom. Then I introduce how we will turn balagtasans into bulosanans.

Balagtasans were held in Tagalog, Spanish, Bikolano, Sibuhanon, Hiligaynon, and even English. The first balagtasan in Tagalog was held in 1924, and one of the first balagtasan contests held in English was in 1927 at the

University of the Philippines. Although "balagtasan" was the common name associated with these contests, there were also poetical jousts in the other Philippine languages. In Pampango, poetical debates were named *crisottan* for the writer Juan Crisostomo Sotto and in Ilokano, *bukanegan,* after Pedro Bukaneg (Panganiban 196). Therefore, based on this tradition of naming poetical jousts after inspirational figures, a poetical joust inspired by Bulosan's writing can be called a "bulosanan."[6]

In this bulosanan assignment, students work in pairs. Students get to choose their own "opponent" and I get to choose their topic. The assigned topics[7] are geared toward initiating particular conversations about Carlos Bulosan's *America Is in the Heart*. The topics range from debates around Bulosan's autobiography actually being a representation of a Filipina/o American collective history all the way to sex and gender representations in the book. One of the last topics that we cover looks at how we relate or do not relate to Bulosan's issues as contemporary Filipina/o Americans.

Students are first asked to define the topic and answer the questions in a joint essay: What does your pair want to say about Bulosan and how he represents the topic? With what thoughts and experiences does Bulosan lead us to understand the topic? Pairing students to write together often decreases the feelings of intimidation or anxiety that some students have toward writing assignments.

As part of their essay, students are required to find two quotes per person to represent their topic. I encourage students to try to find quotes from each of the four parts of the book and explain what they think Bulosan means in their own words. Following their short essay, I ask them to transform their ideas about topic into a bulosanan. I ask the pair of students to choose opposing/critical identities/views to address the topic.

They then each create a poetic verse and perform it as a bulosanan. Each student has two verses with four lines. Each verse should have four lines that play with rhyme and the idea of poetic joust. The verse should be presented in an alternating fashion. The quotes must somehow be addressed in their bulosanan, either as response to the quotes or in representation of the quotes.

Here is an oversimplified example, written on the theme of Romantic Notions of Bulosan as Hero:

Hero:
*Bulosan was a man (a)*
*Who has lots of fans (a)*
*He is a Filipino hero (b)*
*Not a zero (b)*
De-Romanticized:
*Because he wrote a famous book (a)*
*Many years, it took (a)*
*The community to be critical of his story (b)*

*We ask, how could this all be, if he was in a hospital bed with TB (b)*

You may also use a, b, a, b, or a, a, a, a.

When the students have completed their bulosanan, it is time to perform. I let the students know that they could bring costumes, props, and background music/beats. I usually group them together and have five pairs perform their bulosanans one after the other.

If there are enough TAs or returning students (who often come to visit), I have the classroom set up like the reality TV show, *American Idol* style with three lakandiwas (judges). Instead of the lakandiwas being critical of their style, the judges will ask them critical questions about their topics and the book. They can answer the questions with the help of the quotes that they chose prior to creating their bulosanan. After all the pairs/groups have shared their bulosanans, the class will have discussed a wide range of topics.

At the end of this assignment I end with dialogue around E. San Juan's question in his collection, *On Becoming Filipino: Selected Writings of Carlos Bulosan*:

> Given the disparity between his peasant/working class background and the petit bourgeois cosmopolitan milieu of recent Filipino immigrants, what in Bulosan's writings can help us understand the predicament – the powerlessness and invisibility – of being labeled a "Filipino" in post-Cold War America? (2)

I also add, in a post-9/11 America. At the end of the bulosanan lesson plan, students in the class have studied *America Is in the Heart* not just as a representation of Filipina/o American history but they also have created a discourse through Critical Performance Pedagogy about what is included in Bulosan's rendition of history and how it may or may not relate to their current place in the world.

## TEACHING PROJECT THROUGH PIN@Y EDUCATION PARTNERSHIPS

Following the bulosanan lesson plan, one of the major projects that I have the students participate in is the Community Service Teaching Project.[8] Addressing the lack of Filipina/o American Studies content in the K-12 curriculum, this teaching project shares Filipina/o American literature with high school students. The teaching project in Asian American Studies 363 is a project of Pin@y Educational Partnerships.

Established in 2001, Pin@y Educational Partnerships (PEP) is a Filipina/o American Studies curriculum development and teaching-apprenticeship pipeline of

San Francisco State University's Asian American Studies Department in the College of Ethnic Studies. PEP is a service-learning and community-based research and teaching pipeline that aims to create educational partnerships and projects that work toward social justice. PEP partners with San Francisco public schools and the Filipino Community Center located in the Excelsior neighborhood of San Francisco. PEP's main partnerships are between San Francisco State University upper division undergraduates and graduate students who have an interest in pursuing careers in the field of education, and community college, high school, middle school, and elementary school students who are primarily from low-income backgrounds. One of the main objectives for the PEP Program is to reach out to the students who are underperforming their potential. Through all of the projects, PEP's mission is to promote learning, teaching, and research as practices of freedom.[9]

As a project of PEP, the AAS 363 students' Community Service Teaching Project consists of three major assignments. First, they are to work in groups of five to develop a lesson plan in PEP's Critical Creative Plan format that focuses on a specific topic of Filipina/o American literature. Second, they are to teach their lesson plan with a PEP partner teacher at a local high school. And lastly, they are to write a reflection paper about their experiences.

### Critical Creative Plan

To begin the Critical Creative Plan, the students must first develop the purpose of the lesson plan. To change it every semester, I usually give them several choices within a theme. Sometimes I will have them teach about an author and a text that we are focusing on in class. For example, last semester they were instructed to teach the high school students about Pati Poblete's *The Oracles: My Filipino Grandparents in America*. This fit well since I worked with the partner teacher to assign the high school students Poblete's *Oracles* as one of their main texts. During previous semesters they have taught about other authors like Carlos Bulosan, Oscar Penaranda, and Tess Uriza Holthe. Some semesters they focused teaching about the author of focus in their midterm analysis paper. Along with the author and text, I also ask the students to focus on a topic that is relevant to the text and to their personal stories and the possible experiences of the high school students.

Once the author, text, and topic are decided, the AAS 363 students are to develop problem-posing questions that they aim to address while they teach. Then they create a vocabulary list of main concepts to make sure that the high school students walk away with knowing. Then they plan out the following three main parts of the lesson plan:

Part 1: Cultural Energizer
The cultural energizer is like a short ice-breaker to get the students' minds, bodies, and souls working. Music and dance can help facilitate this type of activity. Silent energizers may work too! A written cultural energizer can also get the students to focus on the topic at hand. Cultural energizers should somehow get the students thinking about their personal opinions and experiences with the topic of the day. Make sure the energizers relate to the lesson plan and/or Filipina/o (American) culture. Culture can be static and dynamic and should not be essentialized and assumed. Please explain to the students how the Cultural Energizer relates to what they are learning for the day. Students, teachers, and facilitators should always do the cultural energizer together.

Part 2: Community Collaboration and/or Critical Cultural Production
This is the main part of the lesson plan. The purpose of the Community Collaboration and Cultural Production section is to create opportunities for students to develop relationships with each other and with the teachers or facilitators, while also engaging in activities that will allow students to engage in cultural production. Becoming a community is a process and will take time. Be patient with the students. In this section of the lesson plan, describe how you will encourage the students to work together to solve the problem or answer the question of the day through cultural production and community building.

Part 3: Conclusive Dialogue through Critical Circular Exchange
This part of the lesson plan returns to the purpose of the day. The teachers and students should work together to address the problems and questions of the lesson plan.

After the students finish drafting their Critical Creative Plans, they practice their lesson plan in front of their classmates before they teach it to the high school students. Through their practice there is process of praxis and community building that occurs to help evaluate the effectiveness of the lesson plans.

### Implementation and Reflection

Students have shared with me that although the Community Service Teaching Project is challenging because the preparation and implementation is intense, they have expressed the great value in their participation. Because the project is directly related to the course content and also to Critical Performance Pedagogy, it is well integrated into the overall curriculum of the course. A Pinay student in the class reflects:

> Learning through experience has taught me in different ways than sitting in a class. Although our class is incredibly interactive and participatory, standing in front of others and explaining what I have learned reinforced the lessons in class. Learning seems to be a two-way experience. I have learned so much about the subjects that we taught as well as a good amount about teaching.

As part of the larger goals of PEP, the AAS 363 Teaching Project also addresses the lack of Filipina/o American content and faculty in the schools. It also encourages more Filipina/o Americans to become teachers. A Pinoy student states, "Teaching at Balboa High School made me realize even further that I was meant to become a teacher."

## Multimedia Final Community Show

Similar to the Teaching Project, the Multimedia Final Community Show[10] is about making literature accessible to the community outside of our classroom. The vision of the AAS 363 final show is to tell the stories of the students (and their families) in the class by using the literature as a focal point. We aim to resurrect the spirits of the past while also addressing the present and future of our communities by sharing literature that literally and figuratively tells the story of the Filipinas/os in America. Historically, Filipina/o American literature has focused on struggle, activism, food, music, politics, intergenerational support, interethnic/interracial coalitions, movement, labor, discrimination, spirituality, dreams deferred, homelessness, racism, sexism, classism, families, travel, migration, sacrifice, love, loss, liberation, and life (along with many other concepts and ideas). As part of this continuum our vision is to do our best to include these ideas in the literature that we present in our final project.

The students of AAS 363 aim to use Critical Performance Pedagogy to share Filipina/o American literature with the community. They create the stage (along canvases, screens, cameras, music, and digital media) as a forum for their voices to scream, whisper, sing, and debate about our stories of loss, love, liberation, and living. As part of the mission for our final project, we aim to be poets, storytellers, filmmakers, artists, web designers, editors, photographers, musicians, and educators who will represent, provide commentary, and commemorate the experiences of Filipinas/os in America. The students in the class are designated to one of the following artistic mediums/

expressions, dependent on their creative interests:

    Audio CD
    (maga)Zine
    Poetry/Balagtasan
    Poetry/Creative Video
    Documentary
    Children's Literature
    Skit/Play
    Storytelling
    Website

Prior to the students working somewhat independently on their artistic expressions, they come together with the teaching assistants of the course to develop a theme and title for their show and a name for their class. For example the Fall 2007 class wanted to focus on rearticulating media representations of Filipinas/os so they came up with *Changing Channels: Re(Media)l Misrepresentation Presented by the Oracles of Literature* (see Appendix for final show titles). This final project will be co-sponsored by a community-based organization such as the Manilatown Heritage Foundation and/or Pin@y Educational Partnerships and is often performed in a community location such as the Filipino Community Center in the Excelsior neighborhood in San Francisco.

The Multimedia Final Show is central to the legacy of Asian American Studies 363. Each show is filled with its own characters and themes, but each semester, the students perform with great emotion and purpose to address problems in their communities. Every show is packed with community members, teachers, students, youth, and families. Students from previous semesters come back over and over to support and learn from the current group of 363ers. It is amazing – the culture that has been created through the development of this final show phenomenon.

## The Last Day of the Semester

After the final show is accomplished, I hold class one more time. Each student writes a reflection paper on the course and reads their letter that they wrote to themselves on the first day of class. We also watch a video of the show and reflect on the entire semester. By this time, students have created a community, many of which will continue to be lifetime friends. Some have even created organizations and performance collectives with their fellow classmates.

The last day of the semester is often bittersweet because more than often, the students of AAS 363 have learned so much together, they find that they are often not ready to part. I encourage students to use what they learned through Critical Performance Pedagogy and praxis in their future endeavors and many have come back to me and shared how they used what they gained in this course. Till this day, I continue to critically perform with the students. And till this day, this course continues to transform my identity as a teacher.

## APPENDIX:
## DEDICATION TO ALL THE TEACHERS!

I want to acknowledge all of the people who taught me about literature and those who volunteered to come in and "teach" the class with me, including Dawn Mabalon, Bill Sorro, Al Robles, Jessica Hagedorn, Oscar Penaranda, Joel B. Tan, Rex Navarette, Barbara Jane Reyes, Patty Cachapero, Gayle Romasanta, Lorna Chui, Edwin Lozada, Jaime Jacinto, Luis Syquia, M. Evelina Galang, Michelle Ferrer, Melinda Corazon Foley, Jeannie Barroga, Ricardo Reyes, John Castro, Tess Uriza Holthe, Lakan deLeon, Jose Saenz, Kevin Camia, Allan Manalo, Herb Felina, Sean San Jose, Alan Maramag, Jason Mateo and 8th Wonder, Praxis Rocks, Kiwi, Anthem, Pele, JT, Ed Center, Wei Ming Dariotis, Liza Gesuden, Tony Robles, Michael Hornbuckle, So Trinh, and Marie Romero from Arkipelago Books.

And a special shout out to all the students who came back semester after semester to help me out, including Sarah Baltazar, Ismael deGuzman, Jeff Mallari, Arceli Alvaro, Patty Salumbides, Terry Magapusao, Rozafelle Maontemayor, Nikkie Magsambol, Charles Ramilo, Lyle Prijoles, Jeff Ponferrada, Alan David, Melanie Novenario, Kat Evasco, Fred David, Noel Salunga, Jocyl Sacramento, Melissa Nievera, Katrina Evasco, Grace Burns, Kris Ginez, Dan Tabora, Kyle deOcera, Gen Jaramilla, Tessa Winkleman, and Aristel delaCruz.

This paper is also dedicated to all the semesters of 363 students who have taught me to become a teacher. The following is a list of final show titles that represent each class:

Fall 2000 *Art Aware: To Increase the Awareness of Pinay and Pinoy Literatures through Various Mediums and Community Events*

Spring 2001 *Microphone Symbol*

Summer 2001 *Through the Journey in Cyberspace We Will Explore How Literature Affects, Documents, and Creates Filipino/a American Histories, Identities, Politics, and the Epistemologies/Subjectives of Filipinos/as in America.*

Fall 2001 *If You Want to Know What We Are*

Spring 2002 *Flip the Page*

Fall 2002 *Open the Light*

Spring 2003 *Brown from the Sun*

Spring 2005 *I-Story: Resurrecting the Spirits of the I-Hotel, Presented by Home Grown from the Ground Up*

Fall 2005 *Rolling through the Authorrrs, Presented by Gangstas of Literature*

Spring 2006 *Boxed In, Boxed Out, Presented by the Balikbayan Boxcutters*

Fall 2006 *We Be to Lit What Key Be to Lock, Presented by Hella Voices in the Dark*

Spring 2007 *Seasons by the Yay: A Flipside Story, Presented by the Writers of Tsismis*

Fall 2007 *Changing Channels: Re(Media)l Misrepresentation, Presented by the Oracles of Literature*

Spring 2008 *363 Ways to Decolonize: Choose One, Presented by AAS 363 Like Sure*

## NOTES

1. Pinay is a singing group formed in 1993 and later signed with Classified Records in 1996. They have a soulful sound and are known for their dynamic harmonies (www.pinaydivas.com).
2. AAS 363 is officially titled "A Survey of Philippine Literature" but the course has become more focused on Filipina/o American Literature in the more recent years.
3. This section of the paper was adapted from a lesson plan that is published in Allyson Tintiangco-Cubales, *Pin@y Educational Partnerships: A Filipina/o American Studies Sourcebook*, Vol. 2 (Santa Clara, CA: Phoenix Publishing House International, 2008).
4. Francisco Balagtas, also known as Francisco Baltazar, was born April 2, 1788 in Panginay, Bigaa, Bulacan, Philippines. According to Castillo and Tuazon, due to "poverty and dubious parentage," Balagtas, who was born to Juana de la Cruz and Juan Baltazar, was sent by his mother to live with a distant relative named Balagtas. This relative gave him a home in Tondo, Manila and an education at the Colegio de San Jose and San Juan de Letran. "Hence, Balagtas was his commonly used name. The poet, conscious of his lowly social position and denial of paternal love, made frequent reference to his orphaned state and his sad, unfortunate life" (Castillo and Tuazon 113).
5. The awit is a form of Philippine popular poetry focused on mythical romance, it is written in dodecasyllabic (verse with 12 lines) quatrains and is often sung or chanted.
6. This tool can also be used with other Filipino American writers, such as Jessica Hagedorn, Evelina Galang, Al Robles, Jose Garcia Villa, and R. Zamora Linmark. This example of bulosanan will primarily deal with *Heart*, although this lesson plan works very well with Bulosan's poetry, short stories, essays, and letters.

7. Working Topics and Themes:
   Autobiography versus Collective History
   American Dream versus American Nightmare
   Brotherhood
   Communism/Activism
   Death versus Life
   Education
   Ethnic Solidarity
   Family
   Foreigner
   Illness
   Labor and Class Struggle
   Classism
   Language
   Loneliness
   Nationhood
   Nostalgia of the Philippines
   Racism
   Romantic Relationships
   Bulosan as a Hero: Romanticized and De-Romanticized
   Sexism and Gender Representation
   Sexuality
   Sojourner versus Settler
   Violence
   Filipino versus American
   Immigrant versus American-born
   Bulosan versus contemporary Filipina/o American
8. I received assigned time through the Institute of Civic and Community Engagement (formally know as the Urban Institute) to develop the service-learning component of the course.
9. To find out more about PEP please refer to Allyson Tintiangco-Cubales, *Pin@y Educational Partnerships: A Filipina/o American Studies Sourcebook Series, Vol. I: Philippine and Filipina/o American History* (Palo Alto: Phoenix Publishing House International, 2007).
10. This Multimedia Final Show receives yearly funding from San Francisco State University's Office of Instructionally Related Activities.

## REFERENCES

Bulosan, Carlos. *America Is in the Heart: A Personal History.* 1946. Introduction by Carey McWilliams. Seattle: U of Washington P, 1973.

Duncan-Andrade, Jeffery, and Ernest Morrell. *The Art of Critical Pedagogy: Possibilities for Moving Theory to Practice in Urban Schools.* New York: Peter Lang Publishing, 2008.

Freire, Paulo. *Pedagogy of the Oppressed.* New York: Continuum, 1970.

Gier, Jean N.V. *Groundbreakers: The First Filipino Writers Published in the U.S.*, Philippine Literature Website, 2000 <http://www.geocities.com/icasocot/gier_grounbreakers.html>

hooks, bell. *Teaching to Transgress: Education as the Practice of Freedom.* New York: Routledge, 1994.

Panganiban, Jose Villa, and Consuelo Torres Panganiban. *A Survey of the Literature of Filipinos.* San Juan, Rizal, Philippine Islands: Limbagang Pilipino Press, 1963.

San Juan, E. *Bulosan: An Introduction with Selections.* Metro Manila, Philippines: National Book Store, 1983.

—. *Writing and National Liberation: Essays in Critical Practice.* Quezon City: U of the Philippines P, 1991.

Tintiangco-Cubales, Allyson. *Pin@y Educational Partnerships: A Filipina/o American Studies Sourcebook. Vol. 1: Philippine and Filipina/o American History.* Santa Clara, CA: Phoenix Publishing House International, 2007.

# POP! REFLECTIONS ON REPRESENTING ASIAN AMERICAN CULTURE

*Valerie Soe, Allyson Tintiangco-Cubales, and Wei Ming Dariotis*

## MOTIVATION

In fall of 2007, a group of three instructors – Allyson Tintiangco-Cubales, Valerie Soe and Wei Ming Dariotis – each teaching a section of ETHS 210 (Asian American Culture), decided to collaborate on a performance event assignment, "POP! (Producing Our Power!): Presenting Asian American CULTURE." We created the idea of a collaborative event in order to build on Asian American Studies' history of using artistic expression and performance in the classroom as well as the department's past success in bringing creative work to a broader audience.

Central to the Third World Strike and the movement that led to the creation of the College of Ethnic Studies was a strong commitment to social change, to community engagement, and to cultural preservation and production. Since the beginning of Asian American Studies (AAS) at San Francisco State, our department has offered courses in a multitude of disciplines from social science to the humanities. In addition to our academic growth, AAS has a strong history of literary, visual, and performing arts curriculum in our classrooms, in the community, and on stage. We place great importance on both studying and theorizing art, as well as on making art as a means of empowering AAS students.

Arts education provides a unique way of knowing self, family, and community because it requires delving into one's deep emotional psyche, something that cannot be accomplished only through studying historical facts or through sociological analysis. Hearing someone else's story and understanding it within larger social and historical contexts provides a foundation to students practicing art in Asian American Studies and translating these stories into creative work helps students to find their own voices. In this way, creating art in the context of Asian American Studies helps students to learn in cognitive and emotional ways.

Although our POP! event only recently started in fall of 2007, our department has a long history of performing arts pedagogy in our curriculum. As AAS professor Jeffery Paul Chan recalls about fall 1969:

> Under the guise of oral history, we asked students to interview the "community," then turned the transcribed interviews into skits, most famously, *Three Women,* that was broadcast on KQED, and starred Kathleen Chang, Judy Seto Woo and Jean Wong. Those classes...also produced *Dear Lo Fan Bak Gwai Honey Babe,* an agit prop performance that toured campuses in the fall and spring. (Chan, personal email, June 2008)

Nearly forty years ago students used their creative work as a means of extending the scope and reach of the original oral histories from which their plays originated, as well as engaging others outside of the campus community. In producing and presenting POP! we hoped to continue in this tradition of infusing creative arts into our curriculum and bringing it to a broader audience outside of the classroom. In courses like Allyson Tintiangco-Cubales' AAS 363 (A Survey of Philippine Literature), she uses Critical Performance Pedagogy in her class to engage students to uncover problems in the literature through skits, spoken word, balagtasans, music, movement, and various forms of performance. In many ways, through performance pedagogy the lesson plans come alive. Through performance pedagogy, students learn to creatively analyze the text in our courses and they become part of what they are learning.

Students learn to use their own lives, family histories, and communities as sources for their artistic production. The work thus became generative and not interpretive – students create original work from their own experiences, rather than simply executing the work of others.

## METHODS

Creative work has been an important part of many AAS classes. For example, AAS 363: Pilipino Literature, ends in a public literary event;[1] AAS 603 (Asian American Women) features a fashion show; AAS 304 (Asian American Community Arts Workshop) includes video, visual arts, and literary and performing arts assignments; and AAS 550 (Asian Americans of Mixed Heritage) culminates in Hapa Cultural Night. These contemporary performance projects underscore the pedagogical approach that began in 1969 with projects that led to the development of the Asian American Theater Workshop (now the Asian American Theater Company, formerly Workshop).

Often in these courses, the instructors begin with epistemological pedagogy by encouraging students to draw from their own experiences to help them create a critical analysis their world. This is important because a large majority of the AAS students are Asian American and almost all of them acknowledge that their ethnic history and cultural experiences were left out of their elementary and secondary curriculum. As a response, AAS courses draw heavily from experiential education and project-based learning, which begin with having students study their own epistemology – essentially how they know what they know. Many of the courses in the Asian American Studies Department begin with the study of our experiences.

An example of this is "Final Project Runway," an assignment in the Asian American Women course taught by Tintiangco-Cubales, which involves the production and presentation of a fashion show. Fashion was chosen as a genre because it has played such a dominant role in the oppression of women and their bodies. For Asian American women in particular, cultural/ethnic fashion has been co-opted, essentialized, distorted, and commodified by American industries. This "Final Project Runway" was designed as a symbolic "reclaiming" and "re-imagining" of fashion as a site of self-determination, political education, and community organizing. "Final Project Runway" is usually held in the evening at a nightclub where many students in the class frequent or where Asian Americans attend.

"Final Project Runway" was more than a show to the students and for some it was more than a "service learning" experience; many felt it was an expression of their experiences, their epistemologies, and their engagement in their community. The assignment for this project was for students to create designs; organizing the fashion show allowed them to explore the issues of Asian American women. This is an application of Critical Performance Pedagogy as a form of community education and activism. Students were able to connect the course content through the use of "ARTivism," when the purpose of art is activism toward social justice.

Student outcomes were based on their own words in their reflection papers and their discussions after the show.[2] Through their reflections students expressed the impact of the "Final Project Runway," the course, and their learning of the "I's." One Filipina student in the class stated the following:

> I think "Final Project Runway" really brought to life the various situations that women experience. It's another form of learning. Taking the class out of the classroom and creating a project that students can call their own, is important and should be part of the curriculum in other classes. Oftentimes, teachers are the ones presenting. However, through the Runway project, the students were the ones who were given the chance to present what they learned throughout the semester. It gives the students ownership of the class. It also gives them a chance to pay tribute to the sacrifices and triumphs of Asian American women.

In the AAS 603 course, the students in the class took great "ownership" of the fashion show and they were not only affected by what they learned but also how they learned it. Many in their responses to the fashion show pointed out the "empowering" nature of the final project. One Asian American male student captured the sentiment of many in the class when he wrote, "It was great seeing Asian women in our class claim negative images and smash them! The imagery presented at the runway showed Asian American women as strong, non-subservient, powerful icons who shape their own history." Not only was the show empowering but it also allowed the students, especially the Asian American women in the course to "shape their own her-story." Through this creative project, students had the opportunity to re-write the often painful narratives of Asian American histories, and to regain control of images that have too often been distorted by mainstream media.[3]

As a working artist and filmmaker, Valerie Soe also has incorporated various creative projects into her classes, combining hands-on projects with more traditional critical and analytical requirements such as research papers and exams. Assignments emphasize the primacy of students' personal experiences and reach beyond the classroom into the shared experiences of the Asian American community. In sections taught by Soe, ETHS 210 began with a self-portraiture assignment, in which students created an 8x10 inch image that represented their self-image. In this assignment students were instructed to pick a single word that described themselves. They then illustrated their selected word with images, prose, or poetry. Students could either use personal images (such as snapshots or original drawings) and write their own text, or they could use "found" images and words clipped from other sources such as magazines or downloaded from the Web. They could either place these elements on a scrapbook page, then scan it into a computer, or use a software program such as Adobe PageMaker to build their page directly in the computer. Students then emailed the professor a jpeg file of their self-portrait, which was then presented in class in a PowerPoint slide show. Students could add a brief commentary as their self-portrait is displayed.

The resulting self-portraits were as varied in style and content as the students in the class were diverse. To represent herself, student Jessica Tse chose the word "blurred," which overlay the boundary of adjoining flags from the United States and China. The text read "No definitive line which separates" and "Two different worlds collide," referring to Tse's bicultural identity as a Chinese American as well as some of the benefits and the conflicts arising from this biculturalism. Student Ferwa Kazmi's self-portrait featured the word "intricate," illustrated by a grouping of six colorful found images paired with the words "honest," "fun," "faith," "feminine," "shy," and "observant." Kazmi's project reflected her experiences as a mixed-heritage South Asian woman as well as her personal esthetic, showcasing her eye for bright color and strong visual images. For her self-portrait Crystal Trinh selected the word "memories" which is centered over a multilayered collage including, among several others, images of her family, a statue of the Buddha, the San Francisco cityscape, and small plush toys. She also included supplementary text including her Vietnamese name in both Chinese characters and transliterated text as well as the words "past," "present," and "future." This kaleidoscopic intersection of language and images suggests a deeply rooted and esoteric cultural history.

Supplementing this assignment were readings and presentations of exemplary works by Asian American writers, filmmakers, and visual artists working in self-portraiture, including Carlos Bulosan (*America Is in the Heart*), Ishle Yi Park (*The Temperature of This Water*), Sokly Ny (*aka Don Bonus*) and Marlon Fuentes (*Face Fusion Series*; *Bontoc Eulogy*). This allowed students to place their own work as well as their personal experiences in the context of the artists who preceded them and who share similar issues of identity, culture, and self-definition. The self-portrait assignment emphasizes the significance of self-articulation for Asian Americans while giving students a means for visually expressing ideas discussed in class. In this way students learn a new method for defining themselves and begin to see themselves in relation to their culture and community.

Another course, Community Arts Workshop (AAS 304), also taught by Soe, looks at the relationship between art-making and activism in the Asian American community through creative projects, readings, guest speakers, and internships. The second half of the semester focuses on the production of short video projects dealing with family histories.

After the midterm, students receive video production training, including camerawork, lighting and sound, and editing techniques. The class also views Asian American films and read texts dealing with issues of Asian American immigration, diaspora, and homeland, including Andrew Lam's memoir *Perfume Dreams: Reflections on the Vietnamese Diaspora* and Spencer Nakasako's documentary *Refugee*.

Students are evaluated on the conceptual and technical quality of their video projects, the themes they address, and the effectiveness in relating those themes to issues discussed in class. They are also required to write a reflection essay on the project in which they evaluate the process, methodology, and outcomes of their video projects.

## Manifestation

The first execution of POP! took place in fall 2007 as a means of realizing and expanding the creative and performative work that various instructors in AAS had been individually developing in their classes, bringing together several parallel but disparate elements. These included interpreting theoretical and critical practices through a creative lens, as with the projects described above, as well as bringing students' creative output to a broader audience, expanding on themes of community involvement in scholarly activities. We were also interested in looking at performativity theory, described by Deborah Wong in *Speak It Louder: Asian Americans Making Music*: "The performative is a consequence of performance: performance constructs new critical realities and the operationalization of the process of performance is key to this."[4] This observation provided a framework for connecting the guest artists' presentations in ETHS 210, the course's service learning element, and the students' own eventual performance experience. Wong's description links critical and theoretical analysis with actual creative practice, grounding the students' work in a concrete process culminating in a performance event.

The instructors were also interested in the way in which creating, planning, and performing a public event helped students to gain confidence in expressing their interests and concerns and, by extension, the concerns of the Asian American community. Tintiangco-Cubales' manifesto in the "Final Project Runway" assignment description described POP! in the following way:

The purpose of this show is to explore how Asian Americans produce power through performing culture....The mission of this project is to use the stage as a way to initiate critical dialogue about Asian American cultural past/preservation, cultural (re)presentation, cultural practice/praxis, cultural production, cultural politics, and cultural power.

This echoed themes of empowerment, collaboration, creativity, and critical analysis expressed in all sections of the ETHS 210 course.

The foundation for POP! begins at the start of the semester with basic questions: What is culture? What is "Asian American"? What is Asian American culture? To begin answering these questions, students in Dariotis' section view the documentary, *The Fall of the I-Hotel*, which depicts the seminal Asian American arts organization Kearny Street Workshop and the poetry of Al Robles as an integral part of the struggle to save the International Hotel in San Francisco. Presentations by volunteer coordinators from the Manilatown Heritage Foundation (MHF), built on the site of the old I-Hotel, connect this history to contemporary issues. Students also perform several hours of service learning with organizations such as MHF, the San Francisco International Asian American Film Festival, and Kearny Street Workshop's arts festival APAture. The class includes guest lecturers by local artists such as jazz musician Anthony Brown and poets Barbara Jane Reyes and Robert Karimi, who discussed the ways in which their art relates to both historical and contemporary community activism.

The event itself includes video, dance, poetry, fashion, music, skits, and food. One of the recent performances, *Asian Family Feud*, was a faux version of the game show, pitting the upscale Wong family, whose interests included golf and bragging about their children's academic achievements, against the working class Nguyen family, proprietors of a San Jose pho shop. Another was a dance-off between teams of students performing the cha-cha and the Electric Slide, culminating in a hip-hop revision of both dance styles. A third performance simply showcased spoken word presentations by several students. These and the rest of the presentations underscore the range and diversity of the students' creative output, from elaborate skits and videos to straightforward poetry readings, on topics ranging from media stereotypes to interpersonal relationships and generational conflicts.

Through this process students learn to recognize the ability of performance to change the way Asian Americans are seen and how they see themselves. Student Ben Lau wrote in his reflection essay, "POP! is a tool that is used to teach people about Asian American culture on campus at San Francisco State University." Lau went on to describe the reading of his classmate and fellow poetry group member, Alissa Nakaji, saying "near the end of her poem, she read with such passion that her voice cracked.

It was a very touching moment. I believe that she broke some stereotypes about Japanese Americans that night."

Other students noted the distinct yet fleeting benefits of performance itself. Student Greta Chang observed, "Despite practicing and preparing for such a long period of time, the end result lasted only a few minutes. On the other hand, those few minutes made a strong enough impact to have been worth it. This is what culture should be: a pleasantly surprising experience meant to open the mind and touch the heart." Others related the event to the volunteer work they had undertaken for local Asian American arts organizations. Le Ho noted, "It felt good to see how much passion people have for their culture and that it inspires people to get in on it and be active in their community."

Yet not all students begin the path towards POP! with a positive outlook. Michele Tateyama confessed:

When I first heard of POP! I was honestly not very excited and actually completely dreading it. Prior to POP! I had never done anything having to do with a performance, let alone perform on stage in front of a large crowd. Performing never had any appeal to me because I hate being the center of attention or having attention drawn to me. Also I am not very capable of most performance genres; I cannot sing, I am a horrible poet, I do not dance, and I am not musically talented. I get really nervous and hot when a lot of people are looking at me, which is another reason why performing never appealed to me. I frankly regretted taking Asian American Culture just because of the POP! performance. That was how much I was not looking forward to Performing Our Power!, but by the time it was over I was really glad that I had taken Asian American Culture and kept with it, otherwise I would not have had the experience of being a part of POP!

POP! also included a culinary representation component, in part because we knew the performers would be hungry after spending all night on stage. The Culinary Representation Committees from each class were instructed to create original Asian American dishes. Michelle Tateyama's contribution is illustrative. She wrote:

For POP! I made two things, Asian Chex mix and Asian coleslaw. I chose to cook these dishes because they not only combined traditional Asian foods with American foods, but they remind me of good times with my family. When I was growing up my family and I constantly loved to make different kinds of Chex mixes. One day my grandma and I decided to try the Chex mix with a sweet soy sauce syrup and with Furikake sprinkled on top of it, then of course baked until crispy. This Asian Chex mix turned out tastier than I ever could have predicted. I also made my family's Asian coleslaw, which is a combination of chopped cabbage, ramen noodles, and a sweet sesame vinegar dressing instead of mayo. My family always has these dishes whenever we meet up and have a celebration, without these dishes our get-togethers would not be the same. I also truly enjoyed serving my food to the crowd.... I was really pleased I was able to share my dishes with so many other people, who hopefully enjoyed them as much as I always do.

Everyone liked the idea of including the culinary arts in the event as it helped to bring the classes together in the venerable tradition of a shared meal. After the spring 2008 presentation of POP! this shared meal became an impromptu after-party, giving students the chance to unwind, mingle, and get to know their counterparts from the other class sections, as well as to informally reflect on and review their performances. It was a nice way to wrap up the evening and provided emotional as well as material sustenance.

The excitement of the event may have been the high point of the semester, but in the quieter moments of reflection following POP!, students were able to connect their experience with the larger issues of the class. In her reflection essay, Linda Noeum asked those key questions in her final reflection: "I knew POP! stood for Producing Our Power!, but what does that mean, how do we produce our power? What kind of power is it supposed to be?...As Asian Americans and as students, we the class wanted to inform others of what it is to be Asian American." But what, she mused, does it mean to be Asian American and what is Asian American culture? Noeum answers:

> Asian American culture isn't just one thing; it's the whole experience in general....Growing up Cambodian American I never really thought that there was an Asian American culture; I just was Cambodian American. After taking this class I learned that as Asian Americans we do have a culture, that it is everything from music, to art, to literature, and to food. This experience in POP! and in the class opened [up] the discussion at least in my family [about] what is Asian American culture. Is it something we are or is it something we do? I've come to learn that it is both, that there isn't one specific thing that defines Asian American culture.

In her final essay for the course Michelle Pangelina also asked the question with which the semester began:

> So what it really boils down to is this: what is culture? If it cannot be learned [by] an outsider and if it isn't just all about the food and what not, then what is it? To be blunt, culture isn't just these things. It's more of a sense of community and struggle. Culture is really the blood, sweat, and tears of sorrow of joy that a group of people has faced. Culture is the product of these things. This is why culture cannot be merely picked up or learned like arithmetic. I decided to walk into the performance wanting to learn more about others' struggles and others' true feelings about their lives.

She continued, "I'm really glad that I got this opportunity to participate in something that really did show our power as human beings, as Asians, as students, and as those who are affected by how society looks at and treats us. The culture we showed was a product of us and can't be taken away." This is the ultimate lesson of the course in Asian American Culture: we produce it, and in doing so, we produce our power. Students understand that POP! is an opportunity for the them to create art that reflects their cultural identity and experience showing it to an audience.

The instructors saw POP! as a way for entry-level AAS students to transform their self-identity by planning and performing the event. Because three classes were working on the same performance there were often logistical difficulties, yet the experience was largely positive. The students engaged in a mild competition between classes, but also enjoyed each other's performances and felt, because there were over one hundred students performing, that they were part of a greater event. In addition the instructors became closer as colleagues, building their own community through this process, which is an important model for students to observe. Planning for the assignment and the event required that the three instructors meet regularly, discuss and share readings and assignments, and collaborate on event logistics. In this way they hoped to model for their students the concepts of group work and creative collaboration. The instructors also guest lectured in each other's classes in their fields of specialization – Tintiangco-Cubales on Asian American performance art and poetry, Dariotis on Asian American literature, and Soe on Asian American film and video. In addition to emphasizing their collaborative efforts, this also allowed them to gain greater expertise in each other's areas of interest, strengthening and broadening their knowledge of Asian American arts and culture.

Ultimately, the students have transformed their own reality, much like the original founders of Asian American Studies did through the student strikes. Activism is a kind of performance, and performance is a kind of activism. Through the close association of these ideas POP! became a way for contemporary Asian American Studies students to feel some small part of the energy that sparked the revolution that became Ethnic Studies. POP! and assignments like it will continue to be a significant part of the curriculum because students who experience having their voices heard are students who carry the values of Asian American Studies forward.

## NOTES

1. Please refer to "Open the Light: Performing Filipina/o American Literature" by Allyson Tintiangco-Cubales published elsewhere in this anthology for further details about this course.

2. All students quoted in this essay took classes from Dariotis, Soe, and Tintiangco-Cubales during the academic year of 2007-08 when the three collaborated together as instructors of ETHS 210 (Asian American Culture) to produce POP!

3. Allyson Tintiangco-Cubales, "Final Project Runway: In the I's of Asian American Women," *Gender, Identity, Equity, and Violence: Multidisciplinary Perspectives through Service Learning* (Serling, VA: Stylus Publishing, 2007).

4. Deborah Wong, *Speak It Louder: Asian Americans Making Music* (New York: Routledge 2004) 5.

# Korean American Roots: San Francisco and the University

*Grace J. Yoo*

The history of Korean Americans in the United States spans over one hundred years. War, colonization, and turbulent leaders have all been reasons for Koreans to leave their homeland. For the earliest of Korean immigrant pioneers, San Francisco has represented the beginnings of Korean American history. Moreover, San Francisco State University (SFSU) is symbolic of access to a university education for so many Korean Americans. It is also one of the first universities to offer a Korean American course. As early as the 1980s, SFSU offered "Survey of Korean American Communities" taught by Tom Kim. In 1997, the course, "Koreans in America" was reformulated and instituted as a general education course. Although the Korean American curriculum has evolved over the years to give students an understanding of Korean American history and issues, this course has also evolved to provide service, education, and awareness of Korean American history and issues to students at SFSU, and also the community-at-large.

## San Francisco: Community, Activism, and Resistance

Korean immigration to the United States can be divided into three different waves. The first wave (1903-1905) of Korean immigrants migrated to the United States in 1903 as contract laborers working in the sugar cane fields in Hawai'i and the farmlands along the West Coast. Over 8,000 Korean immigrants arrived through Hawai'i or Angel Island, before Korean immigration was barred due to the 1924 Immigration Act. With the outbreak of the Korean War in 1950, the second wave of Korean immigrants, representing war brides, adoptees, and students, arrived. The largest wave of Korean immigrants arrived after the passage of the 1965 Immigration Act. With the passage of the 1965 Immigration Act, the San Francisco Bay Area Korean American community emerged. Over the last one hundred years, San Francisco has been home to many Korean Americans, old and new.

## Koreans in America at San Francisco State University

Due to the efforts of SFSU Korean American students, a Koreans in America course was institutionalized in 1997. This course is an introduction to the history of Korean Americans in the United States. In addition to the historical experience, this course covers the sociological, political, and economic implications of being a minority and Korean immigrant in the United States. This course discusses the different waves of Korean immigration and provides an understanding of the experiences of different generations of Korean Americans. In addition, this course explores the experiences of second-generation Korean Americans in terms of identity and community. Since its institutionalization, Koreans in America has been taught by several faculty members including Grace Yoo, Emily Han Zimmerman, Doug Kim, Caroline Chung-Wipff, and Min Paek. Each instructor has brought his/her own unique talents in making this course come alive.

Several hundreds of students have enrolled in the course and have grown intellectually and personally. A reentry Korean American student, Kwang Lim, who took the course in 2002 writes:

> The class has been an eye-opening experience for me, as a 1.5 generation Korean American who grew up in San Francisco, but saw nor heard role models and highly successful people of my nationality....I have been introduced to a whole new world and awakened sense of national and ethnic pride I not realize I had. (Lim, personal communication, 10 Sep. 2002)

This course not only educates students through faculty lectures, but utilizes films, guest speakers, texts, service learning, volunteerism, and field research. Over the years, we have utilized the San Francisco Bay Area and its access to well-known community members to come in as guest speakers including Emmy-nominated filmmaker Deann Borshay Liem, prolific novelist Leonard Chang, Chol Soo Lee, award-winning journalist K.W. Lee, and author Helie Lee. This course has also utilized the elders in our community to serve as guest speakers. Dora Kim, a Korean American pioneer, community activist, and co-founder of the Korean American Community Center, served as a regular guest speaker until her death in 2005. Sookie Song, another Korean American pioneer who is now entering her 90s, is still a regular guest speaker. Korean American history has been taught with lived voices brought to the classroom. Chung-Wipff, who taught this course from 2002-2003, writes:

> I loved helping young adults understand Korean history and Korean American history. But my favorite section of it was teaching more contemporary parts, especially how Koreans who first immigrated here had to struggle with racism. I felt that the students came away with a newfound respect and appreciation for those who came before us. These American kids felt a touch of the Asian respect for elders. (Chung-Wipff, personal communication, 10 July 2008)

In addition the course brought in Korean American pioneers as guest speakers as well as Korean War veterans, Korean War survivors, Korean American queer activists, and other guest speakers who represent history and aspects of Korean America.

The classroom has also been a site for talking about issues within the Korean American family. Often students are able to discuss issues that they normally would not bring up in other settings. The classroom opens up students to talk about their Korean immigrant parents and the intergenerational tensions so common in families. Doug Kim who taught the course in 2006 and 2008 recalls:

> I was reading a paper written by a Korean American male who was twenty years old which was entitled "Are all Korean Fathers as F_ _ ked up as Mine?" In the paper he identified a number of pet peeves and ongoing communication impasses he had with his father. He vented his frustration very articulately, but more importantly... based on what he had learned from the course he gained a new appreciation and perspective of his father. It did not make it easier for him to endure much of the friction he was experiencing with his father, but he wrote that the

course had helped him understand better where his dad was coming from, and also what he would do differently and why – when he became a dad. (D. Kim, personal communication, 11 July 2008)

The classroom has also been a place for community building, and about recognizing and tolerating differences within this community. There is diversity even among Korean Americans and this course has brought together Korean Americans who might have not known each other. Zimmerman, an instructor who taught this course for two years, recalls how the course served to bring students together but also create meaningful dialogue about differences among ourselves: "A panel of five students, all of whom were Korean American adoptees, gave a joint presentation on the issue of adoption, illustrating some of their research findings with personal anecdotes. I found it incredibly moving, and a number of other students (non-adoptees) commented on how this presentation affected them" (Zimmerman, personal communication, 12 July 2008).

Grace Yoo, an instructor who has taught the course on a regular basis, also recalls a time in the classroom when a Korean American queer male came to discuss his coming out experience. The guest speaker had mentioned he had done everything right in his life and according to his parents' wishes. He had gone to get an Ivy League education and received a law degree at Stanford University, but he told the class that he could not fulfill his parents' expectations of marrying a woman. Yoo recalls:

> Enrolled in the course at the time was a sixty-year-old re-entry Korean immigrant student who was so upset by this guest speaker, and in Korean, yelled out that he was not a filial son. The students were horrified and engaged in dialogue with this older student. Years later, this student came to visit me and said he was changed by this experience and was no longer homophobic, and realized that everyone had a choice to happiness even if it went against the expectations of parents. (Yoo, 14 July 2008)

### KEEPING KOREAN AMERICAN ISSUES AND HISTORY ALIVE: COMMUNITY EDUCATION, COMMUNITY-BASED RESEARCH AND COMMUNITY SERVICE

The Koreans in America course has worked to educate students, and also to encourage students to involve themselves with serving the community, documenting voices and history, and working on raising issues impacting our community.

## COMMUNITY SERVICE LEARNING

### *Companionship to Korean Immigrant Elderly at Laguna Honda*

Yoo has partnered with Laguna Honda Hospital, a skilled nursing facility in San Francisco to provide companionship to older Korean immigrants. In their weekly journals, students evaluate their learning experience and also challenge their assumptions and perceptions about older Asian immigrants, disability, health, and family. Students come away with a deeper understanding of what it means to be old, Korean, non-English speaking, low-income, and disabled. For example, one student writes about his observations of the resident whom he visited:

> Mr. Park's life in the nursing home is very simple. He basically stays in his room and watches TV, reads his newspaper, or takes a nap. Every Tuesday morning, a Korean minister visits the hospital to share the gospel with Korean elders. I can only imagine how valuable it was for Mr. Park to have us pay him a visit every week.

Through their weekly journals and a final paper on the experience, students write what they have learned. Often many write about their thoughts about how their older Korean immigrant resident has changed because of their visit, but they also write about deeper philosophical, existential questions like the meaning of life, that also surface during this classroom project.

One male student writes about the time spent with his elder:

> One hour visits every week for seven weeks is only seven hours. Within those seven hours, we may not have heard enough of Mr. Park's life stories, but we did have the chance to share our friendship and value the moments of sharing. We may not have had the chances to ask all the questions that we wanted to ask Mr. Park, but we had the chance to ask ourselves the questions about life in general and what life means for Mr. Park as a Korean elder.

Another undergraduate female reflectively asks herself how she will grow old and who will take care of her:

> If I can I make it to be that old, I wonder what I will be like at that age. If I can't take care of myself, who would help me? What would I do? I don't know but I had these kinds of thoughts during my visits at the nursing home.

Despite the difficulties with such an intergenerational program, the students who have been part of this project seem to be drawn to these residents in a very powerful way, and at the same time the students provide a valuable service to the community.

### *Documenting History: Remembering the Korean War*

Upon liberation from the Japanese, Korea was divided at the 38th parallel and shortly afterwards the Korean War ensued. Millions were killed and separated from their families, and even to this day remain separated from their relatives in North Korea. I have encouraged students to do oral histories of various different aspects of the Korean American experience. For two years, I had students who were interested in interviewing older Korean War survivors. These interviews were collected by students and eventually created into a documentary, *Stories Untold: Memories of Korean War Survivors*. This documentary, whose director was a student in my course, has been screened at various film festivals throughout the country, including the Visual Communications Film Festival in Los Angeles and the Asian Cinevision Festival in New York City. The film also was part of a national tour and was later screened at Amherst College and the University of Wisconsin Film Festival. Sulgi Kim, an undergraduate Cinema major, who participated as a volunteer on this project, states that this film provided an educational opportunity for him to view war as a "unique point of view which puts emphasis on the lives of war survivors which had opened up my eyes on many different levels." (S. Kim, personal communication, 10 Sep. 2002)

## COMMUNITY FORUMS

### *Korean American Media Arts Festivals*

The state with the largest Korean American population is California. Over thirty percent of Korean Americans reside in California. Despite these large numbers of Korean Americans in California, the stories of this population are non-existent in the mainstream media, or limited to a few sound bites about the Los Angeles Riots, or most recently around North Korea. Through a partnership with Asian American Studies, the Broadcasting and Electronic Communication Arts (BECA) Department, and Korean Studies in Media Arts, in 2003 and 2006 a Korean American Media Arts Festival helped to shed light on the emerging Korean and Korean American media artists. This was the only media arts festival in the nation that brought together Korean and Korean American films and media makers.

The hope of this festival was to offer the general public a deeper understanding of the diverse experiences of both Koreans and Korean Americans. It was also hoped that the general public will come away with an appreciation of the diversity that exists in California and understand the contributions that Korean American media artists bring to this diverse mosaic. The goals and objectives of this festival were threefold:

1   To tell Korean and Korean American stories through the media arts.
2   To encourage and facilitate dialogue between Korean filmmakers, Korean American media artists, and the general public.
3   To provide an ongoing space for dialogue about Korean and Korean American films.

Thousands throughout the San Francisco Bay Area attended these two festivals. In addition, these forums have also allowed community discussions on Korean American issues and the media.

### Remembering Free Chol Soo Lee Movement

In 1973, Chol Soo Lee was wrongly convicted of murdering a gang member in San Francisco Chinatown. Imprisoned for ten years, four of those on San Quentin's death row, Chol Soo Lee was sentenced for execution until exoneration in 1983. Investigative reporter K.W. Lee wrote over 120 stories about the Chol Soo Lee case, prompting one of the first national pan-Asian American community organizing movements in the United States. Volunteer activists around the country formed the Chol Soo Lee Defense Committee, which was comprised of immigrants, students, seniors, social workers, and church members in cities such as San Francisco, Sacramento, Los Angeles, and New York. The case also inspired the 1989 film *True Believer*, starring James Woods and Robert Downey, Jr.

"Remembering the Movement," a symposium sponsored by the AAS Department in March 2008 was dedicated to commemorating the Free Chol Soo Lee Movement, one of the first Asian American movements in the nation. The movement had occurred twenty-five years ago and one of the symposium objectives was to remember this movement and those involved. Over four hundred students attended this symposium. Guest speakers included Chol Soo Lee; K.W. Lee; Warren Furutani, a California State Assemblyman; Mike Suzuki, a public defender from Los Angeles; Esther Leong and Susan Lew of API Legal Outreach Center; and David Kakishiba from the East Bay Asian Youth Center. This symposium not only commemorated the pan-Asian American movement that advocated for Chol Soo Lee's release, it also examined the impact of the Free Chol Soo Lee Movement on the Asian American community today.

### Korean American Activism: Past, Present, and Future

In collaboration with the Korean Community Center

of the East Bay and the Oakland Asian Cultural Center, the Korean American unit has also worked to put on a symposium on "Korean American Activism for the Ages: A Multi-Generational Symposium of Activism Past, Present, and Future in the Bay Area" that was held in June 2008 in Oakland. This symposium brought together for the first time an extensive network of activists both young and old, and served to bridge the multi-generational and multi-ethnic divide within activism in the Bay Area. The symposium included K.W. Lee as the keynote speaker, panel discussions among important activists in the Bay Area, photo exhibits, and an oral history video presentation, all united around bridging gaps in technology, information, and awareness.

The event featured a photo exhibit courtesy of the Japanese American National Museum entitled, "Remembering the Past: Free Chol Soo Lee Movement and the Korean Immigrant Community"; an oral history of K.W. Lee, the keynote speaker; an opening spoken word performance from Mush; and a closing performance from poet Ishle Park. This event brought together some of the most important activist work from the 1970s with the Free Chol Soo Lee Movement and the Pan Asian Movement including Chol Soo Lee, freedom fighter and activist; Tom Surh, Commissioner of Alameda County Superior Court; Min Paek, Executive Director of the Korean American Women Artists and Writers Association; and Han Yun, founding member of the Korean Community Center of the East Bay. In addition, the event featured leading Korean American activists in the current moment of activism including Yul Kwon, *Survivor* winner and leading Korean American activist; Helene Kim, community activist/lawyer who fought for fair coverage of Asians in the media; Isabel Kang, Shimtuh Director promoting domestic violence awareness within the Korean and Korean American community; and Amie Kim, a leading activist to bring the politics of Korean adoption to the forefront of discussion.

## COMMUNITY-BASED RESEARCH

### Social Support and Korean Immigrant Elderly

Through a collaboration between UCSF and SFSU, Yoo worked with a nurse researcher Sabrina T. Wong on a two-year qualitative and quantitative study examining the meaning of social support among Korean immigrant elderly. As part of this study, they conducted focus groups with Korean immigrant elderly and in-depth interviews with key informants to understand the meanings and definitions of social support.

Through qualitatively understanding these definitions, they developed their own measurement to assess social support within families. Through this measurement, they examined the effects of social support on an older person's general well-being. In doing this project, Yoo networked with several Asian American elderly service providers in the San Francisco Bay Area including On-Lok Senior Services, Self Help for the Elderly, San Francisco Korean Center, Korean Community Center of the East Bay, and several Korean American churches in the area.

Their work has since been presented at several professional conferences such as the American Public Health Association and Gerontological Society of America. Their work was groundbreaking and has been published in several peer reviewed publications in the *Journal of Gerontology: Social Sciences, Ethnicity and Health,* and the *International Journal of Aging and Human Development.* Their work in this area has already been widely cited and has provided a contribution to understanding the meaning of social support among the elderly in different racial/ethnic communities.

## Accessing Health Care

A large percentage of those immigrating after 1965 have experienced downward mobility and language barriers in accessing work regardless of education levels and pre-migration occupations. In response, many Korean immigrants have steered towards self-employment and demonstrate one of the highest propensities among all racial/ethnic groups to enter into business, concentrating in retail and service businesses. Many Korean immigrants have opted for self-employment because they could not find a job commensurate with their education and work experience in the primary labor market. This high self-employment rate may contribute to the fact that many Korean Americans lack job-based health insurance and have the lowest rates of health insurance coverage among all racial and ethnic groups in the United States (Brown, et al. 2005). Ethnic entrepreneurship comes at a cost to the health and well being of Korean American entrepreneurs, families, employees, and communities. With a small grant from the Korean American Economic Development Council, a sociologist colleague, Barbara Kim, and Yoo have been examining the impact of health care access and Korean immigrants. They surveyed over 268 Korean immigrants throughout California. Their findings indicate that there are high rates of Korean immigrants who are uninsured, and those who are insured are underinsured. Their findings, which they worked on equally together, are forthcoming in *Research in the Sociology of Health* and in a book, *Korean American Economy and Community.*

## Carework: Aging Korean Immigrants and Their Adult Children

Through a California State University (CSU)-wide collaborative community-based research grant, Yoo and Barbara Kim from CSULB have been studying how second-generation adult children undertake and negotiate multifaceted financial and caregiving responsibilities for their aging parents in California, home to the largest Korean population in the United States, as a large group of Koreans who arrived in the peak immigration years of the 1970s and 1980s is retiring or poised to retire. This topic is especially crucial as Korean Americans, like the national population, is aging. Between 1990 and 2000, the Asian American population experienced the greatest growth (63%) compared to any other racial and ethnic group in the United States due to immigration and birth rates. Among Asian subgroups, the Korean population experienced over a one-third increase. According to Census 2000, 13% of the Koreans made up of those over fifty-five years of age (US Census Bureau, 2001). The majority of Koreans, aged fifty-five years and older, are foreign-born. Older Koreans usually have less education and limited English-speaking ability.

The importance of family and being able to rely on the family for support remains a core social value to Koreans. The current generation of older Koreans tends to be unprepared for post-retirement life, having sacrificed personal gain for the betterment of their family and committing themselves to the education of their children. There is little information on how family support changes because of migration and the roles of second generation Korean Americans. In addition, there is a lack of community-based research on the challenges and barriers associated with cultural expectations and caregiving between aging Korean immigrant parents and their adult children. This collaborative project explores these understudied areas from the perspectives of second generation adult children who reside in the greater Los Angeles and San Francisco Bay areas, homes to the largest and the fourth-largest Korean populations in the nation, respectively.

This study has three major aims: (a) explore how second-generation Korean American adult children negotiate intergenerational expectations and caregiving practices for their aging immigrant parents, (b) investigate the challenges and barriers faced by second-generation Korean Americans in caring for their aging immigrant parents, and (c) make recommendations to local and national Korean American community-based organizations (CBOs) that identify ways CBOs and other institutions can assist second-generation Korean Americans with elder care issues. Currently, the data is being analyzed and written for peer-reviewed publications but it also has recommendations for Korean American community-based organizations.

## CONCLUSION

Over the course of ten years, the Koreans in America course has brought education and empowerment to SFSU students. The course has also been utilized to jumpstart several different projects, including a documentary project, an oral history project, and several community-serving projects. The Korean American unit has continued to do outreach, collaborations, and education in the community by producing community forums, and by producing community-based scholarship useful for advocates and service providers in the Korean American community.

## REFERENCES

Brown, E. Richard, Shana Alex Lavarreda, Thomas Rice, Jennifer R. Kincheloe, and Melissa S. Gatchell. "The State of Health Insurance in California: Findings from the 2003 California Health Interview Survey." 2005. 20 June 2006 <http://www.healthpolicy.ucla.edu/pubs/files/SHIC03_RT_0 81505.pdf>

US Census Bureau. *Census 2000 Demographic Profile*. 2001. 1 Oct. 2005 <http://www.census.gov/prod/cen2000/dp1/2kh00.pdf>.

# ASIAN AMERICAN STUDIES TOURS AS PILGRIMAGES OF MEMORY

*Russell Jeung*

In the novel, *Journey to the West,* Xuanzang the Tripitaka Master, sets out on a long journey to seek the dharma for China.[1] His disciples, including the Monkey King, join him to gain enlightenment and forgiveness. According to Susan Naquin and Chun-fang Yu, their journey is "an idealized depiction of a real pilgrimage, involving great dedication and self-sacrifice, danger and high adventure, good companionship and spiritual realization."[2]

With somewhat similar aims, the Asian American Studies Department at San Francisco State University has instituted a range of fieldtrips and tours, both locally and transpacific, in order for students to gain truth for and about themselves. These journeys through space and time help all of us reconfigure who we are and where we belong.

The chosen locations, such as Locke, California, or the Pearl River Delta in Guangdong, China, are contemporary sacred sites. They are sacred not in the sense that they are homes to transcendent gods, but in that they are places set apart by communities to be commemorated and valued. These historic places where our ancestors worked and sacrificed themselves for later generations have now become sites that are *ling*, or efficacious.[3] That is, they are communities of memory that have power to offer rootedness and meaning. Students often wonder how their forebears survived and thrived in impoverished or hostile environments, and gain a better appreciation for the strength and resilience of their community. We also commemorate these places – like the I-Hotel or Manzanar – where our families loved and struggled, fought discrimination and established their own culture. Indeed, they are significant markers of Asian American history that become integral experiences to students' own sense of identity.

Just as these historic locations are sacred sites, the trips themselves are like pilgrimages, communal journeys of transformation. As Joanne Doi, a Japanese American

Maryknoll theologian writes:

> It is helpful to recognize similar stages that characterize pilgrimage in general: separation from the status quo, passage through a threshold, regeneration, and a return to social responsibility. At the heart of pilgrimage is the sense of journey...in which spiritual and social transformation take place.[4]

We leave our normal routines at San Francisco State University, to enter new sights and sounds. Crossing borders – sometimes national, sometimes racial or ethnic – we often are no longer sure of how to act or relate. But in the interactions between faculty, students, and the locals, we share and develop new truths and ideas about ourselves, families, and communities. The process ends when we return to SFSU, with better understandings of where we came from and with new visions of where we want our communities to go.

This section of the anthology details two examples of fieldtrips and tours hosted by Asian American Studies, and how they are pedagogical experiences of pilgrimage and transformation. In this essay, Russell Jeung's personal account of the Chinese American history tours to places like Angel Island and Pt. Alones, Monterey reveals the role of these sites.[5] The Chinese American History Migration Study tours, described elsewhere and led by Marlon Hom, illustrate the types of questions that arise in the process of self-discovery across the Pacific Ocean in the Pearl River Delta region of southeast China.[6]

## CHINESE AMERICAN HISTORY TOURS: SITES OF MEMORY AND COMMEMORATION

In order for Ho Lin Chun, my paternal grandmother, to immigrate as the spouse of an American citizen in 1923, my grandfather Jeung Gwai Fong had to prove that his birthplace was California, not China. My great grandparents gave sworn testimonies at the immigration hearing, but their Chinese American statements were insufficient to prove Jeung Gwai Fong's American citizenship. Also required were affidavits of two white witnesses who attested to knowing Jeung Gwai Fong since infancy. While the US government wouldn't recognize the voice of my great grandparents, I fortunately got a greater sense of who they were.

According to these immigration records, my great great-grandfather brought his entire family, including his wife, sons and daughter to Pt. Alones, Monterey in 1868. There, just across from where the Monterey Bay Aquarium now sits, they settled in a thriving Chinese fishing village of families, which had roughly equal numbers of women and men in 1870. In comparison, Chinese women made up only 7% of the national Chinese population in the United States at that time, so this Chinese American enclave must have had a different air. Chinese didn't come here to sojourn, but to settle with their families. My great grandmother, Quong Shee, had married and raised nine children before she was widowed in 1900.

My great grandfather, Jeung Quong Chong (aka Jeung Sam Moy) took a steamship to the United States in January 1882, just four months before the Chinese Exclusion Act was enacted. After two years working in Panama, he too settled in Pt. Alones, working as a fisherman. According to A.W.E. Parker, one of the white witnesses working with American Railway Express Company, Jeung Quong Chong was "one of our largest shippers in those days."[7] Quong Shee remarried Jeung Quong Chong in 1902, and gave birth to Jeung Gwai Fong in 1904.

On May 16, 1906, a mysterious fire broke out at the fishing village, causing all the residents to evacuate. Spectators cheered the fire, and white vandals looted the village. The landlord, the Pacific Improvement Company, refused to let the Chinese return and actually bulldozed the rest of the village into the bay.[8] Like the other two hundred recorded purges of Chinese American settlements, Pt. Alones was now destroyed.[9] My great-grandparents' home of 38 years had been swept into the ocean, and they eventually had to move to San Francisco Chinatown.

Over a century later, I brought my students back to Pt. Alones in fall 2007 as part of our Chinese American history tours. Each semester starting in 1993, this Chinese American Studies program brought students to Angel Island to learn of this key symbol of racist, American immigration history. Like me, a large percentage of students had grandparents or parents who were held at this station prior to entering the United States. Set up like a military prison, detainees had to stay for periods from a week to up to several years. The highlight, besides seeing a reconstructed set of an interrogation room,[10] was viewing the numerous poems etched in the walls of the Angel Island Immigration Station.

Since Angel Island Immigration has been undergoing renovations, we began visiting other historic sites. We attended the Bok Kai Festival and Parade in Marysville, which was the home of the second largest Chinatown in the United States in the 1800s.[11] We have also toured Locke and Isleton, rural Chinatowns on the delta where Chinese lived in segregated communities. On several occasions, students who grew up in Isleton or had family from Locke shared their experiences of growing up in these places. In addition, I have taken several hundred students on the Chinatown Alleyway Tours.[12] Students frequently write that visits to these places not only make history come alive, but also make their families' legacies more real.

Just as these sites hold special meaning for the students from the delta or from Chinatown, the Pt. Alones tour had personal significance for me. It highlighted both the racial marginalization, as well as the educational privilege, that my family and I have experienced. In 1917, Stanford University eventually acquired Pt. Alones for its Hopkins Marine Station. The same Stanford family of robber barons, who exploited Chinese railroad workers and later called for legislation against them, built a research institute over my family's bulldozed village. Ironically, however, I attended Stanford University as an undergraduate, which led my journey to becoming an Asian American Studies professor. In the summer of 2007, a Stanford anthropology graduate student, Bryn Williams, began an archaeological dig of the Chinese village at Pt. Alones, and found dozens of Chinese pottery shards and bottles beneath the Marine Station.[13]

So along with my three-year-old son, a sixth-generation Californian, I brought my students on a tour of this archaeological dig.[14] Williams had us comb the beach, and several students came up with pieces of pottery. He identified them as evidence from the village being bulldozed into the bay, only to return with the waves to the shore. I picked up one shard, and wondered if I held the rice bowl that Quong Shee or Jeung Quong once ate from. Like these pieces of pottery, I had returned to the shores of my family's American, ancestral home.

The Chinese American history tours thus are more than fun educational experiences or fieldtrips to new places. Rather, by taking them to these sites of Chinese American heritage, I hope students can "return home," to spaces and sources of collective memory that give strength and hope. Just as I have rediscovered my family's history and found their place in Monterey, I want students to return to their communities and claim their space in the United States.

Functioning more as pilgrimages than as sightseeing tours, our trips to historic Chinese American locales can tell us as much about who we are than about the places themselves. Going back in time and space, we connect with our ancestors and share their stories to the next generation. What might be more sacred to Chinese than developing this sense of family and home?

## NOTES

1. The dharma, in this case, is the truth found in sacred scriptures.
2. Susan Naquin and Chun-fang Yu, "Introduction: Pilgrimage in China," *Pilgrims and Sacred Sites in China*, ed. Susan Naquin and Chun-fang Yu (Berkeley: U of California P, 1992) 14.
3. I thank Jonathan H.X. Lee for his insights on non-traditional conceptions of the sacred and of *ling* (Personal e-mail, 5 Aug. 2008). Efficacious sites are places where a deity's power is manifest. See Naquin and Yu 11, and Jonathan Lee, "Creating a Transnational Religious Community: The Empress of Heaven, Goddess of the Sea Tianhou/Mazu, from Beigang, Taiwan to San Francisco U.S.A.," *On the Corner of Bliss and Nirvana: the Intersection of Religion, Politics, and Identity in New Migrant Communities*, ed. Lois Ann Lorentzen and Kevin Chun (Durham: Duke UP, forthcoming).
4. Joanne Doi, "Tule Lake Pilgrimage: Dissonant Memories, Sacred Journey," *Reveal the Sacred in Asian and Pacific America*, ed. Jane Iwamura and Paul Spickard (New York: Routledge Press, 2003) 274.
5. AAS Angel Island fieldtrips began in fall 1993, when the Angel Island Immigration Station was under scrutiny with proposals to shut it down and to close it permanently to the public because of poor attendance. A call went out to the community for help with the situation. AAS came up with the idea of getting students from AAS 310 (Chinese in America), 315 (Chinese American Personality), and 322 (Chinese American Culture – Language and Literature) classes to go there every semester in order to guarantee attendance. On the first year (1993-94), AAS received Instructionally Related Activities (IRA) funding for 240 students to visit Angel Island. Philip Choy (AAS adjunct professor at the time) was the docent for this first fieldtrip. The Angel Island fieldtrip started out as an AAS political move to help save an important Chinese American historical site from being closed down.
6. An earlier AAS international program was the Philippine Area Language Overseas Studies (PALOS) Project. It was a special summer curriculum of intensive study developed cooperatively by faculty from Asian American Studies, Danilo T. Begonia and Daniel Phil Gonzales, and International Relations, Devere Pentony and JoAnn Craig, with the support of the Dean of the College of Ethnic Studies, D. Philip McGee, and the Dean of the College of Behavioral and Social Sciences, Joseph Julian, and funding from SFSU President Robert Corrigan. Five students chosen by the PALOS faculty as the best prepared to do well in the rigorous academic environment of the University of the Philippines (UP) were sent to study there for a full semester, with all costs paid from PALOS project funds.

The six-week course, which met daily for eight to ten hours per day, focused on the work of three visiting professors from the University of the Philippines main Diliman campus at Quezon City – each a leading scholar in their field: Anthropology, Women Studies, and Political Science. They were contacted by Gonzales, the principle project designer, with the cooperation of Juan Francisco of the University of the Philippines. The very successful work of the SF State students was evaluated and monitored by Begonia and Gonzales at UP. The students were awarded full credit toward graduation for the credits earned in the Philippines, and all subsequently graduated from SFSU, with two continuing on to graduate studies. (Gonzales, 12 Sep. 2008)
7. A.W.E. Parker, "Hearing of White Witnesses," US Department of Labor Immigration Service, Office of the Commissioner, Angel Island Station, No. 12017/2291: Jeung Gwai Fong, 17 May 1923.
8. Sandy Lydon, *Chinese Gold: The Chinese in the Monterey Bay Region* (Capitola, CA: Capitola Book Company, 1985).
9. Jean Pfaelzer, *Driven Out: The Forgotten War against Chinese Americans*, (New York: Random House, 2007).
10. Dummies from the Fisherman's Wharf Wax Museum were used to portray the interrogation of a Chinese wife. The security guard was doubly villainous: not only was he a symbol of white American racism, but he was the likeness of Mike Piazza, a Los Angeles Dodger baseball player hated by San Francisco fans.
11. Since 1859, Chinese began parading Bok Kai, the God of the Sea, to view his realm. The town continued this tradition, calling the parade the oldest, continuous parade in California. SFSU AAS students joined in these festivities, which include "Bomb Day," where participants chase after lucky rings exploding from handmade bombs.
12. The Chinatown Alleyway Tour is an award-winning program in which local young adults give tours of how they are working to improve the alleys of San Francisco Chinatown. See http://www.chinatownalleywaytours.org/.
13. Bryn Williams also gave me a copy of a census map of Pt. Alones in 1906 before the fire. It shows the home of my great-grandfather Quong Chong as "House No. 86."
14. Sandy Lydon gave a guest lecture and talked about how Chinese used to ship squid packed in salt back to China. Interestingly, the key product was not the dried squid, but the salt, which was heavily taxed by the British and Chinese governments in the 1800s.

# GOING "BACK" TO WHERE OUR ANCESTORS CAME FROM*

*Marlon K. Hom*

*"Go back to where you came from!"

– *a common racist epithet directed at American ethnic minorities*

## PURPOSE

Chinese American Studies (CAS) at San Francisco State University has pursued an independent homeland identity not to be regarded as foreign Asian Studies. It has placed upon itself a nation-state boundary for studying Chinese America, refraining from the Chinese America-beyond-the-United States geo-political border. However, it has also become clear that transpacific Asian America has a rich Chinese American legacy, especially during the period of Chinese Exclusion (1882-1943). Still, there was no curricular or program activity crossing the Pacific Ocean to study Chinese emigration from Guangdong 廣東, China to the United States. It was not until June 1989 that an attempt was made when Chinese American faculty Jeffery Chan, George Woo, and I went for an ill-fated exchange visit to Guangzhou 廣州, only be to be cancelled because of the June 4 student uprising in Beijing. No formal institutional attempt was made since, while individual faculty, like myself, would engage in transpacific activities without institutional affinity.

The Chinese American Migration History Study Tour Program begun in summer 2000 was an outcome of my field-based research activities on the Chinese American migration regions in the Pearl River 珠江 Delta of Guangdong province in southern China. The study tour program had the following objectives:

- To challenge the disciplinary nation-border on Chinese American Studies, by bringing the study of Chinese American ancestral homeland into the Chinese American Studies discipline.
- To question the notion of the frequently mentioned "Chinese diaspora" which suggests Chinese external migration beyond the current Chinese nation-border is a "diaspora" without considering the continuous migration within and beyond the various former Chinese nation-states, i.e., the massive migratory movement from the northern regions to the south, trespassing different Chinese nation-states and different time periods.
- To field test the Ethnic Studies perspective of minority discourse – Asian Americans as a minority in America and China. How do we as Chinese Americans, an ethnic minority in the United States, identify ourselves among the majority ethnic Chinese in China?

Offered as AAS 629, aka "Chinese American Migration History Tour" ("Tour"), it was a fifteen-day field-based travel study program on trans-Pacific Chinese American historical and cultural linkages and ancestral heritage, specifically featuring the Cantonese American ancestral homes/villages of Guangdong Province in southern China. From the Tour's beginning in 2000 to 2007, the program was planned by me with Jeannie Woo as program assistant (2001-06) and Lorraine Dong (2000 and 2007). The itinerary focused mainly on the emigrant regions along the Pearl River Delta, and the area known as the Samyup (sanyi 三邑) and Szeyup (siyi 四邑) regions in early Chinese American immigration history. In 2008, the program expanded its focus to include the Han River (Hanjiang 韓江) Delta in northeast Guangdong Province, in recognition of the fact that since the late 1970s, Chinese Americans of Guangdong origin also include a new generation of settlers – tertiary immigrants whose ancestors from Guangdong settled first in Southeast Asia and later resettled in North America.

## THE CHINESE AMERICAN MIGRATION HISTORY STUDY TOUR, 2000-2007

The program began in summer 2000 with a group of AAS students attending classes at Ji'nan University 暨南

大學 in Guangzhou 廣州 for two weeks. The class was held in the mornings. Four AAS Department faculty participated and presented lectures. Students took tours in the afternoon and weekend to visit various sites. In the end, they also visited Beijing. It was logistically too expensive to continue in the following year. To reduce cost, the summer 2001 study tour program partnered with Taishan City 台山市, the heart of the Chinese American ancestral homeland, to be part of their summer youth outreach program. Unfortunately, the partnership dissolved the next year also due to logistical concerns. Since then, the study tour became a self-supported fifteen-day travel study program to ensure that the program itinerary would be independent from any protocol interference or disruption from China. Program participants numbered from thirteen to nineteen in any given year.

To question whether or not there is a so-called "Chinese diaspora," the Tour uses a geneo-historical approach, by following Chinese American genealogical claims mentioned in most Cantonese American families (i.e., official clan genealogies or *zupu* 族譜) that they were migratory settlers from northern China (i.e., China Proper) centuries ago. They claim that their ancestors migrated southward and settled in Nanxiong 南雄 in northern Guangdong, then migrated southward, and finally resettled in the Pearl River Delta in the twelfth century. Participants were posed this question: Should this earlier "internal" movement, a migration from north to south crossing the different Chinese nation-states under different dynasties and of different geo-political borders, be considered part of the "Chinese diaspora"? Why do Chinese American historians not consider these movements as a "Diaspora" (using the Jewish reference), when the participants were uprooted from one geographical region to another repeatedly in different time periods, and when China as a region consisted of many nation-states and was no different from that of Europe and the Middle East?

The Tour first covers a three-day journey to Nanxiong in northern Guangdong, hiking up the Mei Ling Pass 梅關 and strolling through the narrow streets of the Zhujixiang 珠璣巷 settlement where Chinese American ancestors moved from northern China and settled more than a thousand years ago, as claimed in most Cantonese American family genealogies. The focus is to recognize the role of Zhujixiang as a site of migrant clan (kinship through surname) solidarity. This clan solidarity is best exemplified in Chinese America through the powerful clan (surname-based) *gongsuo* 公所 organizations that represent the integrity of community maintenance. While in Nanxiong, the students also visited the abandoned Guangzhou Huiguan 廣州會館 building, a reference to another Chinese American community institution, the geographical/region-based *huiguan* under the umbrella of the CCBA (Chinese Consolidated Benevolent Association or the Chinese Six Companies). In this building, there were still artifacts indicating how it played a key role in facilitating Cantonese travelers to return home to China, dead or alive. This "sojourner homecoming" service was also a major feature found among the regional organizations of the Chinese American communities before the 1950s.

After being acquainted with the historical precedents of north-south migration and community institutions, the next stops were the various historical sites relevant to Chinese American migration history in the Pearl River Delta. It began with the Opium War battlefield and museum in Humen 虎門 City. The chaos and desperation that followed China's defeat in the Opium War of 1840 pushed Cantonese emigration from the Pearl River Delta, while the California Gold Rush in 1949 pulled these emigrants to North America. Afterwards, the group visited numerous historical sites connecting Chinese America with modern (post-1940) China. Among the numerous sites were the 72 Martyrs Memorial (aka Huanghuagang 黃花崗) that honored the Cantonese Uprising led by Sun Yatsen, the Sun Yatsen Residence, the Chun Afong Residence, the Chin Gee Hee Residence, and various emigrant villages and estates in the Siyi area. In addition, the Tour visited two garden villas in Hoiping (Kaiping 開平) – one completed in 1936 and one just built several years ago, both with American connections.

During this part of the program, participants examined a series of representative emigrant houses in Zhongshan 中山, Zhuhai 珠海, Taishan 台山, Xinhui 新會, Kaiping, etc. The objective was to have the available architecture of these emigrant regions tell the story of trans-Pacific Chinese American family maintenance from the beginning to the present time. From these sites the students learn the differences in Chinese American family maintenance, with respect to different social conditions and time periods, and end with an understanding of emigrant village configurations and features affected by Chinese exclusion in North America. For example, in Sunwui (Xinhui) the group went to the 1892 Gold Mountain Charity Cemetery to witness the physical result of shipping the bones of the deceased sojourners from North America to their ancestral home district for a proper final burial, a role performed by the *huiguan* charity division. In Zhuhai, the group visited the estate of Chun Afong, the "Merchant Prince" of Hawai'i, who built a gated residential compound, part western and part traditional Chinese, surrounded by high walls and a gun-tower. It was built for his retirement. He returned to his first wife and birthplace, Meixi 梅溪 Village, leaving behind in Hawai'i his large Hawaiian family – a wife of native nobility and numerous children.

The Tour also visited the deserted Moy/Mui/Mei Clan Estate in Taishan which was once an awesome grandiose example of trans-Pacific Chinese American maintenance. Built in the early 1930s, this site was formerly a bustling and affluent marketplace, and a self-contained residential-commercial development, rectangular in design and twice the size of a football stadium. This residential-commercial compound was built by Moy clansmen from mostly North America. It is comprised of high-ceiling, three-level western buildings of various but harmonious facades. Without maintenance for over sixty years, the place is now mostly empty – abandoned buildings with peeling paint, falling plaster, broken windows, collapsed roofs, and rusty ironwork that reminded us of its former glory.

The same awe and sadness were again experienced in visiting a series of western-styled high-ceiling homes in the emigrant regions of Taishan and Kaiping, especially at Yong'an Village 永安里 in Kaiping that was built in the early 1930s by the Ong/Deng clan from Phoenix, Arizona and San Francisco. There also exist six extravagant but empty western mansions in Zhongxing Village 中興里, built in the early 1930s by a Tom/Hom/Tan family in San Francisco. Everything is now padlocked and forsaken.

The second portion of the Tour allowed the group to visit their own ancestral home villages after gaining a general impression of the physical environment of the emigrant region. This was always exciting and full of anticipation and beyond expectation. Some of the villages were so far from the main road and isolated from everything that we wondered how our ancestors found their way out to go onward to North America. Everyone had an opportunity to conduct one's own ancestral search, by reaching out and talking to the local villagers – making connections without local official intervention – to find one's ancestral house after arriving at the villages. Some arrived unannounced and caused total surprise because they did not have prior contact with their local village cousins.

When the group reached a participant's ancestral village unannounced, there was always excitement among the villagers; the visitors were warmly received despite being total strangers. After a brief self-introduction, the locals were genuinely pleased and eager to offer assistance with whatever they knew about the participant's family. When ancestor's names were mentioned or photographs shown, connections would be made instantly. Sometimes there would be a confusing start since a Chinese man would have various names, one each for birth, school, marriage, etc. When the villagers did not know a name, they would call other village elders to figure it out. Usually, an elder in his/her nineties would appear and tell us exactly the information we needed. Of course, we made sure that

we were never the inconvenient intruders disrupting the villagers' normal routine and work.

Usually immediately after a participant's ancestral home visit, we would ask the individual to speak to the group, sharing with everybody his/her impression and response on such an experience, taking in the collective experience. Although there was one non-home visiting Tour member who expressed criticism of this public emotional sharing because it may be too personal and private, it was nonetheless extremely welcomed by the group. Everyone volunteered to share with everybody who witnessed this sentimental journey of self-discovery. This voluntary sharing of emotions also bonded the group, as everyone eventually came to realize that every family shared a migratory experience that is universal in the general history of migration movement yet specific in detail to each family.

## THE CHINESE AMERICAN TERTIARY MIGRATION HISTORY TOUR, 2008

Our migration history tour activities on the Pearl River emigration regions impressed and attracted the attention of the Guangdong Overseas Exchange Association 廣東省海外交流協會, a quasi-civilian organization under the official Guangdong Office of Overseas Chinese Affairs 廣東省僑務辦公室. In spring 2008, it offered me the chance to organize an all expense-paid educational summer program for twenty to thirty American university students of Chinese ancestry, preferably those with ancestral roots from Guangdong and whose families resettled in the United States after their initial migration to Southeast Asia (Vietnam, Cambodia, Laos, etc.). The offer is part of their cultural campaign to outreach to young, collegiate ethnic Chinese born outside of China. The Chinese Language and Cultural Education Foundation of China 中國華文教育基金會 in Beijing and the Agile Property Holdings 雅居樂地產公司 were the logistics and financial sponsors.

This opportunity allowed me to reconsider the Tour, which was quite expensive without institutional funding support, and to take another approach to examine Chinese American migration in recognition of a more diverse Chinese American population since the Immigration Reform Act of 1965. For over hundreds of years, ethnic Chinese families from China's southern provinces have been emigrating *en masse* to Southeast Asia – Vietnam, Cambodia, Laos, Thailand, Malaysia, Philippines, Indonesia, etc. – long before coming to the United States. Because of US involvement in the Vietnam War, many ethnic Chinese in Vietnam, Cambodia, and Laos resettled in the United States. Many of these tertiary migration Chinese Americans have ancestral roots in the Han River Delta region in northern Guangdong

Province. Their tertiary migration from their homes in Vietnam, Cambodia, and Laos to the United States since the late 1970s is similar to those Cantonese who were pushed out of their homeland from the Pearl River Delta after the Opium War of 1840. Both were pulled to the United States to begin a new life.

The itinerary for the 2008 travel study program was re-aligned to be a comparative study of the two main emigration regions in Guangdong Province that represent the majority Chinese American population – the Han River Delta in northeast Guangdong and ancestral homeland to most of the post-1970s tertiary migration Chinese Americans from Southeast Asia, and the Pearl River Delta in south Guangdong, ancestral homeland to most pre-1960s Chinese Americans.

The July 2008 Tour cohort grew as the Chinese program sponsors wanted to maximize the professional expertise embedded in our program. In addition to the original US cohort of twenty-six, the budget was doubled to recruit an international group of thirty-three more college students from Southeast Asia (ten from Indonesia, nine from Malaysia, and fourteen from the Philippines), all of whom have Guangdong and, especially, Han River Delta and Pearl River Delta ancestral heritages. There were another seven local Chinese students (four from Sichuan 四川 and two from Guangzhou). Together it was cohort of seventy-nine people, including a film crew and staff. Minh-Hoa Ta, our Chinese Vietnamese American colleague of Han River Delta ancestry, was the tour's co-leader with me.

Because of time restriction and the increased size of the group, individual home visits, the highlight of the earlier tour activities, and the visit to Nanxiong and Zhu-jixiang were eliminated from the 2008 program. This was also due to the fact that many participants, being third or fourth generation born outside of China, did not have sufficient information about their family history (genealogy) to warrant a genealogy-based visit. In lieu of such visits were three lectures given by local cultural experts in Chaozhou, Jiangmen 江門, and Zhongshan.

The Tour of July 2008 also began in Guangzhou, the capitol city of Guangdong Province, and visited the same local sites as the previous study tours did. This was to illustrate the close cultural and historical relationship between Guangdong Province and Chinese America. Instead of going to Nanxiong, the Tour traveled to northeast Guangdong, visiting sites pertinent to emigration in the vicinities of Shantou 汕頭 and Chaozhou 潮州. The group visited many historical and cultural sites connected to emigration, among them were the once bustling but now forsaken Zhanglin Seaport 樟林港 that was replaced by Swatow (Shantou) after the Opium War, the Chao-Shan Remittance Museum 潮汕僑批博物館 that presented a detailed history on the legacy of

how emigrants sent remittances from Southeast Asia to the Chaozhou-Shantou area for family maintenance, and the grand, gated residential compound built by emigrant Chen Ciheng 陳慈黌 that the family never enjoyed after its completion in the 1930s.

After the tour to the Han River Delta, the Tour resumed its itinerary similar to the earlier tours by visiting sites in the Pearl River Delta. The Tour provided the participants with a comparative view to recognize the differences and similarities of the two major emigration regions in Guangdong.

In August 2008, both the Chinese Cultural Education Foundation and the Guangdong Overseas Exchange Association considered the tour an extremely successful program for "overseas Chinese" collegiate students, and have informed us that they are considering sponsoring it again for summer 2009. Since this program has expanded to include ethnic Chinese students from other countries, an adjustment to the program's original Chinese American specific objective is needed to be inclusive of its international participation. Hence a comparative approach to examine the different emigration regions in Guangdong is now a more appropriate approach. Hopefully, the Hakka (kejia 客家) emigrant regions in north Guangdong will also be part of the study-tour program, thus making the Tour a most comprehensive study tour on Guangdong's three major emigrant regions.

## CONCLUSION

All the Tours have been intense experiences of self-discovery. Every participant-observer gained first-hand experience in the process. There were always discussions when we ate our meals and shared among ourselves what was observed:

- If the migratory movement has been a continuous relocation process for the family/clan for centuries in East Asia, why do Chinese American historians ignore this migration from North China to South China as part of the Chinese diaspora?
- The group saw how Chinese American forefathers/ancestors invested and committed tremendously in the community development and family maintenance of their "old" country, i.e., the emigrant regions of the Han River Delta and Pearl River Delta. But these places are now mostly abandoned. The once local grandeur made possible with remittances from Southeast Asia and North America is now mostly gone with ghost towns and deserted communities.
- What would have become of our Chinese American communities in North America had our forefathers and ancestors made a similar commitment and investment in their "new" country/home? For

example: Why did Chun Afong give up this Hawaiian family – a wife who was a Hawaiian princess and seventeen Hawaiian-born children – to return to Meixi and build a gated, western residential compound? Why did Chen Ciheng, an emigrant whose family settled in Thailand and elsewhere, build such an extravagant and elaborate, self-enclosed residential compound back "home"? Why did Chin Gee Hee build a railway and high mansions in Taishan and none in Seattle? Why did Chinese Americans invest in Chin's railroad project in which they saw their investment evaporate after its completion? Why did Chinese Americans build all those fancy mansions and residential gun-towers in Kaiping and nothing comparable in Chicago, Calgary, New York, Phoenix, San Francisco, Toronto, or Calgary where they had resettled? Why did Xie Weili 謝維立 build such a fancy Li Yuan 立園 garden villa in Kaiping and nothing similar in Chicago?

- What is the story behind the massive exodus of inhabitants from the Han River Delta and Pearl River Delta to Hong Kong in the early 1950s and later elsewhere, leaving behind all these well-built residential houses without maintenance for over fifty years?

- Must Chinese Americans wait for the post-World War II period to piggyback on the Civil Rights Movement to have a sense of belonging in North America? Why do so many Chinese Americans give large sums of charitable but unaccountable donations to China today – to build roads, bridges, roadside pavilions, and schools – and not do something comparable or similar in the Chinese American communities?

These are serious questions for Chinese Americans to ponder as lessons on Chinese American civics and history. Through this travel study program, some individuals have found leads to help answer these questions.

# COMMUNITY

Health Town & Gown

ADVOCACY POLITICS

Community Service Learning

# THE NINE UNIT BLOCK AND
# OTHER EARLY COMMUNITY PROGRAMS

*Malcolm Collier and Irene Dea Collier*

The students and community members who created Asian American Studies were especially concerned about addressing the needs of their communities, so in addition to building coursework in Asian American Studies they looked for ways to constructively link college and communities. This essay looks at a project titled "Coordination of College and Community Resources" ("The Nine Unit Block") as an example of an attempt to achieve such linkages.[1] The immediate goal of the program, which started in the fall of 1970, was to place students in community agencies while also enrolling them in a set of linked classes intended to better prepare them for community work. The long-term goal was more ambitious – to "establish a permanent link between the college and community agency personnel...[in which]... the college will become permanent consultant to the San Francisco communities needing its help."[2]

## STRUCTURE AND OPERATION

The program was an interdepartmental project involving Asian American Studies and several Behavioral and Social Sciences (BSS) departments. It was fully funded by the Chancellor's Office of the California State College System. Funding covered faculty time, student stipends, community assistants and consultants, office staff, evaluation, and office supplies. Tenured professors in BSS were listed as project directors, but the project was significantly directed by the Asian American Studies Program.

Students committed to a minimum of twenty hours of community work per week and enrolled in a block of three classes (hence the term "nine unit block") and were provided with a small stipend as well as with units. Each block of courses was comprised of a specific Asian American community seminar (Chinese, Japanese, or Filipino American) and two additional courses from participating departments in BSS. The participating faculty varied

a bit from semester to semester and the BSS offerings rotated each semester, so students took several different BSS courses during the course of their enrollment in the program.[3] Classes met every week in the beginning and less frequently later in the semester, often at social service placement sites in the communities. Classes within each block often met simultaneously, which facilitated team teaching. Students received nine units of credit, with an open acknowledgment that their community work partially counted as academic units.

The project had paid community assistants and consultants, whose jobs included outreach to community agencies, helping to place and supervise students in community work, and coordinating activities between communities and the college. The project opened with fifteen participating agencies (eight from Chinatown, four from J-Town, and three Filipino American community groups), and the number of participating agencies increased over time. By November 1970, the Chinese American block placed eighteen students, the Japanese American block had nineteen students, and the Filipino American block had fourteen.

The intent was that students engage in sustained community work, earning a stipend and units, while benefiting from "relevant research and scholarly information" from different fields in the social sciences. The seminars were to be venues in which students and AAS community instructors would interact with the BSS faculty in a productive interchange of ideas, experience, and knowledge. The BSS faculty would benefit from access to AAS communities and the students would benefit from the professional skills of the faculty.

In practice, the involvement of the BSS faculty was a mixed affair. Many participants mentioned Jean Vance of Geography and Thomas Ryther of Sociology as people who provided useful information and appreciated what they in turn gained from students and communities.

The information provided by other BSS faculty was not considered as useful on a community level. Even so, enrollment in the range of classes provided students with a solid resume of social science coursework to incorporate into majors and transcripts, as well as better understanding of social science jargon, theories, and limitations. Dan Gonzales noted that his experience with the Social Science courses and instructors cemented in his mind the need for AAS to develop its own perspectives and approaches to community needs. He added that the most rigorous methodological training came from Jovina Navarro in the Pilipino American Community Seminar (Gonzales, personal communication, 15 Aug. 2008).

The project provided Asian American faculty and students a testing ground for the relevance of academic theories and methods in community contexts. Regular class meetings were a time during which they could exchange information and engage in substantive practical and theoretical discussions that tested their own perceptions of community needs and possible solutions (Gonzales). The experience exposed many participants to skills needed to run social service agencies and provided opportunities to discuss issues and share frustrations. In addition, the stipends were important, enabling many of the students to put more effort and additional hours into both community work and school and less on outside employment to pay their way through school. This outcome was an explicit goal of the project. A number of former participants later commented that they would never have made it through to a BA without the Nine Unit Block. Moreover, having obtained BAs, some later enrolled in graduate programs which provided them with important credentials with which to establish themselves.

In evaluating the effectiveness of the classes, both from BSS and AAS, it is important to recognize there was almost no research available on Asian American communities and even less on effective community action models in the Asian American context. The history of Asian American social service agencies in 1970 was a very short one; most agencies were new organizations that were still exploring what the most effective approaches might be. All those involved, both in the Nine Unit Block and at the community level, were breaking new ground, so it is not surprising that the courses often did not supply the assistance and answers we may have innocently hoped for.

Participation in the program provided a venue for participants to establish long-term relationships not only within their own communities but also across the different communities. These relationships would be the basis for later community organizing and political activity. Indeed, it can be said that the establishment of a number of well-known community agencies was a direct or indirect result of the program. Kimochi Kai, a Japanese American community service center for seniors, was a direct product of projects started in the Japanese American Community Workshop class in the Nine Unit Block. The Chinatown Resource Center (1977), Chinatown TRIP (Chinatown Transportation Research Improvement Project, 1974), and the Korean Community Service Center all have origins significantly, although not exclusively, rooted in actions of former participants in the Nine Unit Block. Kimochi Kai and the Chinatown Resource Center (now known as the Chinatown Community Development Center) have become nationally recognized for their programs, and model community programs of their type.

The names of some of the participating students are interesting today because many became prominent community leaders. A very incomplete list includes: Jeff Mori, an EOP student who became director of JCYC (Japanese Community Youth Council) for many years and later head of San Francisco Mayor's Office of Children, Youth and their Families, and a major player in J-Town affairs; Steve Nakajo, a founder and director of Kimochi Kai; Gordon Chin, a founder and director of the Chinatown Resource Center (CRC) and the Chinese Community Housing Corporation; Tom Kim, cofounder and director of the Korean Community Service Center; Phil Chin and Lelandy Dong, long-time activists in Chinatown TRIP, CRC, and other organizations; Ed Ilumen and Ed de la Cruz, later instrumental in West Bay Pilipino Multi Service Center and active in I-Hotel affairs; Anita Sanchez, Filipino community activist and later active in city government; Dan Gonzales, now a faculty member in AAS at SFSU; Richard Wada, long time J-Town activist and staff member for Southeast Asian Community Center; Fred Lau, later SF Chief of Police; and Juanita Tamayo Lott, later of the US Census Department. Given the backgrounds and character of many of the students it is likely that many might have engaged in community work anyway but it is also true that the program nurtured those interests. George Woo commented that it was a specific goal of the program to encourage students to stay in college and get their degrees while maintaining strong community interests (interview, 14 June 2008).

### OTHER PROJECTS

The Nine Unit Block did not continue past its funding cycle but was the first of many community-oriented projects between 1969 and the 1980s. An immediate successor was the Asian American Social Work Training Program, which intended to train and license more Asian American social workers. (There were very few at the time.) Some of the faculty and staff involved in this program had also been involved with the Nine Unit block. It was a logical follow-up, to obtain postgraduate degrees for students from the Nine Unit Block. The Social Work Training

Project was funded by the National Institute of Mental Health and provided both stipends and focused training. As with the Nine Unit Block, the lack of useful academic social work theory proved to be a stumbling block. Even with the assistance of experienced Asian American social workers, the bridge between specific agency problems and useful theory was not easy to build.

Additional projects included cooperative endeavors with the San Francisco Unified School District and the College of Education to help train bilingual aides and teachers, as well as develop curriculum. As part of these efforts, the department offered specialized Tagalog and Cantonese classes for a number of years that were aimed at bilingual teachers. Representatives from the department sat on the campus bilingual advisory committee well into the 1980s. They attempted to ensure that training of bilingual teachers include not only languages, but also Asian American history, culture, and community issues. These efforts faded in the later 1980s as changes took place in the credentialing process and the administration of the College of Education.

## CONCLUSION

The Nine Unit Block and later projects reflected certain principles or goals that were close to the hearts of the three Asian American Student groups in 1969. Most important was a focus on community service and community-based perspectives. Explicitly, there was a goal that the community should define what was needed from the college and not the other way around. The Nine Unit Block also manifested one of the major challenges to the linkage of community and college: the difficulty of getting community relevant skills, perspectives, and knowledge from the academic world. The program succeeded in getting students through to their degrees and kept them active in the communities, but practical application of existing social science theory was not as effective as hoped. Academic theoretical knowledge tended to evolve slowly through painstaking, controlled research schemes, while community agencies had to depend on quick, broad, intuitive strokes for program development and delivery. Consequently the practical understanding of staff in community agencies was well in advance of the campus-based, traditional faculty.

This lack of connections would surface as an issue again and again over the years, even with the field of Asian American Studies. An attempt to use a symposium to address the subject at an Association of Asian American Studies conference in San Francisco (2003) illustrates the ongoing challenge. Organized by faculty from AAS at San Francisco State and local community organizations, the session was intended to provide a venue for collective exploration of how Asian American Studies programs might assist Asian American community organizations more effectively. At a very well-attended conference of "Asian Americanists" from all over the country, almost none showed up at this well-publicized session, in which participants from community organizations had concrete suggestions to make. Instead, most participants preferred to attend other sessions on intellectual and theoretical aspects of Asian American Studies. With the exception of three or four individuals and several faculty members from SFSU, everyone else who showed up were from local community organizations, so the purpose of the session was thwarted.

Attempts to maintain different aspects of the Nine Unit Block within our own AAS Department, especially the principle of sustained student work in the community, also faded with time, despite repeated attempts to revive them. This was, in part, due to lack of financial resources, but was also the product of a basic separation of the college world from that of Asian American communities. By the late 1980s, linkages between community organizations and the AAS department became personalized rather than programmatic, with no real venue for students to compare their work experiences and learn from them.

A basic problem was and is that maintenance of any real programmatic link involving the AAS Department with communities is quite difficult and time-consuming. The funding for the Nine Unit Block provided staff money to maintain the connections among community organizations on one hand and the college on the other, but such support did not survive the end of the program. Since the end of the 1970s, neither the Asian American Studies Department nor the community agencies have been able to adequately maintain such coordination on their own. Faculty and AAS Department resources and time are already fully consumed by maintaining campus classes, especially with heavier enrollment loads. Community organizations are likewise stretched thin with regard to resources and are each concerned with their immediate programs. A stable, ongoing program that truly links communities and campus program requires commitment of resources for coordination of community and departmental efforts.

This reality was recognized by AAS in the 1990s and a pilot program to provide such coordination with the Chinatown organizations was run under the umbrella of NICOS (a San Francisco Chinatown-based health care coalition), but stable funding for such efforts, especially across the many Asian American communities, has remained elusive. Efforts to build such coordination using AAS departmental resources have also foundered on lack of money, particularly during ongoing periods of budget cuts. The "service learning" activities now encouraged by the larger campus do not provide an alternative model, as these are too shallow and lack the focused, informed, and community-based direction that is needed.

Within our own AAS Department there have been a number of new projects, most notably the current and very successful Pin@y Educational Partnership (PEP) project between AAS and the San Francisco Unified School District, but these are much more narrowly focused than what was hoped for in 1970. The development of a true community and college partnership, both practical and intellectually informed, remains as elusive as ever.[4] In many ways, the Nine Unit Block has remained a unique and incomplete experiment.

## NOTES

1. This essay is based on archival notes and documents, the memories of several participants in the project, and an extended conversation/interview with George K. Woo (June 14, 2008), a primary person in the planning and operation of the project. We also draw on our own experiences with the project, for which Irene Dea Collier was primary staff person.
2. From mimeographed schedule and description of the AAS Program for fall 1970, titled "Asian American Studies, Fall 1970."
3. Faculty participating in the Nine Unit Block during 1970-71 included Jovina Navarro, George K. Woo, Jeff Chan, and Neil Gotanda from Asian American Studies; Thomas Ryther and Arturo Biblarz from Sociology; Kenji Murase from Social Work; Jack Curtin from Social Science; Jean Vance from Geography; William Becker, Pat Bourne, and Louis Loewenstein from Urban Studies; and Marcelle Kardush from Psychology.
4. See "AAS and CHSA: An Attempt to Merge Town and Gown" by Lorraine Dong in this volume for details of another attempt to coordinate activities between a community organization and the AAS Department.

# ADVOCACY AGENCIES AND POLITICS

*Malcolm Collier*

Historically, the dominant characteristic of Asian American involvement in electoral politics has been its absence. This was largely the product of restrictions on citizenship and other forms of discrimination which served to discourage participation. After 1965, changing immigration laws and the reaffirmation of minority civil rights led to a huge increase in Asia American population and the removal of legal barriers to political activity. Following these changes, participation in electoral politics by Asian Americans increased substantially. An important component of this new activity was the development of "advocacy politics," beginning in the late 1960s.

This essay explores the connection between the development of modern advocacy-oriented agencies and the development of modern Asian American involvement in local politics. It is proposed that the development of modern advocacy agencies in Asian American communities between 1960 and the early 1990s had an important role in providing a political voice for those communities and in laying the foundation for the movement of Asian Americans into electoral political activity and offices. Most examples used come from the context of the Chinese American communities of San Francisco, California but similar patterns are found in other Asian American communities as well.[1]

## NATURE OF ADVOCACY POLITICS

"Advocacy politics" is the use of social service agencies, programs, and community organizations as bases from which to publicly advocate the interests of communities and constituencies before governmental commissions, agencies, administrators, and elected bodies or officials. The goal of such advocacy is to affect government on both administrative and policy levels. Subjects addressed in the advocacy process can range from details of local permit application processes to the character of federal legislation on immigration. Zoning, schools, transportation, health, housing, employment, law enforcement, appointments to boards and commissions, funding of programs, selection of judges, and all forms of local, state, and federal legislation are subject to political influence through such advocacy activities. Involvement in advocacy leads to increased public contact with government officials, politicians, and, ultimately, with electoral politics.

The development of modern Asian American advocacy work can be illustrated by examples from the Chinese American communities in San Francisco. Here, the late 1960s and 1970s saw the formation of a number of new organizations that often provided specific services to clients but which also saw vigorous public advancement of Chinese American needs as a primary activity. Self Help for the Elderly, Chinese for Affirmative Action (CAA), On Lok, Chinatown Neighborhood Improvement Resource Center (CNIRC, later called Chinatown Resource Center or CRC, and now called the Chinatown Community Development Center or CCDC), Asian Inc., and The Association of Chinese Teachers (TACT) are examples of such agencies or organizations and this list is far from complete. Individuals from these groups, most especially the directors or chief officers, were and sometimes still are expected to spend a major part of their time asserting the views of the organization before public officials and bodies. The scope of such activity varies; those with a heavy service emphasis like Self Help may focus more directly on immediate needs of their clients, while other groups, CRC (CCDC) and CAA being good examples, have been more diverse in the range of their advocacy. Over time, older, more traditional organizations in the community have also come to occasionally engage in similar public advocacy. A major focus of efforts is often on a city level, as this is the political entity that most directly affects the Chinese

American communities, but most groups have lobbied and testified on state and federal levels as well.

Advocacy takes a variety of forms. One is direct testimony and comment to governmental bodies, such as that connected with the development of new zoning and planning regulations for Chinatown in the middle 1980s. Representatives from the Chinese Chamber of Commerce, CRC, and Chinese Six Companies (a traditional organization dating from the mid-19th century), and other Chinatown organizations all testified at Planning Department and Commission hearings, presented data, and suggested plans of their own to support their various positions on the subject. Another form of activity involves the use of the press as a means of political pressure, as when Henry Der, executive director of CAA, used a February 1986 press release to charge insensitivity and discrimination in appointive actions by the mayor. The press release was backed up with a research report that detailed the lack of representation of Asian Americans in policy and administrative positions in San Francisco City government. Although the charges were denied by city officials, the press coverage was shortly followed by a number of appointments of Asians to city commissions and administrative positions. Advocacy work can also involve legal action, as in challenges (since dropped) of San Francisco City and County civil service practices by Filipino American community groups or the successful efforts of CAA in the landmark US Supreme Court case Lau vs Nichols. Advocacy also occurs on a state and national level, as in the activities of the Asian Law Caucus and the Organization of Chinese Americans (OCA) with regard to proposed changes in immigration laws that led to new immigration legislation in 1990, or the work of various Japanese American organizations on the issues of redress and reparations for Japanese Americans held in concentration camps during World War II.

It is possible for individuals to perform advocacy roles apart from any formal program or organization but most people believe that advocacy is more effective when associated with an organization or program. Sometimes this leads to the formation of organizations solely for the purpose of creating an illusion of a formal entity. An example was the short-lived Chinatown Improvement Association (CIA). Tom Hsieh, Sr. (later a San Francisco City supervisor), in presenting a pro-development position regarding a planned tower on Stockton Street to city agencies, claimed to speak as a representative of this organization. Although the organization was quickly enveloped in controversy and disappeared when some of the alleged members told the press they knew nothing about its existence, the important point is the need to present the image of advocating for a formal group in order to have more impact.

## THE ORIGINS OF MODERN ADVOCACY

The modern development of advocacy politics in Asian American communities was the product of a particular social and political context. Three federal legislative actions are particularly important: the Civil Rights Act, the Immigration Reform Act of 1965, and the War on Poverty. The Civil Rights Act, and the Civil Rights Movement that produced it, affirmed the right of minority Americans to a political voice and provided models for the advocacy of minority concerns. The Immigration Reform Act for the first time provided for equal immigration from Asia and by 1968-69 there was a rapid increase in Asian American immigrant populations. It was soon evident that existing community organizations and public social service agencies did not have the capacity to properly provide for the needs of this growing population. Individuals and groups within Asian American communities became concerned about the growing gap between needs and services. Concurrently, the Johnson administration had started what was called the "War on Poverty," encompassing a large range of federally funded programs intended to "end" social and economic poverty in America. An important characteristic of many of these programs was guidelines that mandated formation of community advisory and/or governing boards, and encouraged projects that involved advocating for the clientele whom the programs served. Many of the organizations listed earlier were initially funded by such federal programs and incorporated both community boards and advocacy roles.

Actually, the participation of some Asian American communities in War on Poverty programs and funding was itself a product of advocacy. In the case of San Francisco Chinatown, the community was initially not included in Federal War on Poverty plans for San Francisco. It took the concerted effort of Alan S. Wong, Rev. Larry Jack Wong, and Rev. T.T. Tam, including a demonstration and a guided tour of Chinatown for the federal officials, for the community to be included into eligibility for funds and programs.[2]

Another factor shaping these new organizations was that they were generally formed and staffed by a younger generation of Asian Americans, both immigrant and American born. Better educated and raised in environments that promised more rights and freedoms than the periods of extreme discrimination and hostility experienced by the older generation, they were more willing to openly challenge and criticize the social and political structure within their own communities and at large.

It might be noted that, historically, many older and traditional community organizations engaged in vigorous advocacy to protect the rights of Asian Americans. Notable examples in the Chinese American communities are the many court challenges of restrictive laws by Chinese Americans in the 19th century. Some older organizations, like the Chinese American Citizens Alliance (CACA), were formed primarily as advocacy organizations, later became dormant, and have recently become more active again. However, this earlier advocacy took place in a different social and political context than that which exists today; the communities were much smaller due to immigration restrictions, while Asians had little possibility for a real political voice because of restrictions on citizenship and other forms of discrimination. Consequently, earlier forms of advocacy had little potential for leading to further electoral political participation and by the 1950s many older organizations used private rather than public contacts with officials and politicians as a means of influencing the political process, although they encouraged members to exercise their voting rights in elections. The perceptions of the younger generation in the 1960s were that these older approaches were no longer capable of promoting the interests and needs of Asian American communities. Many also felt that the "traditional" groups no longer represented the true interests of the communities and did not allow for participation from new and younger groups.[3]

## POLITICAL PRODUCTS OF ADVOCACY

While advocacy had important immediate results in the creation of new services for Asian American communities, it also produced significant long-term political consequences. Advocacy work led to increased political sophistication and activity because as people engaged in advocacy, they had to become more familiar with government, regulations, politicians, and political processes. Development of contacts and knowledge provides advance information on issues affecting communities and is an important basis for successful advocacy. Advocacy often depends on the political education of agency clients, staff, and governing boards. These people have to be informed about the advocacy work; they may be needed for assistance, and their approval is generally needed if the advocacy work is to continue. Consequently, most agencies and organizations engage in forms of political organizing and education, both formal and informal. These activities have led to a gradual increase in awareness of political processes and issues, which is a necessity if the largely immigrant populations of many Asian American communities are to have a significant political voice.

On a practical level, the agencies and organizations had to use advocacy to compensate for the lack of elected representation of Asian American communities in elected and policy-making positions in government. This placed and continues to place a heavy load on Asian American community agencies and individuals because they have to carry out a larger range of political responsibilities than is necessary in many other communities. Even the best advocacy work cannot, however, make up for lack of people in political positions, whether elected or appointed, as it is such people that ultimately make the political decisions as well as provide much of the information needed for groups to be able to present strong, informed views to other politicians and government entities.

This reality helps promote a belief within advocacy agencies that if Asian Americans are to have impact on political decisions they need to get themselves involved in elections, either to help determine who is elected or to obligate politicians. Because most organizations engaged in advocacy are nonprofit organizations with legal restrictions on partisan electoral politics, it is often necessary for agency staff to act as individuals or to join overtly political organizations or other organizations that can openly participate in political elections. In this manner many members of Chinese American advocacy organizations in San Francisco became active in the membership or political work of the Chinese American Democratic Club (CADC), an organization formed in the 1950s but which became much more active with the arrival of advocacy-based members. Other advocacy-based individuals attempted to start a political group called the Chinese American Political Association (CAPA) when they felt that their political views were not being represented by CADC. CAPA did not survive and some of the individuals involved later developed connections with the Chinese Chamber of Commerce. Other people have been involved with the Chinese Progressive Association (CPA), itself a hybrid political/advocacy/service organization. Political and business organizations can raise money for candidates, endorse people for political office, and engage in the full range of partisan politics.

Similar patterns are found in other Asian American communities in the San Francisco Bay Area. Both the Japanese Community Youth Council (JCYC) and Kimochi Kai, which are social service agencies with advocacy roles, have had individuals active in the Japanese American Democratic Club. There are related connections between political clubs in the Filipino community and Filipino American community agencies. In San Francisco such activity usually focuses on the Democratic Party because, as Jeff Mori (a former director of JCYC) puts it, "in this city, politics is the Democratic Party," although more recently there has been some movement of people into Green Party political circles.

The combination of advocacy and political activity makes politicians and government officials more familiar with individual Asian Americans and gradually more sensitive to the long-range potential political clout of a growing Asian American population. This occurs because they find they may be publicly called to account for their actions which affect Asian American communities. In a few extreme cases officials have lost their positions, as was the case with Thomas Kearny, a former Registrar of Voters for San Francisco (an appointed political position), who lost his position after making unacceptable remarks about Asians.

The character of leadership in advocacy organizations has tremendous impact on the degree to which they are politically active and effective. Chinese for Affirmative Action (CAA) was very active for many years while under the directorship of Henry Der, but when he left for other employment the organization became much less active and similar evolutions have occurred at other organizations with changes in leadership. Often, as organizations become more institutionalized they lose their political edge as newer leadership often has been trained in the context of running an organization rather than in political action. Some organizations never become strong advocacy voices because of the lack of strong leadership.

The tendency toward reduced advocacy activity over time has been aggravated by increased dependence on private corporate funding. Direct services usually provide good public images and are not as controversial while advocacy, if vigorous, is certain to upset someone. Few foundations directly fund advocacy but many do fund direct services. Consequently, fiscal pressure leads organizations to put more emphasis on direct services and less on advocacy, with concurrent changes in who is hired for staff and who is appointed to boards of directors. Increasingly, boards of directors become composed of people perceived as able to assist in fundraising rather than being drawn from the ranks of community activists, as was previously more common.

## ADVOCACY ACTIVITY AND APPOINTIVE POLITICS

Another product of advocacy is an increase in the selection of Asian Americans for appointive political positions such as public boards, commissions, governmental committees, and judgeships. Appointments to such positions are made by elected officials. The decisions of these appointed individuals and commissions often have the most direct impact on Asian American communities. Advocacy activity by Asian American community groups affects political appointments on several levels. First, advocacy activity is often used to inform politicians as to community needs that require representation on boards and commissions. Second, advocacy can also be used to put direct pressure on politicians to respond to those needs through appointments. Third, advocacy activities put people in regular contact with politicians, making politicians more familiar with the pool of individuals available for appointments. Finally, the involvement of individuals associated with

the advocacy agencies in overt political activity begins to obligate the politicians to them, which can also lead to political appointments.

Most of the Asian Americans appointed to city boards and commissions in San Francisco during the 1980s and 1990s had connections with advocacy organizations and the political clubs. Chinese American political appointments by former San Francisco Mayor Agnos during the late 1980s illustrate this point. Of some twenty Chinese American appointments to city commissions, boards, committees and political positions, nine had direct connections to advocacy organizations and at least seventeen had connections to either advocacy agencies and/or associated political organizations. Some examples: Deputy Mayor James Ho was president of the Chinese Chamber of Commerce and a board member of CRC; Lonnie Chin (Library Commission) was a long time member of TACT and a board member for CRC; Wayne Hu (Planning Commission) was a board member for On Lok Senior Health Services and a member of the Chinese Chamber of Commerce; Gordon Chin (Public Utilities Commission) was director of CRC. The activity of these individuals in advocacy organizations provided visibility and credibility, so their appointments were clearly the result of the political aspects of advocacy, both formal and informal. Asian Americans remain, however, underrepresented in appointed political positions in most areas with large Asian American populations.

There are, however, serious constraints on the appointment of people from advocacy agencies to political positions due to conflict of interest laws. Unless the political position is unrelated to the area of policy interest of the agency, appointees usually have to sever their connections with the agency. This reality is one of the reasons why many political appointees come from agency boards of directors (who can readily resign if there are conflict of interest problems) rather than from among advocacy agency staff or directors who might have to give up their jobs if appointed to a board or commission directly related to the area of activity of the agency.

## ELECTORAL POLITICS

Activity in appointed positions can provide the larger political visibility and connections necessary for running for elected offices. This is why an increase in numbers of Asian Americans in appointed political positions is an important step in the direction of increased numbers of elected officials. The function of appointive positions as a "stepping stone" to elected political office is illustrated by the case of former SF Board of Education member Richard Cerbatos. An important member of the Filipino American Democratic Club, Cerbatos was appointed to the San Francisco Board of Permit Appeals and subsequently became an elected member of the Board of Education. Some individuals with political ambitions seek such appointments and then use them to help add political credibility, as with former Police Commissioner Tom Hsieh, who later became a member of the San Francisco Board of Supervisors in the 1980s. More recently, the Chinese Progressive Association has been a starting point for the political careers of Mabel Teng (elected SF Board of Supervisors as well as other elected positions) and Eric Mar (SF Board of Education).

The role of advocacy agencies and activities in this process is important, particularly to the extent that these have led to increased numbers of Asian Americans in appointed positions. However, while some individuals in key advocacy roles as staff of agencies are found on advisory committees and smaller boards, few have shown any signs of running for elected office, in large part because this would mean abandoning their jobs or because they feel that it would undermine their credibility as advocates.

What has occurred, as election to political offices became a real possibility, is that individuals with ambitions for political office or influence associated themselves with community advocacy agencies as board members or important donors in order to enhance their political connections and influence, rather than simply out of interest in the goals of the agencies. This strategy helped speed the election of Asian Americans to political offices but it also raises questions of motivations and responsibility toward the communities.

The impact of advocacy political processes on the political activities of Asian Americans is perhaps confirmed by an examination of who in the Asian American communities engages in public advocacy politics. Throughout the 1960s and 1970s public advocacy in the Chinese, Japanese, and Filipino American communities of San Francisco was largely the territory of the more "liberal/progressive" elements of these communities. By the 1990s, almost all political sectors of Asian American communities attempted to engage in advocacy, in recognition of the importance of advocacy in political relationships between community and the surrounding society. To some people's dismay, this can produce an image of lack of unity, but such diversity of voices probably is a sign of a growing political awareness that was absent in times past when the communities put forth a facade of unity.

## FINAL NOTE, 2008

Recent years have seen a surge in the number of Asian Americans running for political offices and in the number actually getting elected. In San Francisco, Mabel Teng became the first Asian American to be elected to the Board of Supervisors in a citywide election without being appointed to the board first, and the fall 1996 elections resulted in the board having three elected Asian Americans. In Daly City, Filipino and Asian Americans have finally been elected to city offices that Asian Americans have been successful in elections elsewhere in the Bay Area. The number of elected Asian Americans in San Francisco dropped significantly in elections after 2000 for a variety of reasons but the fall 2008 elections reversed that drop, with the election of three Chinese American members, Carmen Chu, David Chiu, and Eric Mar. Carmen Chu, originally appointed to the Board by the Mayor, has no connections to advocacy organizations but Mar and Chiu have roots in advocacy organization. Mar, a former Board of Education member, came into politics following earlier activity with the Chinese Progressive Association and Chiu has been a member of the governing board for the Chinatown Community Development Center. On a broader scale, a recent listing of elected Asian Pacific American officials totals 892 individuals nationally, a figure that would have been unimaginable thirty years ago.[4]

The political role of advocacy agencies described in this essay operated through the 1980s and into the 1990s, but is now in a state of change. As individuals with electoral political ambitions become more numerous in the communities, political activity has begun to shift to more individually oriented agendas. Advocacy agencies continue to provide communities with a political voice in areas associated with their clientele and goals but their broader political role remains to be seen. One of the developing roles for community advocacy agencies will be to remind these new Asian American officials of their roots while also assisting them in attending to community needs. This new role is a product of the reality that people often lose their effectiveness as advocates when they attain political or policy making positions. Community advocacy organizations will have to watch and push Asian American officials with the same vigor as they addressed earlier non-Asian politicians. The degree to which this may be possible is, of course, dependent on their leadership, both collective and individual.

## NOTES

1. This essay is based on personal experience in and with advocacy agencies in both San Francisco and other locales. An earlier version was published in Malcolm Collier, ed., *Asians in America: A Reader* (Dubuque, IA: Kendall/ Hunt Publishers, 1993).
2. Alan S. Wong, personal interview, 18 May 2008.
3. For examples of such earlier community advocacy, see various articles in Sucheng Chan, ed., *Entry Denied:*

*Exclusion and the Chinese Community in America, 1882-1943* (Philadelphia: Temple UP, 1991).

4.  Don T. Nakanishi and James S. Lai, eds., *2007-08 National Asian Pacific American Political Almanac* (Los Angeles: Asian American Studies Center, UCLA, 2008).

# AAS and CHSA:
# An Attempt to Merge Town and Gown

*Lorraine Dong* [1]

In 1989, the faculty in the Asian American Studies Department at San Francisco State University (AAS) began a collaborative community service relationship with the Chinese Historical Society of America (CHSA). At the height of the relationship, this town-and-gown union was considered by some in the academe and community to be a role model for AAS community service. In 2005, somewhat envious and amazed by the success of this sixteen-year-old town-and-gown merger, a caucus of eighteen Chinese American historical societies, centers, and museums at a conference cosponsored by AAS and CHSA made one of its main agenda items to be: how can other historical societies follow in the footsteps of CHSA and find a gown for its town?[2] Shortly after, the many service activities that once held the AAS-CHSA partnership together slowly began to decrease with the changing of the guards and resultant growing pains.

## Necessary Collaboration

CHSA began as an all-volunteer organization with a mission to serve and empower the community with history, a mission necessitated by the exclusion of minorities in America's history.[3] The Society was at the forefront of what became a national movement during the 1960s among ethnic minority communities in the United States. In earnest, a handful of Chinese Americans began to research and study their own history. From the ranks of CHSA came Thomas W. Chinn, who was one of the earliest notable Chinese American community historians, followed immediately by renowned community historians Philip P. Choy and Him Mark Lai. On April 19, 1969, the three co-chaired a CHSA seminar, "A History of the Chinese in America," and co-edited a pioneer publication entitled *A History of the Chinese in California: A Syllabus* that was distributed to the 250 seminar attendees.

With the 1968 Student Strike at San Francisco State College that demanded the establishment of a School of Ethnic Studies and the subsequent establishment of Asian American Studies classes around the nation in the fall of 1969, the Society's mission to research, disseminate, and teach Chinese American history was also being met by the academe. To sustain its mission and existence, CHSA had always depended on the passion and love of history from its volunteer grassroots members to conduct and disseminate its research. With Chinese American history now being researched, written, and taught in the academe, CHSA began to recognize its physical limitations and "competition" from the professional world of Asian Americanists and historians. At the same time, their ambitious decision and goal in 1990 to finally fulfill the dream of acquiring a permanent home or headquarters with a resulting emphasis on fundraising drove them to another level of operation.

Meanwhile, along with the other Ethnic Studies departments at SF State (American Indian Studies, Black Studies, and La Raza Studies), AAS had to deal with resisting or lack of institutional recognition as a legitimate discipline, as well as lack of support and financial resources to develop its various programs and projects, especially for those involving community service. Nevertheless, AAS developed various ways to send its students to the community to do volunteer work in areas such as social work; sociopolitical and community advocacy; mental and physical health; tutorial/educational outreach and retention; and community arts and culture (see article on "The Nine-Unit Block and Other Early Community Programs" by Malcolm Collier and Irene Dea Collier elsewhere in this volume). One area of service that was not sufficiently addressed was history.

The 1960s movement included the call for empowering the community with history. It was clear that the primary goal of K-12 teachers would be to teach and institutionalize Asian American history as an integral part of American history in the K-12 curriculum. The question then arose: other than professionally training K-12 teachers, and lecturing, researching, and publishing for an academic audience, how else could post-secondary teachers and students use their knowledge of history to empower the community? Community service in ethnic historical societies, with its community-based historians, archives, and museums, became an ideal, ready-made venue and source for AAS to fulfill this mission.

At the time, CHSA had a venue but lacked the required human resources to conduct and research Chinese American history for the community while AAS had the human resources but lacked a venue to empower the community with its history. The timing and conditions were ripe for what was considered a natural, beneficial union between AAS and CHSA, two institutions that have the same goal of serving the community with history.

## Creating a Community Service Structure

Under the fundamental principle of serving and empowering the community with history, the AAS-CHSA collaboration attempted to create a structure that would answer the call of the 1968 Strike to topple the ivory tower that isolated the academe from the community. Establishing a town-and-gown partnership based on community service has always posed a challenge for AAS because many town-and-gown service-related unions were made possible through the connection or work of one individual. Once that individual left, the union would end. Such mergers were also short-lived because their duration was based on the length of particular projects. A faculty belonging to a community board of directors would recruit AAS volunteers for a community project. When the project ended or when the faculty left the board, then the department's service relationship with the organization also ended. There were few models, if any, for AAS to institutionalize town-and-gown service relationships on a permanent basis. The plan with CHSA was not to depend on an individual faculty by involving and mobilizing the entire department.

The basic concepts practiced by AAS for this AAS-CHSA service collaboration were not written in a contract but understood and instilled among faculty and students. Service between the two organizations was a two-way street. The town-and-gown relationship is jeopardized if there is an imbalance:

1 To serve the community is not missionary work: Faculty and students must go to the community (i.e., CHSA) without an attitude of superiority where they feel they are more educated and "advantaged," and

are serving the "disadvantaged" community with knowledge or skills that the community "lacks." Reciprocally the community (i.e., CHSA) should not treat faculty and students as mere laborers.

2 Service is mutually exchanged: AAS serves the community with its resources and the community (i.e., CHSA) serves AAS with its resources. AAS faculty and students give back or return to the community with their knowledge, skills, and volunteerism, and CHSA gives to the academe in the form of being a facility where faculty and students can learn and research what cannot be done in a formal academic setting. Both are simultaneously providing for and receiving from each other.

3 There is no class distinction in community service: Within AAS, both faculty and students must be involved in the service project. Students are assigned by the faculty to serve or volunteer, and at the same time, the faculty is integral in serving on that same project. Between AAS and CHSA, members of both institutions are equal because everyone has the same status as a volunteer with the ultimate mission of serving the community.

4 Materialism has no place in community service: CHSA members are not paid to fulfill its mission to promote and disseminate history to the community. Likewise, AAS faculty are not paid to serve the community and should never use the community for retention, tenure, and promotion purposes by serving that community only to leave it once tenure and promotion are achieved. Students also are not paid for their service but because the service itself is integral to their learning experience, they are evaluated and can earn extra credit, a percentage grade if the service is linked to a course requirement, or units if done as a special, independent project.

### Faculty Service

Similar to earlier 1970s AAS community projects, a major distinction between the AAS-CHSA service collaboration and most non-AAS community service projects is the inclusion of faculty in the project as both activists and student supervisors for the service project. AAS faculty are expected not only to be educators and scholars, but also to be community activists. In order to fulfill the ideals of the 1968 Strike, AAS faculty must practice what they preach and serve as a role model for their students in community service. With this expectation, the passion that an AAS faculty has for service and the community will contagiously be transmitted to the students.

The success of the AAS-CHSA community service collaboration was possible mainly because all individuals involved were volunteers. Other than seniority there were no hierarchical differences when both sides joined to work together. For AAS faculty, becoming active in CHSA serves the dual, non-exclusive functions of fulfilling the community service philosophy and politics of AAS, and of enhancing their teaching and professional growth while partially fulfilling the department's and university's retention, tenure, and promotion requirements for community service. Almost all part- and full-time Chinese American faculty, temporary and permanent, have volunteered their services to CHSA.

Appendix A lists the faculty and staff from SFSU who volunteered and served the community via CHSA. It does not include the myriad positions and committees in which AAS faculty have volunteered to serve. The relatively large number of AAS faculty participation was necessary because the all-volunteer CHSA was unable to recruit enough people to join and run the organization. As a result, AAS faculty became integral to CHSA. Of special note is Robert Fung, a lecturer, serving as President of the Board of Directors in 1996 and Lorraine Dong, a tenured, full professor, serving as President for six terms (1998-2000; 2002-04) and as CEO for eight months in 2003 when the Society did not have an executive director. During these years, no one was available or wanted to be president, especially during CHSA's difficult capital campaign years.

At the height of AAS's activism in CHSA, there was at least one and as many as four AAS faculty serving on the CHSA Board of Directors in any given year, but AAS was never close to being a majority on the board. From 1989 to 2008, other Chinese American professors have served on the board; they were from universities such as California State University East Bay (Colleen Fong and David Woo), Stanford University (Gordon Chang), University of California at Los Angeles (Russell Leong), and University of California at Santa Cruz (Judy Yung).

When CHSA decided to include a cultural component to its history museum, individuals from SFSU's College of Creative Arts became another important source of leadership for CHSA. From the Art Department came Irene Poon Andersen, who was an active board member, and Mark Johnson, the Art Department's Gallery Director. In addition to providing invaluable service as unpaid consultants and voluntarily curating exhibits for the CHSA Museum, they recruited volunteer students from the Art Department and Museum Studies.

Another major contribution made by SFSU was financially based. Besides procuring in-kind services and goods, almost all fundraising and grant-writing proposals were written and submitted by SFSU members in the name of CHSA. To the possible professional detriment of faculty members, the years spent helping to raise hundreds of thousands if not millions of dollars for CHSA were not acknowledged in the same manner as service or

contribution to San Francisco State University. Despite the high priority and importance of community service to AAS in its own departmental retention, tenure, and promotion policy, on the university level, AAS faculty's community service and contribution to CHSA were generally ranked not as valuable in service and contribution because they did not bring direct resources and funding to the University.

*Student Service*

In the spirit of AAS faculty volunteering alongside students, AAS faculty and students did the typical volunteer "grunt" work of sitting at the reception desk to greet visitors, answering the phones, filing, stuffing envelopes, and/or cleaning and painting the facilities. Because CHSA did not have a paid staff, these "mundane" activities became tasks that were necessary for the promotion and maintenance of CHSA's mission. Students developed a sense of belonging to the community when they served side by side with CHSA and other community volunteers without the usual hierarchical separation. In some cases, students served on committees as equals to the faculty and community. These "mundane" activities also expanded to become much more meaningful for both CHSA and AAS faculty and students as these activities eventually provided individuals with an opportunity to work on projects in leadership capacities (Appendix B has a detailed description of some major AAS-CHSA service projects). Some SFSU graduates who took AAS classes subsequently became board members or were hired part- and/or full-time at CHSA.[4]

SFSU students provided a service (under the supervision of their professors) that would have cost thousands of dollars that CHSA did not have. The most long-lasting project was the Ching Collection, where over one hundred students from all disciplines who were enrolled in AAS classes volunteered to complete the Society's first major electronic attempt to catalog a collection. Even when classes were finished, students continued to volunteer and curated exhibits on the Ching Collection.

Museum Studies students also played active volunteer roles, especially Tracy Jones-Pomaro who, with CHSA board member William Roop, organized and developed the database in 1995 to preserve and catalog the Ching Collection. For his master's degree in Museum Studies, Stephen Sutley installed the exhibit on Dong Kingman for the November 2001 grand opening of CHSA's new museum on 965 Clay Street.

AAS students were able to use what they have learned in their history classes in a variety of ways for CHSA and the community. Some became student docents and some taught Chinese American history to K-12 students at CHSA's summer programs. While doing volunteer archival and preservation work, many also had firsthand opportunities to research the archives of CHSA and presented/wrote original papers and theses, which were then adapted to lectures, exhibits, and K-12 activities for students and the general public, audiences that have been largely ignored by professional Asian Americanists in the academe. In addition to SFSU "benefitting" from the CHSA archives, many non-SFSU scholars and writers were able to conduct research in CHSA's archives such as Iris Chang, Krystyn Moon, and Jean Pfaelzer, as well as numerous documentary filmmakers and museums. This particular AAS-CHSA service collaboration involving archival preservation helped to fulfill CHSA's mission by making its collections available to scholars, students, and the community, which would not have been possible within the limitations of the Society's volunteer members and resources.

During the years of capital campaign fundraising in the 1990s until the 2001 opening of CHSA's headquarters and museum, AAS students volunteered en masse for its fundraising activities. Of special note is SFSU's Alpha Phi Omega National Service Organization (Mu Zeta Chapter), who volunteered for all, except the first, of the Society's major annual galas (as well as help CHSA move from its rat-infested Commercial Street location to the new museum site). Two AAS students, Voltaire Villanueva and Christopher Banez, as well as Christopher Chow, a former AAS lecturer at the time, volunteered their services by producing original videos on historical topics for three separate gala events. By participating in this multi-year, multi-million-dollar campaign, SFSU students personally experienced the behind-the-scene operation of a fundraising campaign. They learned how it is to be at the bottom of the totem pole as well as how it is to serve as an equal on a fundraising committee. They learned to understand and feel the frustration, stress, and tension that usually accompany this often neglected aspect of the not-for-profit community. During the ten years of service on CHSA's capital campaign, the students learned firsthand the internal workings of community organizing and politics, something that cannot be taught or *felt* in the classroom by reading case studies in textbooks. In the end when the headquarters and museum opened, they were rightfully proud to feel part ownership and to have helped to make it possible.

And, in an interesting give-and-take scenario, these students took their CHSA fundraising and organizing experience back to the AAS Department by planning a very successful 1998 conference that commemorated the thirtieth anniversary of the Student Strike at SF State.[5] They also instituted a structure for their graduation fundraiser that has an estimated $20,000 budget every year. The students' primary goal for this annual fundraiser is to raise money for a graduation celebration dedicated not to themselves but to their families and friends. This graduation planning activity has developed into a "course" on fundraising and event planning, providing students with another valuable learning experience.

## NECESSARY SEPARATION

The conditions for service collaboration between AAS and CHSA were ideal during the 1990s. CHSA was all-volunteer and needed more volunteers, resources, stability, and a staff, while AAS needed a venue to serve and empower the community with history.

Many project opportunities were available in CHSA that provided perfect venues for SFSU faculty and students. Some of these were ideas from AAS faculty when they served on CHSA committees to plan projects, where other members on the committee were not professionally studying and researching Chinese American history. In these planning sessions, AAS faculty would suggest historical dates and events that were used for CHSA programming purposes like conferences, lectures, exhibits, and other special projects and activities. For example, instead of the usual fashion show, CHSA's annual luncheons and fundraisers became popular and distinct from all other social events in the community when AAS faculty members initiated and continued to provide CHSA with historical themes for its various fundraisers. CHSA event program books did not include simply a listing of donors and political proclamations, but historical photos and original essays. The honorees for the events were not those who financially donated or contributed to CHSA, but those who were pioneers and makers of Chinese American history. If the year's theme were sports (as it was in 1996), the evening's honorees were Chinese American pioneers in sports and in the program book would be a historical essay and photos on Chinese Americans in sports. The program books were literally sold for their historical content and some became so high in demand that they are now out of stock. Although not acknowledged as scholarly or academic writings, these pictorial essays have original historical value and serve the purpose of empowering the community and general public with knowledge of Chinese American history. CHSA's annual luncheons and fundraisers with their historical themes also kept the Society in the business of history during a time when their resources and energy were spent mostly on the capital campaign. More important for fundraising purposes, these historical themes educated the donors at the galas and successfully showed how their money was being used.

In addition to the capital campaign, eight major service collaborations (see Appendix B) required tremendous SFSU human and financial resources to accomplish. Keenly aware of the community's constant suspicion of an academic takeover, AAS made sure that all these joint ventures and projects did not involve taking from CHSA and the community. Grant proposals and fundraising for exhibits, programs, and conferences were done mainly by SFSU faculty and staff but under the name of CHSA. There was no line item in CHSA's budget to give SFSU any consultation money or stipend because everything was done as a service to the community. If a faculty or student received any CHSA compensation, it was below minimal to fulfill certain funding requirements and was oftentimes returned as a donation. In contrast, CHSA projects have been line itemed in various SFSU budgets, and for the Ching Project, AAS made it legally clear in an MOU that the collection belonged to CHSA and not SFSU.

Although all AAS-CHSA joint projects were planned with the community in mind, they have been identified by some board members as being too AAS and too academic, mainly because of the presence and involvement of AAS faculty and students. One recent example is the 2005 conference when the CHSA board saw it as an AAS and academic conference despite the fact that out of the 250+ participants making presentations, 58% came from the community, versus 30% from the academe and 12% from high school and college students. In addition, the conference (excluding the proceedings) made a net profit of $75,000, all of which benefitted CHSA and not AAS.

In the beginning of AAS, there was an understanding that the community should define what was needed from the academe and not vice versa. In this case, a community organization was in need of assistance from the academe. When CHSA lacked sufficient board members and volunteers to function and reach its goals, AAS willingly made themselves available and by default became the "leaders" in CHSA. Under such circumstances, a gray area was created as to who was "in control." An important question arose: is AAS acting on behalf of AAS or CHSA? This was followed by another question: Why are AAS faculty and students who joined as CHSA members not seen or treated equally as CHSA members like other CHSA members who are not AAS-affiliated? Because of this gray area caused by both parties' shared, volunteer commitment to the goal of promoting Chinese American history, it was difficult for AAS faculty to be accepted or seen as CHSA members.

Finally, as an all-volunteer organization trying to raise money for its permanent headquarters, CHSA had to fulfill donors' and grantors' main requirement that the organization be stable and permanent in the form of a staff. Hence, the multi-million dollar capital campaign included the establishment of a staff which eventually led to the corporatization of CHSA under new leadership. The constitution of the board slowly became more "professional," no longer hands-on or grassroots. The

services of AAS were not needed in the same manner and were even seen as a monopoly. In 2005, AAS was told by CHSA that CHSA's identity was linked too closely with AAS and that AAS needed to leave because the Society had to develop their own identity and move forward to their next, higher level of development and growth. AAS's departure would open opportunities for other colleges and universities to participate in CHSA. Some AAS students were also told that CHSA wanted more professional and mature volunteers from the corporate world and other universities to do the volunteer "work," rather than students still "in training to be professionals."

As of 2008, there remains one AAS lecturer (Robert Fung) on the board and one AAS faculty (Russell Jeung) on the Society's Editorial Committee, with no other AAS involvement in terms of department-level consultation or student service projects. AAS is no longer cosponsoring the Society's annual journal, *Chinese America: History and Perspectives* (*H&P*). The 2005 conference proceedings published as a special 2007 *H&P* issue marks the last institutional collaborative project between AAS and CHSA. After nineteen years of institutionalizing community service with CHSA, AAS has returned to the individual faculty structure with its usual limitations in service and longevity. Meanwhile, CHSA has outreached to other universities to meet their needs.

AAS failed to "educate" CHSA on the AAS philosophy of community service and to convince CHSA of the value of a town-and-gown merger where both entities can stay grounded in the community together. Further complicating the situation is the acquisition of a permanent headquarters and museum, and CHSA's transition from an all-volunteer organization to an organization with a paid but minimal staff. This has resulted in an annual budget that can only be maintained by grants and fundraising, resulting in a board of directors who are recruited more on the basis of their connection to money or other non-history-related professional skills. A new hierarchical structure is created with a paid staff who plans and handles the Society's general operation and history-related programs, whereas in the past these functions were done by volunteers and a hands-on board. With this changing of the guard in staff and board leadership, and with CHSA's existence relying more heavily on corporate funding and playing the right politics, the path that CHSA has chosen to take is deviating from its grassroots origins and structure.

AAS cannot force the community to understand or accept the concept that faculty and student community service is integral to the paradigm and discipline of Asian American Studies. Community organizations already lacking in staff are not set up with specific employees designated to instruct and oversee faculty much less student volunteers in large numbers. In many cases, they do not understand that the community is a learning ground where students are there to volunteer and more importantly to gain a specific learning experience. Sometimes community organizations might not synchronize with the instructor's intended learning outcome for the students, and vice versa. To alleviate this situation in the past, AAS had at least one faculty serving on the CHSA board. Therefore, it was convenient for AAS faculty to supervise the student volunteers at CHSA and to link the students from academe to community. However, this requires time and energy that mainly senior faculty with tenure and living nearby could afford to commit. Younger faculty with a family and living outside San Francisco would find such intense dedication to volunteer service almost impossible to fulfill in addition to their current teaching, research, and campus service responsibilities. The commitment is further exacerbated with the coming generation of Asian Americanists who are not necessarily from the local community and who would not have the same passion or urgency of service and volunteerism for CHSA as would the AAS faculty from the 1960s-70s who were born and raised in the local community.

The challenges posed by the 1960s and 1970s idealism to unite academe and community are still ongoing. To reiterate, the main reason why the AAS-CHSA service collaboration was successful is because CHSA had no staff and was run by volunteers and a working board of directors. With the few SFSU faculty and staff serving as a small minority on the board, it was not a problem for CHSA to accept and consider AAS personnel and ideas as mutually their own, and to manage the many volunteers coming from SFSU in order to fulfill shared goals. Now with a paid staff to handle CHSA programs, board members no longer need to be hands-on or have any background in Chinese American history, and the composition of volunteers and donors is changing. AAS did not foresee that after serving and helping CHSA to serve the community, maintain the integrity of its (and AAS's) mission, purchase a home, and establish a paid staff, AAS is seen as an outside force and not an integral member of CHSA. AAS's years of membership and service have been interpreted as controlling CHSA and as such, the Society must be "freed" to develop its own identity. AAS will abide by its founding principle that the community defines what it needs from AAS and not vice versa. Until the Society sees a necessity to institutionalize a relationship with AAS again, the separation between academe and community in this case remains real.

## APPENDIX A

### List of SFSU Faculty and Staff Who Volunteered and Contributed Their Services to CHSA

Note: Unless otherwise indicated, all individuals are faculty members from the Asian American Studies Department at San Francisco State University.

*Served on the Board of Directors*

>   Irene Poon Andersen (Art Department)
>   Wan-Lee Cheng (College of Creative Arts)
>   Lorraine Dong
>   Robert A. Fung
>   Madeline Hsu
>   Russell Jeung
>   Vitus Leung
>   Jeannie Woo

*Presented CHSA Lectures, Workshops, and/or Book Talks*

>   Jeffery Paul Chan
>   Chuong H. Chung
>   Malcolm Collier
>   Lorraine Dong
>   Marlon K. Hom
>   Madeline Hsu
>   Russell Jeung
>   Mark Johnson (Art Department)
>   Jeannie Woo

*Wrote for the Society's Monthly Bulletin, Annual H&P Journal, Program Books, and/or Exhibition Catalogs*

>   Irene Poon Andersen (Art Department)
>   Lorraine Dong
>   Robert A. Fung
>   Marlon Hom
>   Madeline Hsu
>   Russell Jeung
>   Mark Johnson (Art Department)
>   Valerie Soe
>   Jeannie Woo

*Served as Editor of the Monthly Bulletin and/or on the Editorial Committee of the H&P Journal*

>   Lorraine Dong
>   Marlon K. Hom
>   Madeline Hsu
>   Russell Jeung
>   Vitus Leung

*Curated Museum Exhibits*

Irene Poon Andersen (Art Department)
Lorraine Dong
Marlon K. Hom
Mark Johnson (Art Department)
Jeannie Woo

APPENDIX B

Major AAS-CHSA Service Collaborations

AAS's first official collaboration with CHSA began in 1989 with AAS's cosponsorship of the Society's annual journal, *Chinese America: History and Perspectives* (*H&P*), the country's oldest, continuously published journal dedicated to the study of Chinese America. Marlon K. Hom served on its Editorial Committee of five, and on the seven-member Production Committee were four AAS members: George Woo as production manager, Michael Hornbuckle as assistant, and Lorraine Dong and Marlon K. Hom as typists.[6] AAS cosponsored the journal for fourteen years, from 1989-2007 (excluding 1993-1997) and Hom served continuously on the editorial committee from 1989-2007. Both AAS faculty and students have contributed articles to the journal.

One year later, Dong joined the CHSA Board of Directors. Woo, Department Chair at the time, suggested to Dong that AAS would support CHSA if she were to develop a collaborative project between AAS and CHSA. An ideal venue materialized in 1993, when AAS and CHSA had its first major collaboration, the November 1993 conference entitled **"The Repeal and Its Legacy: A Conference on the 50th Anniversary of the Repeal of the Chinese Exclusion Acts"** and the publication of its proceedings in 1994. Hom was the Conference Coordinator and by that time, also AAS Department Chair. Unlike past CHSA conferences, this one began with a planning committee comprised of CHSA board members, AAS faculty, and a student representative from the Asian Student Union, where all three entities (community, faculty, and students) were equal partners from the beginning to the end of the project.[7] The three-day conference began at SFSU and ended at the Chinese Culture Center in Chinatown, with the goal of reminding everyone that the conference was both academic and community-based, and that the two venues were a reminder to empower both the academe and community with history and knowledge. Not only were community organizations, academic professionals, and college students invited to attend and make presentations, but high school students were also subsidized to attend the conference. Over 650 individuals participated, and the event became a model for subsequent Chinese American historical and cultural organizations to host their national conferences in collaboration with academic institutions. This also became a model for many other town-and-gown conferences.

The next major AAS-CHSA collaboration came with the bequeathal of the **Daniel K.E. Ching Collection** to CHSA in 1994. CHSA was chosen over other historical societies because Philip K. Choy and the town-and-gown relationship between AAS and CHSA were factors assuring the Ching Estate that the preservation and cataloguing of the collection would be done. An MOU was signed between AAS and CHSA to work together on the collection. This was the first and only legal document signed by both institutions. Philip P. Choy, Lorraine Dong, and Marlon K. Hom became the Project Coordinators. The collection contains about 10,000 Americana artifacts with Chinese and Chinese American images dating from the 1800s to the 1990s. This includes postcards, trade cards, sheet music, piano rolls, records, books, magazines, newspapers, prints, posters, paintings, photographs, stereocards, toys, games, household items, tokens, coins, and stamps. The Ching Project involved SFSU students preserving, cataloguing, and studying the collection for research, exhibition, and publication purposes. Since 1994, over one hundred AAS students and volunteers worked on the project, with some of the students using their research findings to write papers and theses, curate museum exhibitions, present at conferences, and develop K-12 curricular activity kits and workshops.[8] While acquiring hands-on primary research skills, AAS students became better scholars, but more importantly, they gave back to the community with the knowledge and skills acquired from their AAS history classes and the Ching Project.

SFSU's yearlong, citywide centennial celebration in 1999 opened another opportunity for AAS to give back to the community through the Society's museum and monthly lecture series. AAS students under the supervision of SFSU faculty and staff produced an exhibition for the museum entitled **"Dreams, Realities, and Challenges,"** which commemorated the thirtieth anniversary of the founding of AAS at SFSU. The exhibit was on display for the entire year in the community.[9] AAS also cosponsored the CHSA's monthly lecture series for 1999 by recruiting SFSU alumni, faculty, and students to speak year-round on topics pertaining to Chinese America. This **"CHSA/SFSU<in>the Community"** lecture series had the highest monthly lecture attendance in CHSA history to date.[10]

In 2000-01, AAS helped CHSA to set up a Chinese American history summer program. It was known as **ChAMP**, the **Ch**inese **A**merican **M**entorship **P**rogram. Four AAS students, Brenda Eng, Bonnie Li, Lorraine Lim, and Vivian Toy, spent the academic year of 2000-01 taking Chinese American Studies classes at AAS and met regularly to create a curriculum plan for summer school. Besides receiving additional training sessions from CHSA board member Don Chan, AAS graduate student Tseh-sien Kelly Vaughn, who was also a former middle school teacher, conducted workshops that trained the four undergraduate students with teaching pedagogy. These four AAS students became mentors training high school students on Chinese American history who would in turn teach the subject matter to middle school students. Funding for this program came from the department's Asian American Access and Retention Project (AAARP), which had as one of its goals to do outreach activities such as student mentorship and tutorial, educational programs to provide middle and high school students with exposure to and interaction with San Francisco State University. Unfortunately, publicity for the program was unsuccessful, so the total number of participants in ChAMP was less than ten and the program did not continue the following year.

Beginning in summer 2000, AAS began its first **Chinese American Migration History Study Tour,** where AAS faculty led students to China to study Chinese American history and culture (for details on the study tour, see Marlon K. Hom, "Going 'Back' to Where Our Ancestors Came From" published elsewhere in this volume). The program was meant for students, but in its second year, CHSA board and staff were welcomed to join the study tour as a service to help the Society's board and staff learn about Chinese American history from a transnational perspective and to meet their counterpart organizations in China.[11] For several years, the study tour stopped being an AAS course and was billed as a joint CHSA-AAS program. It became an intergenerational program involving college students and individuals of a much older age range from the community. Under this structure, the program gave an opportunity for students and community members to learn and interact with each other. It provided a community service by giving non-students an opportunity to go to such study tours without having to enroll as students. AAS faculty volunteered their services as tour leaders, which resulted in a joint program that also brought in some revenue for the Society where the participants were paying fees to CHSA rather than SFSU. Finally, this resurrected the Society's field trip program but on an international level.

The last major town-and-gown collaboration between AAS and CHSA was the international conference entitled **"Branching Out the Banyan Tree: A Changing Chinese America,"** held on October 6-9, 2005, and its conference proceedings published in the 2007 issue of *H&P*. This joint venture marked two milestones: (a) the conference was held thirty years after CHSA sponsored the first Chinese American conference in the nation and (b) the proceedings were published in the twentieth anniversary issue of the *H&P* journal. The conference mission and concept continued and updated that of the 1993 joint conference. Of the fourteen-member planning committee, five were AAS-affiliated.[12] More than seventy students from AAS classes volunteered as "runners" and to help with logistics. The conference was a huge undertaking with an estimated attendance of eight hundred, three hundred fifty of whom were high school and university students learning and interacting side-by-side with people from both the academe and the community. Over two hundred fifty participants from the academe and community presented their research and thoughts. Of these, 58% came from the community, 30% came from the academe, and 12% came from the student community. About four high schools and sixty colleges/universities were represented, and thirteen panels were individually sponsored by community organizations. The conference, as well as the proceedings, was in both English and Chinese. Panels and papers were presented by people from a variety of backgrounds: professors with doctoral degrees, educators, high school and college students, physicians, health professionals, lawyers, politicians, community activists, artists, writers, filmmakers, and average citizens whose hobby or pastime is to learn about Chinese America in general. Topics of research and interest were no longer simply about immigrant, first-generation Chinese Americans from China. They included Chinese people coming to America from all parts of the world, Chinese Americans who are fourth- and fifth-generation, Chinese Americans of mixed heritage, and LGBTQ (Lesbian, Gay, Bisexual, Transgender, and Queer) Chinese Americans. The conference reflected how Chinese American Studies is no longer monolithic and has expanded from being regional to being global and transnational, not only geographically but also culturally and conceptually.

## NOTES

1. The writer wishes to thank the Editorial Committee, Irene Poon Andersen, Robert A. Fung, Jeannie Woo, and others for providing invaluable suggestions to help with the accuracy and writing of this reflective paper. The writer bears full responsibility for its final content.
2. The conference, "Branching Out the Banyan Tree: A Changing Chinese America," was cosponsored by AAS and CHSA, and held from October 6 to 9, 2005, at the Radisson Miyako Hotel in San Francisco, California (see Appendix B for more details). The caucus had representatives from the following eighteen organizations: Angel Island Immigration Station Foundation, Chicago Chinese American Historical Society, China-town Historical Society of Honolulu, Chinese American Council of Sacramento, Chinese American Museum,

Chinese-American Museum of Chicago, Chinese American Museum of Northern California, Chinese-Australian Historical Association Inc., Chinese Canadian Historical Society of British Columbia, Chinese Historical and Cultural Project of Santa Clara County, Chinese Historical Society of America, Chinese Historical Society of New England, Chinese Historical Society of Southern California, Hawaii Chinese History Center, Museum of Chinese in the Americas, San Diego Chinese Historical Society and Museum, Ventura County Chinese American Historical Society, and Yuba Historical Society.

3. The Chinese Historical Society of America was an idea conceived in 1962 by five men, Thomas W. Chinn, C.H. Kwock, Chingwah Lee, H.K. Wong, and Thomas Wu. The Society's first meeting was held on January 5, 1963 and in 1965, the Society became a not-for-profit 501(c)(3) exempt status organization with the stated purpose of being "educational." According to its mission statement, CHSA's specific focus is to "promote the contributions that the Chinese have made to the United States of America" by "establishing and operating a scientific, literary, and educational organization through a historical society."

4. Examples of SFSU students hired by CHSA when they graduated from SFSU or were still matriculated at SFSU include Liana Koehler, Karl Ma, Ivy Wong, Jeannie Woo, and Hubert Yee. SFSU students who became recent board members after graduation included Cedric Cheng, Calvin Fung, Galin Luk, and Jeannie Woo. Fung was also the Society's Interim Administrator from 1997 to 1998.

5. The conference, "Dreams, Realities, and Challenges in Asian American Studies: Asian Pacific Islander Americans Commemorating the 30th Anniversary of the SF State Third World Student Strike," was held from October 22 to 24, 1998, at San Francisco State University. Besides AAS students, two student groups, Pilipino American Collegiate Endeavor (PACE) and Chi Rho Omicron, were actively involved. The department's Asian American Access and Retention Project provided much of the funding for the conference.

6. Non-AAS members serving on the Editorial Committee were Him Mark Lai, Ruthanne Lum McCunn, Ted Wong, and Judy Yung. The three non-AAS members on the Production Committee were proofreaders Lillian Louie, Robert Schwendinger, and Annie Soo.

7. The Conference Planning Committee was comprised of AAS faculty members Lorraine Dong, Robert A. Fung, and Marlon K. Hom; ASU student Maxwell Leung; and CHSA members Albert Cheng, Bruce Chin, Jean Jew, Him Mark Lai, Madeleine Leong, Enid Lim, and Ted Wong. About one-third of the committee was SFSU-affiliated.

8. Daniel K.E. Ching (1931-1990) was born in Honolulu of Chinese immigrants from Guangdong. An accounting executive for the Pacific Bell Telephone Company by profession, Ching was also world known as a coin collector and later in his life, a collector of Chinese American memorabilia. Most notable among the many SFSU student-related outcomes from the Ching Project that benefited the students, CHSA, and the community were: (a) 1996 presentations of the Ching collection in two national conferences (Hawai'i and Washington, DC) by Ethnic Studies MA students James Chan, Dennis Park, and Dina Shek, who also published their preliminary findings in the 1997 issue of the Society's *H&P*; (b) "StereoView: Chinese Images in Americana," a 1998 exhibit premiering the Ching Collection at the CHSA Museum, involving AAS students Susan Jeong, Soklan Nou, and Jeannie Woo; (c) the new CHSA Museum's grand opening exhibit entitled "Facing the Camera" on early Chinese photographs in the Ching Collection, co-curated by Irene Poon Andersen and AAS graduate student Jeannie Woo; and (d) "'The Heathen Chinee': Stereotypes of Chinese in Popular Music" exhibit with an accompanying K-12 curricular activities kit (2003-04), curated by AAS graduate student Darren Lee Brown with SFSU students Ting Chen, Elan Hom, Vixie Javier, Julia Lam, Allen Lee, and Florence Tu. This exhibit was done in conjunction with Brown's 2003 MA thesis entitled "'All Aboard for Chinatown': Stereotypes of Chinese and Chinatown in Popular Music."

9. AAS students involved in this exhibit were Katherine General, Lynne Wong, and Nancy Yin, who were co-curators with Irene Poon Andersen and Lorraine Dong.

10. The brackets around the word "in" was a graphic design attempt to focus on the town-and-gown connection. Speakers included the following SFSU-related individuals: Robert A. Corrigan (January), Lorraine Dong (February), Lora Jo Foo (March), Arthur Dong (April), Michael Chang (May), Lonnie Chin, Lisa Kwong, Darlene Lim, and Roger Tom (June), Jeffery Paul Chan, Philip P. Choy, Him Mark Lai, and Marlon K. Hom (September), Gordon Chin (October), Judy Yung (November 13), Calvin Fung, Denise Leo, and Allan Yu (November 19), and Jeffery Paul Chan, Frank Chin, Russell Leong, and Shawn Wong (December) (Chin did not make it because he suffered a heart attack on the afternoon before the December lecture).

11. The first staff to join the study tour included Executive Director Melissa Szeto and Administrative Assistant Beth Wilson. Past CHSA President Philip P. Choy was also a participant.

12. AAS faculty members serving on the Conference Planning Committee were Lorraine Dong, Marlon K. Hom, Madeline Hsu, Russell Jeung, and Jeannie Woo, with Him Mark Lai who was an AAS Adjunct Faculty and CHSA board member. Other committee members included CHSA board members Don Chan, Colleen Fong (CSU East Bay professor), and Alexander Lock, with CHSA staff Sue Lee, Marisa Louie, Russell Ow, Leonard Shek, and Ivy Wong (the latter was both an SFSU student and part-time CHSA staff member). Dong, Lock, and Woo were the Conference Co-chairs.

# ASIAN AMERICAN COMMUNITY HEALTH: BRINGING EDUCATION AND SERVICE TO THE COMMUNITY

*Mai-Nhung Le and Grace J. Yoo*

*Power is love implementing the demands of justice.*
*Justice is love correcting everything that goes against love.*
— Dr. Martin Luther King, Jr.

Our health initiative in the Asian American Studies Department (AAS) at San Francisco State University (SFSU) is rooted in the inspiring words of Dr. Martin Luther King, Jr. We believe that a significant role of an educator is to promote justice and civic involvement by providing opportunities for students to work in the community towards these goals. Because of our expertise in Asian American Community Health, we have had the opportunity to collaborate with, write for, consult with, and present to both individuals and groups in local, state, and national organizations in our fields. Although our work has provided opportunities for scholarship, the mission of the Asian American health unit has been about breaking silences around health and social problems unspoken in the Asian American community, providing forums through outreach and education to bring voice to these issues, and about providing community and support around these issues that have been unvoiced and silenced.

There are several silenced and unvoiced health and social issues that impact Asian America. Often the popular press and even the community assume that Asian Americans are a healthy minority; but the data shows they experience numerous social and health problems that impact quality of life and ultimately mortality. This essay will review the role of SFSU AAS in facing the Asian American community and the role of community education outreach efforts and community service learning programs

With growing demand by SFSU students for a course examining health issues among Asian Americans, we created the course AAS 575 (Asian American Community Health Issues). This course is designed to provide students with an introduction to major health issues affecting the Asian American communities. It reviews current research on Asian Americans and health. It also examines how social and cultural factors shape the perception, recognition, and prevention of health issues, and treatment of medical problems. Lastly, it examines the national and community-based Asian American organizations in meeting these challenges. We have established internship opportunities for students with various Asian American community health organizations in the Bay Area, such as the NICOS Chinese Health Coalition, the Asian American Wellness Center, Asian American Recovery Services, and the Chinatown Public Health Department, to name a few.

We also believe that students can be instruments of social change. In our AAS 575 course, we assign students to work on group projects which assess specific health issues or problems in the Asian American communities, and develop interventions and solutions to those health issues or problems. We bring in experts, prominent leaders, organizers, and activists in these fields to discuss relevant issues as guest lecturers. Presentations by these working professionals strengthen the content of our courses and increase the students' interest in the subject matter. We work hard to ensure that the course is always current, relevant, and engaging for our students, and accurately reflects the latest advancements in the field. We provide ample opportunities for students to work in the community through service learning projects. For example, in spring of 2007 we designated the AAS 575 course to prepare and train students for a service learning trip to New Orleans and Biloxi to assist the local Vietnamese community with its rebuilding efforts following Hurricane Katrina. A total of seven undergraduate and graduate students participated in the week-long service learning trip.

Over the years, this course has trained students who want to become doctors, nurses, physical therapists, and psycho-therapists, and other interested students on key issues impacting the Asian American communities. One student, Charlene-Jade Premyodhin, states how the course inspired her to further her understanding of Asian American mental health, and to remain in contact with her professor, which eventually led to a job for this student upon graduation:

> Even after completing her course, she [Le] continued to keep me motivated and excited about studying different avenues of Asian American health.... Her support enabled me to get involved with Asian American Recovery Services (AARS), specifically their youth program in San Francisco. What started as a volunteer position, developed into a job soon after I graduated from San Francisco State.

In addition to building and developing the Asian American Community Health course, a major component of our work has been to provide community service and education to the Asian American communities on a wide variety of health and social issues throughout the San Francisco Bay Area, the state, and the nation. We have partnered with local organizations, and also national organizations, to provide education and support. We have also linked students to these projects as assistants and volunteers. The following are examples of the outreach and education that we have done in our work with the various Asian American communities.

## OUTREACH TO ISOLATED AND FRAIL ASIAN AMERICAN ELDERS

There is a widespread assumption within and outside the Asian American community that Asian American families take care of their own – more specifically that they take care of their aging and sick family members. The literature on Asian ethnic families furthermore promotes this common assumption that there is a willingness of adult children to care for their aging parents and an expectation of the old to be cared for by them. Although the traditional Asian family is seen as strong with filial ties, there is lack of critical discussion of how adult children in a new country who are overworked, lack resources, and lack time and money can provide for the emotional, social, and financial needs of their aging parents. Seventy-five percent of nursing home residents are over the age of seventy-five and suffer from multiple chronic diseases and functional impairment (Kayser-Jones 1995). For most Americans, the nursing home is associated with an unpleasant, depressing environment. As a result, many who enter a nursing home enter reluctantly. Previous research has shown that racial and ethnic minorities have avoided use of long-term care facilities, like skilled nursing facilities, because of cost, stigma of family abandonment,

fear of social isolation, and low quality of care (Hikoyeda and Wallace 2002). For Asian immigrant elderly, three significant losses occur for those entering into a nursing home, including the loss of family, loss of culture, and loss of community (Maclean and Bonar 1986).

Research has shown that a nursing home resident's sense of isolation decreases with companionship. Moreover, visits by friends and family enhance a resident's self-esteem. As a result, the visits by students can be a learning experience for students, but they can also improve the quality of life for many monolingual Asian elderly residents. Simply talking to a resident in his or her language can benefit the elder's well being. Talking with elders has shown to provide stimulation. Other events that students have organized include bringing ethnic food, music, or videos.

In the Asian American Community Health Course, this visitation assignment has been an option for students in lieu of writing a research paper. Many students who take up this option often volunteer to opt out of writing a research paper, and many who take this option grow and learn tremendously. This optional assignment is not limited to bilingual Asian students. In our previous courses, both bilingual and non-bilingual Asian and non-Asian students have been a part of this weekly assignment.

The site of the intergenerational service learning experience has been a county-run nursing home in San Francisco, the Laguna Honda Hospital, which has a large proportion of monolingual Asian elderly immigrant residents. Paired up with a bilingual student, an elder interacts with students in pairs or teams. It is initially challenging having students feel comfortable stepping inside a nursing home. Oftentimes, this is the first time a student has been in a nursing home, and the first time they have witnessed frailty, disability, and dying. There are several things they do each week, including conducting oral histories, simply visiting, or letting elders reminisce. If residents are unable to speak, the students still provide companionship by showing ethnic videos or reading newspapers to the residents.

## RAISING AWARENESS ON SURVIVING CANCER IN ASIAN AMERICAN COMMUNITIES

Cancer is a major and growing problem for Asian Americans in the United States. In contrast to other racial/ethnic groups, cancer is the leading cause of death for Asian American females. It is the second leading cause of death for Asian American males (National Center of Health Statistics 2005). Incidence and mortality rates vary by cancer site, ethnicity, and gender. For example, compared to white American women, the incidence rate of cervical cancer is five times higher among Asian

American women from Vietnam. The lung cancer incidence rate is eighteen percent higher among Asian Americans from Southeast Asian than among White Americans (Mills et al. 2005). The mortality rate from cancers of all sites is growing faster among Asian Americans than in other racial/ethnic groups.

For Asian American communities, culturally appropriate cancer services and resources for emotional support and practical assistance are lacking. Often, only programs and services developed for other populations are available, and what is available varies widely by region and community. We know from personal experience that the resulting gap causes needless suffering, and we are committed to improving this situation by collaboratively developing culturally appropriate and unique support services and resources for Asian Americans with cancer, their families, and their caregivers.

Through a partnership with the Asian American and Pacific Islander National Cancer Survivors Network, we served as Project Directors for a 2001 statewide conference on Asian Americans and Pacific Islanders and breast and cervical cancer, with funding from the Susan B. Komen Foundation and the National Cancer Institute (1R13CA91858-01). This conference focused on issues and needs facing Asian American and Pacific Islander women with breast and cervical cancer. Best practices for support were highlighted, including the Chinatown Public Health Center program and the work of the University of California, San Francisco Comprehensive Cancer Center. Over two hundred persons enrolled, including national, state, and local community-based health and social service providers, state and local researchers, representatives from Asian American health, women, and legal advocacy organizations, cancer survivors and their family members, and pre-health, medical, health education, nursing, and social work students from the San Francisco State University and the University of California, San Francisco.

We co-chaired a 2005 Research/Practice Forum, sponsored by the SFSU Cesar Chavez Institute, "Women of Color: Surviving Breast and Cervical Cancer." The more than two hundred participants included survivors, SFSU faculty, community service providers, and students as well as University of California, San Francisco Comprehensive Cancer Center clinicians and students. Speakers presented the latest research on such issues as culturally competent care, social support, and the role of spirituality. Survivors spoke about their own experiences on these topics, and through roundtable discussions, implications for more effective programs, community action, and policy were addressed.

Currently, we are partnering with the Asian American Cancer Support Network (AACSN) to help identify some of the unmet emotional and practical needs of Asian American cancer survivors, and to develop multifaceted, culturally appropriate intervention services and education that will ultimately better meet the needs of cancer patients and survivors and their families.

## RAISING AWARENESS: ASIAN AMERICANS AND INCARCERATION

Like cancer, those who are at-risk and/or faced incarceration in the Asian American communities are heavily stigmatized and face a lack of support. According to a report by Angela Oh and Karen Umemoto (2005), the issues facing Asian American prisoners include the lack of community and family support. Asian American community organizations lack the capacity to provide services to those coming out of prison. In addition, there exists limited data on this growing population in the prison systems. With funding from the Rosenburg Foundation and the California Wellness Foundation, a daylong symposium was held on the issues impacting at-risk Asian American youth, and those formerly incarcerated. Loan Dao, a lecturer and doctoral candidate in Ethnic Studies at University of California, Berkeley, coordinated this event, "Challenging the Myth, Uniting Community," held in March 2008. This symposium focused on the growing numbers of Southeast Asian youth incarcerated, and also the issues of re-entry.

This daylong symposium brought together individuals and family members who have had to deal with the criminal justice and prison systems, social service providers and community organizers, and legal practitioners. In addition, over two hundred students, community-based organizations and service providers, and the community-at-large participated in this event. Speakers included Michael Kinoshita, San Francisco Public Defender's Office; Peter Kim, East Bay Asian Youth Center; William Poy Lee, author; Eddy Zheng, and Many Chout Uch.

Several workshops were conducted, including "Re-entry Challenges for Asian American Prisoners Coming out of Prison." This session focused on examining the issues around transitioning back into communities, including substance abuse treatment, housing, employment, addressing immigration status, reuniting with family and the Asian American community, forming support networks for reintegration, and avoiding re-incarceration. Another workshop focused on "The Role of Religious Leaders in Supporting Prisoners and Those Facing Re-entry" which examined the role of Asian American religious leaders in supporting prisoners and those facing re-entry. Another workshop discussed "The Criminalization of Sexually Exploited Youth." This workshop discussed the increasing numbers of Southeast Asian women and girls involved in sex work and the criminalization of these sex workers. Other workshops presented on topics such as incarcerated women, life on parole, supporting prisoners and their families, building a bridge between the community and policymakers, and sharing unique outreach efforts with at-risk youth.

## Conclusions

Over the years, we have worked to help fundraise, organize, and develop educational and community outreach activities that provide community and support around issues unrecognized and unvoiced in the Asian American community. These efforts have focused on health and social problems within Asian America. We have worked with those on the front lines to bring information to students and the community. In addition, we have partnered with those on the front lines to provide outreach and support to the unique health and social problems facing Asian Americans.

## REFERENCES

Hikoyeda, Nancy, and Steven Wallace. "Do Ethnic-Specific Long Term Care Facilities Improve Resident Quality of Life? Findings from the Japanese American Community." *Social Work Practice with the Asian American Elderly*. Ed. Namkee Choi. New York: Haworth Press, 2002.

Kayser-Jones, Jeanie. "Decision Making in the Treatment of Acute Illness in Nursing Homes." *Medical Anthropology Quarterly* 9 (1995): 236-256.

Maclean, Michael, and Rita Bonar. "Ethnic Elderly People in Long Term Care Facilities of the Dominant Culture: Implications for Social Work Practice and Education." *International Social Work* 2 (1986): 227-236.

Mills, Paul, Richard C. Yang, and David Riordan. Cancer Incidence in the Hmong in California, 1988-2000. *Cancer* 104.12 (2005): S2969-S2974.

National Center for Health Statistics. *Health, United States, 2005*. Hyattsville, MD: National Center for Health Statistics. 2005.

Oh, Angela, and Karen Umemoto. *Asian Americans and Pacific Islanders: From Incarceration to Reentry*. San Francisco: Asian American/Pacific Islanders in Philanthropy, 2005.

# To Serve the Community:

## The Fourth Decade of Community Service Learning at Asian American Studies, San Francisco State University

*Russell Jeung*

*I was anxious, but excited about the important meeting set up for us. My group and I were nervous about how to approach the passing of a city resolution and what we would say to persuade the councilwoman to pass it. When asked to attend the meeting, I was hesitant at first, but with much thought, I agreed in hopes that I could be part of a resolution that would make a change. I felt as if it was my calling to attend.*

*Before taking this course, I didn't know the situation currently happening in Burma. I was unaware of the fact that the country has been in war for over fifty years, and that many were forced from their homes and ended up in refugee camps located in Thailand.*

*When I found out that they were in refugee camps, I was reminded of my parents and grandparents. Before arriving to the United States, my family was forced out of their homes and stayed in the refugee camps located in Chiang Rai, Thailand. Because of the experience my parents went through, I felt a sense of connection that made me eager to participate in lobbying for Burma.*

- Susan Saechao, SFSU student

This past semester, Susan Saechao and eight of her classmates from the course, "Asian Americans and Public Policy," traveled from San Francisco State University to Oakland City Hall. They went to lobby for a city resolution to support human rights in Burma and to denounce foreign, corporate exploitation of this poor nation. This paper describes their efforts and other class projects in Asian American Studies (AAS) at San Francisco State University. Beyond providing hands-on experiences and critical reflection, our pedagogy especially aims to connect students with Asian communities, both locally and transnationally. As Saechao exemplified, building solidarity with other Asian Americans can lead to student activism.

While my course focuses on public policy, AAS courses ranging from literature and history to health and psychology also provide students with community service learning. Community service learning (CSL), as defined currently by SFSU, is "the combination of academic study with community service so that each is enhanced by the other."[1] Students who enroll in CSL courses can volunteer at organizations officially registered with the school. At the completion of their service learning, their hours are recorded on their official transcripts.

This institutionalization of CSL is a direct result of the initial efforts of Third World students to "establish a permanent link between the college and community agency personnel."[2] While the Nine Unit Block program ended, "diversity" and "equity and social justice" are now "bedrock values" and the first goals of San Francisco State University's strategic plan.[3] Within Asian American Studies, they have become institutionalized in that they are normative values of faculty and students majoring in AAS, and a primary element of our pedagogical practice.

To illustrate how CSL is integral to AAS values and practice, this paper highlights case studies of service learning. Spearheaded more by the initiative of the faculty and students than the university's programmatic efforts, they illustrate three key elements of the successful use of service learning in AAS. First, tenure-track AAS faculty, who have more job stability, are able to develop sustained relationships with community agencies that facilitate partnerships. Second, student-initiated or student-chosen projects encourage greater ownership over service learning and instill a greater ethic of community responsibility than required community service. Third, community-based learning exposes students to a range of experiences that they would not otherwise receive in the classroom. Consequently, they can better apply theoretical concepts, develop concrete skills, and establish their own visions for themselves and their communities.

## LOBBYING IN THE POLITICAL PROCESS THROUGH ETHNIC STUDIES 665: "ASIAN AMERICANS AND PUBLIC POLICY"

Sitting around a huge conference table with the council-woman at the head, the students had prepared most of the semester for their lobbying effort. The entire class of fifty had written letters to the councilmember, noting that oil companies profited both from the cheap natural resources of Burma and from the high gas prices exacted from the students. They expressed their outrage over Burma's sex trafficking, forced labor, and internal displacement of tribal communities. Most of all, they came to support two classmates who had migrated from Burma, but still had family suffering there.

Armed with facts about the abuses in the country, a seven-point resolution for the City of Oakland, and even a press release ready to go, the students were both anxious and excited, as Saechao recalled. Because of my ties with refugee organizations and faith-based communities, other Burmese Americans, representing four community groups, joined our coalition.[4]

The councilwoman welcomed us to City Hall and expressed how impressed she was with our letters. I had worked as a council aide to this district in the past, and personally knew this legislator. I was therefore hopeful that she would be an ally to the students' efforts. Unfortunately, though, she could not support our resolution because she felt the city should not become involved with foreign affairs.[5] I felt blood rushing to my face, angered that I troubled the students and the community members to take the time to come here, only to be so quickly rejected out of hand. We tried to reframe the issue, and discussed the plight of Burmese refugees now coming to Oakland, with their numbers expecting to double in the next year. The councilwoman referred most of our concerns to the county level, and offered to assist in contacting other officials.

While this class project did not turn out as successfully as hoped, it did galvanize the students around a hands-on experience and connected them to a community and issues that they would not have otherwise been aware of. Steven Tsuboi, an Asian American Studies major, explained:

> Most of the time in the classroom is spent passively learning through lectures and presentations. Even when students are presented with an opportunity to actively participate, their involvement is relatively limited. When it was announced in class that we would be involved in lobbying for Burma, I felt that this project would allow me to apply what I have learned so far and gain hands-on experience.
>
> Aside from learning about the processes involved in dealing with public policy, I felt strongly about human

rights violations in Burma. What intrigued me most was a statement from a video we watched saying that "while Burma currently meets and exceeds all the criteria for United Nations intervention, they have yet to have received any support."

Like Saechao, Tsuboi developed a strong empathy for the Burmese after I showed a documentary and brought a guest speaker from the Burmese American Democratic Alliance. He further wrote:

> After hearing this statement I was appalled that they were not receiving aid and for a moment I understood how alone and abandoned they must feel. That is when I knew I had to participate in this project.

Consequently, he elected to help with the media working group. Together, they determined the best way to frame the issue was to relate how Burmese American students at SFSU are affected by military junta's rule.

Along with learning about current issues, this class aimed to provide students with actual public policy skills to effect social change. In working groups, they engaged in a variety of aspects of policy development. Kirsten Mendoza recounted the steps in the process:

> Because it was our first time lobbying, it was an entirely new learning experience. I learned how to state the root of an issue, organize my information, exploit that information to catch the audience's attention, and build alliances with other organizations.

The students working to build coalitions with other groups even developed rap sheets to help them make phone contacts.

Why would San Francisco State University students, in a class focusing on policy issues facing Asians in the United States, be expected to learn about Burma? Furthermore, why should they care? Andy Liang shared what he drew from this class project:

> Through this process, I discovered more about myself and my identity as an Asian American. To be specific, I learned to be more empathetic to other Asian people in undeveloped countries. They share the same government oppression as Asians in the United States have throughout centuries.
>
> I realized that the displacement of Burmese people through the use of force by the government can be compared to recent American immigration policies which deal with deportation and reunification difficulties. Furthermore, I now feel that it is my responsibility to help others around the world who are disproportionately affected by such policies.

Students realized that, as Americans, they have the responsibility to address both domestic issues and American foreign policy concerns. With more at stake with Pacific Rim affairs than most Americans, Asian Americans need to have a voice in foreign relations.

Ultimately, this project aimed to broaden the students' perspectives and possibilities about their role in the community. Like Liang, Mendoza explained that this lobbying opportunity helped her reconsider her vocational choices:

> Coming from a corporate perspective of working capital, volunteering for the lobbying assignment made me a better person. My corporate managers told me I would be successful and that money is everything. After this assignment, I realized that life does not revolve around finances, and I could exert my efforts to help others that cannot help themselves. I had found my identity again....

While this class lobbying project may have made the students more cynical about the political process, perhaps it inspired others to see that they can impact policy. As indicated in this account, my relations in the city government, along with the refugee and faith communities, provided access for students to network and lobby. This advocacy around refugee issues by SFSU AAS students will most likely continue, as I maintain a strong commitment to these communities.[6] Faculty relationships in the Asian American community facilitate service learning, but students also bring their initiative and interests to these projects

### LEARNERS BECOMING TEACHERS THROUGH THE PIN@Y EDUCATIONAL PARTNERSHIP: AAS 685, "PROJECTS IN THE TEACHING OF ASIAN AMERICAN STUDIES"

In Asian American Studies 685, students are teachers in their communities through the Pin@y Educational Partnership (PEP). In 2001, Professor Allyson Tintiangco-Cubales brought a group of eleven SFSU students to Balboa High School in San Francisco, a public high school with a large low-income, Filipino American population. She recalled:

> When I first came to SFSU, I wanted to do something that was *political*. I wanted to develop something that would allow students to challenge their notions of what is political by encouraging them to find their own agency and self-determination. The creation of PEP, a program that not only encourages people to become teachers, but also allows for a space to learn about what type of teachers they hope to become, is inherently political.

Since its first class of twenty-five high school students, PEP has grown to become an award-winning, innovative curricular project. Now in four schools, PEP has thirty-five teachers/coordinators and over 125 students from elementary school age to high school. Tintiangco-Cubales has published a PEP sourcebook, but perhaps what is more remarkable is the tight community of learners/teachers that has emerged over the past seven years. SFSU students have taken ownership of the project, and now direct the program themselves.

Jonell Molina, a SFSU student and current PEP coordinator for the Balboa High School site, explains that the mission of the program is to make teachers of all the students. All students, regardless of their age, have concrete experiences, knowledge and creativity which they can share with their classmates. Because Filipino American Studies is absent from the students' curriculum, PEP makes education relevant by starting from the students' own stories. Molina relates:

> [PEP] has created a space for today's Filipina/o generation like me to be exposed to the richness and beauty of one's culture and identity. Students in the program have become more conscious of how powerful culturally relevant curriculum, based in ethnic studies, can really bring a smile to their face as they learn.
>
> Students have seized the opportunities through their participation in the classroom projects and to emerge as leaders. They start to take responsibility for their actions and thoughts in their own lives as youths of color.

The *PEP Sourcebook* offers thirty lesson plans that illustrate the philosophy of the project. Each lesson plan focuses on a key topic, main concepts, and learning goals that address the mind, body, and soul. These topics include Filipino colonial history, gender relations, and immigration reform. More interesting, though, are the culturally appropriate methods employed by the teachers.

Classes start with a "cultural energizer," "an icebreaker to get the students' minds, bodies, and souls working. Music and dance can help facilitate this type of activity," according to Tintiangco-Cubales. Games, skits, and visual images help students to start relating to the topic of the day. For example, in the lesson plan on gender, an entertaining talk show opens the lesson with the guest being a *Lapu-Lapu* (a masculine chieftain) and a *Babyalan* (a feminine shaman to the spirits). Students then explore why the chief is male and the shaman is female, and other problems related to gender identity.

The students then learn through "community collaboration and cultural production." For the lesson on gender, students share memorable events that contributed to how they felt about being male or female. They plot these events along a "gender lifeline," and connect to each others' experiences. To conclude a lesson, students dialogue about the questions/problem posed at the start, and assess what can be done to address the problem.

Angelica Posadas grew up in the Excelsior district and attended PEP classes at Balboa High School. She is an AAS major and plans to teach Asian American Studies in the future. She recalls:

> If it weren't for PEP, I would have never learned about my people's history, let alone my own family's history. To be given the opportunity to engage in a class where my peers and I could learn about our heritage through literature, poetry, performance, and other interactive forms pushed me to want to give the same opportunity to others.

Likewise, Terry Valen of the Filipino Community Center shares how the community benefits from the service of PEP students:

> The collaboration between the PEP Program and its community home at the Filipino Community Center (FCC) has enhanced the sense of local community empowerment for the Filipino Excelsior community. Over the 4+ years that I have been at the FCC, I have witnessed how PEP Program teachers and students continually enrich the increasingly active and organized Filipino community of San Francisco.

Like the Burma lobbying project, PEP developed from the vision and community relationships of the faculty. The students, though, exerted their own leadership in PEP, and have developed both professional and civic skills in the process. Rather than doing community service as a requirement or for credit, PEP students participate on their own initiative in order to empower their community. This philosophy of learning from and giving back to the community is also reflected in the AAS department's tours and research.

## REBUILDING OUR COMMUNITIES: AAS 575, "ASIAN AMERICAN COMMUNITY HEALTH ISSUES"

Given options of where and how they serve the community, students are much more likely to develop a sense of civic responsibility. Some of these service learning opportunities take students out of their normal context and expose them to experiences, relationships, and perspectives that are new. Having access to and grappling with these experiences often lead to rich, self-discovery and stronger, racial analysis. In the summer of 2007, Mai-Nhung Le brought seven students on another tour, this one to a site where students learned about contemporary racial inequities in the United States.

Two years after Hurricane Katrina, the Vietnamese American communities in Louisiana and Mississippi continue to suffer from this natural and social disaster. The Gulf State region is home to 60,000 Asian Americans, the majority of whom are Vietnamese Americans. Because of language barriers between the disaster relief staff and those with limited English proficiency, this community did not receive accurate information ensuring their timely and safe evacuation. Consequently, many Vietnamese Americans remained stranded and could not secure government help during the disaster, or relief support following the disaster.

To learn about this situation and engage in community-based research, Le and her students traveled to New Orleans, Louisiana and Biloxi, Mississippi. Under the direction of the National Alliance of Vietnamese American Service Agencies (NAVASA), they assisted local parishes and an agency, Boat People SOS for one week. Le reports, "The students were aware politically of racism, but this trip showed them concretely how race and cultural insensitivity severely impact our communities."

On the first three days, the students conducted a survey of the businesses along the Chef Highway in New Orleans, a predominantly Vietnamese American commercial district. Gathering information on the business conditions and whether merchants had received loans or compensation from insurance companies, the students got first-hand accounts of the community's frustrations. They compiled the survey data into a database, which NAVASA will use for policy reports and funding proposals.

This type of community-based participatory research aims to develop knowledge useful for the community. Because of its participatory nature, it also helps the community to voice its own concerns and organize around self-articulated issues. Having established trust while conducting the survey, SFSU students later helped recruit the merchants to a town hall meeting to address local crime. They succeeded in getting over twenty-five business persons out on a stormy night to tackle this issue. AAS student Viet-Thi Ta notes:

> This was definitely the trip of a lifetime. Not only did I absorb and learn a massive amount about the underrepresented communities' experiences post Katrina, but I was also humbled and educated by my peers and Professor Le as well. They taught me what mobilizing under the rain meant, what putting our heads together and listening to each other can resolve, and what dedication and self-determination can impact the people around us.

The SFSU group then drove an hour and a half east

to Biloxi, Mississippi, where they stayed a local Catholic parish. Again working with a local organization, they served a Vietnamese American neighborhood by taking an inventory of the physical conditions of homes. They also interviewed residents for a video documentary.

Locals told the students how casinos have redeveloped the area, ruining local industries such as shrimping that once provided for the livelihood of the community. Following Hurricane Katrina, tourist areas like the French Quarter have quickly been rebuilt, but more isolated areas like this one remain devastated. SFSU student Paul Matsushima learned:

> A really strange occurrence is happening as we speak. In Biloxi, because a lot of houses were washed away, the owners decided it was not worth rebuilding, so they moved away and sold their property, mainly to casinos. So people are moving out, casinos are moving in. Some predict that the Gulf Coast region is going to be the next Las Vegas.

One elderly woman shared that she had home insurance, but not flood insurance, so she could not receive compensation for her lost homes. Having relied on our homes for rental income, she has no health insurance and complained, "It's worse than being a refugee from Vietnam, because I was younger then and could work. Now I'm in my retirement years and have little to live on."

Mark Tran, an AAS graduate student, was so moved by the experience that he obtained a fellowship to intern another year in the rebuilding of the community. Ethnic Studies MA student Holly Nigoriza shares what she gained from the experience:

> I have unfortunately become pessimistic about the government, but not in the faith of the community. By "community," I am speaking of the Vietnamese community hit by Katrina in particular, and the working class folks devastated by Katrina in general. Post-Katrina, it seems that everyone did have to fend for themselves...in terms of water, food, clothing.
>
> But, this "fending" – due in large part to the lack of government support – brought out the beauty in the humanity of the people. I learned of families reciting their final prayers together, who – despite the odds – came out alive post-Katrina, and supported other families despite the fear that "sharing" meant that their own family may have nothing for days. There is a sense of resilience about the people and the areas that we visited.

## Conclusion

These classes, in which CSL is integral, are just a small sample of how Asian American Studies has evolved over the past decades. The institutionalization of CSL

within AAS is not in the form of required assignments or student credit hours. Rather, the ethic of working with the community to effect social change is a value upheld by the current faculty, and expected of new faculty. This ethic is integral to our department subculture, and plays out in our hiring, tenure process, and curriculum.

As the AAS Department has increased and diversified its faculty in the past two decades, applicants are asked about their involvement in local Asian American communities. As described, these relationships with non-profits and organizations facilitate student access to CSL opportunities. Later, in their tenure review process, Asian American Studies faculty give accounts of how their research, teaching, and community service relate to local Asian American communities. In their curriculum, faculty also provide ample opportunities for students to engage in local Asian American events, and highlight community activists as guest speakers. These operating practices ensure that the responsibility of community is communicated to students.

Students remain the department conscience, just as they were forty years ago. While SFSU students overall increasingly come from outside the Bay Area, AAS students remain primarily local. They remained tied to nearby ethnic communities, and can see the relationship between AAS courses, their own lived experiences, and their community's social problems. Consequently, they demand not only courses that are relevant, but also opportunities to engage in pertinent community issues. Given opportunities and options to do CSL, they integrate academic learning with social responsibility.

Malcolm Collier and Dan Gonzales, in this volume (p. 15), wrote of their goals for the Third World strike in 1968:

> We were seeking a change in the character and focus of the college, of academia in general. We wanted a connection between college and communities, believing, hoping, that such connections would be to the long-term benefit of the communities and, secondarily, the college. We wanted the college to serve the communities, not to remove or "rescue" students from their communities.

While far from being fully realized, these goals have been officially adopted by SFSU and they make up the heart of the AAS departmental subculture. With such a rich legacy, we hope to instill the same spirit within the next generation, to serve the community.

### NOTES

1. <http://www.sfsu.edu/~icce/programs/csl_program. html>, accessed 7 Aug. 2008.

2. See Malcolm Collier and Irene Dea Collier, "The Nine Unit Block and Other Early Community Programs," in this anthology.

3. <http://www.sfsu.edu/strategicplan/strategic.html>, accessed 7 Aug. 2008.

4. Organizations represented included Asian Community Mental Health Services, Refugee Transitions, the Oakland Burmese Baptist Church, and the Oakland Karen Baptist congregation.

5. San Francisco, Berkeley, and San Jose had already passed resolutions supporting human rights in Burma, so the students and I thought Oakland would also be open to such a resolution.

6. Besides going to Taiwan on a Fulbright Scholars fellowship in fall 2008 to work on my area of expertise, Asian Religious Studies, I took a tour of unofficial Burmese refugee camps in Thailand on that same trip.

# CONTRIBUTIONS

nomads 木蘭 Legacy?

Mixed DUAL CITIZENSHIP

Diversity Religion

# PREGO

## Jeffery Paul Chan and Scilla Finetti

*Russell Leong, editor of* Amerasia Journal, *asked me to write about the discussion Chinese American literature has generated in the American Studies programs in Italy. I asked my friend and translator, Scilla Finetti, as well as scholars and students I have met over many visits to Italy, to forward their thoughts. Scilla sent the following essay, which was paired with my own for publication in* Amerasia Journal (2008). *Our exchange is reprinted here with some corrections and with the permission of* Amerasia Journal.

– J. Chan

[*Amerasia* 34.7 (2008): 51-53]

### NOMADISM IS OUR DESTINY: TRANSLATING CHINESE AMERICA

*Scilla Finetti*

When I first read Jeff Chan's short story "The Chinese in Haifa," I felt I had found what I was looking for. I was in the throes of giving shape to the subject of my graduation thesis. Being a Comparative Studies student and studying Chinese, I became very interested in the history and experience of Chinese immigrants and in their literature. I am sure that every ethnic group has its own specific ways of adapting to its new post-emigration situation and I was curious to understand how the Chinese had used their ancestors' culture and their former habits in a new reality. *MELUS* gave me very useful suggestions for my research as well as an idea of the complexity of this literature and I soon discovered that Chinese American authors were quite aware that the search for roots could hide subtle ambiguities.

Of course, I had already read *The Woman Warrior* by Maxine Hong Kingston. Later on, I read several other works by women writers such as Amy Tan, Gish Jen, Sky Lee, and Fae Ng etc. My friend Claudia Valeria Letizia was translating this autobiographical novel for the Italian publisher e/o. She told me how impressed she was by the ancient Chinese myths and legends that Kingston used to represent the psychological formation of the protagonist and at the author's ability to intertwine these myths with the development of her personality. However, though the book fascinated me with its way of visiting and revisiting ancient China's traditions, and though I was very very interested in the experience of women and the experience described by Kingston was very thought-provoking, I was looking for something else. And I found it in Jeff Chan's "The Chinese in Haifa." Chan does not describe the difficulties, injustices, and abuses suffered by Chinese immigrants, nor does he go into serpentine feelings of discontent. He just recounts a day in the life of Bill Wong, a young man, neither Chinese nor American, in a moment of passage. Through this account, you are presented with the problems of the new generation and with the challenges they have to face. Having left behind Chinese traditions and their imposing habits, they have to build new points of reference. This story reveals the complexity of the search for identity, for new paths to follow and expresses, in a neat and bare style, not only the feelings of bewilderment but also the awareness of the opportunities the new situation of freedom allows. And all is implicit, nothing is explained in "The Chinese in Haifa": Chan, with the ability of a good photographer, captures the personality and situation of his protagonist in precise pictures (the dream, the empty house, the fishing, the dinner).

I translated Chan's short story for the magazine *Linea d'Ombra* and I was soon contacted by Mario Maffi, professor of American Literature at the University of Milan, who was editing the anthology of Chinese American Literature *Voci dal silenzio* (*Voices from Silence*) for the publisher Feltrinelli. Maffi proposed including "The Chinese in Haifa" in this anthology.

I later went on to discover Chinese American poetry from Angel Island in the book *Island* and from Marlon K. Hom's *Songs of Gold Mountain*. Translating from the Chinese text was a real and intriguing challenge to me. *ACOMA, Rivista Internazionale di Studi Nordamericani (North American Studies' International Review)*, of the University of Rome's English Department, published extracts from *Island* in a special issue dedicated to emigration. Extracts from *Songs of Gold Mountain* came out in *Linea d'Ombra*. For the same magazine, I also translated a few poems by Nellie Wong, a very interesting poet whose work I liked very much. When Empiria decided to publish a collection of short stories by women writers from various countries, I translated Wong's "The Death of Long Steam Lady."

At the time, Chinese American authors were a novelty in Italy: Italian readers were more familiar with African American authors and their struggles. Since then the history of Chinese emigration to the United States has been analyzed much more. Though the larger Italian audience did not pay much attention, the complexity of the Chinese American voices claimed the interest of more demanding readers.

The approach to issues about emigration and the search for identity of Chinese American writers and poets such as Jeff Chan, Frank Chin, Shawn Wong, Fae Ng, Russell Leong, David Wong Louie, Marilyn Chin, and Nellie Wong, among others, presents complex and subtle points of view and ranges quite widely. These authors' ways of relating to their Chinese roots are varied and often intriguing. I feel in them the full force of the contemporary individual's awareness, both melancholy and proud. The search for roots reveals how fragile these roots can be, how, at the same time, they are undergoing a process of continuous evolution where it is difficult to distinguish the fake from the real.

Experimenting with the new can be very hard, but it is the only way to live in our world. Nomadism, as Rosa Braidotti, a feminist philosopher, defines the ability to travel emotionally through different cultures and experiences, is today not only our psychological condition, but a value in itself and, all things considered, our destiny.

[*Amerasia Journal* 34.2 (2008): 37-49]

L'AMA *Non Ci Ama,*
LOST & FOUND IN TRANSLATION

*Jeffery Paul Chan*

[*Slide: We're in Rome. That's Scilla sipping Orzo in Trastevere, just down the hill from her flat in Monteverde Vecchio.*]

I accepted an invitation from Scilla Finetti (see essay above) to visit Rome more than ten years ago. And what was for both of us a mutual interest in Chinese American literature became a great deal more. Her generosity, introducing me to both her friends and family, has forged a lifetime's friendship and provided both of us with experiences and insights unique and rather unlikely as I come to consider what it is to have a close reader translating your life.

My earliest American memories are of North Beach Chinatown, Catholic daycare, catechism at St. Peter and Paul, of Latin mass, days of abstinence, of rosaries, solariums, a Chinatown crèche that stuck around till Chinese New Year with baby Jesus looking vaguely like my just-born cousin Phyllis, the layering aromas of roasting coffee, tomato sauce melding over a low flame, rank cheese, and the smell of *salumi* and sawdust in Guido's deli on the corner where I bought penny candy on my way home from Jean Parker, still under an awning that sheltered the boys' yard from the construction dust of the Broadway Tunnel. So it was that I was imbued with a Catholic sensibility until age seven, the Jesuit requirement, and am forever bound. So my connections to Italy are emotionally starched, layered in pasta. Chow fun in a paper carton after school, the smell of cornmeal and the bricks of lasagna served in my Catholic daycare are comfort foods for my generation of North Beach/Chinatown kids growing up in the 1940s just a little north of Portsmouth Square to the North Beach playground. I date the end of my generation to the end of Exclusion and the first surge of refugees escaping the newly unified PRC. After 1950, a new immigrant wave would erase my generation's hold on an English-speaking Chinatown. It is, it has always been, and will always be, this matter of food and language, fighting for the expression of my own sensibilities, and now a trip to Rome to see how they might translate. I'd never been. *Perche no.*

If the phrase, "to be," resonates, read on. Inventing and re-inventing the Chinese American is the indisputable focus of Chinese American writing, qua literature. And if the arranged marriage of Maxine and Frank is not evidence enough, imagine an opera, libretto by the first-born, a daughter, of course, named Amy. Imitation invites acceptance, equals assimilation, and becomes a hallmark of success. But the quick and dirty reply remains: the stereotypes of acceptable behavior are as attractive as they are unimaginative. Being unique was the key to self-acceptance. But with self-acceptance, the tables turn. And if I finally understand, emotionally speaking, the paradox of being unique paradoxically requires shared recital of history, language, and culture, sense of community, *weltanschaung* that an audience bespeaks, I got it. But the temptation to be the only game in Chinatown is irresistible. So, with a new Fodor's to accompany a used Hugo's

*Italian in Three Months* I rescued from the used bin of the old Compass Books in North Beach, *a Roma*. I would be the first Chinaman to discover Italy.

Fat chance. James Chan Leong, painter, known most famously in San Francisco Chinatown for his Ping Yuen murals, lived in Rome in the fifties and sixties, had worked at Cinecitta, had seen Frederico, Sophia, and Marcello having lunch. Fae Myenne Ng (*Bone*) had spent a warm summer at the American Studies Center in Rome. More recently, Shawn Wong (*Home Base, American Knees*), had completed an envious residency at the Rockefeller centre in Bellagio on Lake Como. I was way too late to be the first, and no way an "only." Resigned to "better than never," I went with my memories of North Beach and the irresistible temptation to be odd, a stranger in a strange land.

Since my first visit, with multiple and ever evolving agendas, trying not to trip over the other ABCs, Scilla and friends have made it possible for me to learn a bit about Italy, but more, to confirm what I already know. Everywhere, anywhere in the world, somebody always introduces himself or herself, wanting to share: "I once met this Chinese guy from California." In the most exotic palaces, the Etruscan galleries, at the Vatican, did I know Shawn, Fae, Frank, the painter Jim Leong? I do. "Small world."

*[Slide: A bust of Marco Polo behind a plant, Venice.]*

Given that I am the perennial tourist (even in California) with language skills a notch above Pavlov's dog, I try to follow whenever I hear or read "*cinesi*," however eclectic the source. In Venice, I bought a used children's biography in Italian of Marco Polo, who I learn was a local from the Venetian hood, the Ca D'oro. So encouraged, I nearly tripped over his eponymous bust, Polo's likeness as an insane clown on the second floor of Museo Correo while reading the takeout menu of the Marco Polo Chinese restaurant I picked up on the street while searching for the gents. The first joke I expected to exchange with a newly met on the issue of Chineseness in Italy revolves around pasta and Marco Polo who, as a matter of fact, did not import Chinese noodles to Italy. Pasta – there's a museum devoted to pasta in Rome – comes from the Middle East, and illustrations of eighteenth century Napolitanos eating noodles with their fingers – no chopsticks – are unrelated to the fifteenth century science fiction of mad Marco, the Venetian. It was like the dog joke. Wealthy neighborhoods in Rome were littered with pet poop as opposed to the Chinese quarter [Esquilino] where the sidewalks were relatively poop-free. "*Perche no*? *Mangialo*!" I'd been here before. Marco Polo jokes, no; dog eating, *si*.

*[Slide: That's me in the turtleneck wearing the berretta.]*

During one extended stay in Italy, I lived alone in a small village, cobblestone streets, a view of monastery perched on a hill that gleamed at sunrise like a birthstone, freezing in my cell-like studio built into the wall that girdled the town. I was up at dawn writing, feeding a wood stove. By noon, forced to re-supply, I would shop, exchange monosyllabic courtesies – almost impossible in a romance language – and repeat phrases cobbled from the vocabulary in my phrase book. "*Sono di California. Fabricante con pezzi cinese.*" California drew smiles; but "manufactured with Chinese "parts" did not work. I was trying to explain something that didn't require explanation. That's the problem with phrase books: you might be able to express an idea, but you will not be able to understand a reply that requires more than yes, no, or a hand signal indicating direction. It was as if I had misunderstood an earlier text from Wong Sam, shopping for pants.

*[Slide: The tall woman with her back turned is Fae Ng, with her Italian translator, Centro Studi Americani.]*

The illusion of being alone was impossible to maintain. Back in Rome, I was invited to participate on a panel to introduce the Italian translation of Fae Ng's *Bone*, and found myself in the company of a professor of American Studies from Naples, and there's Fae. My five minutes of introduction – an inside Cantonese/English pun I described as a "yo' mama" joke ("*Ngo sic negaw mah.*" *Bone*, 8) for which Fae landed a sharp elbow in my side – was followed by an Italian professor's examination of the several themes of cultural and intergenerational conflict that read for an hour in front of 200 increasingly restive scholars in the library of Centro Studi Americani. The Question and Answer segment broke out into a sharp dispute when the Italian translator let slip her notion that dialect/idiomatic expressions might be overlooked in the translation process, provoking a witty but passionate argument (over exactly what I will never know) that included the importance of knowing whose "mama" and why. At least I think that was the gist of the debate.

That should have been a warning to stop translating myself. At yet another literary gathering, I was about to launch into a tedious explanation regarding the first phrase of a tentative title I'd invented for a work-in-progress, "Hey Mambo, Scherzo Italiano," when the entire audience broke out in song. It was the highlight of the evening. I finally got the hint. I stopped trying to explain myself and began listening.

*[Slide: SPQR engraved manhole cover, Esquilino, Rome.]*

My recent stays in the eternal city, living in Esquilino, Rome's version of the eternal Chinatown, have been more revealing. The Esquilino is euphemistically described as "international," never mind the presence of Santa Maria Maggiore, one of the four patriarchal basilicas of Rome crowning the district, or Piazza Vittorio, a landmark square given over to Bangladeshi food shops, telephone call centers, and Chinese supermarkets with adjoining clothing shops and shoe stores all done in marble slab, stainless steel, and plate glass. The *immigranti* can find the latest soap opera episodes, last night's news from home, fresh tofu, bean sprouts, and the ubiquitous internet cafés, several in Chinese, one in Korean across the street from the Korean deli. Hard by Termini, Rome's central railroad station, the neighborhood that traditionally guards the eastern wall houses an uneasy mélange of East Asian and South Asian communities that tolerate one another. Romans point delightedly at a Chinese espresso bar, object to the noise generated by the crowds of men waiting outside the phone shops to call home in the middle of the night. For Rome's municipal government (SPQR, Senatus Populusque Romanus) loves the economic enterprise but despairs the loss of language as well as the traditional wedding shops that once characterized the neighborhood, not to mention the trash left on the sidewalks that nonna swept regularly before selling the family apartment when the real estate market caught fire.

[*Slide: Riccardo Duranti roasting artichokes in a grapevine fire pit in Genzano, May Day.*]

In translation, I'm finally beginning to get it. With Scilla connecting the dots, I'm introduced to the American Studies Department at the University of Rome, La Sapienza (the campus that most recently protested successfully against the Pope's presence – imagine UC Berkeley, the sixties) and Riccardo Duranti, professor of American Studies, a poet and translator who inspired his students to work on Chinese American literature and is thus responsible, in an indirect way, for my presence in Rome. The range of this guy is phenomenal: Raymond Carver, Philip Dick, Richard Brautigan. In an apocryphal encounter translating the early work of Gail Tsukiyama while on sabbatical at San Francisco State's Poetry Center, he opened a door to the examination of Asian American, then Chinese American writing for his Italian students and colleagues who in turn became the translators/critics I have had the pleasure of meeting, people who have translated the Chinese American canon and become the books they have translated like characters out of *Fahrenheit 451*. That they have the skill sets, much less the purpose to do so, humbles me. But it also makes me a bit wary. It is one thing for me to closet myself in fiction, quite another for someone to interpret what I may have meant into a different language. I'm not quite sure how to explain this feeling of unease. At times, I think my translator, Scilla

Finetti, knows me better than I know myself. When we are together, I am sure of it.

[*Slide: Anna and Donatella sharing a glass.*]

Recently, Anna Scannovini, the current editor of *Acoma, Rivista Internazionale di Studi NordAmericani* introduced me to Donatella Izzo from the University of Naples, Oriental Studies. Professor Izzo's critical anthology of *Suzie Wong Non Abita Piu* leads with an essay by her prize graduate student, Manuela Vastolo, on "The Real and the Fake" *autobiografia, fiction e rappresentativita*. The titles alone, assure me of the currency Italian academics proudly foster in their students. Professor Izzo was also kind enough to ask her students at the University of Naples to respond to my queries about their involvement with Chinese American writing. Their responses, in English, are revealing.

First, and probably most telling, students who have taken up Chinese American literature begin and return to the study of Chinese literature. Their own progress is measured by language examinations. Their remarks encompass all of the slips and faults we Chinese Americans debate by simply viewing all three, America, China, Chinese America, as essentially integral as well as distinct. This, of course, requires literacy in both English and Chinese. That is why I feel like a tourist. Their remarks on the broader implications of Chinese American literature strike familiar chords in Italian society, the *fin d'siecle* issues of race and gender. American minority lit resonates with the rising expectations of similarly restricted groups in post World War II Europe, no less resounding as the European Union's material prosperity trickles south, and no more so than in Italy.

In the Italian model that one student, Paola Maddaluno, describes in her e-mail, she recognizes Chinese American literature as a part of American literature and alludes to issues of immigration, assimilation, and ethnic prejudice in Italian society. She supports her responses with examples from the press commenting on the immigrant wave with which Italy contends. The obvious stereotypes abound. Filipinos, Sri Lankans, South Asians in general, send money home. They also show a willingness to speak Italian. The African immigrant is generally disparaged as their numbers grow. The Chinese are notoriously wary, sharing no common language, the older generation known for their general hostility and resistance to anything Italian, right down to the food, which they avoid whenever possible.

From Paola Maddaluno:

When I think about the US literary production . . . Asian American literature is just a container in which I will group, just to simplify, the geographical areas of the subject that deals with the text. Meaning, I will put under European American Literature a writer of European descent that writes about the American experiences of his people in the United States. Meanwhile, I consider Louis Chu an Asian American writer of Chinese descent that writes about the American experiences of Chinese and Chinese Americans. So [I] can consider Asian American literature a genre to qualify it from a wider perspective and to differentiate it between the other American literatures . . . a sort of DNA. I like to think of the unique characterization of the American literature in these terms, [just] as a human being is considered unique through DNA, the same is true for American literature . . . unique by its minoritarian literary productions.

From another student, Maria Pina Gargiulo:

The study of Asian American literature is very productive in terms of discussions about power relationships. Observing how some mechanisms of oppression and exclusion reproduce themselves invariably in a community opposed to the same mechanisms working against it can help to understand how hierarchies form.

Along with the pleasure of reading beautiful texts, studying the Chinese American experience is of great importance to Italian students and Chinese Italian communities which are already a relevant presence in Italy. We have a Chinatown in Milan (with recent episodes of violence) and every little town has a Chinese shop selling clothes and bags. Our institutions, Italian people, are not able to establish a peaceful relationship with them. Anti-Chinese racism is increasing with protectionists railing against Chinese products and the media not giving voice to the immigrants. Knowing about a similar experience (provided the differences in specific historical and social contexts) is extremely helpful in a country that could not even imagine a Chinese-Italian literature.

[*Slide: School kids, mixed races, playground, Esquilino.*]

Maria reads my mind. In the Esquilino, things are changing. On the street, I can see acculturating Chinese Italians, superficially distinguishable from their immigrant counterparts, most noticeably in their interaction with Italians and other immigrants. The Chinese are the second largest Asian population, Filipinos being the largest, and followed by Sri Lankan and Bangladeshi. These latter began to increase when the last Prodi government (liberal, recently fallen) encouraged emigration from South Asia where wages and opportunities are perceived to be lower than in China. The Chinese diaspora, which never relies on underemployment for too long, has invested in property and textile manufacturing, and has landed small communities of Italian Chinese where

families with children are present, the second generation now appearing at University, on Vespas, cursing in dialect, and gesticulating with their hands. The Vatican acknowledges small communities of Chinese Catholics. (In Prato, Catholic Chinese textile workers who have emigrated – read escaped – are a part of a Chinese labor force that comprises twenty percent of the town's population.) At the same time, the Church has recently made peace with the PRC version of Catholicism in China by recognizing government appointed clergy. Implicit in this context is a two-China approach to Chinese people. There is China's Chinese, then there is the Chinese who are not going back, who wish to settle elsewhere, in Italy, the European Union, or the gold ticket to North America. These immigrants find their lives complicated by the attendant acculturation of the Italian-born, the 1.5s, who prefer espresso to bubble tapioca and have been raised in that nether world of self-contempt, cushioned by the admonition that one will not be loved if one does not learn to behave. Sound familiar? I see a few, holding hands with their Italian counterparts while chatting on their *cellulares*.

[*Slide: News photo, Chinese demonstrators, Corriere della Sera.*]

The immigrants responded to these stereotypes in familiar fashion, becoming what popular opinion requires, Chinese, Italian, whatever. In Milan, Chinese garment workers flying the PRC flag demonstrate against what they perceive to be unfair prosecution of parking laws. No one in Italy can be accused of bad parking – bad driving, yes, but not bad parking. Immediately after the photograph of the flag waving above Chinese faces battling the police appeared on TV and in the newspapers, a spokeswoman for the local Chinese business community explained that the flag was merely a convenient symbol and did not in any way express loyalty to China; rather to being Chinese. I felt a kinship in this regard, a first step in the construction of an Italian Chinese identity. (Hey mambo, a strategic move.)

[*Slide: That's me again at the Trevi Fountain pitching a lira.*]

I had not been back to Europe since the sixties when Artie Wong told me his brother went to Spain and became a bullfighter, playing a version of the "dozens," discovering that seat of mutual self-contempt for what we were, what the future held. We were the ABCs, Chinatown with no accent or suburban, overachievers, pre-med/dent engineering majors, too short for the women, and too aware of the absurd imitation we struck, button down collars crowning lambswool V-necks, chinos, penny loafers, passing through Sather Gate a year or two before the tear gas clouds choked the pollarded hawthorns and caught an entire generation in a similar unease. Almost on a whim, I discovered what fun it is to be the only, the exception, a real foreigner versus the fake. But this time, thirty plus years later, the luxury of spending months at a time in Italy surrounded by translators, students of American culture, interested in parsing the sensibilities of Chinese America, who arrive at their interest as a result of studying both English and Chinese, has its price. I have to take myself more seriously just to keep up my end of the bargain. There's more at stake.

*[Slide: Newspaper clippings on the floor.]*

March 2005, Chinese bodies floating off the coast of Sicily evidence the immigration dynamic at work. But the stereotypes are familiar, omniscient, broad, and evolving. This year I saw an ad in our local Banco Popular that featured an East Asian couple looking decidedly middle class, seated at the desk of a friendly loan officer. Jokes about the Italian banking system aside, the imagery of home-buying Chinese Italians coincides with the first black newsreader on Italian TV's RAI 2. My initial introduction to Chinese in Italian popular media some ten years ago featured the scandal of Chinese businesses purchasing apartments and using them to warehouse merchandise, a practice discovered when the flooring in one apartment collapsed, threatening the entire building. There have been numerous stories spun from the threat, now the reality, of Chinatowns rooting themselves in "traditional" neighborhoods in the major Italian cities. In the northern city of Treviso, municipal officials ordered all Chinese restaurants to remove the red lanterns from their façades because they looked too "oriental." The bodies of presumably Chinese immigrants are found floating in the waters off the coast of Sicily, victims of smugglers. Chinese beach gleaners are swept away in a high tide while gathering shellfish. Frank Viviano, an American foreign correspondent and the best read for an English-speaking ex-pat, reports on the rumored arranged marriage between a Mafia prince and a Triad princess. But as a protest to the anti-immigrant Berlusconi policies, post 9/11, an Italian musician has organized la Orchestra di Piazza Vittorio, made up of immigrant musicians to perform in Esquilino.

So what about the Chinese in Italy? The canon of American Studies recognizes the ethnic/racial divides of a country built on immigration and draws a parallel. American Studies in Italy recognizes Chinese American literature as a part of American literature, includes or alludes to issues of immigration, assimilation, race, even ethnic prejudice in Italian society. No surprise there. But I'm beginning to sense what's missing, what my part in

all this might be as an object of interest: Simply to echo the question Maria raises. Where is the point of view of Chinese Italians, the artists, the writers? Who might they be and how might they present themselves? How do they, when and where do they, as this other, meet the expectations for acceptance, the sensibilities of language, then outfit their bespoke identity to satisfy themselves.

*[Slide: The journal, Parole Sopra Esquilino]*

A poster on the support column of the arcade that shades three sides of Piazza Vittorio solicits articles about the neighborhood, writing about Esquilino by its residents, to be called "*Parole Sopra Esquilino.*" *Vero?* University of Rome, La Sapienza has embarked on a community studies activity, inviting anybody who lives in the district to write about their experience in any language, the most interesting to be translated into Italian and published in order to form a linguistic bridge. This effort feels familiar, like home.

In my brief but enlightening discussion with Professor Zhang Tongbing, who holds the position *Lettore di lingua cinese in Dipartimento di Studi Orientali, University of Rome, La Sapienza,* she confirms the opinion that there is as yet no evidence of Chinese Italian writing. Professor Zhang suggests that it is more than Italian literacy that's at stake for the few Chinese Italian students she has observed at her campus. And that is that literary confidence, and all that that assumes, of a history and language, a self-defined point of view, a Chinese Italian audience. "*Parole Sopra Esquilino*" may encourage Chinese Italians to write only if they see this as encouragement; if they see themselves as Italians; if they see themselves as inhabitants of Esquilino; if they see themselves as conveniently as Italians see them. Given such a short presence in the equally short history of modern Italy and the rather, patronizing opportunity for self-expression, they are silent. The popular consensus suggests that Chinese immigrants do not wish to assimilate. After all, those who are legally landed can travel back and forth. The PRC is an economic nuclear reactor. Now why this historically challenged assumption should arise again should be no surprise. There's also the Northern League neo-facist/racist sensibilities at play.

But Italy is after all Italy: Rome, the seat of the Roman Catholic Church, the home of Maria Montessori, who encouraged hands-on learning, as well as Reggio Emilia, who emphasized creative activity as critical to empowering students. Thus, "*Parole Sopra Esquilino*" is not so farfetched. Chinese Italians are a challenge.

The immigrant shop owner minding a storefront warehouse disguised as a retail shoe emporium, the Chinese restaurant waitstaff dealing with busloads of rice famished Chinese tourists and suspicious Italian diners skewering items on chopsticks for closer examination, reinforce a broad divide. At the same time, the kids behind the counter are chattering in Roman dialect, and efforts like "Parole Sopra Esquilino" acknowledge an Italian society poised to acculturate the latest wave, accustomed as it is to all manner of barbarians at the gate, think Visigoths, think Woody Allen and Soon-Yi debarking at the Venice film festival. (One of the charming cultural paradoxes is the ability of the Italians to make iconic the Roman Empire [SPQR] but view native Italians from anywhere south of their immediate location as barbarians.) Teaching behavior, cultural translation, institutions that define what is Italian is as Italian as the study of what is not Italian. Broadly, then, I found a snug fit in Italy as an object of examination. So the complaint headlining a front page editorial in a journal devoted to publishing works about the Esquilino caught my eye: "*L'AMA non ci ama.*" It looks like we're learning to speak Italian. Who doesn't love us? Why?

*[Slide: Irene Duranti with baby.]*

Language kills me. It is not the verb that confuses me; it is the reflexive pronouns, the invisible subject, and here, the initials. Riccardo's daughter Irene comes to the rescue. He gave me SPQR, the Latin and the vulgar. And like her dad, her ear for translation is perfect, although her American accent is better. She laughs, "*L'AMA, Azienda Municipale Ambiente* doesn't love us. The garbage collectors.*" It is an admonishment to keep the streets of Esquilino cleaner. Oh. Got it.

The headline, "*L'AMA Non Ci Ama*" only confirms what I already knew. On one side, the key components, the terms of acceptance, the stereotype, are clearly in place. Italians are willing to accept Chinese Italians on Italian terms, namely, learning to clean up, learning to behave within the constructs of the dual identity syndrome, earn acceptance. Be what the stereotypes require. Be Chinese; be Italian. I can only imagine the difficulties. Scilla and friends took me to see a production of *Turandot* at the futurist (read fascist) Olympic Stadium where a delirious mob demanded that the tenor repeat the opening aria of the third act while they hummed along. I was reminded that Gold Rush 49ers were singing "Ching Chong Chinaman" at roughly the same time Puccini was scoring his libretto. There is no trace yet of an Italian Chinese sensibility that defines themselves in their own terms, certainly not in any literary context as yet. That's the reason for this article. Not to comment on the state of Chinese American literary studies as seen by Italians; certainly they've read it and written about it. Their study remains a sidebar in Chinese Studies, in American Studies. But I have a different point of view, and I don't want to lose it even as my audience expands, contracts, to

fit the times or the customs of place. I always draw a different lesson from the history and texts Chinese America provides, and it's the same in any language, a small, but not inconsiderable conceit.

*[More slides, hundreds more if you have the time.]*

Here is one of me in Rome sitting at an sidewalk café table in Trastevere where the barista asked if I was that Chinese writer in *L'ombra* he'd just read about. That is when I knew I'd died and gone to heaven. Vatican City was just a few blocks away where I could confess my latest sin, vanity. Here's one of Scilla and me in Hoiping waiting for the ferry (a story for another day.) That's Shawn Wong blessing the throng from his veranda overlooking the Campo di Fiori. (Talk about Marco Polo's revenge.) Here I am again with a group of translators who kindly labored over my tortured syntax and ventriloquized as I posed as author for an evening's reading. The Italians are used to this, *strangieri qui non parlano italiano.* Here's a friend, a Franciscan monk from Beijing just back from Prato ministering to a small but devout group of Chinese *immigranti* in the rag trade. Here's my favorite, me leaning against an ancient wall crowned by the Roman Coliseum. Wait, there's more.

## NOTES

1. Following are resources on the Chinese American experience written in Italian. To date, I include here the invaluable advice and friendship of Riccardo Duranti at La Sapienza, University of Roma and Anna Scannavini of Universita dell'Aquila. See also, Mario Maffi and Feltrinelli Milano, *Nel mosaico della città* (City: Publisher, 1992), which includes a chapter on New York's Chinatown; and Donatella Izzo, "Letteratura e/o testimonianza: *Bone* e il canone asiaticoamericano," *Nuova Corrente*, 47 (2000): 327-360 (anche al sito: <http://centri.univr.it/iperstoria/testi35.htm>); and Donatella Izzo, a cura di, *Suzie Wong non abita più qui. La letteratura delle minoranze asiatiche negli Stati Uniti*, (Milano: Shake, 2006). See also Manuela Vastolo, "Schede: La letteratura asiaticoamericana," *Ácoma* 31 (Inverno 2005) and Manuela Vastolo, "Intervista a Jeffery Paul Chan," *Ácoma* 33 (Inverno 2007).

2. For resources in English, see: Serena Fusco, "'Our Inside Story': BodySpaces in Fae Myenne Ng's *Chinatown*," *Igitur* 3 (Jan.-Dec. 2002): 129-144; Elisabeta Marino, ed., *Asia and the West: A Difficult Intercontinental Relationship*, proc. of the Second Asia and the West: A Difficult Intercontinental Relationship Annual Conference, 19-21 Dec. 2001, Sun Moon Lake, Roma (2002). See also Lina Unali, ed., *Talk-story in Chinatown and Away: Essays on Chinese American Literature and on U.S.-China Relationships* (Roma: Sun Moon Lake, 1998); and Lina Unali, ed.,

*The Body, the Gods*, proc. of the Third Asia and the West: A Difficult Intercontinental Relationship Annual Conference, Dec. 19-21, 2002, Sun Moon Lake, Roma (2003).

# To Be "Hapa" or Not to Be "Hapa": What to Name Mixed Asian Americans?

*Wei Ming Dariotis*

## Preface

*I have been struggling for several years with this apparently unresolvable issue: what to do about "Hapa"? I finally decided I had to start writing about it, to start engaging the dialogue. The essays and talks[1] I have been giving on this issue represent my commitment to be fully involved in this dialogue, this journey, no matter where it might take us.*

Asian American Studies was founded by student and community activists in the Bay Area who proposed the revolutionary idea that positionality – how people are situated within, on the edges of, and in opposition to various kinds of groupings – is a valid perspective from which to shape analysis, scholarship, and critical inquiry. The positionality of mixed race and mixed heritage Asian Americans became more solidly located within Asian American communities at least partially through the naming of them/us as a coherent, identifiable group through the use of the term "Hapa." "Asian American" itself is a term of collective identity that grew out of a political movement – before 1968, one was "Oriental" or Chinese, Filipino, Japanese, or Korean. "Asian American" as a term provides a space in which these disparate ethnic communities can come together, but it also creates its own sense of identity – what Espiritu calls "Asian American pan-ethnicity." As opposed to ethnic-specific terms like the Filipino "mestizo" or the Japanese "haafu," "Hapa" is a word that specifically situates mixed Asian Americans within this pan-ethnic Asian American community. "Hapa" also provides the important function of giving mixed Asian Americans a safe space. Growing controversies over the use of the Native Hawaiian word "hapa" to identify mixed race Asian Americans could possibly destabilize this unifying identity – or could provide an interesting opportunity to push out the boundaries we may have drawn around ourselves in the process of coming together.

I am a queer (bi), "mixed race" Asian American woman or, in the words of Beverly Yuen Thompson, a "bi-bi girl." My name is my symbolic passport to both my Asian American and my "mixed race" identities: Wei Ming Dariotis – Chinese and Greek, right up front. My mother told me she chose my Chinese name to balance the Greek, and to give herself the satisfaction of naming her own daughter the way she wished she had been named, with love and care. Names are not to be taken lightly, she told me. My name, Wei Ming, was something she determined would be special. "Wei" contains the characters "book" and "heart" and she translates it to mean both "heart" and "book" knowledge – that is, "be both wise and understanding." The message of my name is: always "know your heart," she tells me. "Ming" combines the characters for "sun" and "moon," which my mother translates as "shining brilliance" – no pressure to live up to that name! My mother told me that Wei Ming was a name I should love calling myself and that I should try to grow into. My mother told me she thought about a child who is told everyday that she is stupid. Eventually, she may come to believe this about herself. My mother wanted me to believe what my name says about me, and through this she taught me that names are important. They are not just randomly assigned labels or markers; rather, names also have the power to shape meaning, identity, and even to create communities.

The queer Vietnamese American poet Truong Tran told me that when he was a young boy his Tolkiensian "ring of power" was the English word "fuck." This word made him American; it was like a secret language, something his parents didn't speak, a word of his own. He used it gleefully, like Bilbo used the ring, to set himself above where he had been as a disenfranchised, alienated immigrant child.

My ring of power was also a word, the word "Hapa."

173

I first learned this word in 1992, when I was 23 years old. I was a second-year English Literature doctoral student at University of California, Santa Barbara, and I was enrolled in the course, "The World of Amerasians," taught by Teresa K. Williams.[2] When I learned the word "Hapa" I felt as though a whole new world had opened up to me. Before this, when anybody asked me, "What are you?" I had to answer, "Chinese Greek Swedish English Scottish German Pennsylvania Dutch." This was a list of my ancestry. It is my heritage. However, this list is not my identity. Heritage does not equal identity. To paraphrase the title of the book on Asian Americans of mixed heritage edited by Teresa K. Williams and Cynthia Nakashima, my identity is something more than the sum of my parts. "Hapa" gave me such an identity. With the word "Hapa" I had a sense of given community for the first time in my life. The word "Hapa" made me something more than just a "half Chinese" or a "fake Filipino." The word "Hapa" allowed me to be a fully recognized member of the pan-ethnic Asian American community because "Hapas" came to be recognized as a legitimate Asian American group. For example, I was invited to give reports at Asian American Department meetings from the "Hapa unit" – in parallel to the "Japanese American unit" and the "Korean American unit." The word "Hapa" allowed me to comfortably identify as Asian American for the first time in my life because it was understood to be an Asian American-focused term; it didn't just mean "mixed" – it specifically signified "mixed Asian or Pacific Islander."

Here I must interrupt my own narrative to trouble this definition of "Hapa" as meaning "mixed Asian or Pacific Islander." Recently, I've been reviewing the shifting article on "Hapa" on Wikipedia.[3] The currently posted definition reads in part:

> In the Hawaiian language, hapa is strictly defined as: portion, fragment, part, fraction, installment; to be partial, less. It is a loan from the English word half. However, it has an extended meaning of "half-caste" or "of mixed descent." This is the only meaning of the term in Hawaiian Pidgin, the creole spoken by many Hawai'i residents.
>
> Used without qualification, hapa is often taken to mean "part white," and is shorthand for "hapa haole." The term can be used in conjunction with other Hawaiian racial and ethnic descriptors to specify a particular racial or ethnic mixture. Examples of this include:
> * hapa haole (part Caucasian/white)
> * hapa kanaka (part Hawaiian)

My dispute with the last part of this definition is implicated in the examples provided, especially "hapa haole," which I understand is the most commonly heard usage of the term "Hapa." The term "hapa haole"

implies that the non-named "part" is Native Hawaiian. This might be contradicted by the other example, "hapa kanaka;" however, I think a comparative history of these two terms and a survey of their actual usage would help determine the nature of the implied "other part" of the term "hapa."

What I have found even more revealing is the "Discussion" board connected to the "Hapa" article on Wikipedia, on which members of the Wikipedia community who have edited or are interested in the "Hapa" article are encouraged to explain their rationales for editing or changing the definitions provided by others.

One poster, writing under the username Ilikea, writes:

> Hapa is a Hawaiian...word of Hawaiian (ethnicity, blood ancestry) origin. Hapa began as a word by Hawaiians... for Hawaiians of part Hawaiian ancestry. Hawaiian dictionaries define "hapa" as "part, fragment, portion" or "an indefinite part of a thing, a few, a small part." Later it was further defined to include "of mixed blood, person of mixed blood." Hapa does not mean "part or partial Asian."
>
> To take a word that is a part of an indigenous language and then redefine it as a word used for part-Japanese people who came from Hawai'i and then further redefine it as "people of part Asian and European ancestry" is ethnocultural theft. At the very least, the article...on Wikipedia that defines and explains the word "hapa" should give credit where credit is due – to the Hawaiian... people of Hawai'i. The word hapa was in use long before any of the foreign Asian and Portuguese immigrants came to Hawai'i. Hawaiians and...Europeans...created the first hapa people of Hawai'i. An example is Princess Victoria Ka'iulani Cleghorn. Later, Hawaiians intermarried with the Chinese...who were the first non-European immigrants to Hawai'i. This then created many people of Hawaiian, European and Chinese ancestry. Hapa is a Hawaiian word, it is not a "Hawai'i Creole" or "Hawai'i Pidgin English" word.
>
> I am Hawai'i born and raised, and am hapa because I am part Hawaiian.... (Posted Reference Desk by User: Ilikea)

In conjunction with the changes argued for by this protestor, the definition of "Hapa" was apparently temporarily re-named, "HAPA-Mainland U.S.A. redefinition of Hawaiian word" (Chameleon Main/Talk/Images 05:27, 27 July 2004).

The question of "ethnocultural theft" is addressed by a user who argues:

> When used as a loanword in English, "hapa" may have a different meaning than the meaning associated with the

word used in the Hawaiian language.

One argument espoused is that it is either morally or at least technically wrong to use a loanword in a manner varying from the meaning given the loanword in the language from which it is borrowed. I respectfully disagree. Many loanwords to English have acquired significant difference in meaning from the original – this process of semantic shift is not of itself either bad or good, but simply a reality of linguistics. (Ryanaxp 21:35, 3 Aug. 2004)

This same user also argues that definitions of a word can and perhaps should include the regional variations in the use of that word. In the case of "hapa" the argument goes that there may well be a difference of meaning in how the word is used in Hawai'i, versus how it is used on the West Coast or even, as the writer notes, "in the eastern United States at least, the term "hapa" is used to broadly denote persons of mixed Asian ancestry. This fact (like all facts) is neither bad nor good – it simply is, and as a fact, this definition of "hapa" is valid in an encyclopedic entry." The writer continues:

Rather than despair at the reality of semantic shift, I invite you, Ilikea, to add your understanding of the term "hapa" to this entry; however, I feel the other definition(s) should not be deleted, as they are equally valid in the regions in which they are used. (Ryanaxp 21:35, 3 Aug. 2004)

In response to this argument, Ilikea writes:

Here in Hawai'i it is understood that hapa has to do with those of mixed Hawaiian blood. However, we also use this word to describe people of mixed or part Asian ancestry.... I use the word for all mixes of people who are either part Asian or part Pacific Islander or both and any other racial/ethnic ancestry.... As someone of part Hawaiian ancestry, I have seen the decline of the Hawaiian people and the passage of many of my full-blooded ancestors. What I hope to achieve by contributing to the "Hapa" article is showing the origins, usage and development of a Hawaiian word that has come to encompass more that what it originally meant. Most people of Hawaiian ancestry are part Asian and part Caucasian. (Ilikea 22:48, 3 Aug. 2004)

Zora, another contributor, writes, "As regards the history of the term hapa – it seems clear that it diffused from Hawaiian into Hawaiian pidgin and thence onto the U.S. mainland, but HOW AND WHEN is not clear" (Zora 00:29, 6 Aug. 2004). Noted Mixed Race Studies scholar Paul Spickard provides a possible history of the term in his "Afterword" to Kip Fulbeck's *Part Asian, 100% Hapa*. Spickard writes:

By the 1970s, Hapa was being used by everybody in Hawai'i to refer to anyone who was mixed. Then Asians from the continental United States visited their relatives in Hawai'i and brought the word back home with them. And they started applying it to anybody who was mixed *and part Asian* [my emphasis]. (261)

Similar to Spickard's version of the history, in the communities in which I have moved, the accepted lore has been that the word "Hapa" moved to the West Coast through the Japanese Hawaiian-Japanese West Coast connection. It was already present by the late 1980s, and it gained traction with the 1992 founding of Hapa Issues Forum (HIF), initially as a student group at University of California, Berkeley in response to statements made in a Japanese American community course to the effect that mixed people were diluting the Japanese American community. I joined the board of Hapa Issues Forum in 1997 and in 2002 we held a conference at San Francisco State University marking the 10th Anniversary of the founding of HIF. In fall 2007, we held "HIF's Last Hurrah" commemorating fifteen years of the organization's work. During the life of HIF, the focus of the organization was on building recognition and acceptance of mixed Asian Americans within Asian American communities (pan-ethnic Asian American communities as well as ethnic-specific communities). HIF was founded not just because mixed Asian Americans sometimes felt marginalized in Asian American communities, but because there was a fear being expressed that our very existence threatened those communities – or at least presaged the inevitable dissolution of those communities through processes of assimilation. The work of HIF had two main foci: (1) HIF functioned to demonstrate to Asian American communities that mixed Asian Americans were a part of – not apart from, these communities, and (2) HIF functioned to create a space where, in the words of Maria Root, author of "The Bill of Rights for People of Mixed Heritage," mixed Asian Americans did not have to "justify our ethnic legitimacy." At one HIF retreat, lead by then Executive Director Sheila Chung, we envisioned this "safe space" as a physical place, a building that would be a "Hapa Cultural Center." Within the building there was a library stocked with books about Asian Americans of mixed heritage, an art gallery for art by Asian Americans of mixed heritage, a theater for gatherings and performances, a space for an afterschool program and a summer camp, and meeting rooms. The organization has folded, and so we never built that building, or perhaps I should say we have not yet built it. Yet the word "Hapa" has functioned as that building for me and for many other mixed heritage Asian Amercians. It has given us a space of our own, a place where we can be us, without having to explain ourselves. Anyone entering the space created by the word accepts our identities as Asian Americans of mixed heritage. In this way it works opposite from Bilbo and Frodo's ring of power, which makes the wearer invisible; the word "Hapa" makes my community visible – that is its power.

The very success of the word "Hapa" has been in some ways its downfall. What I mean to say is that the word "Hapa" as it is used now may never be able to "shift" back to *only* meaning what it once meant: a Native Hawaiian word meaning mixed or part or half. Spickard writes that he sympathizes "with resentments some Hawaiian may have at their word being appropriated by Asian Americans, but," he continues, "that is the nature of language. It morphs and moves. It is not anyone's property" (262). However, I would argue that this is not merely a question of trying to hold on to a word that, like many words used in the English language, has been adopted, assimilated, or appropriated. **This is a question of power.** Who has the power or right to use language? Who has the right to define language? Native Hawaiians, in addition to all of the other ways that their sovereignty has been abrogated, lost for many years the right to their own language through oppressive English-language education. Given this history and given the contemporary social and political reality of Hawai'i, the appropriation of this one word has significance deeper than many Asian Americans are willing to recognize. To have this symbolic word used by Asians, particularly by Japanese Americans, as though it is their own, seems to symbolically mirror the way Native Hawaiian land was first taken by European Americans, and is now owned by European Americans, Japanese and Japanese Americans and other Asian American ethnic groups that numerically and economically dominate Native Hawaiians in their own land. In "Foregrounding Native Nationalisms: A Critique of Antinationalist Sentiment in Asian American Studies," Candice Fujikane argues that Asian Americans are "settlers" in Hawai'i, and therefore "support American colonialism" (76) even while trying to fight racism and discrimination in a "colonial context" (80). She defines the term "settler" in opposition to "native," and argues that Asian Americans "refuse to see themselves as the beneficiaries of [the US] colonial system" (84). Although Fujikane does not here specifically mention the use of the word "Hapa" by Asian Americans, her argument is certainly in line with the critique that Asian Americans have wrongfully appropriated the term in a way that disenfranchises Native Hawaiians from their culture.

On www.realhapas.com, Lana Robbins argues, "Today's rape of the Hawaiian language also implies that the Hawaiian language means nothing and thus the Hawaiian people are nothing." Robbins argues:

> The raping of Hawai'i continues with a new group of Colonizers, the California Wanna Be Hapa. As colonizers, California Wanna Be Hapas raped from Hawaiian Hapas their very identity, culture, and history and called it their own. These colonizers justified their illegal actions by creating organizations such as Hapa Issues Forum and other "Hapa" online forums. They gained allies from elite mixed Eurasians who like California Wanna Be Hapas, stole their term from the wartime and colonial Eurasians while stomping on the rights of Amerasians and Hawaiian Hapas.

My response to first hearing this protest was to say, "But I like the word 'Hapa'; look at everything it has done for us." I was also defensive: my experience of being mixed had never felt like a privileged position. It was a difficult thing, often about feeling rejection and exclusion, and racism, from within my own families and certainly from my "own" communities. Being "Hapa" was a refuge from such feelings of exclusion and alienation. I didn't want to give "Hapa" up. I remembered how hard it was just to get people to begin to use it. When I first began using the word in 1992, I encountered Chinese, Filipino, and Korean people of mixed heritage who objected to using the word "Hapa" because they thought it was a Japanese term. They didn't want to feel colonized by the Japanese language the way their ancestors had been colonized by Japan. When I informed these people that the word was Native Hawaiian in origin, they gladly adopted it for themselves. Native Hawaiians have never colonized anyone. When criticism against Asian Americans using the term "Hapa" first started being raised strongly in 2002, I realized that the fact that Native Hawaiians had never colonized anyone, and that is therefore why mixed heritage Asian Americans are comfortable using the word, was a sign of the relative power of Asian Americans in this context. Maybe, I started to think, the word "Hapa" was a colonizing violence in which I was actively participating. At a 2003 talk at UC Berkeley I mentioned my increasing concerns about using the word "Hapa." I was very surprised when a young man in the audience became visibly upset at the suggestion that the word "Hapa" might be somehow taken away from him. It meant so much to him for the same reasons it meant so much to me – it provides a sense of community and identity in one simple word.

In other words, quite possibly, the word "Hapa," which I had been so happy to wear because of the sense of identity and community it gave me, might have to be destroyed – or like Frodo's ring, which was forged in the fires of Mt. Doom, returned to the point of origin to be destroyed or at least re-shaped. I say this knowing that the word can never be again what it once was. There is a nostalgia here that cannot be satisfied even if everyone were to stop using the word "Hapa" to refer to non-Native Hawaiian mixed Asians. But while I certainly do not have the power to fling this word into a "Mt. Doom" of linguistic destruction, I do feel responsible to participate in the dialogue. I have been silent on this issue for too long, perhaps hoping that it would go away, so I could keep "my" word.

Over time I have realized that the controversy would not go away; rather, it has only grown stronger. It is time for me – and other mixed heritage Asian Americans – to recognize that when we use the word "Hapa" it causes some people pain. What is so difficult about this is that the word "Hapa" was chosen because it was the only word we could find that did not really cause us pain. It is not any of the Asian words for mixed Asian people that contain negative connotations either literally (e.g., "children of the dust," "mixed animal") or by association (Eurasian). And it avoids the confused identity and the Black-White dichotomy implied by English phrases (like mixed blood, biracial). It was adopted to enhance an Asian-focus to our mixed identity, thereby allowing us to use the word to participate more fully in our Asian American communities, and, as I mentioned earlier, is a word that allows us to band together. Individually, as some fraction of a larger ethnic community, Filipino mestizos or Japanese haafus are relatively small in number. Collectively, as Asian Americans of mixed heritage, we are either second or fourth in terms of position in the overall Asian American population.[4]

Languages grow and evolve, and how they do so reveals the traces of power, but is it our lot to merely record and uncover those changes? Or is it our responsibility to shape those changes? I have to acknowledge that through my work with Hapa Issues Forum and as a writer and an educator, I have contributed to spreading the use of the word "Hapa" by Asian Americans, and I thus feel responsible in part for the current contention.

I presented an earlier, far less developed version of this paper in November 2007, at a talk at Occidental College. I was just beginning to grope towards some of the issues that are outlined more clearly in the present essay. At the end of my two hours of sharing my research and my series of "Hapa Poems," a young woman who identified herself as Native Hawaiian and Japanese American, told me that my use of the word "Hapa" felt like a violence – like something was being taken away from her – another piece of Hawai'i, another piece of Native Hawaiian culture and identity. She reminded me that I am part of this problem, that I am responsible and have influence and power in this dialogue. I remembered how, in the early 1990s at UC Santa Barbara, I had joyfully and eagerly talked so many people into using the word "Hapa"; and I realized that she was right. So here is an attempt to send "Hapa," which I have seen as my word of self-empowerment, back into the fire, perhaps to be re-forged to serve the community for which it was originally intended – people of mixed Native Hawaiian heritage. I can no longer use a word to empower myself that in the process dis-empowers – even oppresses – others.

Finding another label that works as well as "Hapa" did to draw together our community and create a sense of shared identity seems an impossible task; even now we are dis-aggregating Pacific Islander Americans from Asian Americans, meaning the unifying label "API" is being dismantled. How can we create community without these collective terms? Should we even try to? What do we lose by doing so and what do we gain? Marianne Maruyama Halpin, the self-identified "white mother of hapa children," reminded me, after reading an early draft of this essay, that "a name, to work, needs to be something loved." Any name we choose for ourselves must be loved the way my mother loved my name. With that in mind, I suggest that we need to find a name we can all love calling ourselves because it empowers us to be fully ourselves and because it also causes no one else any pain. The name we choose must be loved because it empowers all the marginalized members of our communities which, let us not forget, includes mixed heritage Native Hawaiians. As we remove this self-imposed label and prepare to replace it with another, let us use re-positionable glue. There will be times when we need the labels to stick, but we must not let them stick us up. We need to know when to let them go and when to recreate them. For now, I will be calling myself a "mixed heritage Asian American." I don't love this name yet (the abbreviation is "MHAA" – which isn't exactly euphonious), and I certainly hope we can create something better soon, but for now, I'm just happy to not be mis-using "Hapa." I'm looking forward to working with the poets, writers, leaders, and dreamers of our community to find another word that gives mixed Asians our own safe space and also locates us firmly within the borders of Asian America.

## ACKNOWLEDGMENTS

My thanks to the students of Occidental College, San Francisco State University (especially AAS 550: Asian Americans of Mixed Heritage), UC Davis (ASA 120, Spring 2000), and UC Berkeley; the former members, staff, and board of Hapa Issues Forum (especially Andrew Bushaw, Anthony Yuen, Claire Light, Eric Hamako, April Elkjer, and Sheila Chung); my teachers, Teresa Williams-Leon and Kip Fulbeck; Cynthia Nakashima; Paul Spickard; Laura Kina; Farzana Nayani; Camilla Fojas; Marianne Maruyama Halpin; Wesley Ueunten; Stuart Gaffney; Lori Kay; Kent Ono; Sachiko Reed; Aaron Kitashima; Danise Olague; Joemy Ito-Gates; Truong Tran; the many students who have attended my talks and workshops on this topic; and to Native Hawaiian hapa people, and to any others who have contributed to the ongoing dialogue that has led me to write this essay or have acted as sounding boards for these ideas.

## NOTES

1. This essay was previously published in two different versions in December 2007, on both the Mixed Heritage Center website and on the online version of *Hyphen Magazine*'s Hybrid Issue, under the title, "Hapa: The Word of Power." The talks have included one at Berkeley in 2003; another in Fall 2007 at Occidental College; and a third in Spring 2008 as a keynote speech entitled "A Name We Can All Love Calling Ourselves" at the Berkeley API Issues Conference (with thanks to student organizer Brian Lau). This essay was presented as part of a Mixed Heritage Week at University of California at Davis on May 8, 2008. It was organized by the Cross Cultural Center, for which I would like to thank to Dominique Littlejohn and Center Director Steven Baissa.

2. This class is described in detail in: Teresa Williams, Cynthia Nakashima, George Kich, and Reginald Daniel, "Being Different Together in the University Classroom: Multiracial Identity as Transgressive Education," *The Multiracial Experience: Racial Borders as the New Frontier*, ed. Maria P.P. Root (Thousand Oaks, CA: Sage Publications, 1996).

3. In doing research for the current article, I found an earlier version of this article, entitled "Hapa: The Word of Power," which is published on the Mixed Heritage Center website, had been listed as one of the external links to the "Hapa" Wikipedia entry.

4. In my 2003 article, "A Community Based on Shared Difference" for the *The New Face of Asian America*, I defined "Hapa" as including people of Asian and another racial category, as well as Asian Americans of more than one Asian ethnic heritage and people of mixed Pacific Islander heritage. Based on this definition, I added up the relevant Census categories and came up with the determination that as of the 2000 Census, "Hapas" so defined were in number second only to Chinese Americans. Eric Hamako, defining "mixed Asians" as people of Asian and one other race, or people of more than one Asian ethnic heritage, determined the number of "mixed Asians" to be fourth-largest among Asian American communities.

## REFERENCES

Fujikane, Candace. "Foregrounding Native Nationalisms: A Critique of Antinationalist Sentiment in Asian American Studies." *Asian American Studies after Critical Mass*. Ed. Kent A. Ono. Malden, MA: Blackwell, 2005.

Halpin, Marianne Maruyama. Email to Wei Ming Dariotis. 20 Nov. 2007.

Hamako, Eric. "Mixed Asian Workshop." Paper presented at the Association of Asian American Studies Conference, Chicago. 16 Apr. 2008.

"Hapa." Wikipedia. 8 May 2008

Kina, Laura. Email to Wei Ming Dariotis. 30 Nov. 2007.

Robbins, Lana. "The Real Hapa: The Hawaiian Hapa." The Hawaiian Foundation Inc. 2004-06. 15 Nov. 2007 <http://www.RealHapas.com>.

Spickard, Paul. Afterword. *Part Asian, 100% Hapa*. By Kip Fulbeck. San Francisco: Chronicle Books, 2006.

Thompson, Beverly Yuen. "Fence Sitters, Switch Hitters, and Bi-Bi Girls: An Exploration of Hapa and Bisexual Girls." *Asian American Women*. Spec. issue of *Frontiers: A Journal of Women's Studies* 21.1-2 (2000): 171-180.

Tran, Truong. Personal communication. 20 Apr. 2006.

Williams, Teresa, Cynthia Nakashima, George Kich, and Reginald Daniel. "Being Different Together in the University Classroom: Multiracial Identity as Transgressive Education." *The Multiracial Experience: Racial Borders as the New Frontier*. Ed. Maria P.P. Root, Thousand Oaks, CA: Sage Publications, 1996

# MULAN LEAVES CHINA
# 木蘭出塞

*Lorraine Dong*
曾露凌

It is uncertain when Mulan left China and landed in America. It could be as early as the mid-1800s when she came with the first major arrival of Chinese laborers in America, where the legend of Mulan was told to entertain and remind the homesick and isolated Chinese of their ancestral country. Mulan was kept alive in turn-of-the-century America when an emerging generation of Chinese American children was told of her story by their elders or when they had to recite "Mulan ge" 木蘭歌 [The song of Mulan][2] from the Chinese textbooks of their local Chinatown schools. In mainstream Euro-America, hardly anyone knew Mulan unless one was a student or connoisseur of Chinese Studies. Some Sinologists have translated and included the Mulan song or poem in their Chinese literature anthologies. However, these books were not popular literature written for the average American adult or child to read and appreciate.

Mulan's name became more known in the United States when she was mentioned as Fa Mu Lan 花木蘭 in a 1976 novel by Maxine Hong Kingston 湯婷婷 entitled *Woman Warrior*. Three years later, David Henry Hwang 黃哲倫 wrote a play entitled *FOB*, using Fa Mu Lan as a character reference borrowed from "American literature," specifically referring to *Woman Warrior* as that piece of American literature. Over a decade passes before Mulan resurfaces in America, this time mainly in children's literature and animated films. At least six storybooks, one short story, and three animated films have been published and produced in the United States and Canada that attempt to transmit the legend of Mulan. The most popular Mulan in America (and worldwide) is the one created for Disney's 1998 animated feature, *Mulan*. This paper looks at the Americanization of Mulan and how Mulan's departure from China engages the broader issues of cultural appropriation and authenticity versus artistic imagination in a world where the Chinese exists as a minority in a dominant Eurocentric world.

## CHINA'S MULAN:
## SYMBOL OF FILIAL PIETY AND PATRIOTISM

Chinese scholars have been trying for a long time to identify the real Mulan. She is not mentioned in any official Chinese history book written prior to the Song 宋 dynasty (960-1127). Everyone agrees that the sixty-two line Mulan poem was composed during the Northern Wei 北魏 dynasty (386-534) and later collected in the *Yuefu shiji* 樂府詩集 compiled during the Song dynasty.[2] In the poem, the protagonist is known only as Mulan. The Chinese have tried to identify her family name with varying results: Zhu 朱, Wei 魏, Mu 穆, Yuan 苑, and Hua 花. Hua became the most popular surname choice. Its earliest known mention came from Xu Wei 徐渭 (1521-1593), who wrote a play about Mulan and gave her family the surname of Hua. Mulan's origin is also unknown, with scholars identifying Hebei 河北, Henan 河南, or Gansu as her birthplace. The general consensus says northern China, and that Mulan was not Chinese. Recent theories state that Mulan is not an individual but a composite, representative character of the time period. Amidst all these scholarly speculations, one fact is unquestioned: the story of Mulan, whether historically real or not, has been passed down for centuries in a variety of forms and genres, not only in China but now outside of China.

In the Mulan poem, the storyline has the following basic components and development: Mulan has a father, mother, older sister, and younger brother. Her father is drafted to battle by the khan. He is too old to fight and there are no adult sons in the family. Mulan dresses as a man to substitute for her father in battle. She fights one hundred battles in a ten or twelve year span.[3] When the war ends, the emperor promotes her, gives her over one hundred thousand cash, and offers her anything she wants.[4] Mulan does not want to be an official and asks only to return home. When she arrives home, she takes off her military outfit, wears a dress, and puts a yellow flower on her hair. As soon as she steps out, all her fellow soldiers are shocked to discover that they have been fighting side by side with a woman. The poem ends with four lines about a pair of rabbits, one male and one female, and that from afar, no one can tell which one is male and which one is female.

The story of Mulan caught the imagination of the Chinese people and was passed down from generation to generation. She instilled Chinese values of filial piety and patriotism in children. As a filial daughter, she dresses as a man to fight for her father. As a patriot, she fights for her country. Chinese children recited and chanted her poem in schools, and her story was retold in a variety of popular genres from short stories, novels, drama, and opera, to film, television, picture storybooks, and comic books.

From the writer's personal Mulan collection of two plays, ten films, one opera stage performance, three television series, eleven short stories, nine novels, and twenty-two picture books and comic books that were published mainly in the People's Republic of China, with some in Hong Kong and Taiwan, one can find a good sampling of how Mulan stories have deviated from the original poem down through the ages. The many different Chinese Mulan stories usually embellish the original plot with additional characters and details. For example, some versions have one or more of the following changes: Mulan has bound feet; the emperor wants Mulan to marry his daughter or the princess falls in love with Mulan; soldiers discuss Mulan's sexual orientation; Mulan marries a fellow soldier; Mulan does not get along with her mother-in-law; Mulan has a fight with her ugly husband and is kicked out of the house; and/or Mulan and her husband wake up one morning to discover that she is a man and he is a woman. People in China reading or watching these Mulan stories do not condemn them or challenge their authenticity, but rather read and watch them for their entertainment value and with the understanding that these are creative departures from the original Mulan poem. In almost all instances, the basic themes of filial piety and patriotism are kept constant.

## AMERICA'S EARLY INTRODUCTION TO MULAN

In America, where the Chinese is a minority existing in a dominant Eurocentric society, Mulan's story has a different impact and significance. Due to a basically Eurocentric education and environment, Mulan's story does not exist in popular American culture, until recently. Unlike in China, Chinese Americans are rarely introduced to their ancestral heritage unless they learn about it through their elders, community, or Chinese language schools.

Maxine Hong Kingston is the earliest popular Chinese American writer to bring attention to Mulan in the United States. Her award-winning novel, *Woman Warrior: Memoirs of a Girlhood among Ghosts* (1976),[5] describes how some Chinese Americans learn about their Chinese heritage through oral tradition:

> After I grew up, I heard the chant of Fa Mu Lan, the girl who took her father's place in battle. Instantly I remembered that as a child I had followed my mother about the house, the two of us singing about how Fa Mu Lan fought gloriously and returned alive from the war to settle in the village. I had forgotten this chant that was once mine, given me by my mother, who may not have known its power to remind. She said I would grow up a wife and a slave, but she taught me the song of the warrior woman, Fa Mu Lan. I would have to grow up a warrior woman. ("White Tigers" 20)

Of immediate note is Kingston's transcription of Mulan's name which reveals a common linguistic situation for most people living in an English-only America, which is not to be able to read, write, and speak well in a language other than English, in this situation, Chinese. In transcribing Mulan's name, Kingston uses two dialects, Cantonese (Fa 花) and Mandarin or Putonghua (Mu Lan 木蘭). If Cantonese were the dialect, then the name should be transcribed as "Fa Muklaan," and if it were Mandarin, then the name should be "Hua Mulan." The dialectal mix-up is not corrected and is perpetuated by American writers like David Henry Hwang, Robert D. San Souci, and the Disney team of writers who continue to spell the name as "Fa Mu Lan" or "Fa Mulan."

This linguistic error does not raise as major a concern as America's understanding of a Mulan that is based on *Woman Warrior.* Immediately after the above quote from the novel's "White Tigers" chapter, the narrator goes into her fantasy martial arts journey where she trains with a pair of elders for fifteen years and dresses as a man to substitute for her father who is conscripted by the local wicked baron. Her father carves "revenge," "oaths and names," and a list of grievances on her back so that she would not forget the evil events that have happened. The narrator meets her lover-turned-husband while in battle, becomes pregnant, and with the baby on a sling tied behind her back, she continues to fight battles. She eventually sends her husband home with the baby. When she encounters the baron, she shouts "I am a female avenger" and chops off his head (43). In the end she returns to her parents-in-law, husband, and son. Kneeling before her in-laws, she says "Now my public duties are finished. I will stay with you, doing farmwork and housework, and giving you more sons" and the villagers would make "a legend about my perfect filiality" (45).

This story eventually became Mulan's story in America. The general American populace had no knowledge of the original Chinese Mulan poem to make a literary comparison between "The Song of Mulan" and the narrator's journey in *Woman Warrior*. What Kingston has done was to incorporate story elements from several famous Chinese legends into one fantasy story: Mulan, Meng Jiangnü 孟姜女 (ca. Qin 秦 dynasty, 220-207 B.C.), Guan Yü 關羽 (ca. Three Kingdom Period, 220-280), Yue Fei 岳飛 (ca. 10th century, Song dynasty), and Ren Yongchun 任永春 (ca. 1700s, Qing 清 dynasty). These legends represent the storytelling and oral tradition passed down from the Chinese elders to the next generation. In *Woman Warrior*, the narrator creatively blurs the line between authenticity and fantasy by imagining herself as a superheroine fighting injustice in America, but an ignorant America appropriates the narrator's story and becomes fixated with making this the story of Mulan.

Three years later in 1979, David Henry Hwang published a two-act play entitled *FOB*.[6] This was his first play, and it borrowed Fa Mu Lan from *Woman Warrior*. In the play, Fa Mu Lan's story is described as almost identical to the fantasy story told by Kingston's narrator. In a role play scene, Grace, a first-generation Taiwanese Chinese American, becomes Mu Lan and Steve, a Chinese newcomer, becomes Gwan Gung 關公 (aka Guan Yü). "Mu Lan" accuses "Gwan Gung" of killing her father and family for sport. They fight and she uses an invisible sword to thrust his heart.

In his "Playwright's Note" to *FOB*, Hwang states:

> The roots of *FOB* are thoroughly American. The play began when a sketch I was writing about a limousine trip through Westwood, California, was invaded by two figures from American literature. Fa Mu Lan, the girl who takes her father's place in battle, from Maxine Hong Kingston's *The Woman Warrior*, and Gwan Gung, the god of fighters and writers, from Frank Chin's *Gee, Pop!*
> This fact testifies to the existence of an Asian American literary tradition. (3)

Hwang claims that the Fa Mu Lan and Gwan Gung in his play are taken from American literature, i.e., Kingston's *Woman Warrior* and Chin's *Gee, Pop!* respectively. It is crucial that he does not acknowledge Fa Mu Lan to be from Chinese literature. For him, Fa Mu Lan, with its mixed dialectal transcription and a new imagined story, is an American creation. To be more specific, it is an Asian American creation by an American of Chinese ancestry whose cultural heritage is trying to survive in a dominant Eurocentric environment where cultural authenticity is extremely difficult to control and maintain for a minority people. In the situation of Fa Mu Lan, Kingston had

no control over how mainstream America would appropriate Mulan from her novel. Hence, Fa Mu Lan is not Fa Muklaan or Hua Mulan. Fa Mu Lan is Fa Mu Lan, distinctly American, not Chinese.

The issue of a fake versus real Mulan is addressed by writer Frank Chin 趙健秀, who harshly criticizes Kingston and Hwang for their revisionist stories of Mulan:

> In *The Woman Warrior*, Kingston takes a childhood chant, "The Ballad of Mulan," which is as popular today as "London Bridge Is Falling Down," and rewrites the heroine, Fa Mulan, to the specs of the stereotype of the Chinese woman as a pathological white supremacist victimized and trapped in a hideous Chinese civilization. The tattoos Kingston gives Fa Mulan, to dramatize cruelty to women, actually belong to Yue Fei, a man whose tomb is now a tourist attraction at West Lake, in Hanzhou [sic] city. Fake work breeds fake work. David Henry Hwang repeats Kingston's revision of Fa Mulan and Yue Fei, and goes on to impoverish and slaughter Fa Mulan's family to further dramatize the cruelty of the Chinese.
> Kingston, Hwang, and [Amy] Tan are the first writers of any race, and certainly the first writers of Asian ancestry, to so boldly fake the best-known works from the most universally known body of Asian literature and lore in history. And, to legitimize their faking, they have to fake all of Asian American history and literature, and argue that the immigrants who settled and established Chinese America lost touch with Chinese culture, and that a faulty memory combined with new experience produced new versions of these traditional stories. This version of history is their contribution to the stereotype.[7]

As seen in the above quote, Chin also uses "Fa" to refer to Mulan. He equates Kingston's narrator to Mulan, which understandably explains in large part why he condemns Kingston for writing a fake Mulan story that is misleading an America that is ignorant of the "real" Mulan, and supporting an America that demonizes China.

Chin's comments bring up a crucial dilemma for the Chinese American minority artist: Must Chinese minority artists be "real" or authentic and bear the responsibility of educating everyone in America about Chinese culture? If "yes," then one needs to think about white majority artists in America and Chinese majority artists in China who do not have such a responsibility within their own countries because a majority people do not need to be reminded of something they already know. If "no" to the above question, then one must ask who in America has the power to educate and ultimately be responsible for educating the people about a minority culture. More important, can a minority artist boldly express his/her creativity and imagination between a dominant Eurocentric culture and a gagged minority culture, and still avoid accusations by one or both of being a "fake" or co-conspirator to demonize the other? Under such pressures, a Chinese American minority artist has hard choices to make, sometimes involving compromises that yield extreme displeasure from the very community where he/she belongs. In some cases, the artist's creative work is ignored for its art over a minority people's desperate search and need for a "real" heritage, regardless of the fact that many times the work is appropriated by mainstream America, sometimes becoming a product beyond the artist's control. There is nothing fake about living in the real world of a minority.

## AUTHENTICATING MULAN IN AMERICA

Over ten years after the publication of *Woman Warrior*, America begins to see the emergence of Mulan's story in the form of children's literature and animated films. Unlike the early Fa Mulan written about or imagined in literature for adults, these works attempt to present a more authentic Mulan story in a multicultural mission to introduce Chinese heritage to American children.

Among the earliest of these children's books is *The Legend of Mu Lan: A Heroine of Ancient China* 花木蘭的故事, 中國古代女英雄 (1992), written and illustrated by Wei Jiang 姜巍 and Cheng An Jiang 姜成安. It was part of the Heroines in History series.[8] Publisher and translator Eileen Hu packaged this Chinese/English bilingual book with an audiocassette and a Mulan doll that she designed herself. The book was marketed with a "Multicultural Education Council Seal of Approval," citing that it was required reading for University of California at Berkeley and San Francisco State University. It was also translated into Spanish and Vietnamese. Despite using a variety of marketing strategies, Hu's ambitious attempts to make her version of the Mulan story as popular among the children in America as it is in China failed.

In addition to *The Legend of Mu Lan*, three other Mulan picture books were published bilingually in Chinese and English: *China's Bravest Girl* 巾幗英雄花木蘭 (1993) by Charlie Chin 陳建文, *The Song of Mulan* 木蘭歌 (1995) by Jeanne M. Lee, and *The Ballad of Mulan* 木蘭辭 (1998) by Song Nan Zhang.[9] The presence of a Chinese text, along with historical and cultural notes of an explanatory nature at the end of some of these books, adds to the appearance of authenticity. The 1995 and 1998 storybooks reprint the original Chinese poem. The 1993 and 1998 books have also "translated" the original poem into Chinese prose. (The 1998 book has two Chinese texts, one in poetry and one in prose.) More interesting is *China's Bravest Girl* where Chin retells his version of the Mulan story which is then translated into Chinese by Wang Xing Chu 王性初 (or perhaps vice versa). This partially explains why the English stories in these three books do not match the storyline of the original Chinese poem; for example, Jiang and Jiang's Mulan story describes the usage of goats in a battle scene; *China's Bravest Girl* has a love interest for Mulan who proposes to her in the end (a popular ending in later Chinese versions); and *The Ballad of Mulan* resolves the inconsistent mention of how many years Mulan fought by ignoring "twelve" in the Chinese poem and saying "ten" in the English text that follows the Chinese "translated" prose. These three bilingual picture books prove that the inclusion of a Chinese text does not ensure authenticity to the original Mulan poem.

The most popular Mulan to appear in America is the one created by Walt Disney Studios in its animated feature entitled *Mulan*. It was released on June 19, 1998, and was nominated by the Academy of Motion Picture Arts and Sciences for an Oscar in the category of best musical or comedy score.[10] The ending credits show that the film is based on a story by Robert D. San Souci and that the screenplay is by Rita Hsiao, Christopher Sanders, Philip LaZebnik, Raymond Singer, and Eugenia Bostwick-Singer. At least nine official Disney storybook versions of the *Mulan* film have been published, each written by different authors.

As with the case of David Henry Hwang's Mulan character, Disney's Mulan is not based on a Chinese story but on a story created by an American, Robert D. San Souci. His picture book, *Fa Mulan*, was published on the same year as Disney's *Mulan*.[11] In his "Author's Note" at the end of the book, San Souci explains:

> For my retelling, I go back to the earliest versions of *The Song of Mulan*....I follow the traditional sequence of events; but retelling (as opposed to translating) allows me to fill out briefly sketched scenes and to "read between the lines," by drawing on my study of the poem in its historical and cultural context. (n. pag.)

San Souci uses Kingston's spelling of "Fa Mulan" and tries to add authenticity to his version of *Mulan* by providing an historical account of what was happening in China during Mulan's time.

In "retelling" and not translating, and in his "reading between the lines," San Souci makes four basic changes to Mulan's original story. First, he says it "seems logical" that in becoming a general, Mulan must have studied *Sunzi bingfa* 孫子兵法 [Sunzi's Art of War] that was written during 6th century B.C. Therefore, he hints at Mulan having learned from *Sunzi bingfa* in his picture book [16]. Next, he thinks that "Mulan might well have taken the Maiden of Yueh as a role model," so the Maiden of Yueh is mentioned throughout the story as Mulan's source of inspiration, with her father saying in the end that his daughter's fame will "outshine and outlive" that of the

Maiden of Yueh [29]. In addition, San Souci draws upon both Chinese scholars and Frank Chin to explain why he ends Mulan's story with a hint of marriage by a companion soldier:

> Commentators over the centuries have suggested that the image of paired male and female rabbits running together suggests domesticity and a marriage bond. Moreover, Frank Chin, in *The Great Aiiieeeee! An Anthology of Chinese-American and Japanese-American Literature*, notes, "The poem ends with the Confucian ideal of marriage. In Confucianism, all of us – men and women – are born soldiers....Life is war. The war is to maintain personal integrity in a world that demands betrayal and corruption....Marriages are military alliances." This telling image points up "the romantic drama found between the lines." (n. pg.)[12]

Finally, San Souci has one new and unnecessary addition that the Disney version adopted and highlighted in its film version, which is the act of Mulan cutting her hair in order to disguise herself as a male soldier. This act to be a man was unnecessary because Chinese men had long hair at the time.

While the ending credits say Disney's *Mulan* is based on San Souci's story, a bilingual Disney Hyperion publication that translates the original Mulan poem states in its subtitle that the poem "inspired the Disney animated film."[13] To further add authenticity to their work, a Disney Special Collector's Edition of *Mulan* describes how Disney sent a team to China in 1994 to conduct research for the film. They studied China's culture, people, landscape, architecture, and clothing in order to make *Mulan* as true to the Chinese as possible.[14]

As a result of adapting an American Mulan story by San Souci and not a Chinese one, the Disney team of writers wrote yet another American Mulan story.[15] The film opens with a tomboyish Mulan who is fighting various attempts to match her with a husband. She has four talking animal companions: Mushu 木須 her guardian dragon, Khan 汗 her horse, Cri-Kee 蟋蟀 her pet cricket, and Little Brother 小兄弟, her dog. Disguised as a man named "Ping" 平, Mulan fights under the command of Captain Li Shang 李翔 and befriends three fellow soldiers, Yao 堯, Ling 寧, and Chien-Po 金寶. In a snowy battle, Mulan is wounded after she saves Li Shang. She is then discovered to be a woman and is banished from the military. On her way home, she accidentally overhears the enemy's plans to invade the imperial palace and races to warn Li Shang. Yao, Ling, and Chien-Po disguise themselves as women to infiltrate the palace with Mulan. With additional help from Mushu and Cri-Kee, a female Mulan defeats Shan-Yu 單于, the evil Hun leader. In appreciation, the emperor of China bows before Mulan

and presents her with his pendant and Shan-Yu's sword. When Mulan returns home, she gives the pendant and sword to her father. Li Shang follows her home and she asks him to stay for dinner.

Following a recent trend of producing sequels to some of its popular animated features, Disney Studios produced a DVD sequel to *Mulan* that was released on February 1, 2005. Entitled *Mulan II*, the story begins one month after Mulan saves China from the Huns, which obviously does not follow the storyline in the original poem.

As expected in a typical Disney musical animated feature, *Mulan* has animals and spiritual beings. In this film, they sing and dance to disco and rap music, eat bacon and eggs for breakfast, and brush their teeth with a modern-day toothbrush. These characters and scenes provide comic relief and are obvious indicators that Disney's *Mulan* is not meant to be a serious historical documentary or work of non-fiction about Mulan. Nevertheless, the American audience is led to believe that the portion of the story involving human beings is based on the true Chinese story of Mulan.

Since there are no official histories written about Mulan, many use the Mulan poem composed in the Northern Wei dynasty as the standard by which one gauges the authenticity of a Mulan story. For the audience in China where the mainstream Chinese majority knows the original poem, the question of authenticity is not a major concern. Reading or watching more Mulan stories from outside China like Disney's *Mulan* only adds to the repertoire of the many Mulan stories already in existence in China.

However, in America, the majority of the children grow up with little knowledge or exposure to a minority culture. If an individual wants to learn more about Chinese culture, he/she would normally go to the library or Internet to seek and find information, most if not all of which would be written and read in English. In many cases, very little English-language information about Chinese children's books would be found. If any were to be found, the dangers of works being translated from one language to another need not be explained. More crucial is the interpretation, analysis, and presentation of Chinese culture through the lens of English-language works that do not necessarily come from a Chinese perspective and might affect authenticity.

Disney's *Mulan* has slowly become *the* Mulan in the eye of an America that does not know the Mulan of the original poem. Every year during Chinese New Year when the American elementary school curriculum calls for the obligatory one week's worth of lesson plans to study Chinese culture, many teachers would insert Disney's *Mulan* into a DVD player for students to watch. If the harm done by such ignorance is not corrected, Disney's *Mulan* can easily be perpetuated in America as the real Mulan, a phenomenon that might reach global proportions because of America's strong cultural influence around the world. Recently, Houghton Mifflin Reading has attempted to offset the situation. Instead of Disney's *Mulan*, it has chosen Song Nan Zhang's Mulan storybook version as the source of their Mulan curriculum activity kit for third grade students in the United States.[16]

The possibility of Disney's Mulan becoming *the* Mulan is likely because of Disney's aggressive marketing strategy, both domestically in the United States and internationally. In America, before the film was released, store shelves were already stocked with Mulan dolls, action figures, games, and toys made by Mattel. There were also Mulan books, CDs, stationery kits, cups and plates, clothing, jewelry, phone cards, and even dog and cat collars. Cereal, candy, and toothpaste companies featured Mulan logos on their products. And, in conjunction with the film, another one of America's corporate giants, McDonald's, began selling Mulan happy meals and toys.

Internationally, Disney has produced *Mulan* in several languages like Chinese, Japanese, German, and Italian. Its powerful influence is evident in China where Disney's *Mulan* film has been translated into Cantonese and Mandarin in VHS, VCD, and DVD formats, and where its book version has been published in at least nine different Chinese translation editions (versus at least twelve different Chinese Mulan picture book versions published in China since 1998). Other Disney products like Mulan toys, games, and activity books were sold in Chinese stores. During the Hong Kong premiere of Disney's *Mulan* in July 1998, a huge Mulan billboard stood on the corner of Jordan Road and Nathan Road, and a carnival-like "World of Mulan" took over the Harbour City Shopping Center at Ocean Terminal in Kowloon. The success of Disney's global commercialization of Mulan can be further seen when the image of Disney's Mulan has dominated all other Chinese images of Mulan. The world instantly identifies Disney's image as Mulan but none of China's own Mulan images can instantly be identified as Mulan. If Disney's story of Mulan does not become the "real" Mulan story worldwide, then its image of Mulan is becoming the most acknowledged, if not the most "real" image of Mulan.

## AMERICA'S MULAN: FROM SOCIETY TO SELF

In China, a majority of popular Mulan stories end with a restoration to societal norms. Mulan begins by challenging a system that did not include women in the military and does so only in order to fulfill her daughterly duties. She disguises herself as a man not to prove a woman can be equal to a man, but to save her father. In the end she does not want to stay as a soldier or influence policy changes to include women in the military, even though she has proven a woman can be a good soldier and leader. Instead, she returns home to be a woman again and to continue fulfilling her filial piety as a daughter. Later versions that add a male character and end with a marriage advance the Mulan story to the next level of societal expectations for women – to marry and bear children for her husband's family. In all these stories, Mulan begins and ends by doing what society expects of a woman. She does not change society and society does not change because of her.

Once a creation is released to the public, it has a life of its own. "The Song of Mulan" sparked the imagination of generations of Chinese writers, resulting in numerous versions of Mulan that reflect changing times and a changing society. This creative activity is not confined to China, as Mulan's arrival in America also sparked the imagination of Americans who began recently to write Mulan stories.

Kingston's Mulan story was never told explicitly in *Woman Warrior*. Because there are similarities between Mulan's poem and the narrator's fantasy story in the novel, the latter was easily and quickly appropriated as Mulan's story. The narrator is never identified with a name. However, the "coincidental" naming of the three sisters in the novel – Brave Orchid, the narrator's mother, Moon Orchid, and Lovely Orchid – provide the reader with a hint of whom this narrator might be. "Orchid" is Kingston's chosen English translated word for "lan" 蘭, the same "lan" in "Mu Lan," which can be translated as "Sylvan Orchid." The narrator is not the "real" Mulan but a reincarnation or spirit of Mulan. She represents the continuation of the Chinese heroic tradition transmitted from China to America.

It should also be noted that when the narrator mentions how Brave Orchid passed down the story of Mulan to the daughter, Mulan is said to be a "warrior woman," where Mulan is identified by the noun "woman," with the adjective "warrior" to describe what kind of woman she is.[17] However, when Moon Orchid arrives to America, she says Mulan "was a woman warrior, and really existed."[18] Being the strongest of the sisters, Brave Orchid identifies Mulan as a woman and being the weakest of the sisters, Moon Orchid sees Mulan more as a warrior. In the end, Kingston's narrator becomes a "female avenger," a "woman warrior," where the nouns and focus are on "avenger" and "warrior," active and not passive. Although the basic theme of filial piety is maintained from the original Mulan poem when the narrator returns to "perfect filiality" after her revenge, the narrator fantasizes herself mainly as a "superwoman" who makes her own decisions and fights injustice accordingly.

Thus begins the entourage of American Mulan stories and films that place womanhood as the major theme with filial piety and patriotism as secondary themes. Of particular note is filial piety, which is a rare theme in American children's literature. The two words "filial piety" do not even exist in the vocabulary of American children. More popular are themes highlighting individuality and overcoming obstacles in life. And in recent decades, as a result of studies that reveal how girls have been ignored in literature and the K-12 education system, children's stories and films with female protagonists have become the foci for American publishers and educators.

In two American children's books and one short story, Mulan is maintained as a daughter fulfilling her filial duties. The two bilingual picture books by Lee (1995) and Zhang (1998) reprint "Mulan ci" in the text and are faithful renditions of the original poem. However, Lee's book does stress the story and theme to be for women by adding a dedication page that says, "To all women, young and old." The short story by Susan Lynn Peterson entitled "The Ballad of Mu-lan" (2003), is also faithful to the original characterization of Mulan. Mulan goes to battle for her father: "If she wanted to save her father's life, she would have to go to war herself....What she did, she did for him [father]."[19] In the end when she returns home, she gives her father the scroll she got from the Khan and hangs her medal around her father's neck (47).

Among the animated Mulan features produced in 1998, *The Secret of Mulan* has kept patriotism as the theme.[20] In this version, all the characters are insects. Mulan and her "people" are caterpillars and butterflies. The evil Mala Khan is a beetle with ants and wasps for soldiers. Starting out as a caterpillar in the cartoon, Mulan's secret is not only her female identity, but also her butterfly identity. Before she reports to duty dressed as a man, she is depicted as a rebellious and independent female caterpillar who loves her country, "For honor, for country, I'm told to keep my place....Because I love this land.... The time has come to fight for what I know is right....I'm ready to do what I must do." After metamorphosing into a butterfly and defeating Mala Khan, she and the butterfly prince fly over the kingdom with Mulan singing, "My land is a beautiful land....My heart is this homeland....So it's here I'll remain in my land." Together the two merge to become a heart. Patriotism or love for one's country is definitely stressed in this animated feature.

Four picture books published in America deviate from the original Mulan storyline and de-emphasize the themes of filial piety and patriotism. They focus on being a strong, independent woman. In Jiang and Jiang's version, Mulan begins as "smart and brave" (1), well versed in military strategy (13), and already possessing martial arts skills taught to her by her father since she was young (2). As commanding general she comes up with a strategy of using goats to attack the enemy which results in a final victory for the Chinese empire. In the scene when the emperor asks her for anything she wants, she "politely declines" and requests to be sent home (29). She returns with no mention or picture of her father or family. The reader is shown and told only how surprised the accompanying soldiers are to see that she is really a woman (30). The focus in Jiang and Jiang's version is on Mulan. Although the story begins with a father-daughter relationship, it does not close with a father-daughter reunion scene. Filial piety, the reason for Mulan's disguise, is de-emphasized. Instead, Mulan's intelligence and military prowess are highlighted throughout the story. The theme centers on overcoming obstacles, in this case, a woman overcoming a law that "says females are not allowed to join the army" (6).

In Charlie Chin's *China's Bravest Girl*, a big change occurs in the scene when Mulan reveals to her soldier companions that she is really a woman. One of her comrades says to her, "How many times in danger did you turn to save my life? We were always the best of friends. Why not become husband and wife?" (26). In response, Mulan says, "If I become your wife...we will play a different game. You treat your friends with honor. Can your wife expect the same?" to which he says, "Yes, I will honor you...in all I do and say" (28). This exchange reveals two elements not in the original poem: Mulan has a life-saving relationship with a particular male soldier and Mulan insists on mutual respect between husband and wife. The latter is crucial because the author has gone one step beyond in depicting Mulan as a woman: she insists on female-male equality in the battlefield as well as in marriage. Hence, although Mulan returns to social normalcy by becoming a wife, she does so with feminist conditions.

Six years later, Lucille Lui-Wong wrote another Mulan story that has obvious signs of being influenced by Chin's picture book. In the scene where Mulan appears as a woman before her soldier companions, "One of the soldiers went to Mu-lan and said, 'All this time we have fought together, I have admired you so much. I never guessed you were a woman. I'd like to ask you to be my wife.'" Mulan answers, "'When I was your general, you honoured me. Will you also honour me as your wife?'" When the soldier "promises" in the affirmative, she replies, "Then I will marry you."[21] The story continues with a wedding ceremony and "Mu-lan and her soldier husband lived a long happy life" (19).

San Souci's *Fa Mulan* creates the strongest Mulan of all the American picture books. The book begins with Mulan "slicing the air with a bamboo stake" and saying, "'I am a swordswoman like the Maiden of Yueh!'" [2]. Similar to Jiang and Jiang's Mulan, this Mulan is not only well versed in martial arts but also in military strategy with an added implication by San Souci that she knows *Sunzi bingfa* [16]. Elder sister's statement that Mulan "acts like a man" [6] further reinforces why Mulan can pass and survive as a man in the battlefield.

Unlike story writers who focus on Mulan's masculine abilities, San Souci reminds the reader that Mulan's strengths are both feminine and masculine. Mulan refers to women in her war strategies when she tells the soldiers, "We will follow the classic wisdom that says, 'Act like a shy maiden to make the enemy think you are no threat. Then surprise them like a hare just let loose, and catch them off guard'" [22]. And, when one veteran soldier notes that she has increased her strength and improved her sword fighting, he says, "'You excel because you balance female and male energies....A good swordsman should appear as calm as a fine lady, but he must be capable and quick action like a surprised tiger'" [16]. Mulan's softer side is especially revealed when in the battlefield: "...sometimes one or another of the brave, handsome young men would touch her heart. She would dream of leaving the battlefield for the fields of home, of becoming a bride, a wife, a mother. However, duty to family and country, and her sense of honor, pushed all these dreams aside" [18].

Note should be taken that Mulan's own "sense of honor" has been added to filial piety and patriotism as an important reason for maintaining her disguise. This is a Mulan who is more individualistic than past Chinese Mulans.

Finally, when San Souci's Mulan returns home and becomes a woman again, she talks about not being able to tell the difference in gender between two rabbits. One soldier, with whom Mulan "felt closest to," says, "'In the field, what is the need of telling he-rabbit from she-rabbit? But when they return to their/burrow, the rabbits know which partner is husband and which is wife. So they build a life together.'" To Mulan, these words "hinted at a bright, shared tomorrow" [28-29], which imply a return to the social normalcy of marriage. However, San Souci's *Mulan* breaks tradition when the soldiers bow before a female Mulan in acknowledgment of their loyalty to her, their former general, and for all she has done [29]. This is significant because bowing to a woman during a time when "the Khan does not let women serve as soldiers" [6] symbolizes that society in the end has changed by recognizing and honoring a woman despite the fact that she went against societal rules. This reaction is in sharp contrast to the ending in the original poem, as well as in all the other American and Chinese picture books, where the soldiers are only expressing surprise and shock at seeing a female Mulan.

In adapting San Souci's *Mulan*, Disney's team of writers created a stronger and more individualistic female protagonist who literally makes China change its ways. In the beginning of the story, Disney's Mulan character is consistent with the traditional Mulan. Her reason for disguising as a man is to save her father, in other words, filial piety. But in a song entitled "Reflection" (lyrics by David Zippel), Mulan shows signs of doubt when she questions her identity and what she is doing:

> Look at me,
> I will never pass for
> a perfect bride
> Or a perfect daughter
> Can it be
> I'm not meant to play
> this part?
> Now I see
> That if I were truly
> To be myself
> I would break my family's heart.
>
> Who is that girl I see
> Staring straight
> Back at me?
> Why is my reflection someone
> I don't know?
> Somehow I cannot hide
> Who I am
> Though I've tried
> When will my reflection show
> Who I am inside?
> When will my reflection show
> Who I am inside?

A major turning point for Disney's Mulan occurs after she is discovered to be a woman. Disgraced and sad because she is now banished from the military, she says to Mushu, "Maybe I didn't go for my father. Maybe what I really wanted was to prove I could do things right. So when I look in the mirror, I'd see someone worthwhile. But I was wrong. I see nothing." Then she throws her helmet onto the snowy ground. At this point of failure to maintain and bring honor to the family, Mulan begins to realize that it is no longer about fighting or living for her father but for herself. She is evolving into an individual. She feels like a failure not because she failed her father but because the reflection on the "mirror" of her helmet shows she is nothing and has failed herself. The throwing of Mulan's helmet is symbolic of her character development in two ways: First, she discards the last of her disguise, which has held her back in terms of physically being a woman. Second, she is embarking on her next phase of life, which is to prove her own worth as a woman. To continue with this focus on individuality and being a woman, Mulan ends by no longer being a woman disguised as a man but as a woman fighting as a woman to save her country.

Mulan returns home victoriously and gives to her father the sword and pendant that the emperor has bestowed upon her. She has fulfilled her filial piety on her own grounds as a woman and is acknowledged accordingly when her father says, "The greatest gift and honor is having you for a daughter." This is significant in a patriarchal society where sons/men are preferred over daughters/women. Finally, when Li Shang shows up at her house with an obvious implication of wishing to wed Mulan, Mulan responds simply by saying, "Would you like to stay for dinner?" and Mushu saying in the background, "Would you like to stay forever?" As a woman, she takes the initiative to invite Li Shang to dinner before a tongue-tied Li Shang is able to say another word. In the background, her guardian dragon finishes the implied marriage proposal made by a woman and not a man.

The boldest change in Disney's *Mulan* happens when the emperor and all the people of China physically bow to a female Mulan in respect and gratitude for saving China, after which Mulan gives the emperor a big hug. The Disney team has gone beyond San Souci's picture book of soldiers bowing to Mulan. One can easily question the historical and cultural possibility of a Chinese emperor bowing to anyone or of anyone being able to hug an emperor publicly, but Disney's version ignores cultural practice and authenticity, and chooses to dramatically show how Mulan has changed China to the point that everyone bows to her as a woman. Unlike previous stories where Mulan returns to societal norms, Disney's Mulan is an agent who has changed society.

While Disney's *Mulan* deals with filial piety, *Mulan II* continues with the other important Mulan theme: patriotism. One month after returning home, Li Shang officially proposes to Mulan. But before they marry, the emperor assigns the two to escort his three daughters to a blind marriage ceremony with the sons of the Mongol lord in order to avoid war. Mulan's former three soldier companions, Yao, Ling, and Chien-Po, also accompany this entourage. During the journey, the three princesses and three soldiers fall in love with each other. The main conflict of the story, as expressed in conversations between the princesses and Mulan, is how to decide between heart and duty. According to the princesses, their duty is to sacrifice and serve one's country, so they must be filial to their emperor father and go through with the blind marriage in the name of patriotism. But for Mulan, "my duty is to my heart." The story ends with everyone doing what's right for one's heart and not what's considered right for the emperor father or country. This completes the characterization of Disney's Mulan: Societal expectations such as filial piety and patriotism are not priorities in Mulan's life. Priority is the individual self.

In America, Mulan has evolved from being a woman fighting for her father and country to a woman fighting for what she wants and not for what society wants or expects of her. Due to different value systems, the perennial conflict of society versus self in literature is resolved differently in the two countries/societies from where the

Mulan stories are created. The majority of Chinese stories favor society over self whereas the majority of American stories favor self over society. The former honors family /country and maintains status quo in society; the latter honors the individual and changes status quo. Both are women with different personalities and strengths.

## Mulan Returns to China

In 1998, Mulan returned to China not as a Chinese American Mulan but as an American Mulan. Of all the American versions of Mulan, Disney's *Mulan* has the biggest recognition in China. With the exception of Rita Hsiao, a Chinese American born in Poughkeepsie, New York, who makes up one-fifth of the *Mulan* writing team, the combined Disney production teams of *Mulan* and *Mulan II* are the creative voices of mainstream Eurocentric America and not of minority Chinese America. Powerful Disney commercialization and marketing strategies have proven to be effective in the country where Mulan was born. At least twenty-one different picture book versions of Mulan have been published in China from 1998 to 2007, nine of which are different translated editions of Disney's *Mulan*. This equates to 43% of Mulan picture books published in China to be Disney's *Mulan*.

Although Disney's *Mulan* appears to be the most popularly published version of the Mulan story in Chinese children's literature since 1998, there is no indication that China's Mulan focuses on the self. The majority of the twelve post-1998 Chinese stories have been fairly loyal to the traditional themes of the original Mulan poem. One 2004 Chinese version does borrow elements from the Disney story, like having a dragon named Mushu and having a Mulan discovered to be a woman during battle.[22] However, this version does not follow Disney's themes for the story. It ends when the evil Khan is killed by the rocket. There are no scenes depicting the emperor bowing to Mulan or of Mulan returning home.

The didactic function of Mulan's story continues in China as evidenced in one (among many other) 21st century Mulan stories published in China, where the editor's comments at the end of the story maintain the Chinese focus on society rather than self in the Mulan stories:

A filial Hua Mulan fights in place of her father in the military. While in the military, she fought hard and brave, and ended up being a successful woman warrior. Boys and Girls: We must also be like Hua Mulan – be filial to our parents, and be strong and brave children.[23]

This particular Mulan story is contained in a collection entitled *Bansui nühai kuaile de 108ge haogushi* 伴隨女孩快樂成長的108個好故事 or "108 good stories accompanying girls to grow up happy." The Chinese book title alone identifies the didactic theme of Mulan's story.

Of further note is that in America, Mulan's story is deemed acceptable by educators to be read and studied at the third grade level, versus in China where Mulan's poem is read and studied in the middle school level as serious literature. Almost every Chinese study book ranks the poem as one of the "must know" and "must memorize" poems for middle school students. The commentaries and analyses in these study books emphasize and praise Mulan's filial piety, patriotism, and recently, her humble nature for not wanting any glory or wealth from the emperor except to go home and live a peaceful, ordinary life.[24] This is in contrast to the American education system where Mulan is presented to elementary school students in picture storybooks as a role model to be a strong, individualistic woman.

With the popular Chinese translations of Disney's *Mulan* and its accompanying commercialization in China, the American Mulan themes have been introduced to China. How big an influence the American Mulan has on China is yet to be determined. To date, none of the Chinese Mulan tales being retold and revised have boldly deviated from the traditional thematic focus on society and family, and only a few individuals in China have seriously challenged the authenticity of Disney's *Mulan*.

Have both mainstream China and minority Chinese America embraced a Mulan that "fakes" Chinese culture and places more value on the self? In light of the fact that from 1998 to 2007, 56% of the sixteen Mulan storybooks in America are different versions of Disney's *Mulan* and 43% of China's Mulan picture books are translations of Disney's *Mulan,* and that these percentages are expected to increase respectively in the future, is it possible that the world might one day acknowledge Disney's Mulan as the "real" if not the "best" Mulan? For now, what cannot be denied is that Mulan has left China. Her ancestral roots stem from China but her present and future belong to the creative domain of the world.

## NOTES

1. This paper is abridged from a longer work-in-progress study on the evolution of Mulan. Beginning in 1997, portions of the writer's Mulan research project have been presented in various conferences and venues. The latest presentation was at the November 19-21, 2007 international conference on overseas Chinese culture sponsored by the Universidade de Macau. Missing for discussion in this paper is a more detailed comparative study of the different Chinese Mulan versions published in the People's Republic of China, Hong Kong, and Taiwan, and a comparative study on the commercialization of Mulan in the United States and China.

2. Depending on which Chinese version or edition of the Mulan story is used, the word "ge" 歌 can be "ci" 辭 or "shi" 詩. There are slight deviations among the various Chinese editions but not enough to cause major concern for the purposes of this paper.

3. Line 34 of the poem mentions ten years in battle but on line 56, the soldiers say they were in battle for twelve years with Mulan.

4. Two different words are used in the poem, *kehan* 可汗 ("khan") in line 10 and *tianzi* 天子 ("son of heaven" or "emperor") in lines 35-36.

5. Maxine Hong Kingston, *Woman Warrior: Memoirs of a Girlhood among Ghosts* (New York: Alfred A. Knopf, 1976).

6. David Henry Hwang, *FOB and Other Plays* (New York: Plume-New American Library, 1990).

7. Frank Chin, "Come All Ye Asian American Writers of the Real and the Fake," *The Big Aiiieeeee! An Anthology of Chinese American and Japanese American Literature*, ed. Jeffery Paul Chan, Frank Chin, Lawson Fusao Inada, and Shawn Wong (New York: Meridian-Penguin Books USA Inc., 1991) 3.

8. Wei Jiang and Cheng An Jiang, *The Legend of Mu Lan: A Heroine of Ancient China*, illus. by authors, tr. Eileen Hu, Heroines in History series (Monterey, CA: Victory Press, 1992). Other Chinese heroines listed as part of this series include Wu Zetian 武則天, Mencius' Mother 孟母, Ban Zhao 班昭, and Li Qingzhao 李清照. As part of a series on famous Chinese generals and officials, this Mulan version was published in Chinese with some minor differences: Jiang Cheng An, ed., *Hua Mulan daifu congjun* 花木蘭代父從軍, illus. Luo Genxing 駱根興 (Hong Kong: Sesame Publication Co., 1998).

9. Charlie Chin, *China's Bravest Girl: The Legend of Hua Mu Lan*, illus. Tomie Arai, Chinese tr. Wang Xing Chu (Emeryville, CA: Children's Book Press, 1993); Jeanne M. Lee, *The Song of Mulan*, illus. by author (Arden, NC: Front Street, 1995); Song Nan Zhang, *The Ballad of Mulan*, illus. by author (Union City, CA: Pan Asian Publications (USA) Inc., 1998). Zhang's storybook has been translated into Spanish, Vietnamese, and Hmong.

10. The Disney team that received the nomination for best music includes Matthew Wilder for music, David Zippel for lyrics, and Jerry Goldsmith for orchestral score.

11. Robert D. San Souci, *Fa Mulan*, illus. Jean and Mou-Sien Tseng (New York: Hyperion Books for Children, 1998).

12. Chin 6. San Souci's "Author's Note" does not provide full citation for Chin's quote.

13. Lei Fan, tr., *The Legend of Mulan: A Folding Book of the Ancient Poem That Inspired the Disney Animated Film* (New York: Welcome Enterprises, Inc.-Hyperion, 1998).

14. Russell Schroeder, "Artistic Inspiration," *Disney's Mulan: Special Collector's Edition* (New York: Disney Press, 1998) 9-15.

15. Chinese names used here for the Mulan characters follow the Chinese names used in Disney's official Chinese translation of *Mulan*.

16. See Houghton Mifflin Reading's Kids' Place website (eduplace.com/kids) for Grade 3 level.

17. Kingston 20.

18. Kingston 120.

19. Susan Lynn Peterson, "The Ballad of Mu-lan," *Legends of the Martial Arts Masters* (Boston, Rutland, VT, and Tokyo: Tuttle Publishing, 2003) 44.

20. *The Secret of Mulan*, prod. Bill Schwartz, United American Video Corporation, 1998. Mulan animated features were also produced the same year in Australia, the Netherlands, and Thailand.

21. Lucille Lui-Wong, "The Legend of Hua Mu-lan," *Tales Near and Far*, Collections 2 (Scarborough, Ontario, Canada: Prentice Hall Ginn, 1999) 17-18.

22. *Hua Mulan* 花木蘭, Donghuacheng gushi 動劃城故事 series, ed. Kang Honglei 康宏磊, 2$^{nd}$ printing (Xi'an: Shanxi lüxing chubanshe, 2006) 4-51.

23. "Hua Mulan" 花木蘭，*Bansui nühai kuaile chengzhang de 108ge haogushi* 伴隨女孩快樂成長的108個好故事 [108 good stories accompanying girls to grow up happy], ed. Cui Zhonglei 崔鍾雷 (Changchun: Jilin shying chubanshe, 2007) 128.

24. For example, "Mulan shi" 木蘭詩, *Chuzhongsheng bibei gushici wushi shou* 初中生比背古詩詞五十首 [50 ancient poems that middle school students must memorize], Xiao Dusong 肖篤宋, ed. (Hunan: Hunan shaonian ertong chubanshe, 2003) 22-26; "Mulan shi" 木蘭詩, *Chuzhongsheng wushi shou bibei gushici* 初中生五十首必背古詩詞 [50 must memorize ancient poems for middle school students], Huang Yongguang 黃永光, ed. (Guangzhou: Guangdongsheng yuyan yinxiang chubanshe, n.d.) 29-36.

# 民族使命感與個人選擇權：
## 從美國華人研究角度看近代中國留學生的"回歸"

## 譚雅倫
*Marlon K. Hom*

CHINESE STUDENT-IMMIGRANTS'
RECENT QUEST FOR DUAL CITIZENSHIP:
AS SEEN FROM AN ASIAN AMERICAN PERSPECTIVE
(ENGLISH ABSTRACT)

Chinese students have been studying abroad since Yung Wing's graduation at Yale in 1854. They have studied in the United States, Europe, and Japan. Studying abroad in America eventually became the most ideal and popular choice when the United States made its influence in post-secondary education with American missionaries establishing numerous private universities in China beginning in the early 1910s. Thousands of Chinese students have attended top-ranked colleges and universities in the United States. This international educational experience changed the fate of China. These students – engineers, philosophers, scholars, artists, economists, politicians, and revolutionaries – would return to China and make changes and contributions in China's quest for modernization.

Political struggles in China and social movements in the United States during 1950-1979 created a situation where there were hardly any students coming from Mainland China because of the hostility between China and the United States. But thousands came from Taiwan and they chose not to return to Taiwan because of its political instability. They considered the United States conducive for resettlement as America's domestic Civil Rights Movement provided better opportunities for people of color in the United States. These students would find ideal employment, raise their families, and become naturalized citizens in America.

As China began its quest to "open and reform" and modernize after the mid-1980s, thousands of Mainland Chinese students resumed coming to study in the United States, with many settling down in America, especially after the June 4, 1989 Incident. They were able to change their legal status under a presidential executive order, and eventually became naturalized US citizens.

Beginning in the late 1990s, the Chinese government outreached to this population of highly educated Chinese Americans by appealing to their sense of cultural patriotism and allegiance to their homeland. Thousands – mostly with MBAs, science or engineering degrees, and armed with US or Canadian citizenship – have returned to China, some representing Western business interests, to carve out their niche in this new Chinese market-driven economic development.

However, China does not recognize dual or multiple citizenship, so these returnees have lost their Chinese birthright citizenship when they naturalized as citizens of their adopted country. They are considered "foreigners" in their homeland and they are subject to a cumbersome bureaucracy aimed against non-Chinese citizens in China.

At the same time, these student-immigrants are unwilling to forfeit their naturalized US or Canadian citizenship because of their distrust of the Chinese political structure. They want to make sure that there will be a survival option if anything undesirable were to happen in China. So a new movement developed: the quest for dual citizenship – an appeal to the Chinese government to recognize their Chinese citizenship despite naturalization in their adopted country. They profess their allegiance to China, but they want to keep their foreign citizenship.

This generation of student-immigrants represents a new population of Chinese Americans whose quest for dual citizenship highlights a continuous struggle in Asian America: What does it mean to be Asian American? What is their sense of citizenship and identity? Is this a self-interest-driven act, oblivious of social and political implications in both China and the United States? Will this be used by anti-immigrant advocates in America to call into question Chinese American allegiance to the United States? Japanese Americans with their dual citizenship paid a high price in the 1940s when their allegiance and loyalty to the United States were questioned. What price might Chinese Americans have to pay for these student-immigrants' quest for dual citizenship?

I.

　　美國華裔研究，對象是美國的華人，也包括跨越太平洋有關美國華人的人物事物。此項研究是美國亞裔研究 (Asian American Studies) 的一部分，也是與非洲裔，拉美裔，印第安裔等研究領域聯盟爲所謂的美國少數民族研究 (American minority studies) 或是美國族裔研究 (American ethnic studies)。

　　少數民族研究是一項新興的學術專業；隨著第二次世界大戰後二十多年間美國本土非洲裔族群伸張民權的社會運動 (Civil Rights Movement) 的時代產生。1968年秋季，美國加州的舊金山州立大學學生運動成功挑戰美國白人爲主的主流學術，創辦族裔研究學院 (School of Ethnic Studies, 1990年後改稱College of Ethnic Studies) 開始美國少數民族族群的課程與研究項目。這個新學術項目立刻得到熱烈響應，隨即美國西岸數間著名大學也相繼成立美國少數民族研究的課程與項目，因此得以扎根。在以後二十多個年頭，漸漸自然而然地蔓延到美東及美中的主要學府。

　　這個研究領域，是基于美國非白種人的少數民族的族群使命感所産生，以大學課程和學術研究來否定美國白種主義對少數民族的不客觀學術研究，　重新認可及保存自己民族在美國的歷史與貢獻，　爭取作爲美國人的認同與美國憲法所賦予的平等民權，　挑戰及取締社會各階層所存有種族歧視。另一方面，也要把學術研究從白人爲主的象牙塔裏解放出來，走向服務群衆和少數民族的族群社區。

　　從這一個華裔研究專業的大前提和角度觀看近百多年的中國留學美國的中國學生和海外華人歷史，使我對早期的中國留學生和早期海外華人民族情操和社會的使命感非常敬佩崇拜。他們一開始便以行動改變了中國的近代歷史，改變了中華民族的命運。他們的貢獻，實在數不勝數；舉例說：當年容閎接受了美國教育，雖然歸化了美籍，但他沒有放弃他的民族教育改革的使命感。詹天佑留學美國後回國，改造了中國的鐵路交通。伍廷芳雖是出生于南洋，但回到祖國成爲出色的外交家，出使美洲等地。孫逸仙（孫中山）雖是幼年隨孫氏家族移民夏威夷，但他長大後沒有因此而隨其家族落籍夏威夷，反而爲鼓吹和領導中國的國民革命運動而奔走世界各地，成功推翻封建專制的中國皇朝制度。胡適當年留學美國，回國後搞的白話語文（新文化）運動，實在是洋秀才以筆爲槍，成功展開名符其實的中國文化大革命；不流血，不像六十年代生靈塗炭，民不聊生的中國政治鬥爭的文化大革命。留學其他國家中國留學生也是一樣。郁達夫在日本的留學遭遇使他意識到他應有的民族的尊嚴。魯迅也是留學日本時明白到中華民族尊嚴的失落，使他放弃學醫的志願，回國後以創作文學，投身醫治中國人民靈魂的偉業……還有勤工儉學留學法國的周恩來，鄧小平等中國青年，都像庚子賠款留學美國的清華學生，他們一批一批的出國，一批一批回國；學成（有學位）回來，不完成學業（沒有學位）也都回來。參與改造中國，建設中國的行伍。因爲，他們在國外留學的經驗，讓他們認識到他們出國留學所應有的民族使命。

　　當年這些中國留學生群裏，他們所懷有的民族情操與意志，跟我們六十年代美國少數民族運動的族群情操與意志是一致的：大家都有爲自己國家民族服務的使命感而投身自己的社會和社區，不躲在象牙塔裏頭與社會脫節。當年一些中國留美學生和六十年代的美國華裔大學生，生活在種族矛盾尖銳的白人爲主時代，對種族歧視的問題很敏感，也積極地以各種方式批判，挑戰，抗議，或是以行動企圖消滅這種不平等社會環境。早在在美國排華時代（1882-1943），很多留學美國的中國學生和美國華人都感到，中國祖國的强盛是消滅歧視華人的最有效武器。他們都注意到美國社會歧視華人的現象。當年紐約港自由神像建設期間，在美國各地社區籌款時，就有紐約華埠的美國華人質疑：這個自由女神的象徵，是否也保護受到歧視的華人？留學生的聞一多，在二十年代也感到美國種族歧視的華人羞恥，在其詩篇疾呼：下賤的洗衣工作你們肯幹？你們肯幹？三十年代的美國土生華裔，他們有一個全國性的論壇，討論他們的將來（前途）是在出生地的美國還是祖籍的中國？其中最明顯的，大家有了共識：中國需要建國人才；若能回國建設，使中國強盛起來，他們在美國的被歧視的地位也就會有改善。曾經留學日本的蔣介石在抗日戰爭時，也對美國種族歧視作了相應立場，要求美國政府廢除《排華法案》，作爲合作條件，聯合成爲太平洋戰區盟邦向日本軍國主義反攻。這立場推動了美國國會在1943年底廢除了執行了六十一年的《排華法案》，讓華人有權移民美國和歸化美國籍。而美國華裔當年也在美國軍隊服役和在後勤單位工作，以效忠美國憲法中的公民責任的行動面對美國的種族歧視與排斥。除了在歐洲戰場，他們也到了中國戰區，參加飛虎隊等戰時“救中國”工作行列。美國本土的華人社區，有“一碗飯”(Rice Bowl Campaign) 拯救中國戰時苦難同胞的運動。這是華埠社區的保衛和支援祖國抗日的民族行動。這一切都是海外華人的民族尊嚴和使命感驅動下的反應與表現。

　　抗日戰爭結束，中國學者學生恢復留學美國。不過，中美兩國的內部都產生了急劇大變化。美國有反對共產黨的保守派的麥加錫時代抬頭：視馬克思主義爲顛覆美國自由思想的最大敵人；任何支持或親近共產主義的活動，就是反對美國的“非美國”行爲 (un-American)。一連串清算行動戰後展開。同時期，中國內戰結束，共產政權勝利，統治中國。不久中美兩方絕交，繼之是韓戰爆發，中美兩國爲朝鮮半島戰場上的敵對國。無數當年拿中華民國護照來美的訪問學者與留學生，變成了美國聯邦政府當年對抗中國共產政權而修正了的 “難民法案” 所公認的政治難民。

　　當年很多決定留居在美國的華人和中國學者及科學家，在五十年代始也受到了美國極右的麥加錫主義者的調查與壓害。美國聯邦調查局局長胡佛 (J. Edgar Hoover) 也公然說了詆毀所有美國華裔和華人的言論；他說在美國的華人都不可信賴，因爲他們只會效忠中國，不會效忠美國。（其實，這個論調是重複了在第二次世界大戰時對待美國日裔的種族政治籍口， 指美國日裔在祖籍國保存有日本國籍，只忠于日本天皇，不會效忠美國；當年就以 “戰事所需”(military necessity) 的理由，把美國西岸十二萬無辜的美國日裔關進集中營。）

　　當年在各種各式的無理調查與壓害下，美國華人社區開始是消極地抵抗，後來積極地面對這個挑戰，集資聘請憲法律師告上美國聯邦法院伸張憲法保護的公民權益。同時期也有很多有強烈民族感情的中國知識分子和科學家毅然離開美國，響應周恩來呼籲海外中國知識分子回祖國參加建設新中國的行伍。這情形當時很普遍，很多留學生感到這是自然而然的中國留學知識分子責任。在六十年代文革還沒有全面展開之前，連一些來自臺灣的中國留美學生，包括來自東南亞的華人，響應海外知識分子回來祖籍国建設新中國的號召也回到中國大陸。

　　不過，很多懷著民族情操回國的留學生們，在反右，整風，文革等運動中，因爲他們的西方教育背景和海外關係遭受到無情的中國極左政治勢力衝擊。他們像其他的中國知識分子，遭下放到“五七幹校”勞動改造，不能在他們的專業領域發揮建設性的社會功能。他們受到懷疑，歧視，被隔離，生活在恐慌害怕的日子裏，并不好過。有的更是被逼害至家散人亡或是妻離子散。一位舉世著名的留英回國在外文出版社工作的翻譯家，不但夫妻受罪，兒子也瘋了。七十年代起，一些能够再次出國的，也就紛紛離開。好幾位更在歐美出版傳記或小說，把當年回國服務的各種痛苦遭遇，公諸于世。對我們海外華人和研究學者來說，對當時信息封閉，現在也是信息禁區的文革時代，從這些回憶文字上，知道了當年回國的留學生的遭遇，對當年中國社會有了人性化的認識和瞭解。

　　當然也有很多中國留學生與訪問學者選擇留居在美國，在當年的種族歧視與反共社會形態下生活謀生存。他們的生活條件也并不容易或是理想。一位戰前中國天津名牌大學的外語系主任，五十年代時期也只得栖身在美國的大學裏美國國防部建立的語言訓練項目，教美國軍人學生基本漢語。到了韓戰後美國政府認識到國家安全與全球化戰略需要， 國會動過了 “國防教育法案”(National

Defense Education Act)；把中國研究列爲國防（國家安全）全方面的大學教育項目，撥款支持中國研究。很多中國學者才有機會在大學亞洲研究系拿到教授身份任教。可是，他們教授的是中國語文，并不是他們本來的西方語文專業。不過他們的民族使命感沒有因爲居留歸化美國社會而湮滅，專業上的中國研究使他們的民族情操變得濃厚。記得七十年代初"保釣運動"在美國各地大學展開，很多華人學者在背後鼓勵支持活躍于保釣運動的中國留學生（活躍的學生多是來自香港）。　中美兩國開始學術交流對話時，有些學者很早便成爲交流前綫的橋樑分子。其中有些老留學生，還有些像1880年代的容閎，文革後從中國安排新的留學生出國到美國大學留學。不過，也有人在文革後期因爲研究項目在中國是敏感題材而受到壓害；像舊金山州立大學的許芥煜（已故），他的專長研究是周恩來；他早在1972年夏天中美關係暖化后便回到中國訪問探親及做研究。那還是文革批鬥的年代；同年秋天他被拘禁，全家被驅逐出境，至今還沒平反。不過在九十年代以後這近十幾年，有很多年老退休的國際級的美國華人教授，在中美之間飛來飛去；亦有的選擇了回祖籍中國養老，享受高等海外華人的特殊規格待遇。

　　這兩種上一代的留學生在祖國與國外的生活遭遇，其民族意識情操與個人生活選擇的表現，是非常強烈的對比與啓示。

　　五十年代末期到六十年代初的臺灣，因爲十多年來海峽敵對局勢不穩定，很多家庭決定把就學年齡的晚輩送出國外念書，出現了大批學生以留學美國方式出國，然後在美國定居，出現了大批留學生畢業而不回原籍國家的現象。雖然臺灣國民黨政府後來實行禁止本科生出國，男生本科畢業更要服了義務兵役才可以申請出國深造（研究生），也擋不住當年要到美國留學的熱潮，反而造做了美國社會吸收了大批來自臺灣的中國精英研究生人才，在美國大學的研究院畢業後定居美國。這也就是開始了當年臺灣的人才外流 (brain drain) 的現象。

　　中國大陸在八十年代起，也開始出現了相同的留學美國熱潮；而中國大陸的人才外流的現象，比當年臺灣的情形，簡直是小巫（臺灣）見大巫（大陸）。不過中國政府沒有像臺灣政府一樣用兵役制度駕馭在男生留學的制度上，也沒有意識到留學外國是嚴重知識人才資源外流。相傳開放當初有中央領導人說中國人才多，出國留學不回來也不要緊的論調。看來中國政府開放出國留學政策時沒有適當地瞭解或借鏡臺灣六七十年代的人才外流現象；現在才有明顯的考慮如何挽留，鼓勵精英留學生人才回流的策略。再者，開放初期，首批出國者多是有影響力，有身份和背景的高層高幹子弟。這個早期出國留學現象，成了下層階級向上層效仿而形成的一種風氣。不過幾年後美國政府相對地意識到很多中國留學生跟臺灣的留學生一樣，以留學簽證作爲移民美國的捷徑，連一些學者也用學術交流簽證而一去不返。八十年代末期美國領事館便對中國留學簽證嚴厲審批，動不動便以"有移民傾向"而拒絕中國學生的留學簽證申請。據本人所知，九十年代中期，就有一位中國學生往廣州美國領事館申請簽證五次遭拒，還是不甘心放弃；在第六次却終于獲到簽證。這個情況并不是特殊例外。很多中國學生不止一次地重複申請，期望幸運時刻光臨。這種美國簽證難和獲到簽證到美國是成功形象的現象，加深了中國學生學者前往美國留學或交流的無限欲望，更形成爲獲得美國留學簽證是一種高難度的成就或榮譽。

　　不過儘管美國留學簽證困難，每年都有成千成百計的精英中國學生到美國留學。拔尖中國學府如北大清華，跟六，七十年代的臺灣大學情況一樣，畢業生前往美國研究深造的比例，相信是世界任何國家的頂尖大學無可以相比。1989年六月"六四"事件後老布殊總統 (President George H. Bush) 作反應而頒發的總統行政指示命令時，當時就有數以萬計的留美中國學生立即申請。他們很快獲得到美國永久居留權（綠卡）；數年後便歸化爲美國籍。當然也有一小部分公費留學生保持其原國籍，學成回國，高官厚祿。總之，一般中國精英學生認爲留學美國然後留下美國是理所當然的現象，是局外人難以想像的狂熱。

II.

　　五，六十年代美國本土的民權運動，帶出了法律條文和司法程序推廣美國社會的種族平權；在教育，就業，宗教信仰，居住方面給與少數民族各種平等機會。六十年代中期，詹桑總統(President Lyndon Johnson)推行他的"偉大社會"(Great Society)計劃，改善民生；也把歧視性質的移民法律也革新了。1965年新的移民修正法例 (Immigration Reform Act of 1965)，移民配額不再是以1920年代的美國人口的種族比例爲配額基礎，而是世界每一國家都有兩萬名的同數量配額，更以美國公民的家庭團聚爲移民主旨，每年五十多萬人的移民總額，先到先得。因爲當時美國跟中國沒有邦交，這兩萬名的配額倒方便了來自臺灣香港的中國留學生，學成後非常容易改變留學生身份留居美國，找到工作便可拿到綠卡，數年後便可以依照移民條例歸化成爲美國公民。1990年修正的移民法加多了每年數萬技術移民的配額，高深專業教育的中國留學生，當然受益不淺；畢業後順理成章地留下了。

　　1979年中美關係正常化以後，美國聯邦移民局在移民法例執行上實際采取的是兩個中國的政策：臺灣和中國大陸都有相同數量，等於兩個國家的配額。因此，中國人每年移民美國的配額，比任何國家多一倍。加上香港的特別配額，華人移民美國每年可以達到五萬多人。所以說，雖然中國外交上批評美國的臺灣海峽的兩個中國的國際政治，中國政府沒有抗議或有效地回應這個美國處理中國國民移民美國的兩國中國政策。中國海峽兩地的公民，也確實充分地享受了這個公開的兩個中國的美國移民政策，三十多年來一直大比數地利用這個國家配額移民到美國。留學生畢業後申請移民居留的配額也因此比其他國家多。這也是多年來這個臺灣中國大陸人才外流的根源。中國政府也沒有在外交上有效地處理此項美國對中國的移民政策上的兩國中國立場。

　　以教育而言，六十年代後很多美國大學才有透明的入學規則，之前的透明度并不高。很多優秀的華裔學生都不能進入心儀的理想大學。筆者的兩位土生華裔同窗，都是品學兼優，名列前茅的華裔。一位中學畢業申請斯坦福大學 (Stanford University) 讀本科遭拒絕，因爲她的父親是沒有社會地位的華埠工人。另一位讀完州立大學的本科及碩士班，學歷成績驕人，她并拿到加省政府的四年獎學金報考斯坦福大學亞洲研究的博士班，保證四年在斯坦福無經濟顧慮；可是斯坦福大學不收錄她。她認識該校中的資深亞洲研究系教授後來告訴她：原來不是她的成績學歷不優，而是因爲她的家庭背景不理想：爸爸只是酒樓服務員，媽媽是華埠工作的車衣女工。雖有她獲得加省政府獎勵，提供四年全免獎學金也不獲取錄進入私立的貴族學府斯坦福攻讀博士。

　　公民權法案推動下，各種相關的聯邦法律禁止了此類種族，階級及性別歧視性質的入學決定：更有《教育機會項目》(Educational Opportunity Program)提供少數民族及家庭經濟低微的學生上名牌公立和私立大學。《落實行動項目》(Affirmative Action Program)及《就業平等機會委員會》(Equal Employment Opportunity Commission)更嚴密監察各大學，機關和行業，要求在同等資歷的申請者之間，過去在美國社會上曾被歧視過的民族，在取錄程序上，應該落實獲得優先取錄的待遇和機會來補償以前不平等待遇所造成的今日弱勢族群的社會現象。法律監察下七十年代的美國大學入學和求職取錄程序漸漸明朗了，種族歧視不能過分明顯違反聯邦民權法案。八十年代初期華人大學生人數激增。

　　很多大學裏的學系，尤其是文科，藝術，社會科學等學系，在七十年代還是不願意聘用華人爲教授。就是在80年代，算是較爲開明的舊金山州立大學，其英文系因爲歧視華裔應徵者被告上法庭，隨而喪失了其獨立招聘教授的權利數年。一般公立私立大學在民權法案的推動下，加上幾場官司訴訟失敗的司法教訓，漸漸開始聘請少數民族的教授，華人在七十年代的專業就職機會也相對地開始增加了。在這個民權運動轄管的美國社會，廣推本土的種族平等內政，來自中國的留學生畢業後也沾了利益，容易找到自己專業的工作。因此在七，八，九十年代提供了一批又一批中國（臺灣與大陸）留學生畢業後留在美國的理想就業機會。有了職業也有容易申請到永久居留權（綠卡）；有了綠卡，幾年後就歸化成爲有美國籍權的美國公民。有了公民權，就可以申辦家屬移民美國；有了專業經驗，同時也可以利用機會在美國創業。這個現象，也是七十年代的臺灣和今日的中國大陸所稱的人才外流 (brain drain) 到美國本土因素。

　　相對來說，自六，七十年代起，民權運動推動下的美國開放社會，跟留學生們本土國家（臺灣，大陸）的情形相比，在各種民生與政治條件的比較下，他們選擇留在美國，是明顯的理性個人選擇與決定。早期（四，五十年之前）中國留學生的使命感與民族情操，加上國外的種族歧視，驅使他們回國建設，發奮圖強。現代的留學生，享受了美國少數民族運動帶來的所謂平等民權的個人本身之基本利益。所以他們在個人前途的選擇上，主要是要考慮到在外國的個人的物質享受愛好和專業待遇和機會，使他們對民族情操和使命感的看法加上了新的注釋：愛國在心，個人權益的考慮與選擇也重要。居留在國外也可以愛國。所以大多數選擇了在國外定居及歸化爲外國的公民。這種六七十年代起，留學便成爲移民途徑，留學成功選擇留下當地國家的現象，是不是超越了留學生的基本使命或教育精神？出國留學的目的是爲了什麼？這是一個令人深省的研討題目。

　　從美國華裔研究角度來說，中國留學生留居美國，在美國本土社會帶來了一定的影響。一般來說，他們的高等教育程度，專業地位，經濟條件，只求踏入白人社會被接受，而不會正面挑戰白人優越感和歧視他人的新移民生活方式，是美國人所認定和贊許的 "少數民族模範" (model minority) 的典型之一。美國一些種族主義者，就常用這些亞裔新移民的成功 "模範" 來批評及貶低其他美國少數族裔，離間少數民族之間的關係。更以此類 "成功" 數據來削減對經濟底綫以下的貧窮亞裔百姓的社區補助。這是我們在美國種族研究領域中所關注的一個相當嚴重的美國種族關係問題。

## III.

　　另一個令我們美國華裔研究者非常關注的新發展，就是這近十年來一些拿到了美國（或是其他國家）的國籍（公民權）或居留權（綠卡）才回來中國的留學生，他們是現在所謂的 "海歸" 華僑華人，近十幾年來，中國政府積極統戰他們。他們在 "回國" 投資創業的行動中，提出了他們想擁有 "雙重國籍" 的願望，建議中國把不承認雙重國籍的憲法修改，恢復他們在歸化外國國籍時喪失了的中國公民權，方便他們回到中國建設創業。也同時他們也保留他們是外國公民的身份和他們在國外居留地的公民權益。

　　雖然很多人坦白地公開討論種種原因，主要是圍繞在今日中國對外籍人士在中國有諸多管制，和建國初年在萬隆會議的中國國籍立場和今日中國憲法的條文；因此要求修正，確認今日的 "海歸" 人士是今日中國發展中所需要的特殊階級人士而必須提供與他們特別權利的方便。

　　但大家都意識到，這個雙重國籍的建議，涉及不單只是他們一群人的特殊身份那麼簡單，還有國際關係與國內法制，其中涵義非常嚴重複雜。最表面的是反映出了中國本土政府對非中國籍人士在華創業就業有困難的程序；中國官僚體制對外籍人士管理關卡重重。若是 "海歸" 者在中國能重獲其中國籍公民身份，這些 "海歸" 的外籍華人可以一邊享受中國對待外資機構的特別利益，也可以不接受那些專對外資機構的嚴謹監管機制。這些監管，也實在是嚇人。就以本人以加州州立大學系統派來北京大學交流工作一年的經驗爲例：駐美的中國領事館（外交部）認爲單是加州州立大學校長發出的來華工作委任證明不合乎中國外交部的工作簽證條件；要求數份個別中國機關單位發出的認可文件才可以辦理入境簽證。抵達北京後，又要立刻奔走于各政府機構，交款重新做體檢（美國做的不算）拿本地發出的健康證明； 又要申請外國專家局頒發的外國專家證（領取此證有何實際作用?除了說是規定條例，沒一個人能說明白）； 北京公安局又取消中國領事館（外交部）發的工作簽證（爲何要取消工作簽證?爲何工作簽證入境後無效?），要再付款申請外國人在華工作的居留證，再到區內的公安局作居留地址登記...處處蓋章收費。外籍人士在華短期任職的簡單事情也變得複雜如此，若是在華創業，重複機制所造成的難度可想而知。

對在華的外籍人士來說，客觀的觀察，就發現種種機制對在華工作或創業的外籍人士的要求，只是勞民傷財，浪費時間;除了收費養活一群官僚，根本沒有其他任何實際作用。若果"海歸"人士認爲雙重國籍建議是針對和避免此等濫權監管機制，表面上是有相當好的理由。不過，這些機制是中國國內應該改革的本土官僚行政現象，雙重國籍則牽連上國際及外交問題;不應混二爲一。在這方面，中國政府若能面對現象，精簡此等節外生枝式，以收費爲主的對外籍人士的國內監管機制，不是更有效的現代制度嗎?

其二，是那些承認或是默可公民可以持有雙重國籍的國家，在國籍認同上是一視同仁而不只是針對某一類特殊身份人物或是某一種特殊階級的公民。若中國政府只給與這些已經歸化外國籍的"海歸"人士中國公民權，也要考慮提供相等權益與其他在華做同類工作的華裔和其他族裔的外籍人士。因爲在國際角度來說，大家都是外籍，在華的法定身份都是一樣的。國家立憲或修正憲法，對外籍人士處理立場應該一致，不能厚此薄彼。否則，這是含有歧視性的待遇，也象徵了中國還是停留在人治而不是法治的不公平封建制度裏。

其三，雙重國籍的建議是反映出了近代中國歷史遺留的嚴重國籍與政治認同問題。 幾十年來國內國外的各種變遷，這些留學生背景的海外華人，雖然有中華民族情操和使命感，但是對祖籍中國沒有個人的安全感。生活在國外後，他們回來中國有了各種的個人利益的要求與安全的考慮; 要安排後路，要有選擇權。這都是對歷史事件的必然回應，原因是他們再也不願意重複前輩留學生在民族使命感驅使下回國後所遭遇到的命運。雙重國籍的身份，對他們來說，也許是他們的人身自由與安全的保障的表達。這個心態，當然是很多早年回國留學生所沒有的，就算有，也不是那麼突出的因素，也沒有演變成爲討價還價的回國條件而達到在國家策略階層上的公開討論。它反映的也不單是針對中國的發展需要他們的專業技能， 更是反映了今日的回國留學生在民族情操與個人生活選擇兩方面都有了相對平衡的觀察與考慮而作出的反應。這種現象令人聯想到，也可以說今日一些"海歸"人士，擁有了魚與熊掌要兼得之的個人特權心態。也是美國諺語所指的 "have the cake and eat it" （拿到了蛋糕還要吃掉）的個人中心主義要擁有一切的表達。

IV.

最後，要是從美國華人研究的角度看來自美國的"海歸"人士對雙重國籍的要求，這個情況似乎是證實了美國在十九世紀中葉以來那些排斥華人的歷史言論： 來自中國的華人移民是不可以信賴，是不能同化的异種民族;他們不會完全忠誠地效忠美國。華人入籍美國只是取其利益，只想享受美國的高度物質文明與憲法的保護。他們不會投入美國的社會;留在美國的幾年是坐"移民監"。等歸化美國籍，公民權這些東西拿到了手，有了美國政府保護外海公民的安全感以後，便拿著美國護照離開，回祖籍中國。現在更要求重獲中國國籍，要擁有雙重國籍的身份方便他們個人在兩個國家的生活方式。

當然，在美國加拿大這些尊重個人行動自由的國度，這個留與去的選擇是任何一個公民的絕對權利。不過，在美國有接受公民歷史教育，有公民意識和社會責任感的美國公民，都認識到他們的國家

是一個複雜的多元化移民社會。祖籍歐洲的白種民族移民的後裔在美洲新大陸排斥歧視其他非白種
民族的移民後裔數百年；排斥華人也有百多年的歷史。第二次世界大戰後美國少數民族大聯盟，在
四，五十年前的民權運動和少數民族平權運動中，成功地挑戰當年的社會種族不平等現狀，打垮了
歧視排斥性的白人社會意識和制度，確實了我們的應有的國籍身份的地位與認同，憲法的權益與公
民義務；爭取給予新一代的美國華人和移民，在教育職業居住等等方面，比前一代較爲平等的待遇
和機會。也讓近三十年來在美國的中國留學生享用了這個美國社會的新貌，可以普遍地在美國求學，
就業與居留，他們實在得益不淺。

　　然而近年來這個由有留學生背景的"海歸"人士提出的雙重國籍主張，反映了他們的個人利益
選擇是大前提的態度；這也無形中吻證了美國的歧視人士對移民背景的美國華人的看法，這更漠視
和否定了四十多年來美國華裔在美國的少數民族認同的艱苦鬥爭運動中爭取到的成果。

　　現在的發展，不但是中國留學生的定義在變形，也是中國的社會，教育與政治氣氛所形成的一個
現象。我個人認爲，中國政府不單只是要在爲了目前經濟發展需求的考慮來處理這個情況，而是更
要嚴肅，客觀，適當地面對這個國內人治，政治與法治有關的討論，和處理海外華人與祖籍國關係所
應該採取的國際立場。

　　值得一提的是2008年春，香港特別行政區政府委任了一批高層政治問責的副局長與政治助理。開
放的香港傳媒爆出了其中五位政治委任的副局長和幾位政治助理都是曾經留學外國，在外國定居落
籍，後來又持外國護照回流香港工作的高深教育人物。他們與家人都持有外國國籍----美國，英國，
加拿大等國籍。香港立法局民選議員隨著跟進，質疑這些新政治委任的官員對政府的忠誠，拿的美加
英護照是否是鋪後路，雖然在香港政府工作高官厚祿，但是政治上對香港沒有安全感。香港特區政府
為他們辯護，指出《基本法》容許副局長持有外籍；國籍更是個人私隱而不加評論。不過在傳媒的
廣泛報道下，結果這些新委任副局長經不了這種國籍與政治效忠質疑立刻作了決定，放棄了他們個人
持有的英國加國美國籍權。（當然，退任或退休后他們還是可以離開香港與其外國籍的家人團聚。）
其中位持有美國國籍的一位新副局長，事前曾對傳媒說這不僅是其個人的職業決定，還要考慮家庭
家人的取捨。三位政治助理拒絕放棄其外國籍權。整個事件是一場國籍效忠與責任承擔的政治質疑，
反映出香港的情形跟中國大陸高層"海歸"人物差不多，個人在經濟利益，社會責任承擔，與政治
安全感之間的不協調的現象。他們選擇放棄英美加國籍的政治利害決定，是不是也肯定了那些排斥
華人，質疑華人歸化他國國籍不是效忠該國而是爲了個人利益的言論？這是值得我們深思其背後的
含義。

　　留學美國是大多數中國留學生的志願。從留學美國變成留下美國也是大多數中國留學生的決定。
歸化美國籍是這些留學生的留居美國的必經歷程。這也是我們對美國移民群眾的公民權益意識與
歸屬感的討論範疇。所以這個現象也實在是我們美國華人研究者所應該要關注的情況。

# THE USE OF RELIGIOUS REPERTOIRES IN ASIAN AMERICA

*Russell Jeung and Marian Wang*

## INTRODUCTION

*When asked about the views of the famed Chinese philosopher, Confucius, my seventeen-year-old nephew, Kevin, replied, "I don't know." Being a sixth-generation Chinese American attending private Catholic school, Kevin has every reason to know more about St. Ignatius than Confucius.*

*Queried, however, about the Chinese God of War Kuan Kung,[1] Kevin immediately answered, "Kuan Kung is a character from* Romance of the Three Kingdoms. *I think he was known for being loyal to his brothers." Kevin's knowledge about Chinese popular religious figures impressed me. I hadn't heard of Kuan Kung's name, although I've seen his red-faced statue at Chinese businesses and even on my own living room shelves while growing up. Surprisingly, Kevin learned of Kuan Kung's values through playing the Three Kingdoms video game. This Chinese god has migrated transnationally, not as a cultural relic, but as a part of popular culture.*

Jeung's vignette raises the question: who is the more popular religious figure among Chinese Americans – Confucius or Kuan Kung? Tu Wei Ming, noted Professor of Confucian Studies at Harvard, suggests that Confucianism is the core of Chinese cultural identity, influencing core ethnic practices of family devotion and perseverance in academics.[2] Confucianism is used as an ethnoreligious explanation of a wide range of Chinese American behaviors and attitudes, shaping issues such as education, generational conflicts, health, and sexuality.[3]

On the other hand, another Chinese American scholar, Joe Fong, downplays the role of Confucianism. He notes that its traditional texts are unread and irrelevant to the common Chinese person. Instead, this community college professor theorizes that higher Chinese achievement is attributable to this group's adherence to Kuan Kung, the God of War, and his *yee hay* or *yiqi* (righteous) code of conduct. He argues:

> To the students, Kuan Kung embodies the Chinese folk model of doing the right thing. Doing the right thing means going to school, staying in school, and finishing school. This folk model is more representative of modern ideals than Confucius.[4]

So, who's right? What Chinese religious figure is better followed, Confucius or Kuan Kung? This debate on the influence of religion on Chinese Americans illustrates two major issues in Asian American religious studies that are addressed in this paper. First, how can we understand, define, and then theorize the religious/spiritual life of Asian Americans? Second, what effects do these varied religious traditions have, especially on Asian Americans' sociopolitical engagement?

While Chinese often assert that Confucianism is not a religion but simply an ethical system, we employ a broad definition of popular religion, one that examines "what matters" – the ultimate values, practices, and cosmology of people.[5] Likewise, Chinese sociologist Anna Sun employs the metaphor of a "religious tool kit" to understand Chinese religious life as more than a syncretic blend of individual traditions. In her framework, Chinese have a range of ritual resources and practices from family and community that can be used for different purposes.[6] Given a practitioner's access to this repertoire of religious resources, she can strategically use them in her religious practice. Religious repertoires, then, include the beliefs, symbols, objects, and practices available for innovation and use by Asian Americans.[7]

Exploring Asian American religious repertoires in this framework of ultimate values and practices seems to be right in line with the objectives of Asian American Studies. By examining "what matters" in the Asian American community, we can better serve the community and mobilize for social change. Through clarifying what religious resources Asian Americans utilize and hybridize, we develop better theoretical perspectives about how Asian Americans practice their faith and traditions.

However, up until only recently, Asian American Studies scholars have seen religion as irrelevant to our racialized experiences and to progressive politics. In fact, in Jeung's own graduate classes in Asian American Studies, students are quick to criticize Ethnic Studies research that neglects class, gender, or sexuality. But when he raised the significance of religion in our communities, they merely smirked at the idea. And they may be correct in overlooking religion; Asian Americans are the most likely group to state they have "no religion" in national surveys.

Among all American ethnicities, Chinese Americans rank the most secular, with 39% claiming no religious affiliation.[8] Historian David Yoo suggests two additional reasons why Asian American religions are marginal to Asian American Studies.[9] Early Asian Americanists, influenced by Marxist thought, viewed religion as the opiate of the masses. Other scholars shaped by postcolonialist approaches negatively see Christianity as part of Western capitalist imperialism. Consequently, both groups dismiss religion's complex relationship with Asian America.

This paper first explores Asian American religious affiliation and repertoires – both how they identify with institutional religion, and how they might express their ultimate values and beliefs in other forms. It then examines how their religious beliefs matter. Just as Confucianism has been shown to be correlated with a range of behaviors, other religious traditions also have strong causal influences on Asian Americans and their experiences. In particular, we consider the sociopolitical consequences of Asian American religion for this chapter. In the spirit of the 40th anniversary of the founding of Asian American Studies, we review how Asian American religion and religious movements can affect social change in the community.[10] By showing how religion relates to community development, we hope to introduce the significance of religion to Asian American Studies.

## THE RELIGIOUS BELIEFS, VALUES, AND PRACTICES OF ASIAN AMERICANS

Because of social science survey limitations and the reasons cited above, the religious beliefs and practices of Asian Americans are not well known. According to the most recent and largest surveys of Asian Americans, 27% of Asian Americans were Protestant Christians (17% Evangelical, 9% Mainline Protestant), 17% were Catholic, 9% were Buddhist, 14% were Hindu, and 4% were Muslim. In addition, 20% of Asian Americans stated that

they had no religion. These significant populations of Asian Americans who are non-Christian or non-religious distinguish them from other racial groups in the United States (see figure 1).

Interestingly, Asian American youth (ages 13-17) report higher percentages of Catholic and Buddhist affiliation. This phenomenon may be attributable to the fact that youth are naming the religion most linked to their ethnic heritage. For example, Cambodian and Thai American youth may consider that to be Khmer or Thai is to be Buddhist.[11] Similarly, Filipino American youth may consider their ethnoreligious heritage as Catholic. These cases illustrate how religion is seen as central to ethnic identity, and even ethnic authenticity.[12]

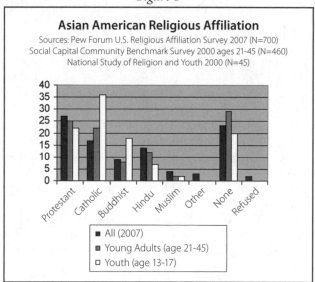

*Figure 1*

Another startling fact about Asian American religious affiliation is the high percentage of those who state that they have no religion. Asian American young adults ages 21 to 45 especially claim a secular outlook. This non-religious orientation may be attributable to the large numbers of Asian Americans with technical and scientific backgrounds. Given the selective immigration of highly educated Asians due to preferences in the 1990 Immigration Act, a greater percentage of the Asian American population are in the science and engineering fields. Since scientists are much more likely to claim no religious affiliation (52%) than the general American population (14%), Asian Americans as a group are also more likely to be less religious.[13]

However, another explanation for the reported secularism of Asian Americans may be due to Western conceptualizations of religion. These understandings of religion, largely based on Judeo-Christian thought, focus on doctrinal statements and congregational worship. Religious affiliation, then, is based on what you believe and where you attend church. Western religion also tends to have exclusive truth claims, so that an individual holds to one religion. Eastern religious repertoires, on the other hand, focus more on household practices and moral values that can be inclusive of multiple systems of meaning. Consequently, Chinese might not affiliate with just one religion, but with multiple traditions such as Confucianism, Taoism, Buddhism, and Chinese folk religion. They might be less likely to claim one tradition in a survey and thus have high percentages identifying with no religion.

Further, claiming no religious affiliation does not necessarily imply that Asian Americans are not spiritual in their individual outlooks or non-moral in their ethical practices. [14] New work on Asian American religious repertoires must take into account the complex ways that religion shapes the lives of individuals and communities. Even for those who do not affiliate with any religion, Asian American spiritual traditions still can influence this group's moral attitudes and community orientations. For example, sociologists Stephen Fugita and David O'Brien explain that the Japanese cultural values of hierarchical and inclusive relationships (*iemoto*) structures their household community lives. [15] This value, of course, stems from the Confucian tradition. Anthropologist Nancy Smith-Hefner similarly demonstrates that Cambodian American parenting and educational orientation are shaped by this group's Theravada Buddhist moral teachings.

Anna Sun's approach for classifying Chinese religions has strong applicability to the Asian American religious experience. The imposition of Eurocentric religious categories on Asian Americans fails to account for the large percentages of Asians who report no religion, as even they make wide use of religious repertoires. Instead, researchers should first start with Asian Americans' own religious life, and identify the diverse beliefs and ritual practices of the community. These resources make up the religious tool kit for Asian Americans. Then we identify how these resources are used (i.e., at home or at the temple), and for what purposes (i.e., to deal with suffering, to celebrate one's heritage, or to honor ancestors). Through this grounded method, better theoretical concepts may be developed for our communities. These new concepts would also be more useful in examining the impact on Asian American religious repertories on other key social behavior. Particularly for Asian American Studies, how religion might influence movements for social change is critically significant.

## THE SOCIOPOLITICAL CONSEQUENCES OF ASIAN AMERICAN RELIGIONS

The popular religions of Asian Americans have long been influential in the development of their local community,

as well as transnational political movements. [16] For example, historian Judy Yung describes the significance of Christianity on the acculturation of Chinese American women:

> Through church, school and the popular media, the second generation was encouraged to challenge traditional gender roles at home and outside, to shape a new cultural identity and lifestyle for themselves. All three factors, to some degree, influenced Chinese American women to reevaluate their gender roles and relations, to move into the public sphere and become involved in the labor, social and political issues of their community. [17]

Three significant studies examine the specific ways that religious actors can encourage community engagement and political action. Not only do religious repertoires provide the motivations and convictions to spur social change, but they also offer schemas, or worldviews, by which spiritual adherents relate to society.

Sociologists Elaine Howard Ecklund and Jerry Park found that the religious affiliation of Asian Americans does indeed significant correlate with their amount of community volunteerism. [18] They found when controlling for age, gender and education, Catholic and Protestant Asian Americans volunteer more than the non-religious, but surprisingly, Buddhist and Hindu Asian Americans actually volunteer less than those with no religious affiliation (see figure 2). [19]

*Figure 2: Community Volunteerism of Asian Americans by Religion*

| Religious Affiliation of Asian Americans | Percent Participating in at Least One Nonreligious Organization [20] |
| --- | --- |
| Protestant Christian | 69 |
| Other Religion | 65 |
| Catholic | 54 |
| Nonreligious | 45 |
| Hindu | 40 |
| Buddhist | 26 |
| Total Sample | 51 |

The authors discuss three possible reasons for these differential impacts of religious affiliation. First, Hinduism and Buddhism have less congregationally oriented worship, so they may have less group-based pressure to volunteer. Second, Hindu and Buddhist Asian Americans are double-minorities, both racially and religiously, so that their practices might not translate well into volunteering. Third, the religious institutions of those with lower volunteer rates, including Catholics, may not be conveying social teachings that encourage voluntary participation.

These reasons relate to the social capital held by co-religionists that might bridge them to the community. We suggest that these religions may also offer differing types of spiritual capital, in that they may have different religious content that spurs volunteerism and community engagement.

Whatever the reason, religion does seem to affect community engagement, and it shapes political behavior significantly as well. Political scientists Pei-te Lien, Margaret Conway, and Janelle Wong also surveyed Asian Americans on their politics, and found that religious participation especially affected their political attitudes (see figure 3). Hindus and Muslims are more likely to be liberal, while Catholics and Protestants are more likely to be conservative than the average Asian American. Beyond shaping attitudes, religious affiliation affects political participation. In general, becoming a citizen, registering to vote, and voting are all correlated with religious affiliation, as well as church attendance. They summarize:

> [Church attendance] turns out to be one of the most critical determinants of voting, even when compared to other types of institutional affiliation, such as membership in an Asian American organization.[21]

Religious affiliation correlates with community engagement and political behavior, but specifically how does it spur these behaviors? Claudine del Rosario, in her Asian American Studies master's thesis at San Francisco State University, examined St. Augustine's Catholic Church in Daly City, California, the largest church in the archdiocese that is also a majority Filipino American congregation.[23] Along with addressing planning and education issues, this church organized mass protests on behalf of airport workers who were laid off after 9/11 because they were not American citizens. She found that the politically progressive leadership of the church offered theological and political teachings to spur

"counter-hegemonic projects." Further, the church was able to mobilize easily by working through "Small Christian Communities," groups which were already formed for fellowship and bible study. According to del Rosario, this congregation led members from apathy to activism by integrating Filipino values of *kapatiran* (brotherhood) and Catholic teachings of social justice.

Given the major role of popular religion within the Asian American community and in its relationships with broader society, more work needs to be done in exploring how Asian American non-profit organizations and advocacy groups could work with religious congregations.[24] Since congregations are the community sites where Asian Americans have the most regular face-to-face interaction, doing community organizing work where people are at seems to be the most logical step for activists. This type of work is especially relevant as the American empire racializes non-Christian religions.[25]

In his own research with Kathleen Garces-Foley, Jeung has found that Asian American evangelical ministers are also very conscious of the racialization process in the United States.[26] For example, they are much more likely to explain that racial inequality is a result of structural factors, such as institutional discrimination and lack of educational opportunities, than whites do. They also understand that Asian Americans have higher incomes than the total population because of selective immigration, in which new immigrants have higher educational attainment and more social networks to utilize.

These viewpoints, in which Asian American ministers are more likely to understand the marginalization of people of color than their white counterparts, exemplify a discourse Garces-Foley and Jeung term "racialized multiculturalism":

> Distinct from White/Black discourses, the discourse of racialized multiculturalism employs three primary assumptions: (1) the United States is a racialized society, in which

*Figure 3: Political Ideology of Asian Americans by Religious Affiliation*[22]

|  | Protestant Christian | Catholic | Buddhist | Hindu | Muslim | None | All |
|---|---|---|---|---|---|---|---|
| *Very Liberal* | 4 | 8 | 6 | 18 | 8 | 10 | 8 |
| *Somewhat Liberal* | 27 | 32 | 21 | 43 | 50 | 22 | 28 |
| *Middle of the Road* | 33 | 24 | 41 | 17 | 12 | 35 | 32 |
| *Somewhat Conservative* | 25 | 24 | 12 | 14 | 17 | 15 | 18 |
| *Very Conservative* | 4 | 4 | 6 | – | 8 | 3 | 4 |
| *Not Sure* | 7 | 7 | 14 | 8 | 4 | 13 | 10 |

race shapes life opportunities; (2) the United States has a racial hierarchy, divided especially between Whites and African Americans; and (3) "ethnicity matters," meaning that cultural differences should be acknowledged and celebrated. It is this combination of sensitivity to racialization and appreciation of ethnic identity that characterizes the leadership of Asian American ministers.

Asian American Christians thus can impact the changing face of American evangelicalism by offering a perspective than introduces social justice concerns to a morally conservative religious group.

## CONCLUSION

Despite the rich and varied religious repertoires of Asian Americans, little is still known of exactly what Asian Americans believe about the transcendent and supernatural, how they practice their faith, and why they hold to their ultimate values. Unfortunately, Asian American Studies has ignored this increasingly significant topic, and Eurocentric sociology fails to capture the hybridized and innovative ways that Asian Americans practice their religion. New research is needed to simply document the religious resources of Asian Americans, especially those who claim "no religion." We suspect that even those who do not affiliate with any religion still employ the resources of their religious toolkit derived from their family or community.

Once these repertoires are documented, we can then better assess specific mechanisms by which religion impedes or promotes social change within Asian American communities. Though researchers and activists recognize the significance of the social capital developed within Asian American congregations, the spiritual capital of these faiths have yet to be explored.[27] We theorize that beyond the congregational networks that enable Asian Americans to promote education and business development, congregations also offer spiritual capital that can be accessed for material returns. Religious teachings of values, beliefs, and schema motivate members to engage in the community and seek peace and justice. Spiritual practices, such as prayer and meditation, also sustain members in this engagement.

In his own activism, Jeung has experienced how the power of God and faith spurred his own community to stand up for its rights.[28] Despite fears of eviction, deportation, and retaliation, forty-four low-income Cambodian and Latino families joined together to sue the landlord. In a landmark settlement, this unlikely tenants association eventually won brand new housing that is permanently affordable. Support from local Buddhist temples, Catholic organizers, and evangelical college ministries were critical to this community organizing effort. Were it not

for the religious resources in the community, this victory would not have been possible.

Continued research on this topic is urgently needed. It is our hope that the findings of future studies will yield further insight on how Asian Americans can harness their various religious repertoires and religious communities to pursue greater sociopolitical involvement. The results may bring tangible benefits for our Asian American communities, as we seek to do justice – both inside and outside of our ethnic and racial groupings – and to make our voices heard in today's political landscape.

## NOTES

1. Kuan Kung (aka Gwan Gung in Cantonese or Guan Gong in pinyin/"Mandarin") is also known as Guan Yu, the Taoist God of War and the Buddhist Protector of the Dharma.
2. Tu Wei-Ming, ed., *The Living Tree: The Changing Meaning of Being Chinese Today* (Stanford, CA: Stanford UP, 1995).
3. See Susie Chan and Cynthia Leong, "Chinese Families in Transition: Cultural Conflicts and Adjustment Problems," *Journal of Social Distress and the Homeless* 3.3 (July 1994): 263-281; Wilbur Aaron Lam and Laurence McCullough, "Influence of Religious And Spiritual Values on the Willingness of Chinese-Americans to Donate Organs for Transplantation," *Clinical Transplantation* 14.5 (October 2000): 449-456(8); Chin-Yau Cindy Lin and Victoria Fu, "A Comparison of Child-Rearing Practices among Chinese, Immigrant Chinese, and Caucasian-American Parents," Child Development, *Spec. Issue on Minority Children* 61.2 (Apr., 1990): 429-433; Connie Chan, "Issues of Sexual Identity in an Ethnic Minority," *Lesbian, Gay, and Bisexual Identities over a Lifespan*, ed. Anthony R. D'Augelli and Charlotte J. Patterson (New York: Oxford UP, 1995) 87-101.
4. Joe Fong, *Complementary Education and Culture in the Global/Local Chinese Community* (San Francisco: China Books and Periodicals, 1993) 145.
5. According to Robert Orsi, popular religion is more than the sacred rituals, practices, and faith of the people, but is also "defined as the totality of their ultimate values, their most deeply held ethical convictions, their efforts to order their reality, their cosmology.... More simply stated, *religion* here means "what matters." Orsi suggests two ways to study popular religion: asking the people themselves, and observing how people express their deepest values. Robert Orsi, *The Madonna on 115th Street: Faith and Community in Italian Harlem, 1880-1950* (New Haven, CT: Yale UP, 1985) xvii.
6. Anna Sun, "A New Approach to the Classification of Chinese Religions," paper presented at the annual meeting of the American Sociological Association, New York, New York City, 11 Aug. 2007.
7. Through this theoretical approach, whether Confucianism

is a religion or not is a moot point. Instead, the focus aims to understand how Chinese Americans use Confucian ethics, symbols, and values for spiritual or ultimate purposes.

8. Pei-te Lien and Tony Carnes, "The Religious Demography of Asian American Boundary Crossing," *Asian American Religions: The Making and Remaking of Borders and Boundaries*, ed. Tony Carnes and Fenggang Yang (New York: New York UP, 2004). Perhaps because they do not consider Confucianism as a religion, Chinese Americans may be more likely to identify with "no religion" on surveys. In 2001 World Values Survey of China, 55.3% of respondents stated they were "not a religious person." However, compared to the 2004 Taiwan Social Change Survey, 84.8% stated they "worshiped gods (baishen) or ancestors (baizuxian)."

9. David Yoo, *New Spiritual Homes: Religion and Asian Americans* (Honolulu: U of Hawai'i P, 1999).

10. On the aim of Asian American Studies to effect concrete changes in our local communities, see "Origins: People, Time, Place, Dreams" by Malcolm Collier and Dan Gonzales published in this anthology.

11. Nancy Smith-Hefner, *Khmer American: Identity and Moral Education* (Berkeley: U of California P, 1999).

12. Joshi observes that devout Hindus are seen as more truly authentic Indian. Khyati Joshi, *New Roots in America's Sacred Ground* (New Brunswick, NJ: Rutgers UP, 2006).

13. Elaine Howard Ecklund and Christopher P. Scheitle, "Religion among Academic Scientists: Distinctions, Disciplines, and Demographics," *Social Problems* 54.2 (May 2007): 289-307.

14. Given our use of Orsi's definition of popular religion, we equate spirituality with religiosity.

15. Stephen Fugita and David O'Brien, *Japanese American Ethnicity: The Persistence of Community* (Seattle: U of Washington P, 1991).

16. For an example of the role of Asian American religion in transnational politics, see Brian Hayashi, *For the Sake of Our Japanese Brethren: Assimilation, Nationalism, and Protestantism among the Japanese of Los Angeles, 1895-1942* (Stanford, CA: Stanford UP, 1995).

17. Judy Yung, *Unbound Feet: A Social History of Chinese Women in San Francisco* (Berkeley: U of California P, 1995) 6.

18. Community volunteerism was measured by a range of questions dealing with an individual's participation in neighborhood projects, art, health, youth, and humanities organizations. See Elaine Howard Ecklund and Jerry Park, "Religious Diversity and Community Volunteerism among Asian Americans," *Journal for the Scientific Study of Religion* 46.2 (June 2007): 233-244.

19. Ecklund and Park 235.

20. Ecklund's and Park's data come from the 2000 Social Capital Community Benchmark Survey with 711 Asian American respondents.

21. Their Pilot National Asian American Political Survey polled 1,218 individuals of the six largest Asian American ethnic groups. See Pei-te Lien, Margaret Conway, and Janelle Wong, *The Politics of Asian Americans: Diversity and Community* (New York: Routledge, 2004).

22. From Pei-te Lien, "Religion and Political Adaptation among Asian Americans," *Asian American Religions: The Making and Remaking of Borders and Boundaries*, ed. Tony Carnes and Fenggang Yang (New York: New York UP, 2004).

23. Claudine del Rosario, "The Power of Prayer and Action: Counterhegemony in the Filipino American Church," MA thesis, San Francisco State University, 2004. For other examples of immigrant religion and activism, see Pierrette Hondagneu-Sotelo, ed. *Religion and Social Justice for Immigrants* (New Brunswick, NJ: Rutgers UP, 2007).

24. Another rich area for research is the relationship between Asian American religious movements and internal community politics. For example, see Diane Haithman, "Ties to Falun Gong Add Controversy to the Chinese New Year Spectacular," *Los Angeles Times* 7 Jan. 2008.

25. In light of the United States' current war with Iraq and fight against terrorism, religious studies scholar Khyati Joshi comments the religious racialization of South Asians is a major issue facing the Asian American community today. Lumped together and seen as Muslims simply because they are brown, South Asians can face severe reactions when interacting with broader society. Racialization is the process of categorizing phenomena on the basis of race or imposing a racial character to groups. Racialization of religion, then, is to understand religion through racial lenses.

26. Kathleen Garces-Foley and Russell Jeung, "Asian American Evangelicals in a Multiethnic World," paper presented at The Changing Face of American Evangelicalism Consultation at Wheaton College, Wheaton, IL, 13-14 Oct. 2005.

27. As an example of how Vietnamese Catholic parishes offer social capital that helps their youth, see Min Zhou and Carl Bankston, *Growing Up American: How Vietnamese American Children Adapt to Life in the United States* (New York: Sage Press, 1999).

28. Russell Jeung, "The Oak Park Story: Organizing a Faith-based, Multi-ethnic Community," *Religion and Social Justice for Immigrants*, ed. Pierrette Hondagneu-Sotelo (New Brunswick, NJ: Rutgers UP, 2006), 59-73. This story is being made into a video documentary produced by Jeung and Valerie Soe.

# TODAY AND TOMORROW

*Isabelle Thuy Pelaud*

*In the 1990s, we can afford to rethink the notion of racialized ethnic identity in terms of differences of national origin, class, gender, and sexuality.... In the 1990s, we can diversify our practices to include a more heterogeneous group.*

— Lisa Lowe[1]

This 40th anniversary of Ethnic Studies is a wonderful occasion to acknowledge those who have contributed to the development of an important program, and to recognize the significance of a job well done. The department of Asian American Studies at San Francisco State University can indeed be proud of its remarkable growth, its ability to attract students and improve its curriculum over the years, and its efforts to address gender representation among faculty. Celebrations also offer an opportunity to assess the present situation and look to the future. I venture to do this here from a Vietnamese American Studies perspective.

## DIVERSITY IN OUR THINKING

Our department is well-known in the country for its early investment in cultural nationalism.[2] Not all faculty today are concerned with cultural nationalism however, or in Hirabayahsi and Alquizola's terms, an "ethnic nationalist ideology" that "highlights 'unique' and authentic cultural traits based on language, history, and values" prioritizing cultural preservation.[3] I, for instance, focus class discussions around the notion that identities are constructed, always in flux, change with time, and are affected by various axes of power such as race, class, gender, and sexuality.

As a critic of Vietnamese American literature, this view raises fundamental questions: How does one critically address the formation of identities, denounce the pitfalls inherent in this very quest, *and* yet retain the ability to use broad categories such as "Vietnamese Americans" as a means toward social justice, fair representation, and full inclusion in American society? How can the term "Vietnamese American," so loaded with memories of the Viet Nam War and US guilt over that conflict, be disassociated from systems of representation and history of that event without denying its legacy? How can a Vietnamese American narrator's memory of the past be analyzed without replicating a problematic law of origin as arbiter of both content and form? Those questions and issues are not about uncovering an authentic account of Asian American culture, but about understanding the various factors that impact its development through time.[4]

To retain the term Asian American as a viable category but depart from fixed notions of identity, I have embraced Lisa Lowe's call to move away from binary opposition set by notions of nativism and assimilation, and instead replace notions of identity with those of multiplicity. Only then, she argues, can the emphasis be shifted from cultural "essence to that of material hybridity," and the construction of race be made more visible.[5] Borrowing from Gayatri Chakravorty Spivak's notion of "strategic essentialism," I thus use ethnic and racial terms only as means to contest and disrupt racist discourses and practices. In this manner, I can address upfront the contradictions inherent in our work, and be careful of the problems that can emanate from abiding by and utilizing terms that categorize and separate people based on their racial attributes.[6]

But regardless of how we view identity, Asian Americanists tend to agree on the following. Most of us see the State as an active agent responsible for shaping the history and experiences of Asian Americans. We do not, however, see power as located only within the State. We teach that social change is achieved through organizing at the local level. We work to effect social change by educating the youth about the importance of creating equal opportunities for Asian Americans, of putting an end to institutional and de facto racism, and of freeing the self from the colonization of the mind. We address in our classrooms the discrepancies between national ideals and what Asian American students experience. And we attempt to construct and develop analytical and practical tools to expose the disjunction between normative narratives and Asian American people's daily lives, experiences, and history.

Aligned with the original vision of the field, our teaching at San Francisco State University is linked to community activism. For instance, it is not enough for me, a teacher of Vietnamese American literature, to underscore that Vietnamese American writers' freedom of creative expression is limited by the outcome of the Viet Nam War and its normative representations. I have to put theory into practice by organizing inside and outside the university walls. I aim to help Vietnamese American writers to be free to create on their own terms.[7] As Asian American Studies scholars, we seek in short to participate in a shift in the structure of feeling and of thinking within American society, and by extension, change the structure of that society itself. Our analytical skills and activism motivate and engage students for whom we serve as role models.

The majority of our students are Asian Americans of many different ethnic backgrounds, with many different histories, languages, cultures, and politics. Many of their parents are immigrants or refugees. We as faculty and staff come also from different backgrounds, from different generations, and have different responsibilities and priorities. As years go by, with new faculty and a changing student population, new questions are inevitably raised and new paradigms considered. New hopes are articulated.

## LOOKING TOWARD THE FUTURE

*Vietnam appears to be well on its way to become yet another "satellite regime" of the ever-expanding American empire. In this "New World Order," Vietnamese refugees, and their insistent demand for "history," are cast aside, yet again.*
                                              – Yen Le Espiritu[8]

Universities – institutions that circumscribe "what can be said and how it can be said"[9] – have made good progress in accepting and incorporating Ethnic Studies into their fold. The department of Asian American Studies at SFSU is unique in its level of self-determination, power and autonomy.[10] I hope that in the future the University will recognize even more of Asian American Studies' vision and approach to knowledge and provide more support for the inseparable endeavors of teaching, community work, and scholarship.

We will continue in turn to be responsible teachers, community activists, and researchers. My hope is that unreflexive cultural nationalism will dissipate and that divisions marked by racial criteria will no longer exist. Mixed race faculty should not have to worry for instance about proving that they are "Asian" enough or be pressured to identify themselves in certain ways. They should not have to fear harassment when adopting different academic strategies. To push back against unfair and unfounded suspicions, exclusionary practices, or disrespectful language and treatment, is not the same thing as being a whistleblower. Faculty of mixed race descent and their perspectives contribute to the development of the department; they increasingly represent the complex formulation of identity evident on every campus in the country. The goal of Asian American Studies should be to produce sites of resistance that do not reproduce the logic of domination we seek to dismantle. In Frantz Fanon's words, our intent is not to replace a white policeman with his counterpart of color. Our job is to invent new paradigms.

With University support and good leadership that privileges constructive communication over conflict and offers a consistent intellectual vision, we will be better able to do our part as accountable teachers, community activists, and researchers. We will continue to adjust to our current context; for instance, openly discussing how globalization, the changes in demographics among Asian Americans, and the rise of China impact our teaching and our thinking. In this process, our class, race, gender, and sexuality analyses will be beneficially deepened and our teaching enriched. Our undergraduate students are not always as prepared as they could be to enter graduate school. A stronger emphasis on writing and early introduction to critical analysis would help get them ready to enter the workforce or pursue their education. Far from being the counterpoint of political empowerment and community understanding and involvement, theories provide explanation for what happens in our communities. Asian American students have the ability to read and understand them. They have the right and deserve to have access to theoretical ideas during their secondary education. To regard race as a continually evolving category on its own right *is* a theoretical claim.[11]

In the future, I hope we will address changes in our student population more directly. I was attracted to the field of Asian American Studies in part because many of the issues of the field spoke to my own experience of racism, to politics geared toward social justice, and to the ideal of combining knowledge with action. But what I learned and now teach does not always touch students of the new generation in the same way.

Cultural nationalists have fought hard to bring stories of racial discrimination into the classroom. These stories and their analyses are extremely important. They empower students and equip them to fight for their rights. One of the assumptions is the correlation between the retrieval and validation of one's experience with the "recovery of wholeness."[12] According to Sucheng Chan:

> Children who grow up under the specter of racism suffer from a loss of self-esteem. Some find it difficult to become whole persons who can contribute productively to the progress of our communities. Adults who had repressed or oppressed childhoods tend to eschew the risks of self-expression lest the guts we place onstage for public scrutiny get thrown back at our face to taunt us.[13]

Interiorized racism and self-hate impact Asian Americans who have been treated as an inferior minority and view themselves as such. When I taught at research institutions it was clear that many of my Asian American students came from privileged backgrounds. They grew up in white suburbs, but were eager to learn of the hardship and oppression experienced by Asian Americans. Vulnerable and marginal among a majority of white students, these stories strengthened their identities. They were empowered by their newfound anger against historical and social injustices experienced by the broader group. Many eagerly volunteered to do community work to help "their people," which always meant the poor but also the unknown. They were doing good work and everyone benefited from these activities.

Some of my students at San Francisco State University have received these stories differently. Many come from working-class backgrounds and grew up surrounded by Asian Americans and other people of color. They do not experience or relate to the topic of self-hate and racism in the same way. Every semester some students in my Asian American Culture class express frustration with the readings: "We are tired of reading these depressing stories," they say. "We want to be inspired and have hope that we will be able to escape our current conditions," they add. When pressed, they explain that they know about racism but it does not seem to bother them in the same way that it did me, or my more privileged students.

As faculty, we have to take in account this new generation while remaining true to our mission. I noticed that my Filipino American students, who comprise the majority in my general Asian American Studies classes, respond intensely to the documentary film *Refugee*.[14] *Refugee* tells the story of three young Cambodian Americans growing up in poverty in the Tenderloin, a poor neighborhood of San Francisco, and who return to Cambodia to meet family members who never left. Students related to the ruptures between family members and the vast cultural gap between the youth here and the people "back home." Transnational linkages speak to their experiences and they

seem empowered, or at least very alert, when I address the global contexts that lead to these unwanted separations that they themselves are experiencing. Discussions of racism in the context of poverty, colonialism, wars, globalization, and empire resonate with them. Many are 1.5 or second-generation immigrants who have immigrated with only one parent, who have visited their families abroad, or share resources with people they hardly know and who live very far away.

A fundamental goal of Asian American Studies is the empowerment of students through the validation of their experience and learning critical history. This task is incredibly important in the context of American history marked by racial inequalities. But as a teacher of Vietnamese American literature, this assertion at times seems insufficient in working with a student population whose parents have experienced civil war. My class has more international students from Viet Nam every year. These include the children whose parents may have killed or imprisoned the parents of other students in the same class, and who have grown up with opposite versions of history. In extreme cases, they may even have been physically attacked by the students sitting in the opposite side of the room. The assumption that understanding their culture will help them be more "whole" seems at times odd, when my Vietnamese American students, inspired by our teaching, go to Viet Nam to volunteer with humanitarian organizations only to discover upon their return to the United States that they are now seen and treated as traitors by their community, and in extreme cases, rejected by their families, who see their actions as helping communism.[15]

As Asian Americanists, I recommend that we be highly aware of community political dynamics when promoting empowerment and encouraging Vietnamese American students to publicly take a stance in regard to local issues linked to Viet Nam. We must be conscious that Vietnamese American students, loyal to their newly assimilated ideas, may risk being blacklisted by the community they deeply and sincerely want to serve. These students do not need more ruptures in their lives. Thirty years after the Viet Nam War, the resulting tensions, mistrust, and anger persist in certain segments of Vietnamese American communities. War does not end with its official ending. In 2004, poet Barbara Tran wrote as she was selecting stories for a journal: "It is not the right time to 'move on' from the war, for there are still too many who cannot do so because the past has gouged too deep a hole in their lives. They keep falling back in."[16] Some Vietnamese American identities are still crafted today in relation to Viet Nam War politics; and although this segment of the population does not represent the group as a whole, it cannot be simply dismissed either as "crazy" or "conservative." To uncritically apply immigrant paradigms to all

Asian Americans, regardless of their immigration status and history, can not only results in unfounded conclusions, but also has the potential to produce real hurt.

What we can do as faculty is help Vietnamese American students make sense of the intense emotions which may have surrounded them as they grew up, hatreds that are fostered by *their* people against *their* people as a result of civil war. At this juncture in their lives, working class Vietnamese American students can be helped to make better sense of their lives and of these pressures by also spending more time improving their writing skills and learning to express themselves in an organized and persuasive fashion. Too many in my classes are weighed down by family obligations and work, torn between family expectations and individual dreams.[17] Some of these students have grown up speaking Vietnamese, and parents simply could not support them with homework. Some can barely write a coherent essay; and yet they are the ones who serve as translators, taking care of bills and paperwork in their family, and as childcare providers or managers of family business. These students need our help and the help of students from more privileged institutions and backgrounds. Some students may not always have a lot of extra time to help others, because they also need help to survive, let alone thrive, in an academic setting. Other university programs in the country would serve this population well by following the lead of the department of Asian American Studies at SFSU and include Vietnamese American history and experiences and a special emphasis on composition as integral parts of their curriculum.

State budget cuts, universities' lack of support for Ethnic Studies in carrying out its vision, and internal pitfalls inherent in identity politics that rely on laws of origins have traditionally caused division between community activists and researchers in Ethnic Studies programs. The Asian American Studies Department at SFSU could become a model for other departments and programs in the country. In the next five to ten years, we can work on creating a more positive work environment characterized by transparency, equal and respectful treatment of all faculty, and a more healthy balance between teaching, community work, and publishing. More ideas can be shared among departments to serve our students, and to improve their level of writing and analysis. Like our predecessors who fought to create Ethnic Studies forty years ago, we need courage to ask questions and affirm what we believe in. As Edward Said stated, the choice for us is always between "actively" representing the truth to the best of our ability or passively allowing a patron or authority to direct us. "For the secular intellectual," Said reminds us, "*those* gods always fail."[18] For a more efficacious and harmonious future in Ethnic Studies departments and elsewhere, we will serve best by honoring the diversity within the unity. In celebrating ourselves, let us remember to listen to and respect the multiple voices within our communities, and the various perspectives that can form bridges to create social justice for all.

## NOTES

1. Lisa Lowe, *Immigrant Acts: On Asian American Cultural Politics* (Durham: Duke UP, 1996).
2. See Lane Ryo Hirabayashi and Marilyn C. Alquizola, "Asian American Studies: Reevaluating for the 1990s," *State of Asian America,* ed. Karin Aguilar-San Juan (Boston: South End Press, 1994) 357.
3. Hirabayashi and Alquizola 358.
4. I have raised these questions in an unpublished manuscript titled "History, Identity, and Survival: Reading Vietnamese American Literature" (currently under review by Temple University Press).
5. Lowe 65.
6. Lowe 82.
7. With my work with the Vietnamese American Studies Center (VASC) and more recently with the Diasporic Vietnamese Artists Network (DVAN).
8. Yen Le Espiritu, "Thirty Years AfterWARd: The Endings That Are Not Over," *Amerasia Journal* 31.2 (2005): xvi.
9. See David Harvey, *The Condition of Postmodernity: An Enquiry into the Origins of Cultural Change* (Cambridge: Blackwell, 1990) 47.
10. Hirabayashi and Alquizola 253.
11. See Michael Omi and Howard Winant, *Racial Formation in the United States: From the 1960s to the 1980s* (New York: Routledge & Kegan Paul, 1986).
12. Sucheng Chan, *In Defense of Asian American Studies* (Urbana and Chicago: U of Illinois P, 2006) 33.
13. Chan 33.
14. *Refugee,* dir. Spencer Nakasako, 2003, 11 Sept. 2008 <http://www.pbs.org/independentlens/refugee/guys.html>.
15. See Isabelle Thuy Pelaud, "Win, Lose or Draw Your Community at 3rd VA NGO Conference," *Nha Magazine* Nov./Dec. 2007: 96-99.
16. Barbara Tran, "Viet Nam: Beyond The Frame," *The Michigan Quarterly Review* 18. 4 (Fall 2004): 482.
17. See Isabelle Thuy Pelaud, "The Plight of Vietnamese American Students at SFSU," Nha Magazine July 2006: 118-120 [title not mine].
18. Edward Said, *Representations of the Intellectuals* (New York: Vintage Books, 1994) 221.

# THE "LEGACY" OF EDISON UNO

*Wesley Ueunten*

Writing this essay on the late Edison Uno has been difficult, to say the least. The idea for the article came when Ben Kobashigawa and I decided to revive and restructure the former Nikkei Studies Center and Edison Uno Institute at San Francisco State University into the Edison Uno Institute of Nikkei and Uchinanchu Studies or EUINUS. In the Japanese American community, Uno's name comes up often as one of the first to teach a Japanese American Studies course at SF State and as an early advocate of compensation for Japanese Americans who were in the internment camps during World War II. It was because of his pioneering work that we decided it was important to keep his name in our newly restructured institute. Thus, I chose "The Legacy of Edison Uno" to be the title of my essay.

However, after writing and re-writing this essay so many times that I lost count, something dawned on me: I was looking for *the* "legacy" of Edison Uno as if it were *the* Holy Grail that would tell us how to set up EUINUS and how to solve issues that now face Japanese Americans.

After going through this arduous process, I would venture to say that Uno would question the use of the word "legacy" with his name. If he were alive today he might warn me about using the word "legacy" with his name, since a legacy could also refer to those students who get into Ivy League schools without having to try hard because of what their parents or grandparents or great-grandparents were. Using the term "legacy of Edison Uno" would invite similar inaction since people might believe that struggles are things in the past and not ongoing.

Standard English is the medium of expression that *pidgin* English (or more officially, Hawaiian *creole*) speakers like me have had to learn as a second language. In this language that is still foreign to me, nouns that end with "y" seem to have tyrannical control over our thoughts. As mentioned earlier, "legacy" leads us to think in terms of

past achievements disconnected from the present. When we talk about Japanese American "identity" or "community" we tend to imagine entities that are formed *a priori* to and separately from our existence.

If it is not nouns that end with "y" that rule over us, the words that end with "ture" do. We often explain Japanese American behavior in terms of "nature" as in the discourses of Japanese American identity: "A Jap is a Jap" was the justification for putting Japanese Americans into internment camps during World War II even though most of them were American citizens. Now that such blatant racism has, at least publicly, gone out of style; Japanese American "culture" is seen as the reason for their being "successful," "passive," or "quiet." I am not really sure, however, if we have collectively been able to distinguish between nature and culture since both suggest that there is some anciently rooted "something" that determines the behavior, ability, potential, and even loyalty of Japanese Americans.

In any case, when speaking or writing in this language called Standard English, I notice that nouns seem to have priority over the verbs. They become the last words in our conversations. Just as nature and culture become explanations of what Japanese American do and what we are, and legacy is chosen to represent Edison Uno, we invest in nouns the power to be *the* answer. Words such as "Manifest Destiny," "military necessity," and "national security" also come to mind. They have been used to explain and justify anything from genocide, slavery, and imperialism to incarceration, internment, and invasion.[1]

It's no wonder I have struggled to write this essay. How can you write about a person who spent his life challenging and resisting anything that confined him and other fellow humans to any constricted place or position in such a language that contains the seeds of our own subordination?

I would like to apologize in advance to the people

who knew Edison Uno for this far-from-complete essay on him. There are more people I need to talk to who knew him that I simply did not make the time and effort to. There are still more materials written by and about him that I have not gone through. I take full responsibility for this essay's shortcomings and every bit of criticism is deserved.

However, as we embark on this endeavor to establish EUINUS, I would like to suggest humbly that if there has been any lesson that I have learned in this search for a "legacy" of Edison Uno, it would simply be: "Take nothing for granted."

Easier said than done – but that is the point.

### DIGNITY VS. MILITARY NECESSITY

*Lissen Uno*

*You Don't like conditions here, in the good ol' U.S.A. then GET THE HELL OUT!!! GO BACK TO JAPAN, YOU GOOK!!!*

*ALSO, SLOPE, Practice what you preach and take all the NIGGERS to JAPAN with you, you DINK HYPO-CRITE!! Its FUCKERS like you who'll turn San Francisco into another Wash., DC, or New York City – fuck this beautiful City up, raise our taxes sky high!! You SHIT talk an act like you speak for all us SAN FRANCISCANS!!! WAKE UP, YOU FUCKIN JAP!! IT JUST AINT GOIN TO WORK!! CANT YOU SEE THAT? You fuckin JAP, nice and cozy in a white neighborhood, and smug, – PRACTICE WHAT YOU PREACH, JAP, an MOVE TO HUNTERS POINT OR THE FILMORE!!*

*Signed*
*Hard-workin, Law Abidin WASP who MINDS HIS OWN BUSINES!!!*

[Letter postmarked August 11, 1971 sent to Edison Uno from San Francisco. From folder entitled "Hate Mail – 1968-1975" in Edison Uno Papers kept at UCLA Special Collections]

Edison Uno was not from Japan. He was born in Los Angeles in 1929 and attended public schools there until 1942, when – in the name of military necessity – his family was relocated to the Amache Relocation Camp in Granada, Colorado and then incarcerated in a Department of Justice internment camp in Crystal City, Texas. While three of Uno's older brothers had left camp to serve in the Pacific and European wars, he and his father remained interned until after the war ended. His mother and sisters had been released after the truce with Japan. When his brothers returned from their overseas assignments, they found Edison and his father still incarcerated.

Thus, the majority of Uno's teen years were spent confined to an internment camp ironically run by the

Department of Justice in the country of his birth. Citizenship and the military service of his elder brothers were no guarantee for freedom. An excerpt of a 1973 interview of Uno gives us an indication of how the interment experience impacted his life as well as a lesson in dignity from his mother:

> The junkman came to haul the stuff away. Everything. But like most people of her generation, my mother had gotten one thing she couldn't part with, because it was worth more than it really was. In her case it was a second-hand piano she'd bought for $175 – a fortune in those days – and all it did, really, was collect dust and she'd pile all kinds of knick-knacks on it. Nobody in the house could even play it.

> Anyway, the junkman saw the piano after he had shoved all our stuff into his truck, and asked my mother how much she wanted for it. But she just shrugged – her English wasn't too good – so he offered her $5. She began weeping. He said $15 was all he could give her for it, you know, he said it was used and all that. My mother suddenly straightened up, her fists clenched, then hurried to a neighbor's to use the telephone. She told someone at the USO if they needed a good piano, they could come over and take it away.

Uno's release from camp also marked the blossoming of his ambitious energy. After returning to Los Angeles, he graduated high school with scholastic honors and had even been elected senior class president. After serving fourteen months in the US Naval Reserve (1951-52), Uno attended Los Angeles City College (AA in government/minor in public administration) and Los Angeles State College (BA in political science/minor in government). Around this time he attended the first national YMCA conference held in Iowa, where he was elected to be the chairman of 5,000 delegates.

Along the way, Uno became active in the Japanese American Citizens League in 1947. He served as president of the East Los Angeles Chapter of the JACL from 1950 to 1951. At 19, he was the youngest chapter president in the organization's history.

From 1955 to 1958, Uno represented people who were claiming war-time losses suffered during the evacuation before the Department of Justice Claims Division in San Francisco. The claims were successfully adjudicated. He actually moved to San Francisco in 1956 and attended law school there from 1957 to 1958. His work in the community continued as he was a charter member of the Nisei Voters League of San Francisco in 1959.

If that was not enough, Uno managed an import-export firm and was a manager of a national mail-order business that specialized in judo and karate supplies from 1958 to 1964. He was also editor for the first national directory of the Judo Black Belt Federation of the United States.

As overwhelming as Uno's activities were, this is only a partial listing that I gleaned from interviews and documents. There is a feeling of urgency that is reflected in his record of service – a need to make up for lost time spent incarcerated, which was by his own accounting, "four-and-a-half years – 1,647 days, to be exact."

However, Uno was not simply making up for lost time. Around 1959, before he reached the age of 30, Uno suffered a heart attack. Following the attack he entered a period of intense brooding during over the question of having "to end one's days so soon." When he was interviewed in 1973, he recalled that he eventually gained a sense of awareness of the world and the people around him. Realizing his mortality seemed to liberate him as he revealed, "After I overcame my fear of death, I really began to live."

## NURTURE VS. NATURE AND CULTURE

*"People still ask me why I do these things," Uno said dryly. "I can't give them a ready answer. It seems that after all the years I've been beating my head against the wall, I've gotten calloused, you know, more stubborn. What the Japanese call* katai-atama. *Still, I see myself as a farmer casting seeds into the wind; some will germinate and others won't. Or, to put it another way, I use the green-stick technique.*

*"You bend a green twig and if you're careful enough, the stick will retain its curve when it sets. Too much pressure and it snaps; too little, you don't have any effect at all. I guess you can say I try to change people, especially the young, by changing their ways of looking at things. And you know, I get my comfort when some kid whose name I don't even remember comes up to me after a talk and shakes my hand, saying 'I know you don't remember me, but seven years ago I heard you talk....' And, you know, that really makes me feel good." And here, his face lights up with a big, warm smile.[2]*

Much of Uno's work was directed at the next generations. In 1964, he became operations manager at the Student Union at University of California, San Francisco (UCSF). In 1968, he became a financial aid officer at the San Francisco Medical Center and was responsible for the administration of student financial aid. From 1969 to 1974, he was Assistant Dean of Students at UCSF. In 1973, he was dismissed shortly after he publicly charged his superior with indifference toward the housing needs of the students. His firing was met with a large outpouring of support from the students who supported him for his dedication to their needs and for his work to improve student services, which few other administrators did. The greater community also supported him as he received letters of support from politicians, minority

organizations, co-workers, professionals, and other people of all backgrounds. The settlement of his grievance was made three months after his dismissal notification.

Despite the support he got from the larger community, Uno was seen as a "radical" within the Japanese American community for not fitting into the "quiet American" stereotype that many Japanese Americans themselves actively encouraged. It was understandable that they would do so since it was related to the racism against Japanese Americans that was manifested in the internment experience. However, Uno refused to succumb to any notion that Japanese Americans are quiet by nature or culture, especially when social justice was at stake.

Richard Wada, one of the participants in the SF State Strike, points out that Uno had definitely been influenced by his internment experience: He could see that the internment experience was not an isolated event, but that there was a social continuum that linked Japanese Americans with other Asian Americans and other people of color. Wada points out that we need to keep in mind that the African American community was much larger than it is now. It was still a big force in San Francisco and had deep relations with other communities. It is hard to understand activism in San Francisco without understanding the Civil Rights Movement and other social protests that were taking place at the time. Uno was involved in such struggles as the protest against the House of Un-American Activities Committee meetings in San Francisco and with protests against the racist hiring practices at the Sheraton Palace Hotel and automobile dealerships on Van Ness which were notorious for not hiring African Americans.

The late 1960s was a busy time for Uno. During this time, Uno contributed over 200 voluntary hours to investigate the SF police department, police commission, courts, and jails as part of his duties as an appointed member of the San Francisco Committee on Crime. Simultaneously, he was an active member of the SF JACL Chapter's Civil Rights Committee.

In the same years, Uno had worked with a small handful of Nisei to repeal the Emergency Detention Act of 1950, also known as "Title II," which continued to give legal justification for actions similar to the internment of Japanese Americans during World War II. Title II was repealed in 1971 and Uno received one of the pens used in signing the measure to repeal it from President Nixon.

Uno also began publicly supporting the student strike at SF State. His support simultaneously marginalized and energized him:

They [the Japanese Americans] used too many cultural crutches to avoid changing their archaic views and to promote creative independent thought. But I'd always looked at myself as an agent of change. Here were the students – particularly the Third World ones – literally getting their heads knocked in, and there was the administration. Nobody from my community was saying anything. So I began organizing an Asian coalition against the administration. We had our first meeting right in my living room.

In the same year, Uno was asked by SF State students to teach one of the first courses on Japanese American history. Uno also taught at Stanford University, Lone Mountain College, and the California School of Professional Psychology. Through his courses, many students, including Japanese Americans, learned for the first time of the internment camps. More importantly, however, they were exposed to his activism that went beyond teaching about what happened, but also provided examples of what can and has been done.

### EDISON UNO VS. EARL WARREN

*WAAAAAAAAA!!! BOOO HOOO!!!*
*OH BOOOO HOOOOO HOOOOO HOOO!!!*
*BOOOOO HOOOO!!*
*...*

*ALL RACISM MUS GO!! DOWN WiF RACISM!!*
*ALL JAPANISE ARISE!! NO MORE RACISM!!*
*DOWN WiF WHItE RACISM, including iffEN*
*JAP Racism!!! BOOOOO HOOOOO!!!*
*EEEEeeeeeeeeeehh!!!*
*...*

*I FiL SORry FO Myself!!!*
*NO MO Racism!! AAA WA MA MAMA!!!*
*...*

*SANGA BISHI!! SANGA BISHI!!!*
*SANGA BISHI!!! MOOOOteM!!!*
*DO GAATS!!! GAAAAHH!!!*

*eRL WARRN STIL HAF NOT*
*ApoLOGISEd HuMbly TO Edson*
*Uno!! EDSon Uno Cant save Fas! Waaa Hooo!! Hooo!*
*...*

*Edson Uno fo*
*CHIFF Justis of*
*SUPRIMM Cott*
*banZai!!!*

*PS Edson – ITS wAteR UNDA*
*DA BRIGE! FoGet iT!!*
*DON Go stiring UP HOSS MANUR!!*
                              *Good GRIFF!!*

[Letter sent to Edison Uno on July 17, 1969 (scrawled in

pencil). From folder entitled "Hate Mail – 1968-1975" in Edison Uno Papers kept at UCLA Special Collections]

For seven years, Uno corresponded with the retired Supreme Court Chief Justice Earl Warren. In 1942, as California State Attorney, Warren implemented the mass evacuation of Japanese Americans under Executive Order 9066 signed by President Franklin Roosevelt. It is widely believed that Warren wanted to consolidate his political base for his quest to become governor by organizing the evacuation of the Japanese Americans.

Ironically, Warren, who was known as a "hanging judge" before the war, established a reputation after the war as a great civil libertarian and defender of civil rights as Chief Justice.

The letters that Uno sent to Warren asked him to publicly admit his motivations for implementing the mass evacuations of Japanese Americans during World War II. Uno actually respected Warren and said that he felt that he was a "great man" whose burden of the past would be lifted by an admission of guilt. Until his death, Warren never made that admission despite Uno's relentless seven-year pursuit. Uno recalls, "Well, for seven years I kept writing. I have an Earl Warren file two inches thick!"

Uno actually met Warren soon before his death in 1973. When Warren came to San Francisco to address an American Civil Liberties convention, Uno patiently waited to see him. Uno remembered the moment:

> *"Ah, so you're Mr. Edison Uno," he said. "I remember you from your letters. Well, within a short while, Mr. Uno, you'll be pleasantly surprised."*
>
> *Whether he had a premonition of his death, I can't say. When he passed away in May of this year, I still felt a tinge of dissatisfaction about my fruitless efforts. You never really get used to that, you know. About a week later, however, a reporter from the* Washington Post *called me and told me he had read about my correspondence with the Chief Justice. I mentioned Justice Warren had written an autobiography to be published after his death by a New York publisher. It'll come out in January.*
>
> *Anyway, the reporter checked it out, and, sure enough, Earl Warren, the great man that he was, admitted in that book he had been torn with anguish by what he had done, and that its memory had haunted him all his life.*
>
> *"But you know," Mr. Uno reflected, shaking his head thoughtfully. "It really takes a great man to admit his wrongdoing.*

Many times students being confronted with our history of racism will ask, "Why bring the past up?" or "Why talk about something that happened a long time ago?" Or as the writer of the letter above stated, *"ITS wAteR UNDA DA BRIGE! FoGet iT!!DON Go stiring*

*UP HOSS MANUR!!Good GRIFF!!"*

As a pidgin speaker might say, however, "Dis not pau yet." To paraphrase using the words of William Faulkner, the *past* is not dead. In fact, it's not even *past*.

As Uno wrote in 1973, we are not *there* yet.

> ...Japanese Americans must constantly ask themselves: "Who are we?" "What do other Americans think I am?" "Why do they draw the erroneous conclusion that I am something I am not?" The whole question of dual identity results from what I call the quasi-American status of Japanese Americans.

At this juncture of the establishment of EUINUS and the 40th anniversary since the SF State Strike, instead of ending our dialogue with those fancy words that end with "y" – mo bettah we start with such questions as "Who," "What," and "Why."

## NOTES

1. I imagine that someone with a good education might just read this and dismiss my rant about a "tyranny of the y-nouns" as being Foucauldian or as just another way to talk about "social constructions." My knowledge of Foucault is limited so I cannot comment on the first point, but I could not agree more with the second point: I am not saying anything new or special about how words (social constructions) *do* hurt people and how they become the reason and justification for us to use sticks and stones to break people's bones. Further, when I redefine the legacy of Edison Uno in terms of what he *did*, I am not saying something that has not been written using the term "agency."

   However, I think that the menace of the "tyranny of the y-nouns" is found in their tendency to become the definitive words on a lot of subjects. For example, when we talk or write about social constructions such as "race," "class," "gender," "sexuality," "nationality," and "ethnicity," I seriously wonder if we give too much agency to the ambiguous entity called "society" and not enough to human subjects. That is, "society" rather than ordinary individuals becomes the culprit or hero in our portrayals of social reality. "Society" is what either "messes us up" or saves us, not the ideas, intentions, choices, and actions of the people who make up that "society."

   In other words, I am afraid of getting trapped in a tautological realm of "social constructions" by using social constructions to explain other social constructions.

2. Richard Akutagawa, "Edison Uno, The Un-Quiet American," *Zenger's* 9 Oct. 1973.

# APPENDICES

## APPENDIX 1

STUDENTS, INSTRUCTORS, AND COMMUNITY MEMBERS INVOLVED IN THE 1968 STRIKE
AND DURING THE FIRST TWO YEARS OF THE PROGRAM

The creation of Asian American Studies at San Francisco State was the collective effort of many people – students, instructors, and community members. The lists that follow are our incomplete attempt to provide some token acknowledgment of their activities. These lists are based on notes, minutes, and people's memories, and are certainly incomplete. We apologize to those whom we have overlooked as well as for any misspelling of people's names. We have grouped people as students, instructors, and community members. Some people are listed in several categories, as their roles changed with time or they belonged to more than one student group.

**Students** active in student organizations, planning groups, and the creation of AAS from 1968 to 1971 (organized by groups with which they were most associated):

(a) Students in **AAPA** (Asian American Political Alliance) and/or the Japanese Planning Group 1968-1971

Cindy Fukagai, Mike Ikeda, Bette (Inouye) Matsuoka, Daro Inouye, Betty Kimura, Kris Kiyomura, George Leong, Jane Maki Tabata, Nori Mayeda, Penny Nakatsu, Donna Nomura, Kay Nomura, Jeff Mori, Steve Nakajo, Lloyd Nekoba, Janice Ogawa, Bruce Oka, Francis Oka, Marian Okamura, Miyo Ota, Roger Oyama, Masayo Suzuki, Terry Terauchi, Sharon Uratsu, Richard Wada, Alfred Wong, Stan Wong, and Paul Yamasaki.

(b) Students in **ICSA** (Intercollegiate Chinese for Social Action) and/or the Chinese Planning Group 1968-1971
Connie Chan, Dorothy Chen, Herbert Chew, Laureen Chew, Alan Chin, Eddie Chin, Gordon Chin, Phil Chin, Wanda Chin, Garret Chin, Julia Ching, Paul Chinn, Malcolm Collier, Curtis Choy, Irene Dea, Jeannie Dere, Jim Dong, Lelandy Dong, Danny Eng, Lincoln Fong, Lora Foo, Bob Gin, Jane Gin, Judy Gin, Lolan Ho, Spencer Joe, Berwyn Lee, Nathan Lee, Rose Lee, DiDi Leong, George Leong, Russell Leong, Tony Leong, Kuo Lew, Arthur Lim, Fred Lau, John Lum, Kendrick Lum, David Quan, Robert Quon, Judy Seto, Benjamin Tong, John Wichman, Alfred Wong, Coleman Wong, Mason Wong, George K. Woo, Rowena Wong, May May Wong, Dorothy Yee, Herbert Yee, Robert Yee, Stan Yee, Vicki Yee, Michael Yep, and Frank Young.

(c) Students in **PACE** (Philippine American Collegiate Endeavor) and/or the Pilipino Planning Group 1968-1971

Rosalie Alfonso, Sonny Aranaydo, Danilo Begonia, Regina Calacal, Ray Cordova, Evelyn Dacanay, Arika Dacumas, Rodney Dela Concepcion, DeLynda DeLeon, Edward de la Cruz, Manuel Difuntorum, Charles Dionisio, Eleanor Evangelista, Virginia Evangelista, Bruce Gali, Isidro Gali, Mingnon Geli, Daniel Phil Gonzales, Tony Grafilo, Eleanor Hipol-Luis, Tedirenio Hipol, Edward Ilumin, Robert Ilumin, Orville Jundis, Ferdinand Lucky, Benjamin Monico Luis,

Bayani Mariano, Carlwood Mendoza, Madeline Mendoza, Karlene Palomares, Alice Patacsil, Oscar Peñaranda, Ronald Quidachay, Magdalena Ramirez, Francisco Rosario, Edna Salaver, Patrick Salaver, Anita Sanchez, Alex Soria, Bles Soriano, Luis Syquia, Serafin Syquia, Samuel Tagatac, Juanita Tamayo, Dennis Ubungen, Val Valledor, and Marilyn Zarsa Ilumin.

**Instructors** from fall 1969 through spring 1971. This list includes individuals who actually taught the classes, regardless of their official status. Many instructors were also active on the planning groups:

Danilo Begonia, Carolina Borromeo, Jeffery P. Chan (coordinator/chair, 1970-72), Frank Chin, Philip P. Choy (also History Department), Malcolm Collier, Edward de la Cruz, Luz DeLeon, Moon Eng (coordinator/chair, 1970), Daniel Phil Gonzales, Neil Gotanda, James A. Hirabayashi (coordinator/chair, 1969-70), Kai-yu Hsu, Joe Kamiya, Rev. Dainem Katagiri, Saichi Kawahara, Him Mark Lai (History Department), Joaquin Legaspi, Karl Matsushita, Celia Mora, Kenji Murase, Penny Nakatsu, Jovina Navarro, Lloyd Nekoba, Sam Tagatac, Juanita Tamayo, Edison Uno, Felicissimo Velasquez, Alan S. Wong, Rev. Larry Jack Wong, George K. Woo, Ken Woo, William D.Y. Wu, Mary Yang, and James Dudley Yasuda.

Note: AAS did not have department status in the early years, so there was no official position designated as "chair" of AAS.

**Community members** who provided assistance from 1968 to spring 1971:

Nestor Aquino, George Araki, Nancy Araki, Alice Barkley, Fred Basconcillos, Carolina Borromeo, Richard Cerbatos, Philip P. Choy, Alex Esclamado, Isidro Gloria, Sue Hayashi, James A. Hirabayashi, Tom Kim, Him Mark Lai, Gordon J. Lau, Rolland C. Lowe, Karl Matsushita, Julita McLeod, Janice Mirikitani, Kenji Murase, Jovina Navarro, Philippine Consul General Samson Sabalones, Anicia Tamayo, Lazaro Tamayo, Rev. Anatalio Ubalde, Edison Uno, Emil Urbiztondo, Jason Villafuerte, Yori Wada , Rev. Lloyd Wake, Alan S. Wong, Rev. Larry Jack Wong, George K. Woo, and Joyce Yamamoto.

**SF State administrators, staff, and faculty** who provided assistance from 1968 to spring 1971:

George Araki, Daniel Feder, Donald Garrity, James A. Hirabayashi, Kai-yu Hsu, Ted Jitodai, Donald Lowe, Kenji Murase, Urban Whitaker, Jr., and Hideo Yanenaka

# APPENDIX 2

## THE STRIKE DEMANDS AND
## SAN FRANCISCO STATE COLLEGE RESPONSES

The following Strike demands and the corresponding settlement responses from San Francisco State College (SFSC) are reprinted from *After the Strike: A Conference on Ethnic Studies, Proceedings*, 12-14 Apr. 1984 (San Francisco: School of Ethnic Studies, San Francisco State, 1984). The wording of the five Third World Liberation Front (TWLF) demands listed here differ slightly from the five demands in *The Strike and You* (pages 7-8), a pamphlet written and distributed in January 1969 by the TWLF and the Strike Support Committee.

### The Demands of the Black Student Union (BSU) and the SFSC Settlement Responses

1 That all Black Studies courses being taught through various departments be immediately part of the Black Studies Department and that all the instructors in this department receive full-time pay.

SFSC Response: All courses have been transferred with the exception of one in Anthropology and one in Drama; all instructors employed full-time will receive full-time pay.

2 That Dr. Hare, Chairman of the Black Studies Department, receive a full professorship and a comparable salary according to his qualifications.

SFSC Response: The apparent failure to rehire Dr. Hare is irrelevant to the institution of the Black Studies Department. The Department Chairman shall be selected by the usual departmental process and Dr. Hare shall be eligible for selection.

3 That there be a Department of Black Studies which will grant a Bachelor's Degree in Black Studies; that the Black Studies Department chairman, faculty, and staff have the sole power to hire faculty and control and determine the destiny of its department.

SFSC Response: President Robert Smith created a Black Studies Department on September 17, 1968; the Trustees approved the Bachelor of Arts Degree in Black Studies on October 14, 1968; on December 5, 1968, the Council of Academic Deans recognized the Black Studies Department as having full faculty power commensurate with that accorded to all other departments of the College.

4 That all unused slots for Black students from fall 1968 under the Special Admissions program be filled in spring 1969.

SFSC Response: 128 EOP students were admitted for the spring 1969 semester.

5 That all Black students wishing so, be admitted in fall 1969.

SFSC Response: The College agreed to admit approximately 500 qualified non-white students for the fall 1969 semester and was actively recruiting such students. There were also to be about 400 non-white students as special admittees; the College committed itself to funding and staffing for an Economic Opportunity Program (EOP); the College agreed that parallel admissions standards are necessary for Third World People if the College is to fulfill its educational responsibilities in an urban environment.

6 That twenty (20) full-time teaching positions be allocated to the Department of Black Studies.

SFSC Response: 12.3 positions were allocated to the Black Studies Department (11.3 unfilled positions); more positions would be allocated in accordance with need and available resources.

7 That Dr. Helen Bedesem be replaced from the position of Financial Aid Officer and that a Black person be hired to

direct it; that Third World people have the power to determine how it will be administered.

SFSC Response: The College appointed a Black administrator to the newly created position of Associate Director of Financial Aid. He would make the final decision in the College Work Study Program and would make final decisions on financial aid packages for all Black students who wish their decisions made by a Black administrator; the Office of Financial Aid already had a Spanish-speaking administrator who would function in the same way as the Black administrator.

8    That no disciplinary action will be administered in any way to any students, workers, teachers, or administrators during and after the strike as a consequence of their participation in the strike.

SFSC Response: The Select Committee members, and representatives of the TWLF-BSU recommended the following to the President concerning all cases pending on March 17, 1969: students charged solely with acts of non-violence shall receive a written reprimand; students charged with "violent acts" shall, if found guilty by the hearing panel, receive a penalty of not more than suspension through the end of the fall semester of 1969-70; students charged with "instructional disruption" shall, if found guilty by the hearing panel, receive a penalty of no more than suspension for the remainder of this (1968-69) academic year.

9    That the California State College Trustees not be allowed to dissolve any Black programs on or off the San Francisco State College campus.

SFSC Response: This resolution was not implemented.

10   That George Murray maintain his teaching position on campus for the 1968-69 academic year.

SFSC Response: This decision would be referred to the community advisory board.

## The Demands of the Third World Liberation Front and the SFSC Settlement Responses

1    That a School of Ethnic Studies for all of the ethnic groups involved in the Third World Liberation Front be set up with the students in each particular ethnic organization having the authority and control of the hiring and retention of any faculty member, director, or administrator, as well as the curriculum in a specific area of study.

SFSC Response: The College will endeavor to establish a School of Ethnic Studies to begin operation in the fall semester 1969. The College will need additional funding for this purpose; the School will equal existing Schools of the College in status and structure; the College would establish a community board to recommend faculty appointments to the President.

2    That 50 faculty positions be appropriated to the School of Ethnic Studies, 20 of which would be for the Black Studies program.

SFSC Response: Allocation of faculty positions to the School of Ethnic Studies will follow upon spring planning and resources acquired by the College.

3    That, in the spring semester, the College fulfill its commitment to the non-white students in admitting those who apply.

SFSC Response: 128 EOP students were admitted for the spring 1969 semester.

4    That, in the fall of 1969, all applications of non-white students be accepted.

SFSC Response: Same as the response to BSU Demand #5.

5   That George Murray and any other faculty person chosen by non-white people as their teacher be retained in their positions.

SFSC Response: Same as response to BSU Demand #10.

## Further Points of Agreement

A   That a committee of students, faculty, and staff, ethnically mixed, be formed immediately to advise the College on how to deal with the charges of racism at the College. A first task for this committee will be to recommend procedures for dealing with claims of racism within the College.

B   That the procedure for appointing an ombudsman be started again and pressed to as rapid a conclusion as possible.

C   The College shall establish, through its Academic Senate and the Council of Academic Deans, a small committee to expedite decision making and action concerning all aspects of this agreement.

D   In recognition of the urgency of the present situation, we recommend that the Chancellor and Trustees expedite in every way possible the consideration of any requests for special resources presented by the College President which arise from the extraordinary needs of the College at this time.

E   In instances where differences of interpretation occur in the precise meaning of any part of this agreement, final and mutually binding decisions upon all parties shall be made by a three-man group composed of one person named by the President of San Francisco State College, one person named by the Dean of the School of Ethnic Studies and the Chairmen of the various Ethnic Studies Departments, and a third person selected by these two.

F   Staffing and admission policies of the School of Ethnic Studies shall be non-discriminatory.

G   Police will be withdrawn immediately upon the restoration of peace to the campus.

H   The state of emergency on campus should be rescinded immediately upon settlement of the strike, together with the emergency regulations restricting assemblies, rallies, etc.

I   The College shall resume planning for a Constitutional Convention and for a student conference on the governance of the urban campus.

J   The students and the administration together recognize the necessity of developing machinery for peaceful resolution of future disputes, arising from conditions or needs outside the terms of this agreement.

K   The student organizations' signatory to this agreement and the College agree that they will utilize the full influence of their organizations to insure an effective implementation of this agreement.

Signed by the representatives of the Third World Liberation Front, the Black Student Union, and members of the Select Committee, March 20, 1969

# APPENDIX 3

### ORIGINAL AAS GOAL AND DESCRIPTION –
### FALL 1969

The Asian American Studies program will be offered under the auspices of the School of Ethnic Studies during the fall semester, 1969. The Asian American Studies program is open to both Asian American and other students interested in Asian American Studies. The curriculum is designed to meet the needs of students (1) who wish to pursue a personal interest in Asian American Studies; (2) who will be teaching Ethnic Studies subjects in elementary, secondary, and college level institutions; (3) who plan to work in ethnic communities in a professional capacity as lawyers, health socialists, psychologists, social workers, sociologists, and counselors.

The Asian American Studies curriculum is thus designed to serve people and to understand people who have unique experiences in the American society. The primary focus is to look at the "whole human being" within relevant context. It is an interdisciplinary approach; a humanistic, historical, and social science convergence for the understanding of the Asian Americans in our society. The individual and his community are viewed at the primary level and more importantly, from the Asian American perspective. It is necessary to examine the cultural heritage and the historical development of the Asian American communities in the American setting. Further, a re-examination of various past and prevailing views of Asian American minorities must be developed from the Asian American perspective. Finally, there must be a continual re-synthesis of meanings and experiences as Asian Americans in the total American society.

Within this context, this perspective is different from both the traditional middle class view of the minorities and the view of the traditional peoples and cultures of origin offered by regular Asian departments. It is complementary with the latter for it is important to study the traditional cultures in their own settings but for us, the focus becomes one of understanding whereby selected cultural forms are re-formulated in the new cultural setting here in the United States. The focus is on the relation between the traditional cultural forms and the migrants so as to lead to knowledge of the adaptive processes of the Asian Americans and for the thorough understanding and meaning of these processes, both for the Asian Americans and others from the perspective of the Asian Americans.

# Appendix 4

## Outline of Department
## Structure and Process (circa 1971)

The following outline of structure and process is believed to date from spring 1971. It may be the earliest written description of the AAS structure and process. Spelling has been corrected but it is otherwise unchanged.

Department Structure

Components

I. The General Planning Group.
The General Planning Group is the basic decision-making body for the department as a whole. The General Planning Group is composed of representatives of individual ethnic area Planning Groups.

II. Area Planning Groups
There are separate Planning Groups for each ethnic group (three at present). The composition and structure of area planning groups is determined by those groups themselves.

III. Chairman
The chairman is the official head of Asian American Studies, and the only component recognized by both the University and the Planning Groups.

Powers and Basic Procedures

I. General Planning Group
a) Decisions in the General Planning Group are by unanimous vote. Each Area Planning Group has one vote. Any group has the right of veto.
b) All matters relating to the Studies as a whole are decided in the General Planning Group. Any decision affecting more than one ethnic area is made in the General Planning Group.
II. Area Planning Groups
a) Decision-making procedures in Area Planning Groups are determined by those individual groups themselves.
b) All matters relating to a single ethnic group are handled by that Area Planning Group.
c) Ultimate power resides in the Area Planning Groups as represented in the General Planning Group.

III. Chairman
Day-to-day administrative decisions are made by the chairman based on policies set by the General Planning Group.

IV. Basic Procedure for General Planning Group Decisions
a) Matter is brought to the attention of the Area Planning Group (generally by being brought up in a General Planning Group meeting).
b) Area Planning groups discuss and reach decision.
c) Matter is returned to the General Planning Group and discussed. Decision is reached when all three groups agree.
d) Specific procedures, deadlines, and information requirements for various types of decisions may be made by the General Planning Group. Area Planning Groups may also set requirements of their own before they will make a decision.

# APPENDIX 5

ACADEMIC ROLE OF AAS
(AAS ACADEMIC PROGRAM REVIEW SELF-STUDY REPORT – 2005)

The primary role of the Asian American Studies Department is to provide academic and scholarly knowledge to students for the intellectual recognition and understanding of the Asian American experience within the structure of the University. This process includes student instruction and faculty professional development. Activities associated with this purpose will benefit Asian Americans individually and collectively, while people of other ethnic background will enjoy equal opportunity in the AAS program to become better informed of the Asian American experience. The goals of the Department are as follows:

Provide a comprehensive instructional curriculum for students to study and develop a greater understanding and awareness of the Asian American experience, inclusive of its history, culture, and communities;

Integrate knowledge and skills from a variety of academic disciplines into a coherent body of knowledge and methodology of intellectual inquiry in the field of Asian American Studies;

Establish a general body of information and knowledge that reflects unique Asian American sensibilities;

Encourage and promote the application of skills and knowledge acquired from Asian American Studies to the needs of Asian American communities and the larger society.

# APPENDIX 6

## FALL 1969 CLASSES WITH INSTRUCTOR NAMES

AA  20    Conversational Cantonese  – *Mary Yang*

AA  60    Introductory Pilipino  – *Felicissimo Velasquez*

AA 105    Practical English Skills for Asian Americans – *Jeffery Chan*

AA 110    Asian American Community Urban Crisis  – *Kenji Murase*

AA 115    Asian Perspectives on the Western Literary Tradition  – *Kai-yu Hsu*

AA 116    Asian Perspectives Contemporary Literature+Ideas  – *Jeffery Chan*

AA 117    Asian American Workshop Creative Writing – *Jeffery Chan*

AA 119    Curriculum, Research, and Evaluation – *James Hirabayashi*

AA 120    Chinese in America* – *Alan S. Wong*

AA 130    Chinese Art – *William Wu*

AA 135    Chinese American Community – *Larry Jack Wong*

AA 140    Japanese American Social Psychological Profile – *two sections: one with Dudley Yasuda, one with Karl Matsushita*

AA 145    Japanese Americans in the United States – *Edison Uno*

AA 155    Selected Topics in Japanese American Studies – *Joe Kamiya*

AA 160    Introduction to Ancient Philippine History – *Carolina Borromeo*

AA 165    Philippine Arts – *Joaquin Legaspi*

AA 175    Pilipino Community Workshop – *Jovina Navarro*

* Two Chinese American history courses were offered in fall 1969, one offered by AAS that was taught by Alan S. Wong and the other by the History Department as an experimental course co-taught by Philip P. Choy and Him Mark Lai. The two courses collapsed into one, offered by AAS in spring 1970 and taught by Choy.

# APPENDIX 7

## FALL 1970 ASIAN AMERICAN STUDIES COURSES

This is a list of all the courses developed and approved for offering. Those offered for fall 1970 are italicized and followed by name(s) of instructor(s) who actually taught the class, and not necessarily listed officially in the schedule. The courses are grouped by the category of General Studies requirements for which they had been approved by the college.

Summary: 44 total; 15 pan Asian American courses, 7 Chinese American courses plus 4 Cantonese courses, 7 Japanese American courses, and 7 Pilipino American courses plus 4 Pilipino language courses.

Summary of fall 1970 offerings: 5 pan Asian American courses plus independent study, 5 Chinese American courses plus 2 Cantonese courses totaling 3 sections, 4 Japanese American courses, and 4 Pilipino American courses plus 1 Pilipino language course.

### General Studies Basic Subjects Approved Courses

AAS  20  *First Semester Cantonese*
         *(two sections: Yang and K. Woo)*

AAS  21  *Second Semester Cantonese (Yang)*

AAS  22  Third Semester Cantonese

AAS  23  Fourth Semester Cantonese

AAS  60  *Introductory Pilipino (Velasquez)*

AAS  61  Pilipino II: Intermediate Pilipino

AAS  62  Pilipino III: Advanced Pilipino

AAS  90  *Introduction to Methodology of Asian American Studies (team taught by Nakatsu, Gonzales, and Collier)*

AAS 101  *Practical English Skills for Asian Americans (Chan)*

### General Studies Humanities and Arts Approved Courses

AAS 113  The Oriental in Literature and Film

AAS 114  *Asian American Media Workshop (Eng)*

AAS 115  Asian Perspectives on Western Literary Traditions

AAS 117  *Asian American Workshop in Creative Writing (Chan)*

AAS 125  Chinese American Language and Culture

AAS 130  *Chinese Art (Wu)*

AAS 138  *Selected Topics in Chinese American Studies (Chan)*

AAS 142  Sources of Cultural Traditions in Japanese American Life

AAS 153  Japanese Art

AAS 155  *Selected Topics in Japanese American Studies (Kawahara)*

AAS 163  *Pilipino Literature (Velasquez)*

AAS 165  *Pilipino Art (Begonia)*

AAS 178  *Selected Topics in Pilipino Amercan Studies (Navarro; although listed in Humanities and Arts, the topic for the semester was Pilipino community issues)*

**General Studies Social Science Approved Courses**

| | |
|---|---|
| AAS 103 | Sociology of the Asian American |
| AAS 104 | The Asian American: A Psychological Profile |
| AAS 105.1 | Social Change in the Asian World I |
| AAS 105.2 | Social Change in the Asian World II |
| AAS 107 | Politics and the Asian American |
| AAS 108 | Asian American Economic Patterns |
| AAS 109 | Caste, Nationalism, and Sex Roles in Asian American Society |
| AAS 110 | Asian American Communities in Urban Crisis |
| *AAS 120* | *Chinese in America (Choy)* |
| *AAS 133* | *The Chinese American: A Sociologixal Profile (Eng)* |
| AAS 136 | Mental Health Problems in the Chinese American Community |
| AAS 140 | The Japanese American: A Sociological Profile |
| *AAS 141* | *Japanese American Personality (Yasuda)* |
| *AAS 145* | *Japanese Americans in the United States (Uno)* |
| *AAS 160* | *Pilipino History (Velasquez)* |
| AAS 162 | Introduction to Modern Pilipino History |
| AAS 172 | Pilipino Political Science |
| AAS 174 | Pilipino Social Science |

**General Studies Senior Integrative Seminar
Approved Courses**

| | |
|---|---|
| *AAS 119* | *Curriculum, Research, and Evaluation for Asian American Studies (Eng)* |
| *AAS 135* | *The Chinese American Community (G. Woo)* |
| *AAS 150* | *Japanese American Community Workshop (Gotanda)* |
| AAS 175 | Pilipino Community Workshop |

**Not in General Studies**

| | |
|---|---|
| *AAS 199* | *Independent Study* |

# APPENDIX 8

## FALL 1977 ASIAN AMERICAN STUDIES COURSES

This is a list of all the courses that AAS had in place that could be offered; many were not actually scheduled. Additional information in parenthesis is provided when the course content is unclear from the course title.

<u>Summary</u>: 52 total: 10 plus 1 special study pan Asian American courses, 13 Chinese American courses, 11 Japanese American courses, and 17 Pilipino American courses. All but 5 of the courses could be used for General Studies credit.

| | |
|---|---|
| AAS 100 | General Studies Colloquium in Pilipino American Studies |
| AAS 101 | Cantonese Language Experience I |
| AAS 102 | Cantonese Language Experience II |
| AAS 201 | Conversational Pilipino |
| AAS 250 | Introduction to Asian American Studies |
| AAS 260 | Survey of Chinese American Community |
| AAS 280 | Photo Cultural Exploration of Pilipino American Experience |
| AAS 300 | Chinese in America: Beginning to Exclusion |
| AAS 301 | Chinese in America: 20th Century Chinese Americans |
| AAS 305 | 20th Century Chinese Political Thought |
| AAS 310 | Seminar on Chinese American Community |
| AAS 320 | Current Issues in the Chinese American Community |
| AAS 330 | Chinese American Personality |
| AAS 350 | Chinese American Culture: Language and Literature |
| AAS 375 | Research and Production (research, production-related Chinese experience with visual emphasis) |
| AAS 385 | Chinese American Oral History Fieldwork |
| AAS 390 | Selected Topics in Chinese American Studies |
| AAS 400 | Introduction to the Japanese American Community |
| AAS 410 | Concentration Camps, USA |
| AAS 415 | Laws, Legislation, and Japanese Americans |
| AAS 420 | Japanese American Sociological Profile |
| AAS 425 | Japanese American Personality |
| AAS 430 | Racism and Japanese Americans |
| AAS 455 | Japanese Americans in the United States |
| AAS 460 | Japanese Americans in Hawaii |
| AAS 480 | Seminar on Japanese American Community |
| AAS 485 | US-Japan Relations and the Japanese Americans |
| AAS 490 | Selected Topics in Japanese American Studies |
| AAS 535 | Pilipino Psychology |
| AAS 540 | Pilipino History (PI not US) |
| AAS 541 | Pilipino History II (PI not US) |
| AAS 542 | Pilipino Ako: The Making of Filipino Identity (PI not US) |
| AAS 544 | Pilipinos in America: Problems of Transition |

AAS 545    Pilipino Political Science: Government, Institutions (PI not US)

AAS 548    Westernization of the Pilipino

AAS 552    The Literature of the Philippine Revolution I

AAS 553    The Literature of the Philippine Revolution II

AAS 555    Pilipino Literary Development (PI not US)

AAS 557    Modern and Contemporary Pilipino American Writing

AAS 572    Pilipino Creative Arts Workshop

AAS 580    Seminar on Pilipino American Community

AAS 590    Selected Topics in Pilipino American Studies

AAS 600    Practical English Skills for Asian Americans

AAS 620    Introduction to Asian American Women

AAS 621    Seminar on Asian American Women

AAS 645    Community Problems and Issues

AAS 650    Curriculum and Instruction in Asian American Studies (focus on secondary school level)

AAS 662    Asian American Media Workshop

AAS 666    Asian American Workshop in Creative Writing

AAS 690    Selected Topics in Asian American Studies

AAS 695    Asian American Studies: Curriculum, Research, and Evaluation

AAS 699    Special Study

# APPENDIX 9

## 1980 ASIAN AMERICAN STUDIES COURSES

A total of 52 AAS courses were listed in the SF State *Bulletin*. (Strike-through listings were courses offered earlier but "banked" and no longer officially listed in the *Bulletin*. Students who took these courses could still use them for General Studies credit.)

GS        =  General Studies
Stat      =  Statutory
BSS       =  Behavioral and Social Sciences (then called the Social Science) requirement
HCA       =  Humanities and Creative Arts (then called Humanities and Arts) requirement
SIS       =  Senior Integrative Seminar
Hist/Gov  =  US History, Constitution, and Ideals requirement
ENG/Comp  =  Lower division Written English requirement

| AAS 101 | Cantonese I | (All Cantonese courses in GS Basic Subjects) |
| AAS 102 | Cantonese II | |
| AAS 103 | Practical Cantonese | |
| AAS 105 | Cantonese I Language Lab | |
| AAS 111 | Practical English Skills for AAS | |
| AAS 201 | Conversational Pilipino I | (Both Pilipino courses in GS Basic Subjects) |
| AAS 202 | Conversational Pilipino II | |
| AAS 214 | Second Year Written English Comp: AAS | ENG/Comp for GS/Stat |
| AAS 250 | Introduction to AAS | GS-Basic Subjects |
| AAS 255 | AAS and American Ideal/institutions | Hist/Gov-Stat |
| ~~AAS 260~~ | ~~Survey of CA Community~~ | ~~BSS~~ |
| AAS 265 | Survey Pilipino Art | HCA |
| AAS 300 | Chinese in America | BSS |
| AAS 305 | 20th Century Chinese Political Thought | BSS |
| AAS 310 | Seminar Chinese American Community | SIS |
| AAS 319 | Cantonese Grammar for Bilingual Teachers | |
| AAS 320 | Current Issues in Chinese American Community | BSS |
| AAS 330 | Chinese American Personality | BSS |
| AAS 322 | Interdisciplinary Analysis Chinese Americans | BSS |
| AAS 350 | Chinese American Culture, Language, and Literature | HCA |
| AAS 375 | Research and Production Chinese America | HCA |
| ~~AAS 380~~ | ~~CA Community Visual Arts Workshop~~ | ~~HCA~~ |
| AAS 385 | Chinese American Oral History Fieldwork | |
| AAS 390 | Selected Topics in Chinese American Studies | HCA/BSS |
| AAS 400 | Introduction to the Japanese American Community | BSS |
| AAS 410 | Concentration Camps, USA | BSS |

| | | |
|---|---|---|
| AAS 420 | Japanese American Sociological Profile | BSS |
| AAS 425 | Japanese American Personality | BSS |
| AAS 455 | Japanese Americans in the United States | BSS |
| AAS 460 | Japanese Americans in Hawaii | BSS |
| AAS 468 | Creative Expression of Japanese Americans | HCA |
| AAS 480 | Seminar on Japanese American Community | SIS |
| AAS 485 | US/Japan Relations and the Japanese Americans | BSS |
| AAS 490 | Selected Topics in Japanese American Studies | BSS/HCA |
| AAS 519 | Pilipino Grammar for Bilingual Teachers | |
| AAS 535 | Psyche and Behavior of Pilipinos | BSS |
| AAS 540 | History of the Philippines I | BSS |
| AAS 541 | History of the Philippines II | BSS |
| AAS 544 | Pilipinos in America | BSS |
| AAS 545 | Politics and Government of the Philippines | BSS |
| AAS 548 | Muslims and Tribes of the Philippines | BSS |
| AAS 549 | Westernization of the Pilipino | BSS |
| AAS 553 | The Literature of the Philippine Revolution | HCA |
| AAS 555 | Pilipino Literary Development | HCA |
| AAS 557 | Modern and Contemporary Pilipino American Writings | HCA |
| AAS 560 | Pilipino Education | |
| AAS 580 | Seminar on Pilipino American Community | SIS |
| AAS 590 | Selected Topics in Pilipino American Studies | BSS |
| AAS 620 | Introduction to Asian American Women | BSS |
| AAS 621 | Seminar on Asian American Women | BSS/SIS |
| AAS 645 | Community Problems and Issues | |
| AAS 661 | Modern Expository Cantonese | |
| AAS 662 | Asian American Media Workshop | HCA |
| AAS 666 | AA Workshop in Creative Writing | HCA |
| AAS 690 | Selected Topics in AAS | |
| AAS 695 | AAS: Curriculum, Research, and Evaluation | SIS |
| AAS 699 | Special Study | |

# APPENDIX 10

## LATE 1980s ASIAN AMERICAN STUDIES COURSES

<u>Summary</u>: 26 total (23 out of 26 fulfilled General Education or statutory requirements); ethnic specific courses included 3 Chinese American courses, 4 Japanese American courses, 3 Pilipino American courses, and 1 Southeast Asian American course.

### Lower Division AAS "Top" Courses

| | | |
|---|---|---|
| AAS 101 | Introduction to AAS | |
| AAS 110 | Critical Thinking AA | GE-Basic Subjects |
| AAS 200 | History of Asian Americans | Stat-US Hist |
| AAS 205 | AAS and American Ideals/Institutions | Stat-US/Calif Gov |
| AAS 206 | Introduction to Asian American Literature | GE-HCA |
| AAS 214 | Second year Composition | GE-Basic Subjects |
| ETHS 210 | Asian American Values and Culture | GE-HCA |
| ETHS 220 | Asians in America | GE-BSS |

### Chinese American Courses

| | | |
|---|---|---|
| AAS 310 | Chinese in America | GE-Segment III |
| AAS 315 | Chinese American Personality | GE-BSS |
| AAS 322 | Chinese American Culture – Language and Literature | GE-HCA |

### Japanese American Courses

| | | |
|---|---|---|
| AAS 331 | Japanese Americans in US | GE-Segment III |
| AAS 335 | Japanese American Personality | GE-BSS |
| AAS 434 | Concentration Camps, USA | |
| AAS 444 | Japanese American Art and Expression | GE-HCA |

### Pilipino American Courses

| | | |
|---|---|---|
| AAS 355 | Pysche and Behavior of Pilipinos | GE-BSS |
| AAS 363 | Survey of Philippine Literature | GE-HCA |
| AAS 456 | Pilipinos in America | GE-Segment III |

### Southeast Asian American Course

| | | |
|---|---|---|
| AAS 370 | Southeast Asians in America | GE-Segment III |

### Upper Division AAS "Top" Courses

| | | |
|---|---|---|
| AAS 308 | Photographic Exploration of Asia America | GE-HCA |
| AAS 406 | Asian American Creative Writing Workshop | GE-HCA |

| AAS 603 | Asian American Women | GE-Segment III |
| AAS 680 | Community Change/Development | GE-Segment III |
| AAS 693 | Asian Americans and the Mass Media | GE-Segment III |
| AAS 695 | Seminar on Contemporary Asian American Communities | GE-Segment III |
| AAS 699 | Special Study | |

# APPENDIX 11

## FALL 1981 AAS FACULTY

**Permanent or Probationary Faculty**
Danilo Begonia
Jeffery Paul Chan (split appointment with English Department)
Laureen Chew (split appointment with School of Education)
Daniel Phil Gonzales
James Okutsu
George K. Woo

**Lecturers**
Marilyn Alquizola
Malcolm Collier
Carole Hayashino Kagawa
Tom Kim
Lilly Loh Lee
Steve Nakajo
Benjamin Tong
Alfred Wong

# Appendix 12

## 2008 Asian American Studies Courses

**Summary:** 41 undergraduate courses total (33 out of 41 fulfill General Education or statutory requirements) with 3 in Chinese American Studies, 3 in Japanese American Studies, 3 in Pilipino American Studies, 3 plus 2 language courses in Vietnamese American Studies, 1 in Asian Americans of Mixed Heritage Studies, 1 in Korean American Studies, and 2 in South Asian American Studies. There are 11 courses listed under the MA program.

The following notations indicate an additional graduation requirement that AAS courses fulfill:

AERM = American Ethnic and Racial Minorities requirement

CESD = Cultural, Ethnic, and Social Diversity requirement

LLD = Lifelong Development requirement

### Lower Division Courses

| AAS 171 | Speak Vietnamese I | GE-Languages Other Than English |
| AAS 172 | Speak Vietnamese II | GE-Languages Other Than English |
| AAS 200 | History of Asian Americans | Stat-US Hist |
| AAS 205 | Asian Americans & American Ideals/Institutions | Stat-US/Calif Gov |
| AAS 206 | Intro of Asian American Literature | GE-HCA |
| AAS 214 | Second Year Written Composition: AAS | GE-Basic Subjects |
| ETHS 210 | Asian American Culture | GE-HCA/AERM |
| ETHS 220 | Asians in America | GE-BSS/AERM |

### Chinese American Courses

| AAS 310 | Chinese in America | GE-Segment III/CESD |
| AAS 315 | Chinese American Personality | GE-BSS/LLD |
| AAS 322 | Chinese American Culture – Language & Literature | GE-Segment III |

### Japanese American Courses

| AAS 331 | Japanese Americans in the United States | GE-Segment III/CESD |
| AAS 335 | Japanese American Personality | GE-BSS/LLD |
| AAS 444 | Japanese American Art and Expression | GE-Segment III |

### Pilipino American Courses

| AAS 355 | Psyche and Behavior of Pilipinos | GE-BSS/LLD |
| AAS 363 | Survey of Philippine Literature | GE-Segment III |
| AAS 456 | Pilipinos in America: Problems of Transition | GE-Segment III/CESD |

## Vietnamese American Courses*

| | | |
|---|---|---|
| AAS 370 | Vietnamese in America | GE-Segment III/CESD |
| AAS 372 | Vietnamese American Literature | GE-Segment III |
| AAS 375 | Vietnamese American Identity | GE-BSS/LLD |

*see also AAS 171 and 172 above

## Asians of Mixed Heritage Course

| | | |
|---|---|---|
| AAS 550 | Asian Americans of Mixed Heritage | GE-BSS/LLD |

## Korean American Course

| | | |
|---|---|---|
| AAS 380 | Koreans in America | GE-Segment III |

## South Asian American Courses

| | |
|---|---|
| AAS 340 | South Asian Diaspora in the United States |
| AAS 657 | South Asian Diaspora (cross-listed as ETHS 657) |

## Other Upper Division Courses

| | | |
|---|---|---|
| AAS 300 | Asian Americans in California | GE-Segment III |
| AAS 304 | Asian American Community Arts Workshop | GE-HCA |
| AAS 308 | Photographic Exploration of Asian America | GE-HCA |
| AAS 406 | Asian American Workshop in Creative Writing | GE-HCA |
| AAS 502 | Asian American Children/Teen Literature | GE-Segment III |
| AAS 575 | Asian American Community Health Issues | |
| AAS 603 | Asian American Women | GE-Segment III/CESD |
| AAS 622 | Asian American Women Literature and the Arts | GE-HCA |
| AAS 629 | Travel Study in China | |
| AAS 680 | Community: Changes and Development | GE-Segment III |
| AAS 685 | Projects in the Teaching of Asian American Studies | |
| AAS 688 | Community Internship | |
| AAS 693 | Asian Americans and the Mass Media | GE-Segment III |
| AAS 695 | Seminar on Contemporary AA Communities | GE-Segment III |
| AAS 697 | Proseminar in Asian American Studies | |
| AAS 699 | Special Study | |
| ETHS 665 | Asian American Community and Public Policy | GE-Segment III |

**Graduate Courses**

| | |
|---|---|
| AAS 710 | Critical Approaches to Asian American Studies |
| AAS 800 | Seminar: Contemporary Asian American Discourse |
| AAS 810 | Seminar: Asian American Immigration |
| AAS 822 | Seminar: Asian American Literature and Arts |
| AAS 833 | Seminar: Asian American Family and Identity |
| AAS 865 | Asian American Community and Public Policy |
| AAS 875 | Asian American Community Health Issues |
| AAS 895 | Field Study |
| AAS 896 | Directed Reading in Asian American Studies |
| AAS 898 | Master's Thesis |
| AAS 899 | Special Study |

# APPENDIX 13

## 2008 ASIAN AMERICAN STUDIES FACULTY

Note: Year in parentheses indicates when faculty was first appointed either as lecturer or tenure/tenure track faculty.

**Professors**
Danilo Begonia (1970) – MA, San Francisco State University; AAS Chair, 1972-75; School of Ethnic Studies Acting Director/Dean, 1976-78
Laureen Chew (1981) – EdD, University of the Pacific; College of Ethnic Studies Associate Dean, 2006-present
Lorraine Dong (1987) – PhD, University of Washington; AAS Chair, 2008-present
Marlon K. Hom (1986) – PhD, University of Washington; AAS Chair, 1993-2008
Ben Kobashigawa (1986) – PhD, University of Edinburgh
Grace J. Yoo (1996) – PhD, University of California at San Francisco

**Associate Professors**
Daniel Phil Gonzales (1971) – JD, University of California, Hastings College of Law
Russell Jeung (2002) – PhD, University of California at Berkeley
Mai-Nhung Le (1997) – DrPH, University of California at Berkeley
Isabelle Thuy Pelaud (2001) – PhD, University of California at Berkeley
Allyson Tintiangco-Cubales (2000) – PhD, University of California at Los Angeles

**Assistant Professors**
Wei Ming Dariotis (1999) – PhD, University of California at Santa Barbara
Valerie Soe (1996) – MFA, School of the Arts Institute of Chicago
Wesley Ueunten (2002) – PhD, University of California at Bekeley

**Approved Tenure/Tenure Track Searches to Be Filled**
Specialist in Asian American Family, Gender, and Sexuality Studies
Specialist in Chinese American Studies
Specialist in Chinese-Vietnamese American Studies

**Lecturers**
Jeanne Batallones (2008) – MS, San Francisco State University; BA in AAS, San Francisco State University
Darren Lee Brown (2003) – MA and BA in AAS, San Francisco State University
Irene Faye Duller (2008) – MA in AAS, San Francisco State University
Robert A. Fung, Esq. (1990) – JD, New College of California School of Law
Betty Kano (1999) – MFA, University of California at Berkeley
Gordon Lee, Esq. (2007) – PhD, Pacifica Graduate Institute; JD, University of Hawai'i at Manoa
Eric Mar, Esq. (1997) – JD, New College of California School of Law
Minh-Hoa Ta (1994) – EdD, University of San Francisco
Alice Tam (2008) – MA and BA in AAS, San Francisco State University
Bac Hoai Tran (1999) – MA, San Francisco State University
Jeannie Woo (2003) – MA in AAS, San Francisco State University

**Adjunct Faculty**
Philip P. Choy (1969) – BA, University of California at Berkeley
Him Mark Lai (1969) – BSME, University of California at Berkeley
Dehua Zheng – PhD, University of Hong Kong

**Emeritus Faculty**
Jeffery Paul Chan (1968) – MA, San Francisco State University; AAS Coordinator/Chair, 1970-72; 1975-1984
Malcolm Collier (1980) – MA, San Francisco State University
James A. Hirabayashi (1959) – PhD, Harvard University; AAS Coordinator/Chair, 1969-70; School of Ethnic Studies Director/Dean, 1970-76
George Kee Woo (1970) – BA, San Francisco State University; AAS Chair, 1984-1993

# AUTHORS

**Batallones, Jeanne**

Jeanne Batallones was a student who led the campaign to establish the Asian American Studies major at San Francisco State University in 1997. She was a co-founder of the San Francisco Veterans Equity Center and the founding Director of the South of Market Community Action Network. Jeanne currently works as a counselor at City College of San Francisco and teaches a community course in the AAS Department at SF State.

**Brown, Darren Lee**

Darren Lee Brown is pursuing a doctorate in American Studies at Michigan State University. His MA thesis was entitled "'All Aboard for Chinatown': Stereotypes of Chinese and Chinatown in Popular Music" (San Francisco State University, 2003). He wrote a book review of Josh Kun's *Audiotopia* (*Journal of American Ethnic History,* Winter 2007) and a forthcoming essay in *Diasporic Counterpoint* (Northwestern University).

**Chan, Jeffery Paul**

Jeffery Paul Chan is Professor Emeritus, San Francisco State University, and a founding member of the Asian American Studies Department. He co-edited *Aiiieeeee!* and *The Big Aiiieeeee!*, and writes short fiction. His award-winning novel, *Eat Everything before You Die* (University of Washington Press), was published in 2004.

**Chew, Laureen**

Laureen Chew received her BA, Elementary Teaching Credential, and MA from San Francisco State University, and her EdD from University of the Pacific. If she has to say anything about herself, this is her statement: "you can take the girl out of Chinatown, but not Chinatown out of the girl."

**Choy, Philip P.**

Philip P. Choy was born Poon Choy on December 17, 1926, and lived at 714 Pacific Avenue on the northwest corner of Grant Avenue above Rex Meat Market (Wo Lung), where his father Choy Yow Chee, a paper son, was in partnership with fellow villagers from Nam Hoi, Gow Gong, China. Because Phil's mother was native born, the place of business was purchased under her name. Phil spent his early years attending Jean Parker School by day and Nam Kue Chinese School at night using his real surname "Woo." He attended Marina Junior High and graduated from Galileo High. The YMCA was his place of recreation. When Phil entered military service, he used "Poon" as his middle name to match his birth certificate to insure proper identification in case of death. Following a year of service in Germany, Phil returned and obtained his architectural degree under the GI Bill and spent fifty years in that profession. Being in private practice gave him flex time to teach Chinese American history. Married fifty-six years to Sarah Owyang (alias a Wong), Phil and Sarah are blessed with three children and five grandchildren.

## Collier, Irene Dea

Born in Guangdong Province, Irene Dea Collier grew up in San Francisco Chinatown. She has been an activist in community educational issues and is currently a middle school teacher in San Francisco.

## Collier, Malcolm

Malcolm Collier is a native of New Mexico, and was educated in Peru, New Mexico, and California. He is a founding member and Lecturer Emeritus of Asian American Studies at San Francisco State University. Malcolm is also active in photography, visual anthropology, and cross-cultural education.

## Dariotis, Wei Ming

Wei Ming Dariotis is Assistant Professor of Asian American Studies at San Francisco State University, focusing on Asian Americans of Mixed Heritage and Asian American literature and culture. Her publications include "Developing a Kin-Aesthetic" in *Mixed Race Literature*, "'My Race, Too, Is Queer': Mixed Heritage Chinese Americans Fight for Race and Gender Marriage Equity" in *Chinese America: History and Perspectives*, and "Crossing the Racial Frontier: Star Trek and Mixed Heritage Identities," in *The Influence of Star Trek on Television, Film, and Culture.*

## Dear, Jerry

Information strategist and librarian/instructor Jerry Dear helps patrons and students foster online research strategies at the San Francisco Public Library and City College of San Francisco, while spending his remaining time indulging in Asian American literature. He holds an MFA in Creative Writing and an MLIS in Library Information Science.

## Dong, Lorraine

Lorraine Dong was born in San Francisco's Chinese Hospital and raised the daughter of immigrant parents (a waiter and sewing factory seamstress). She attended public and Chinese schools in Chinatown, and received her BA (*summa cum laude*) and MA in Chinese from SF State, and her PhD from the Department of Asian Languages and Literature at the University of Washington in Seattle. She is currently AAS Department Chair at SF State.

## Finetti, Scilla

Scilla Finetti is a translator and writer, born in Milan and residing in Rome. She has published translations and critical commentary on a number of Chinese American subjects, poems from Angel Island, Nellie Wong (the poet), and others. Her latest publication is a translation of contemporary Chinese short stories, *CINA, Undici Scrittori della Rivoluzione Pop* (Zhang Tong Bing, co-translator), Isbn Edizioni, Milano, 2006.

## Gonzales, Daniel Phil

Daniel Phil Gonzales has taught, researched, written, and recorded video since participating in the founding of Asian American Studies and the School (now College) of Ethnic Studies at San Francisco State in 1969. He has been historical advisor to several print projects, films, and television programs about Asian Americans and American legal, political, and social processes, Filipino American history, and Philippine-US relations. He received his BA, International Relations, from SFSU, and his Juris Doctorate from Hastings College of Law.

## Hirabayashi, James Akira

Jim Hirabayashi was incarcerated at Tule Lake during World War II. He was the first Coordinator/Chair of AAS and later Director/Dean of Ethnic Studies. He is Professor Emeritus, Anthropology and Ethnic Studies at San Francisco State University. He has a PhD in Anthropology from Harvard and served in research and professor positions at University of Tokyo, University of Alberta, Canada, and Ahmadu Bello University, Nigeria. He has also been an actor in the Asian American Theater Company and Senior Program Advisor for the Japanese American National Museum, Los Angeles.

## Hom, Marlon K.

Marlon K. Hom teaches Asian American Studies at San Francisco State University.

## Jeung, Russell

Russell Jeung has written *Faithful Generations: Race and New Asian American Churches* (Rutgers University Press, 2004). With a Sociology PhD from University of California, Berkeley, he has taught at San Francisco State University since 2002. He lives in Oakland, California with Joan and Matthew, his spouse and son.

## Lai, Him Mark

Him Mark Lai is Adjunct Professor of Asian American Studies at San Francisco State University; researcher and writer on Chinese American history; editorial committee member of the Chinese Historical Society of America's *Chinese America: History and Perspectives*; and cofounder of the In Search of Roots Program (1991) sponsored by the Chinese Culture Foundation and Chinese Historical Society of America.

## Le, Mai-Nhung

Mai-Nhung Le is an Associate Professor in the Asian American Studies Department at San Francisco State University. She was trained in the field of public health (MPH, Yale University and DrPH, University of California, Berkeley). She teaches courses in Asian American history, Vietnamese American experience and identity, and Asian American community and health issues. She has extensive knowledge of women's health issues among the Asian American population, and has conducted a significant amount of research on the spread of sexually transmitted diseases in both Vietnam and the United States.

## Lott, Juanita Tamayo

Juanita Tamayo Lott authored *Asian Americans: From Racial Category to Multiple Identities* and *Common Destiny: Filipino American Generations*. She advocates for policy data for the underserved populations in the federal statistical system, from senior positions at the US Census Bureau, the National Academies, and the US Commission on Civil Rights. Her current work is global migration of human capital and institutional knowledge transfer.

## Matsuoka, Bette (Inouye)

Bette (Inouye) Matsuoka lives in San Francisco with her husband, Ken, and their two dogs. After graduating from San Francisco State and the Pacific Fashion Institute, she spent thirty years designing clothes. Upon retiring from her fashion career, she returned to SFSU and is currently the budget coordinator for the College of Ethnic Studies

## Pelaud, Isabelle Thuy

Isabelle Thuy Pelaud is Associate Professor in Asian American Studies at San Francisco State University. As a community organizer, she promotes Vietnamese American cultural work. Her essays and short stories have been published in *Making More Waves, Tilting the Continent,* and *Vietnam Dialogue Inside/Out.* Her academic work can be found in *Mixed Race Literature, The New Face of Asian Pacific America, Amerasia Journal,* and the *Michigan Quarterly Review.* Her book manuscript, "History, Identity and Survival: Reading Vietnamese American Literature," is under review.

## Soe, Valerie

Valerie Soe is a filmmaker and Assistant Professor in Asian American Studies at San Francisco State University. Her productions include *Snapshot: Six Months of the Korean American Male* (2008), *art/film/revolution* (2007), *Carefully Taught* (2002), *Picturing Oriental Girls: A (Re) Educational Videotape* (1992), and *All Orientals Look the Same* (1986), among others.

## Ta, Minh-Hoa

Minh-Hoa Ta began her community activism in the East Bay and worked many years as an immigration counselor. She started her advising profession at City College of San Francisco (CCSF) in 1990 and her teaching profession at San Francisco State University in 1993. Minh-Hoa is currently the Director of the Asian Pacific American Student Success Center (APASS) at CCSF, and the Co-director of the Vietnamese American Studies Center (VASC) in Asian American Studies at SFSU. Recently, she has extended her teaching interest to overseas studies.

## Tintiangco-Cubales, Allyson

Allyson Tintiangco-Cubales is Associate Professor of Asian American Studies and an affiliated faculty in the EdD program in Educational Leadership at San Francisco State University. She is the founder and director of Pin@y Educational Partnerships (PEP), a service and teaching pipeline focused on the marriage between critical Filipina/o American Studies and critical pedagogy. She is also a senior research associate with the Educational Equity Initiative in the César E. Chávez Institute and an Urban Fellow with the Institute of Civic and Community Engagement.

## Ueunten, Wesley

Wesley Ueunten is a third generation Okinawan born and raised in Hawai'i. After living in Okinawa and Japan for several years, he entered the Ethnic Studies PhD program at University of California, Berkeley, which he completed in 2007. His dissertation was on Okinawan identity in Hawai'i as it has been shaped by the homeland of Okinawa being colonized by both Japan and the United States. Wesley is an Assistant Professor in the Asian American Studies Department in the College of Ethnic Studies at San Francisco State University, and is active in the Okinawan and Japanese American community through his involvement in Okinawan music.

## Wang, Marian

Marian Wang is a journalist living and working in Chicago. Formerly a television reporter, she is shifting gears to work on print and multimedia news pieces centering on local issues of race, poverty, and justice.

## Wong, Alan S.

Alan S. Wong is a native of San Francisco Chinatown. He is a community activist with a Masters of Social Work from San Francisco State. Alan has a long career with the Chinatown YMCA, eventually becoming its Executive Director. He was also a staff person for the first Chinatown-North Beach Economic Opportunity Council and has been associated with several major Chinatown social services agencies for many years.

## Wong, Shawn

Shawn Wong's first novel was *Homebase* (1979). His second novel, *American Knees* (1995), was made into a movie titled *Americanese*, to be distributed by IFC Films in theaters in 2009. Shawn is also the co-editor and editor of six Asian American and American multicultural literary anthologies including the pioneer anthology *Aiiieeeee!* (1974). He is currently Professor of English at the University of Washington in Seattle.

## Yoo, Grace J.

Grace J. Yoo is a second generation Korean American from Southern California who has been involved in bringing voice to Asian American issues for the past twenty years. She is a community-based activist, researcher, and teacher devoted to teaching and understanding the social and health problems impacting Asian America. Grace is also the co-editor of the forthcoming publication, *The Greenwood Encyclopedia of Asian American Issues Today*.